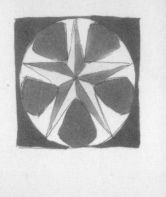

I was finally able to reach the final arc! The entire *Bleach* story has been leading up to this point. I hope you stick with it until the end!

-Tite Kubo

BLEACH is author Tite Kubo's second title. Kubo made his debut with *ZOMBIEPOWDER.*, a four-volume series for *WEEKLY SHONEN JUMP*. To date, *BLEACH* has been translated into numerous languages and has also inspired an animated TV series that began airing in the U.S. in 2006. Beginning its serialization in 2001, *BLEACH* is still a mainstay in the pages of *WEEKLY SHONEN JUMP*. In 2005, *BLEACH* was awarded the prestigious Shogakukan Manga Award in the *shonen* (boys) category.

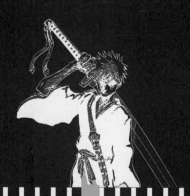

BLEACH
VOL. 55: THE BLOOD WARFARE
SHONEN JUMP Manga Edition

STORY AND ART BY
TITE KUBO

Translation/Joe Yamazaki
Touch-up Art & Lettering/Mark McMurray
Design/Kam Li
Editor/Alexis Kirsch

Printed in the U.S.A.

Published by VIZ Media, LLC
P.O. Box 77010
San Francisco, CA 94107

10 9 8 7 6 5 4 3 2 1
First printing, February 2013

PARENTAL ADVISORY
BLEACH is rated T for Teen and is recommended
for ages 13 and up. This volume contains
fantasy violence.
ratings.viz.com

www.viz.com

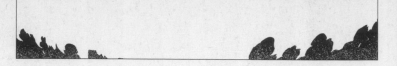

Take one step in and never return
The sea of blood of the universe

BLEACH 55 | THE BLOOD WARFARE

Shonen Jump Manga

ALL STARS ★ AND

石田雨竜
イシダウリュウ

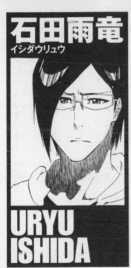

URYU ISHIDA

ORIHIME INOUE

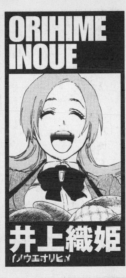

井上織姫
イノウエオリヒメ

黒崎一護
クロサキイチゴ

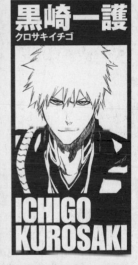

ICHIGO KUROSAKI

plot

Ichigo Kurosaki meets Soul Reaper Rukia Kuchiki and ends up helping her eradicate Hollows. After developing his powers as a Soul Reaper, Ichigo enters battle against Aizen and his dark ambitions! Ichigo finally defeats Aizen in exchange for his powers as a Soul Reaper.

With the battle over, Ichigo regains his normal life. But his tranquil days end when he meets Ginjo, who offers to help Ichigo get his powers back. But it was all a plot by Ginjo to steal Ichigo's new powers! Ginjo, who was the first-ever Deputy Soul Reaper, then reveals to Ichigo the truth behind the deputy badge. However, even after learning the Soul Society's plans for him, Ichigo chooses to continue protecting his friends and defeats Ginjo.

BLEACH STORIES

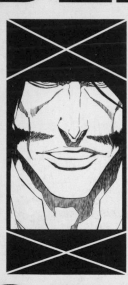

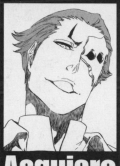

アズギアロ・
イーバーン

**Asguiaro
Ebern**

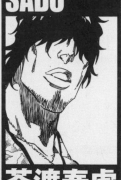

YASUTORA
SADO

茶渡泰虎
サドヤストラ

BLEACH 55

THE BLOOD WARFARE

CONTENTS

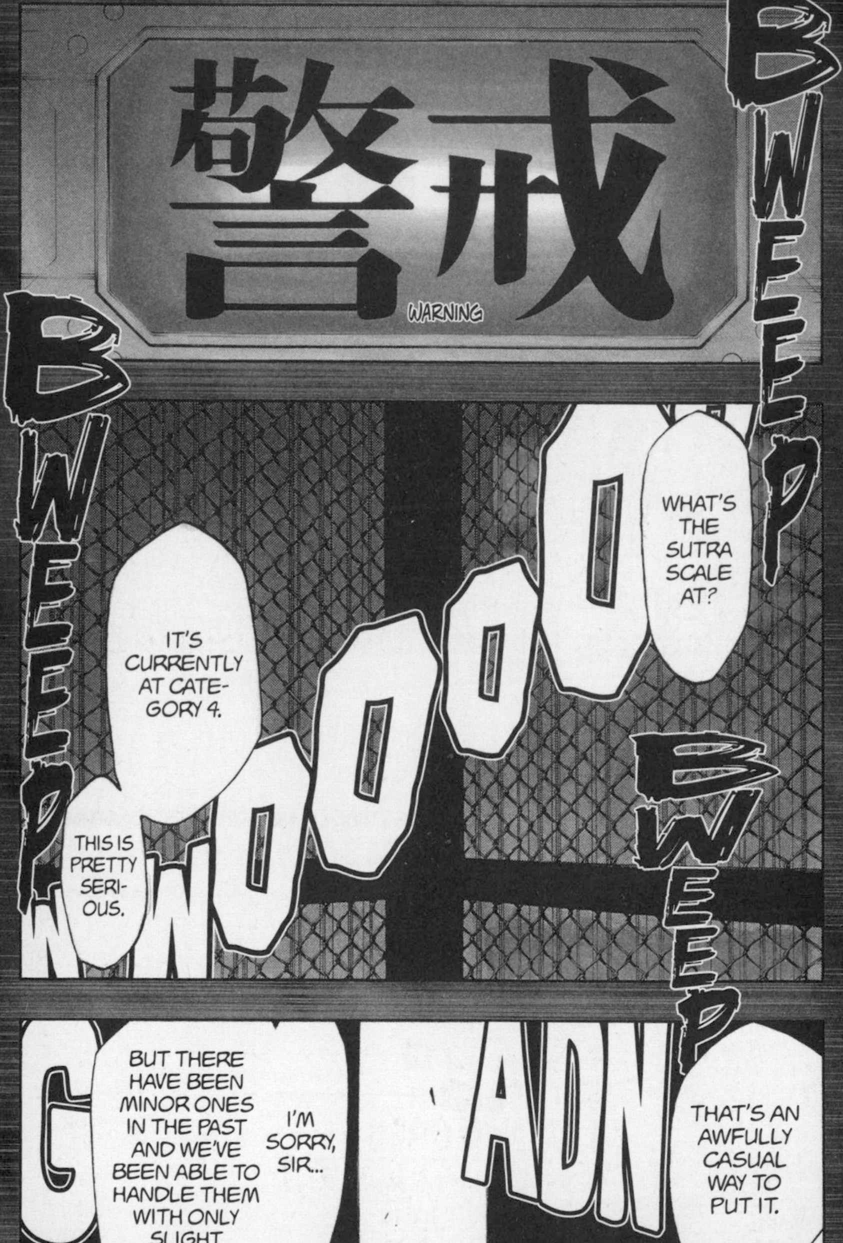
警戒
WARNING
BWEEP
BWEEP
WHAT'S THE SUTRA SCALE AT?
IT'S CURRENTLY AT CATE-GORY 4.
THIS IS PRETTY SERI-OUS.
BWEEP
THAT'S AN AWFULLY CASUAL WAY TO PUT IT.
I'M SORRY, SIR...
BUT THERE HAVE BEEN MINOR ONES IN THE PAST AND WE'VE BEEN ABLE TO HANDLE THEM WITH ONLY SLIGHT ADJUST-MENTS...

480.THE BLOOD WARFARE

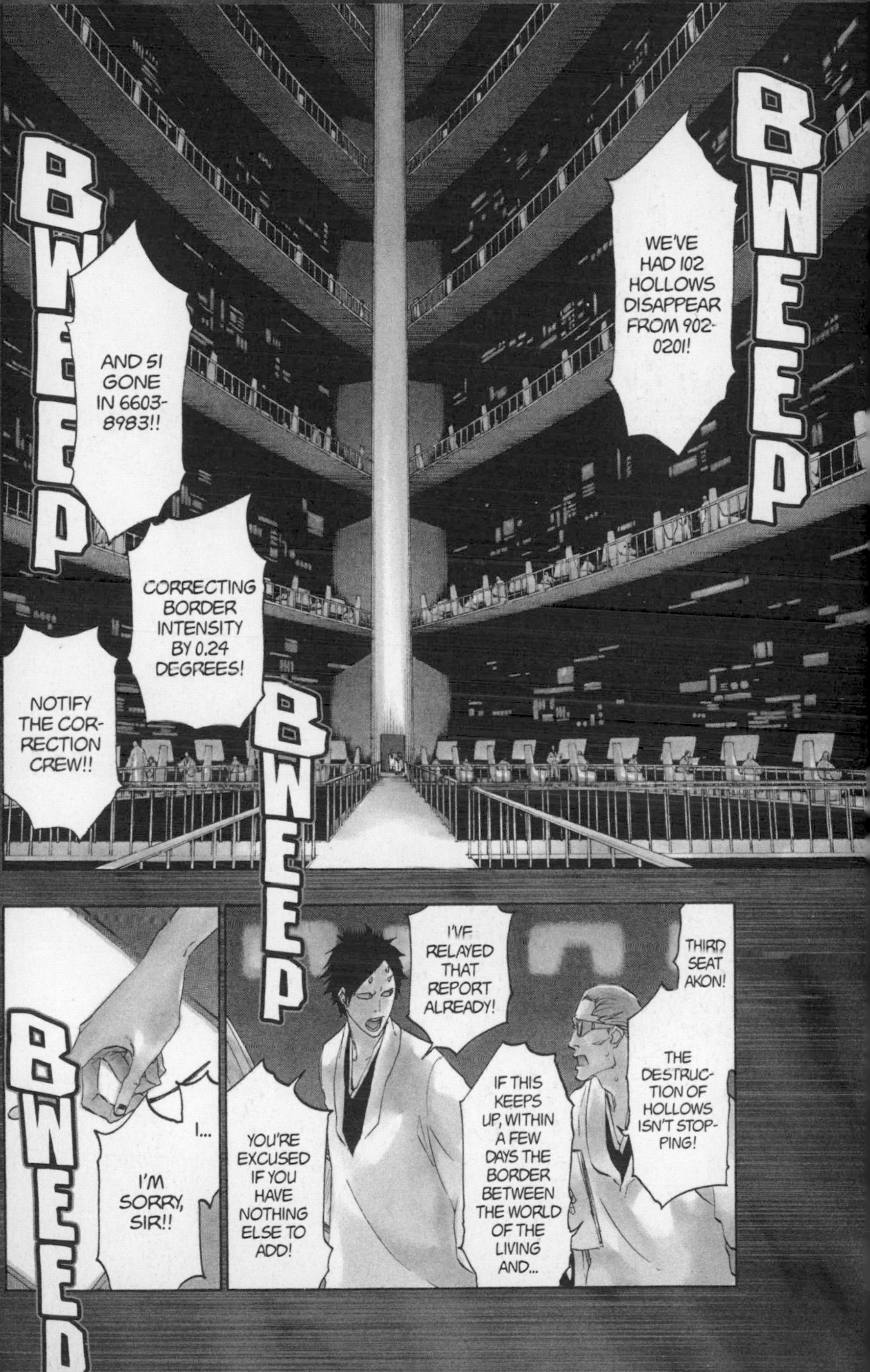
BWEEP
WE'VE HAD 102 HOLLOWS DISAPPEAR FROM 902-0201!
BWEEP
AND 51 GONE IN 6603-8983!!
CORRECTING BORDER INTENSITY BY 0.24 DEGREES!
NOTIFY THE CORRECTION CREW!!
BWEEP
THIRD SEAT AKON!
THE DESTRUCTION OF HOLLOWS ISN'T STOPPING!
I'VE RELAYED THAT REPORT ALREADY!
IF THIS KEEPS UP, WITHIN A FEW DAYS THE BORDER BETWEEN THE WORLD OF THE LIVING AND...
YOU'RE EXCUSED IF YOU HAVE NOTHING ELSE TO ADD!
I...
I'M SORRY, SIR!!
BWEEP

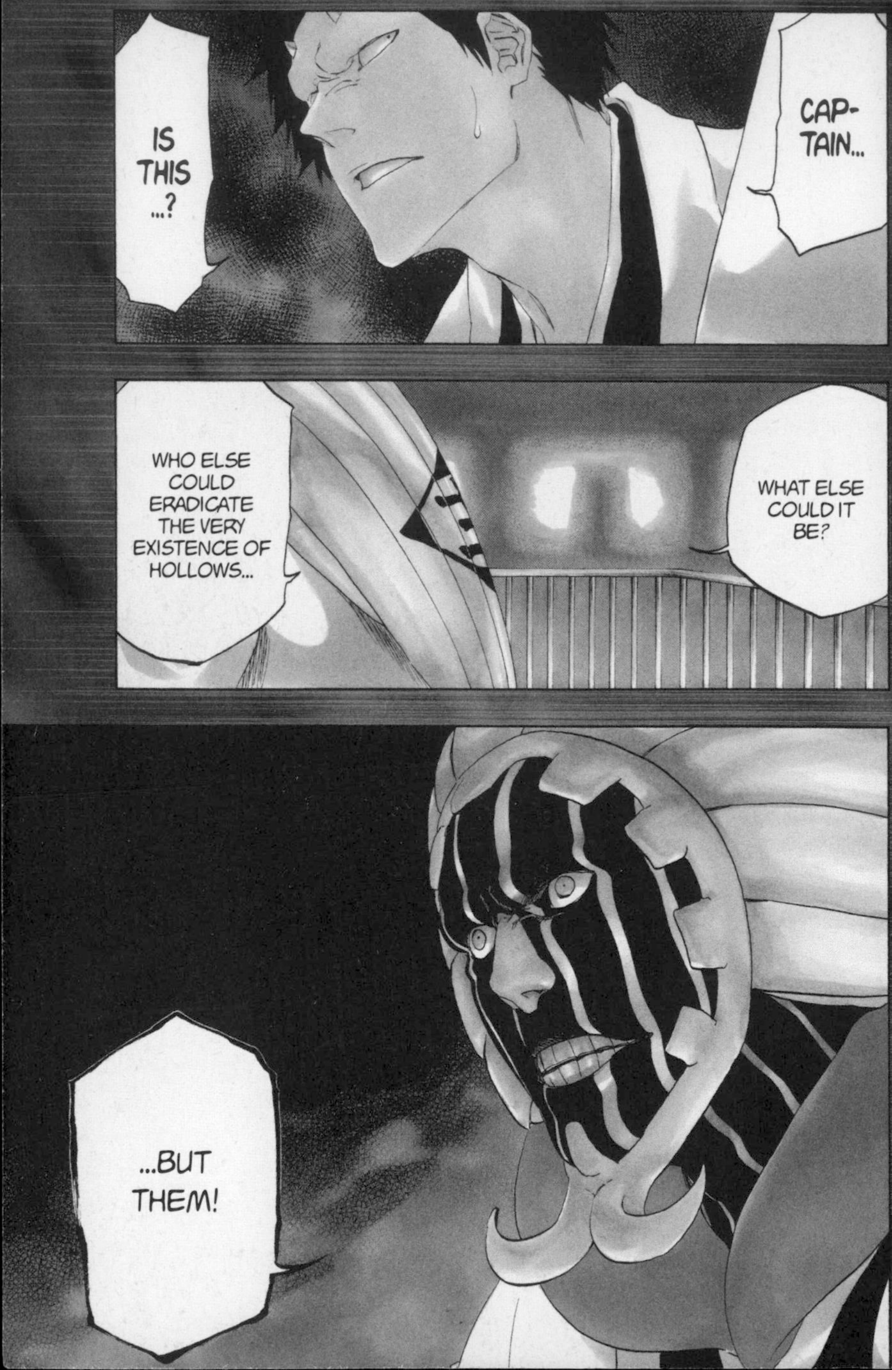
CAP-TAIN...
IS THIS ...?
WHAT ELSE COULD IT BE?
WHO ELSE COULD ERADICATE THE VERY EXISTENCE OF HOLLOWS...
...BUT THEM!

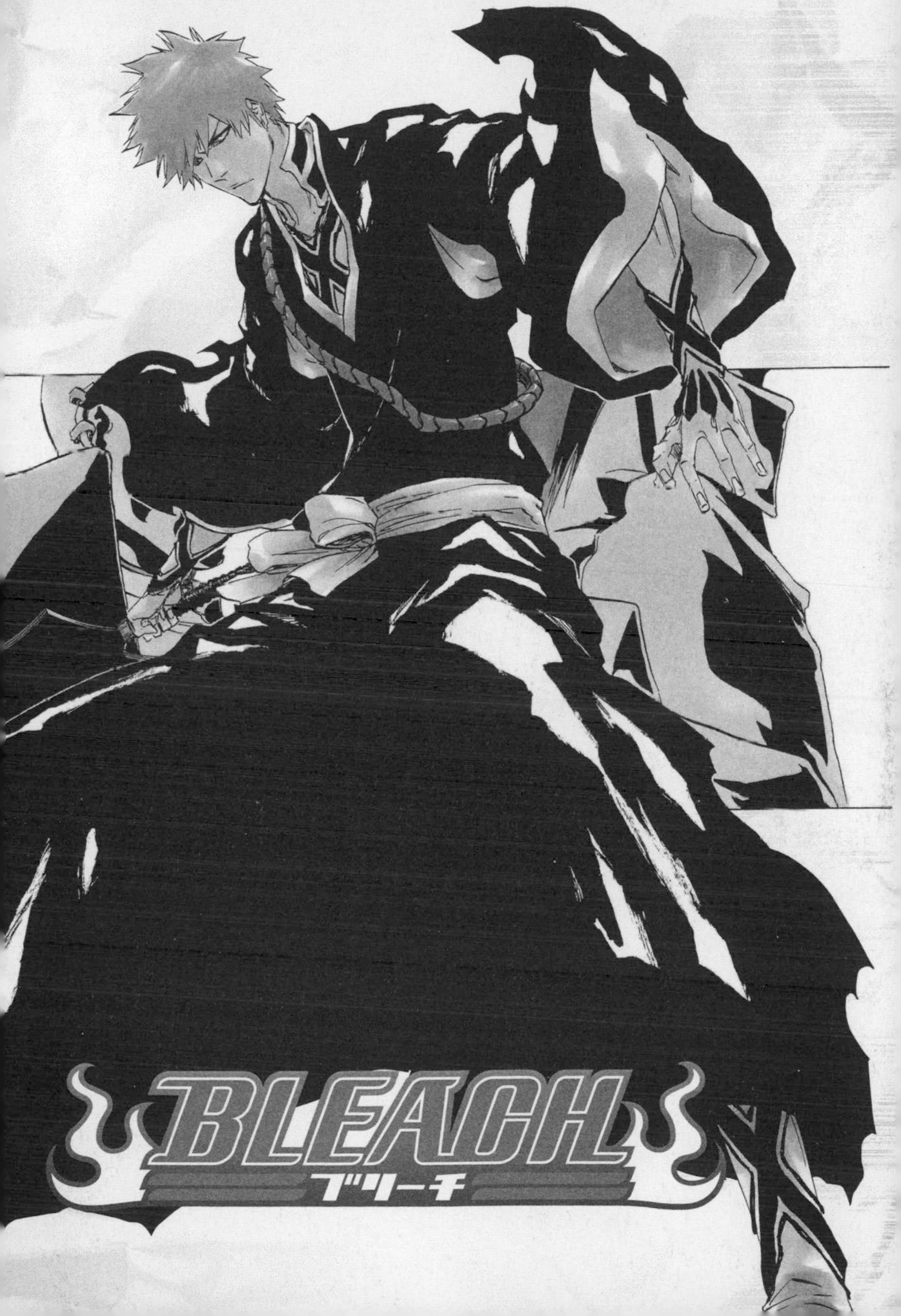
BLEACH
ブリーチ

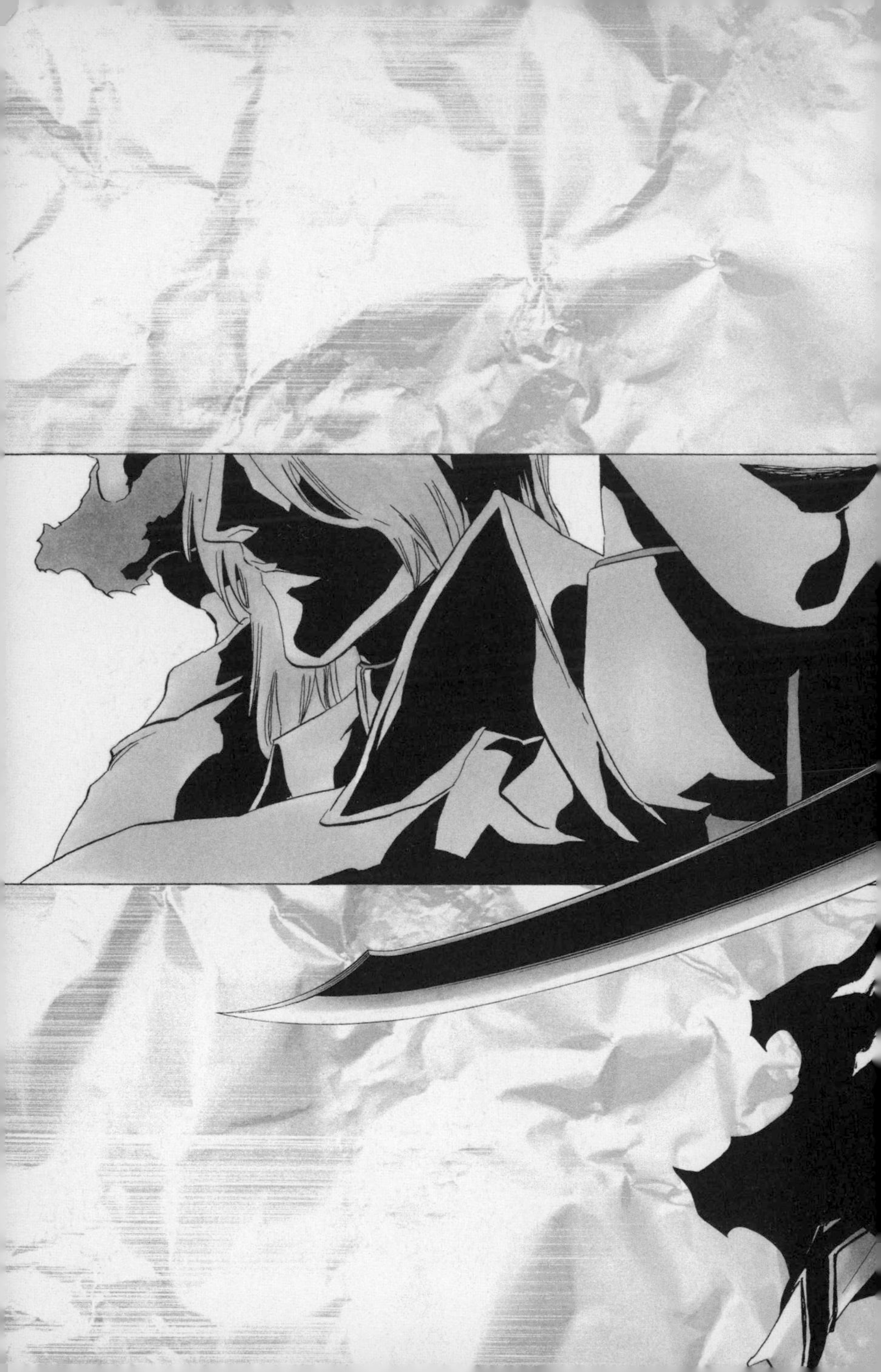

BLEACH
ブリーチ

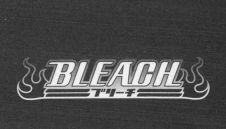

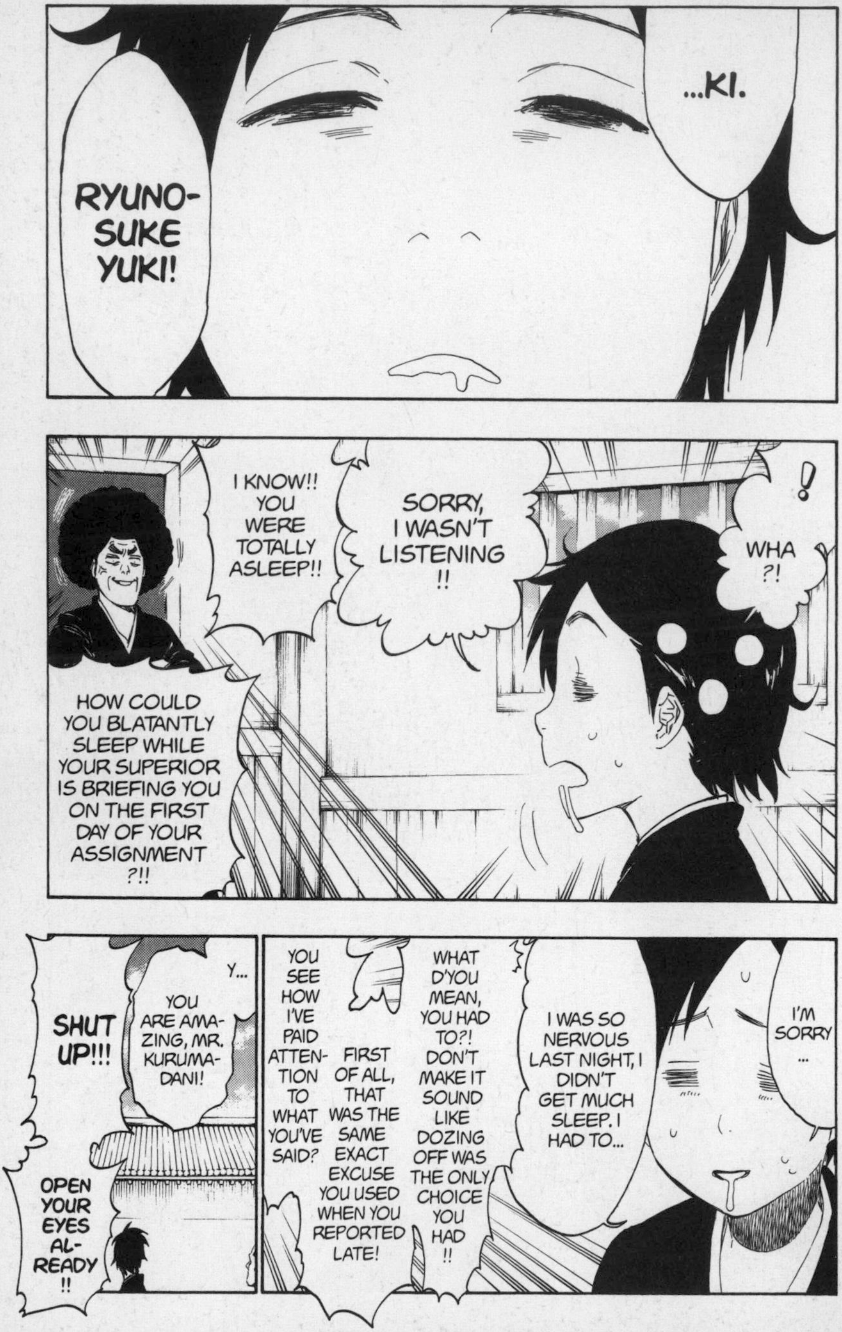
...KI.
RYUNOSUKE YUKI!
!
WHA ?!
SORRY, I WASN'T LISTENING !!
I KNOW!! YOU WERE TOTALLY ASLEEP!!
HOW COULD YOU BLATANTLY SLEEP WHILE YOUR SUPERIOR IS BRIEFING YOU ON THE FIRST DAY OF YOUR ASSIGNMENT ?!!
I'M SORRY ...
I WAS SO NERVOUS LAST NIGHT, I DIDN'T GET MUCH SLEEP. I HAD TO...
WHAT D'YOU MEAN, YOU HAD TO?! DON'T MAKE IT SOUND LIKE DOZING OFF WAS THE ONLY CHOICE YOU HAD !!
FIRST OF ALL, THAT WAS THE SAME EXACT EXCUSE YOU USED WHEN YOU REPORTED LATE!
YOU SEE HOW I'VE PAID ATTENTION TO WHAT YOU'VE SAID?
Y...
YOU ARE AMAZING, MR. KURUMADANI!
SHUT UP!!!
OPEN YOUR EYES ALREADY !!

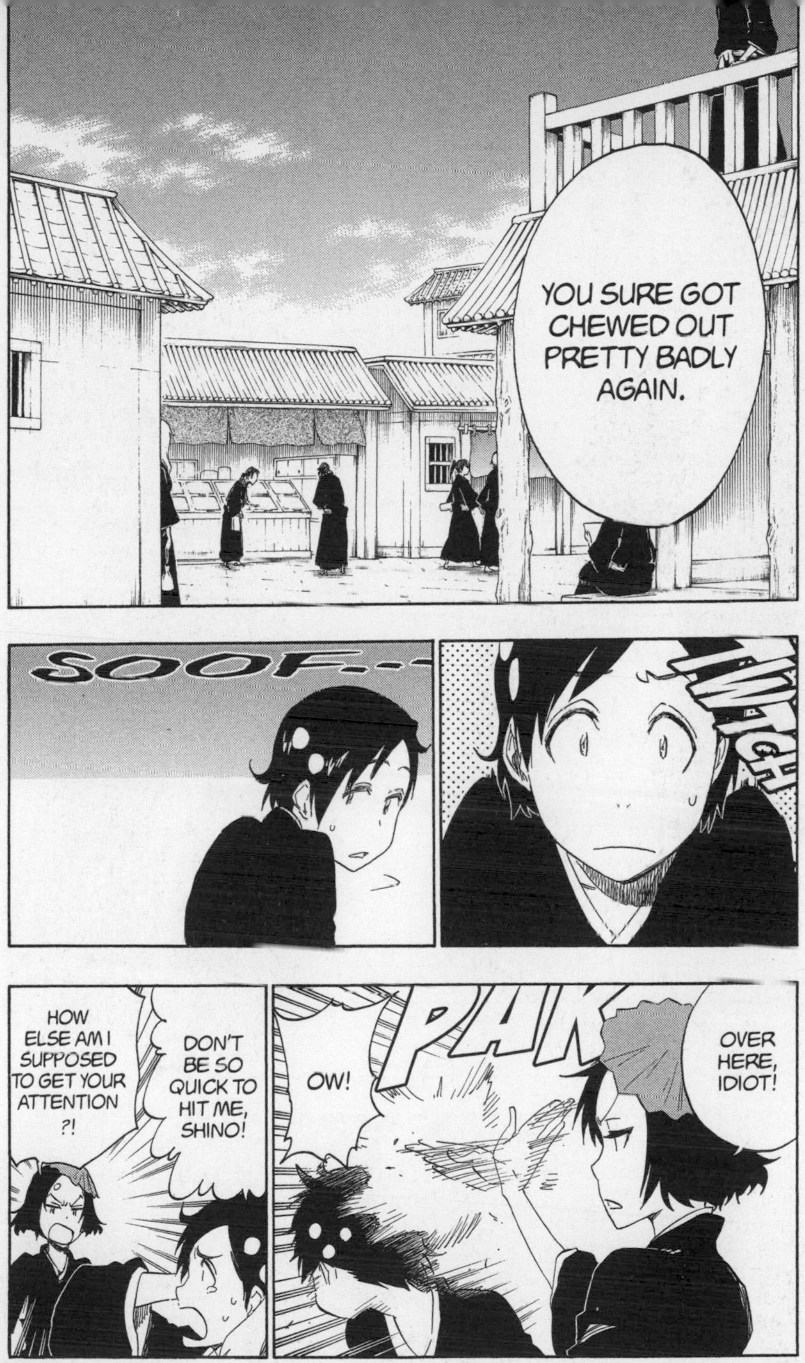
YOU SURE GOT CHEWED OUT PRETTY BADLY AGAIN.
TWITCH
SOOF...
OVER HERE, IDIOT!
PAK
OW!
DON'T BE SO QUICK TO HIT ME, SHINO!
HOW ELSE AM I SUPPOSED TO GET YOUR ATTENTION ?!

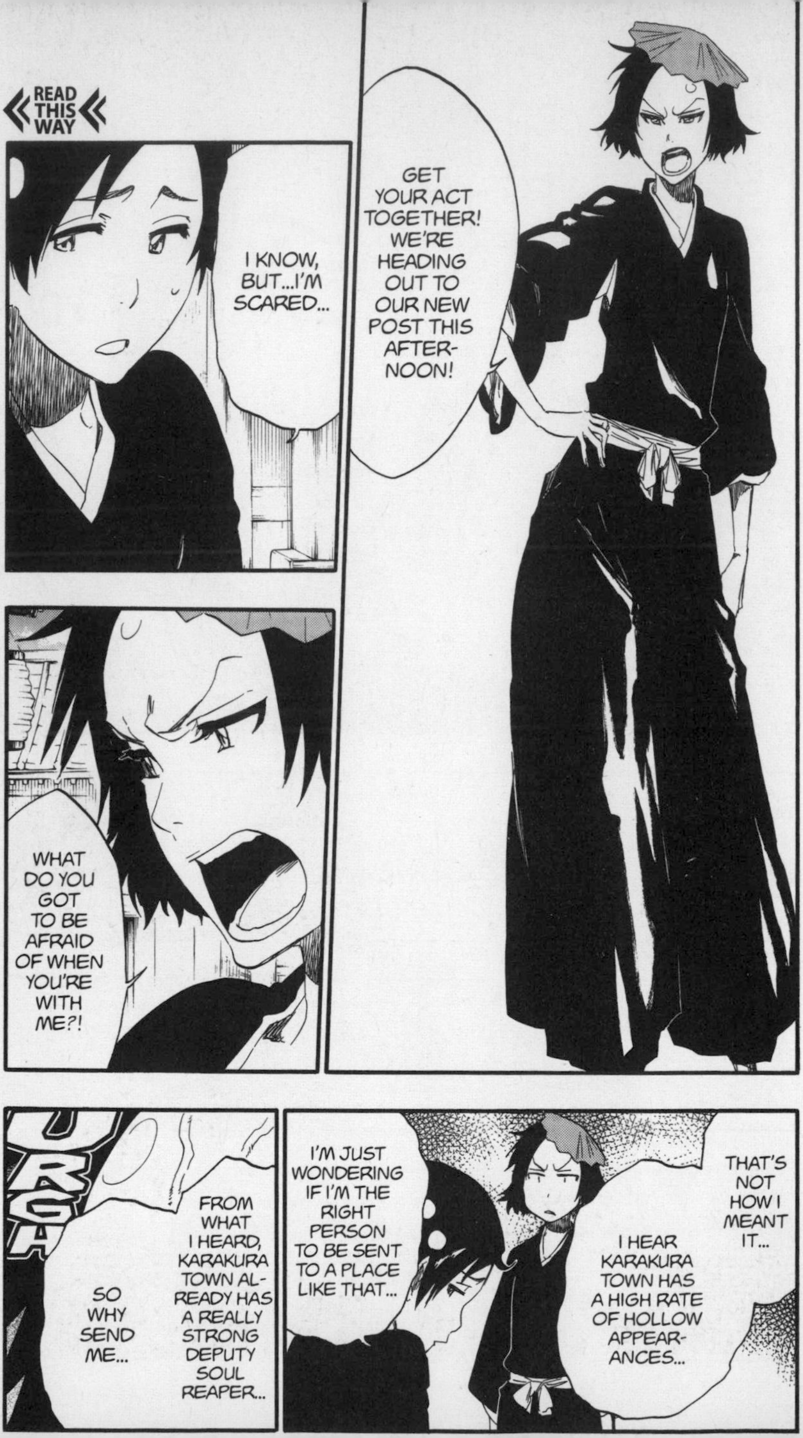
READ THIS WAY
GET YOUR ACT TOGETHER! WE'RE HEADING OUT TO OUR NEW POST THIS AFTER-NOON!
I KNOW, BUT...I'M SCARED...
WHAT DO YOU GOT TO BE AFRAID OF WHEN YOU'RE WITH ME?!
THAT'S NOT HOW I MEANT IT...
I HEAR KARAKURA TOWN HAS A HIGH RATE OF HOLLOW APPEAR-ANCES...
I'M JUST WONDERING IF I'M THE RIGHT PERSON TO BE SENT TO A PLACE LIKE THAT...
FROM WHAT I HEARD, KARAKURA TOWN AL-READY HAS A REALLY STRONG DEPUTY SOUL REAPER...
SO WHY SEND ME...
URGH

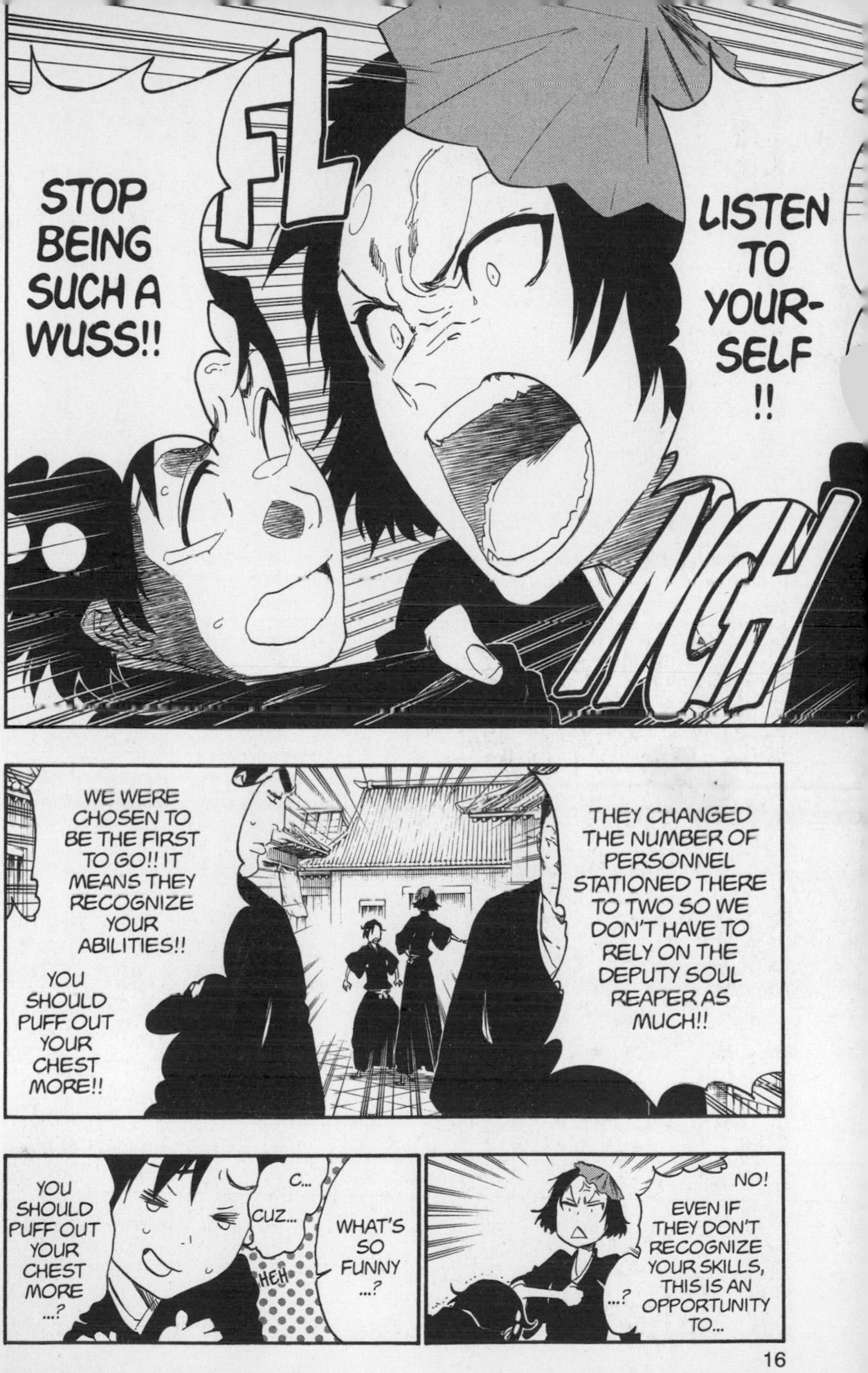
LISTEN TO YOUR-SELF !!
FL
NGH
STOP BEING SUCH A WUSS!!
THEY CHANGED THE NUMBER OF PERSONNEL STATIONED THERE TO TWO SO WE DON'T HAVE TO RELY ON THE DEPUTY SOUL REAPER AS MUCH!!
WE WERE CHOSEN TO BE THE FIRST TO GO!! IT MEANS THEY RECOGNIZE YOUR ABILITIES!!
YOU SHOULD PUFF OUT YOUR CHEST MORE!!
NO!
EVEN IF THEY DON'T RECOGNIZE YOUR SKILLS, THIS IS AN OPPORTUNITY TO...
...?
WHAT'S SO FUNNY ...?
C...
CUZ...
HEH
YOU SHOULD PUFF OUT YOUR CHEST MORE ...?

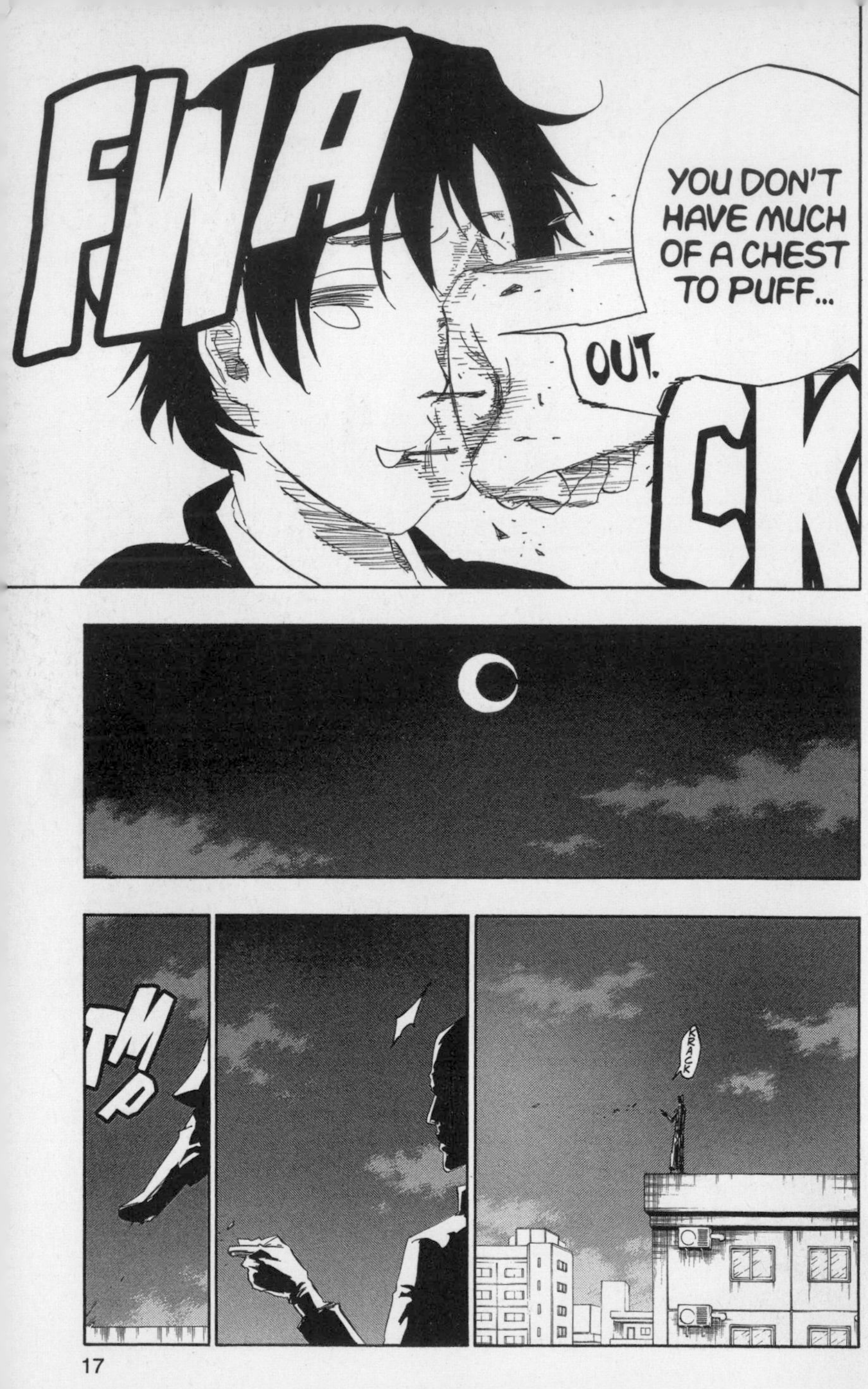
YOU DON'T HAVE MUCH OF A CHEST TO PUFF... OUT.
FWA
CK
KRACK
TMP

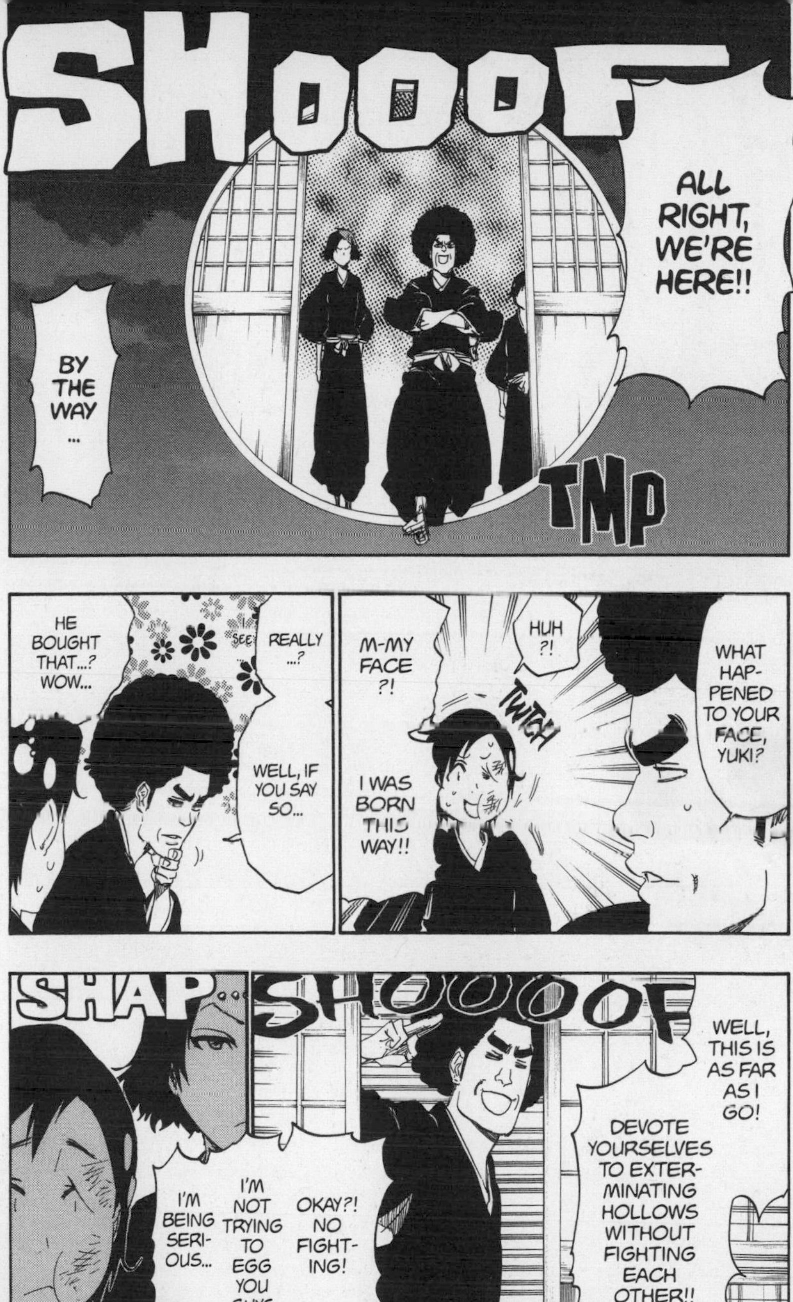
SHOOOF
ALL RIGHT, WE'RE HERE!!
BY THE WAY...
TMP
WHAT HAP-PENED TO YOUR FACE, YUKI?
HUH ?!
TWITCH
M-MY FACE ?!
I WAS BORN THIS WAY!!
REALLY ...?
I SEE...
HE BOUGHT THAT...? WOW...
WELL, IF YOU SAY SO...
WELL, THIS IS AS FAR AS I GO!
DEVOTE YOURSELVES TO EXTER-MINATING HOLLOWS WITHOUT FIGHTING EACH OTHER!!
SHOOOOOF
OKAY?! NO FIGHT-ING!
I'M NOT TRYING TO EGG YOU GUYS ON!
I'M BEING SERI-OUS...
SHAP...

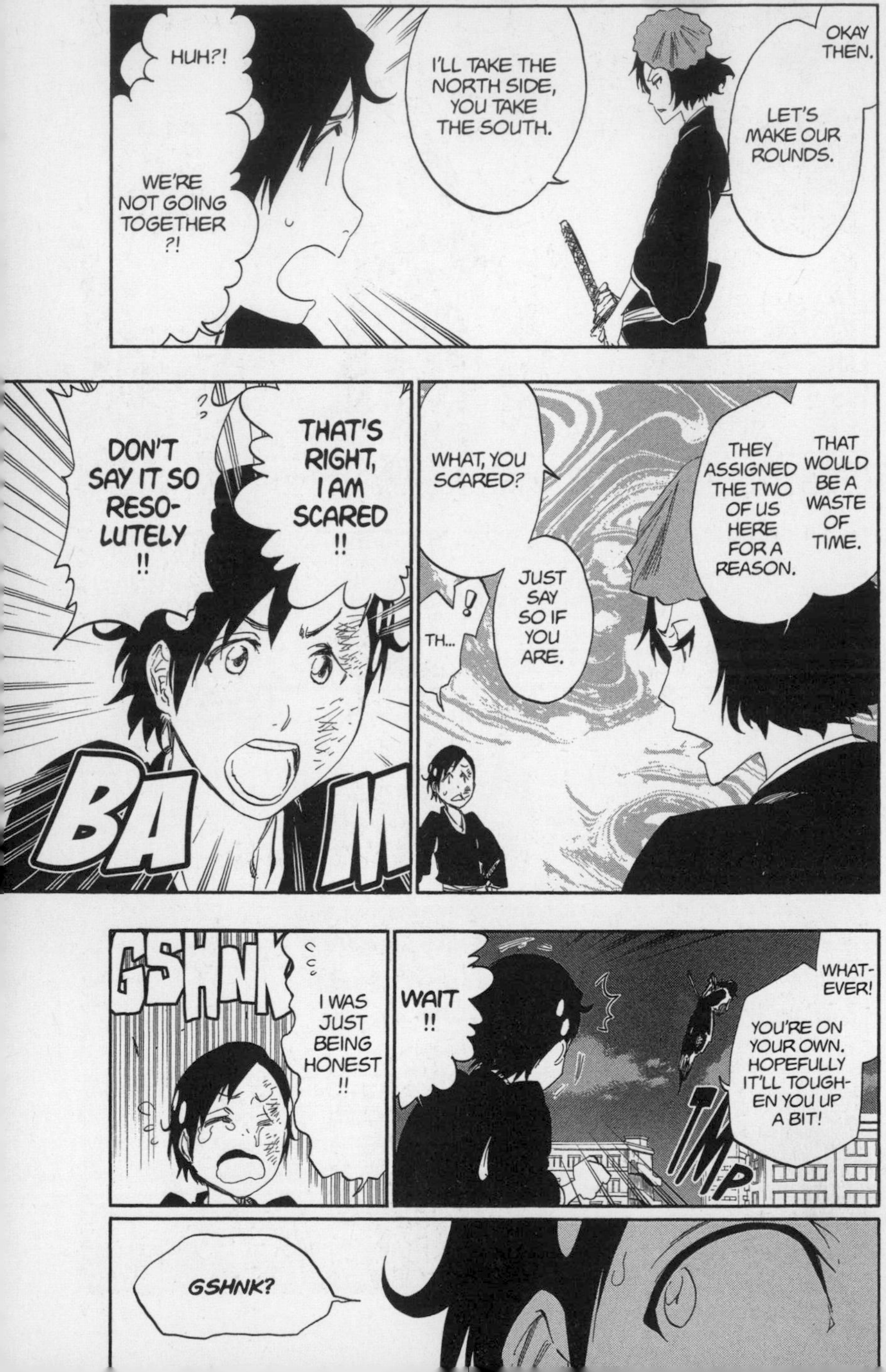
OKAY THEN.
LET'S MAKE OUR ROUNDS.
I'LL TAKE THE NORTH SIDE, YOU TAKE THE SOUTH.
HUH?!
WE'RE NOT GOING TOGETHER?!
THAT WOULD BE A WASTE OF TIME.
THEY ASSIGNED THE TWO OF US HERE FOR A REASON.
WHAT, YOU SCARED?
JUST SAY SO IF YOU ARE.
TH...
THAT'S RIGHT, I AM SCARED!!
DON'T SAY IT SO RESO-LUTELY!!
BAM
WHAT-EVER!
YOU'RE ON YOUR OWN. HOPEFULLY IT'LL TOUGH-EN YOU UP A BIT!
TMP
WAIT!!
I WAS JUST BEING HONEST!!
GSHNK
GSHNK?

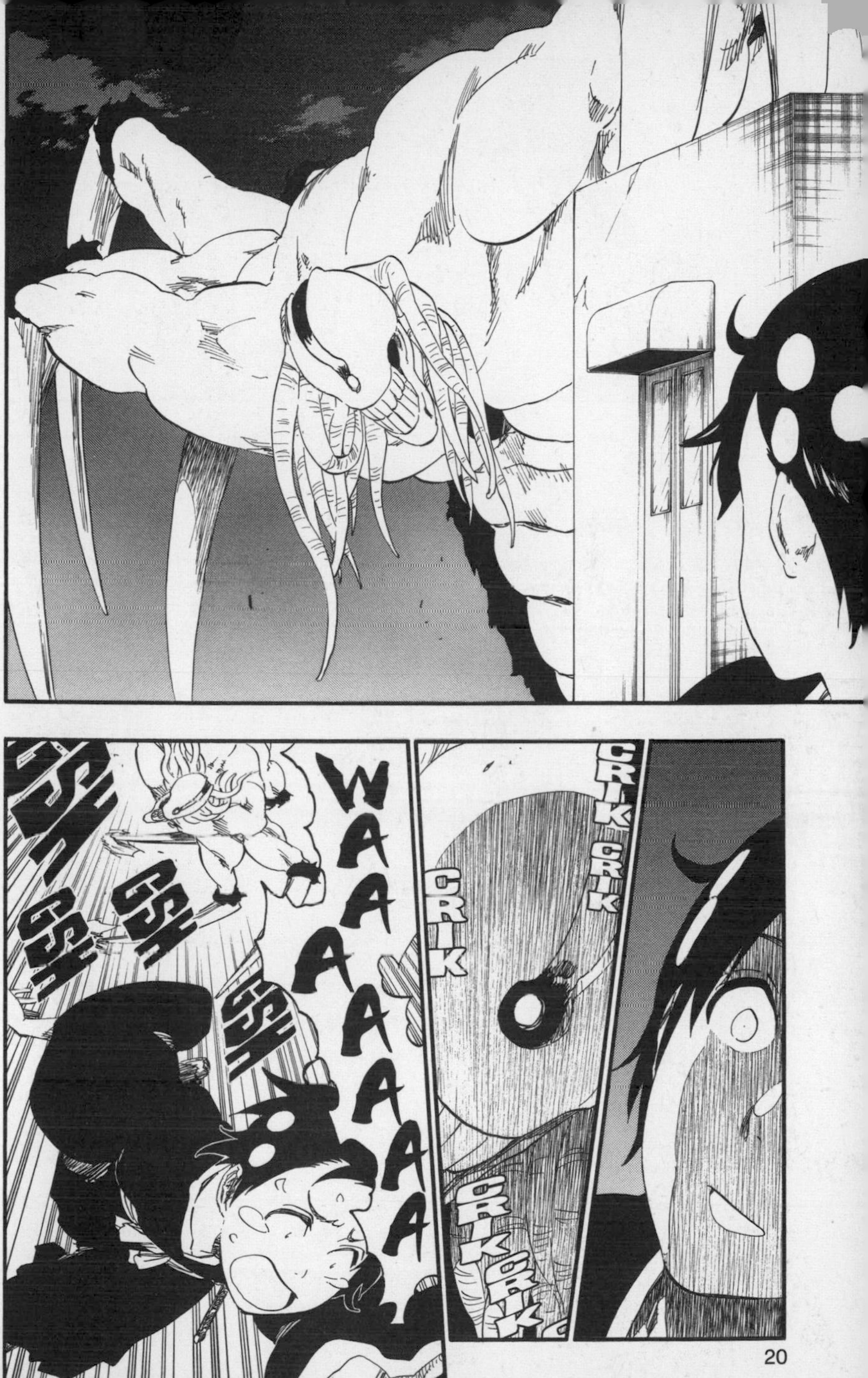
CRIK CRIK
CRIK
CRIK CRIK
WAAAAAAA
GSH
GSH
GSH
GSH

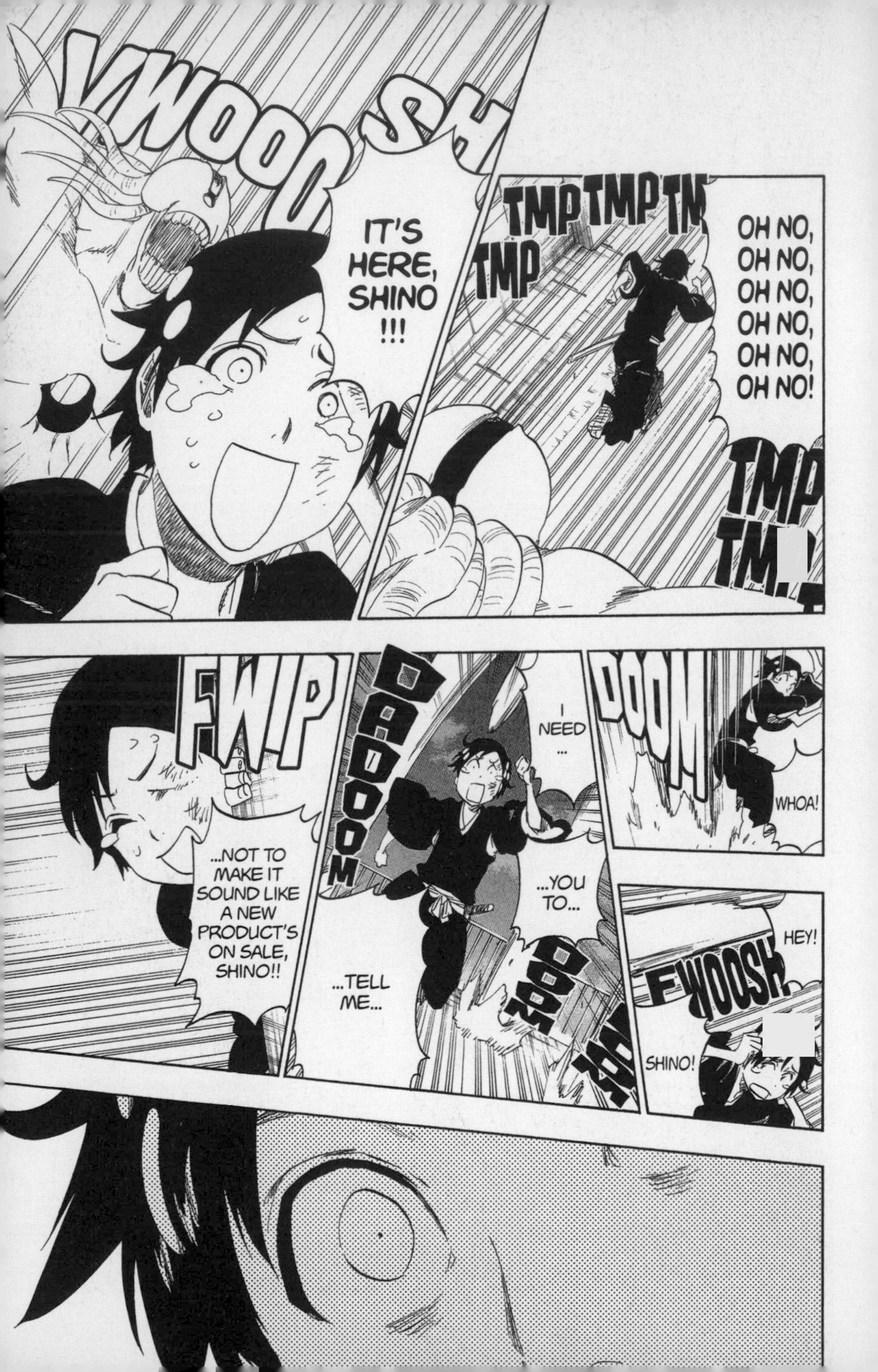
TMP TMP TM
TMP
OH NO, OH NO, OH NO, OH NO, OH NO, OH NO!
TMP TM
VWOOOSH
IT'S HERE, SHINO !!!
DOOM
WHOA!
HEY!
FWOOSH
SHINO!
I NEED ...
...YOU TO...
DADOOM
...TELL ME...
FWIP
...NOT TO MAKE IT SOUND LIKE A NEW PRODUCT'S ON SALE, SHINO!!

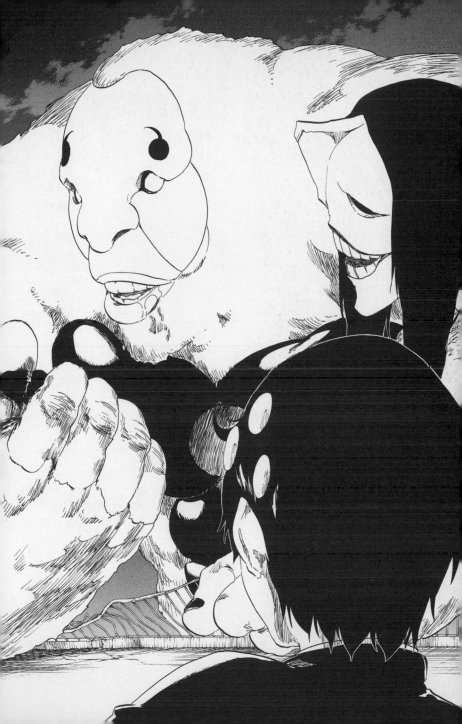

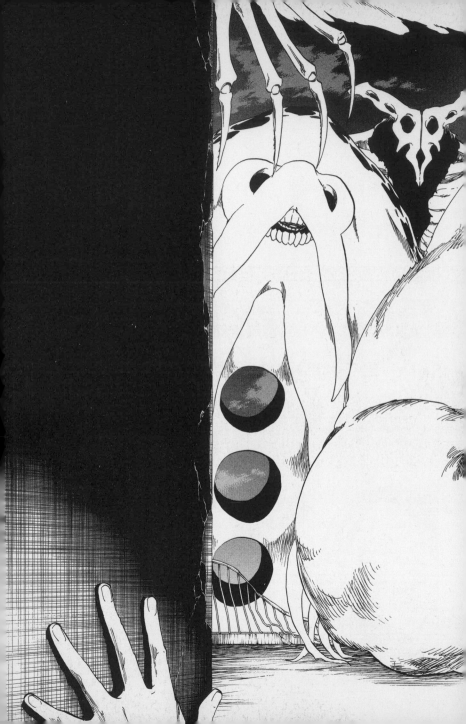

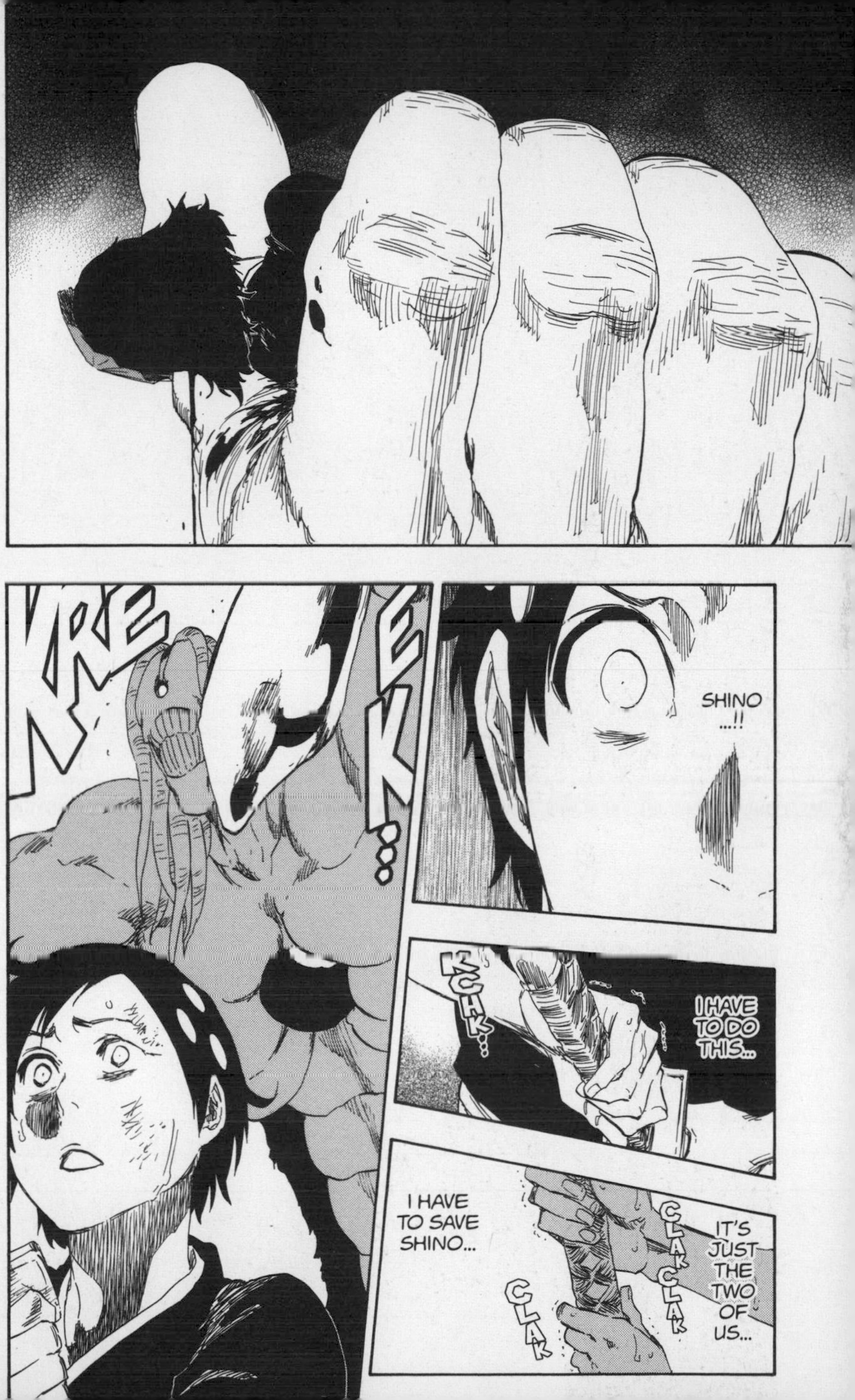
SHINO ...!!
KCHK...
I HAVE TO DO THIS...
IT'S JUST THE TWO OF US...
CLAK CLAK
I HAVE TO SAVE SHINO...
CLAK

« READ THIS WAY «

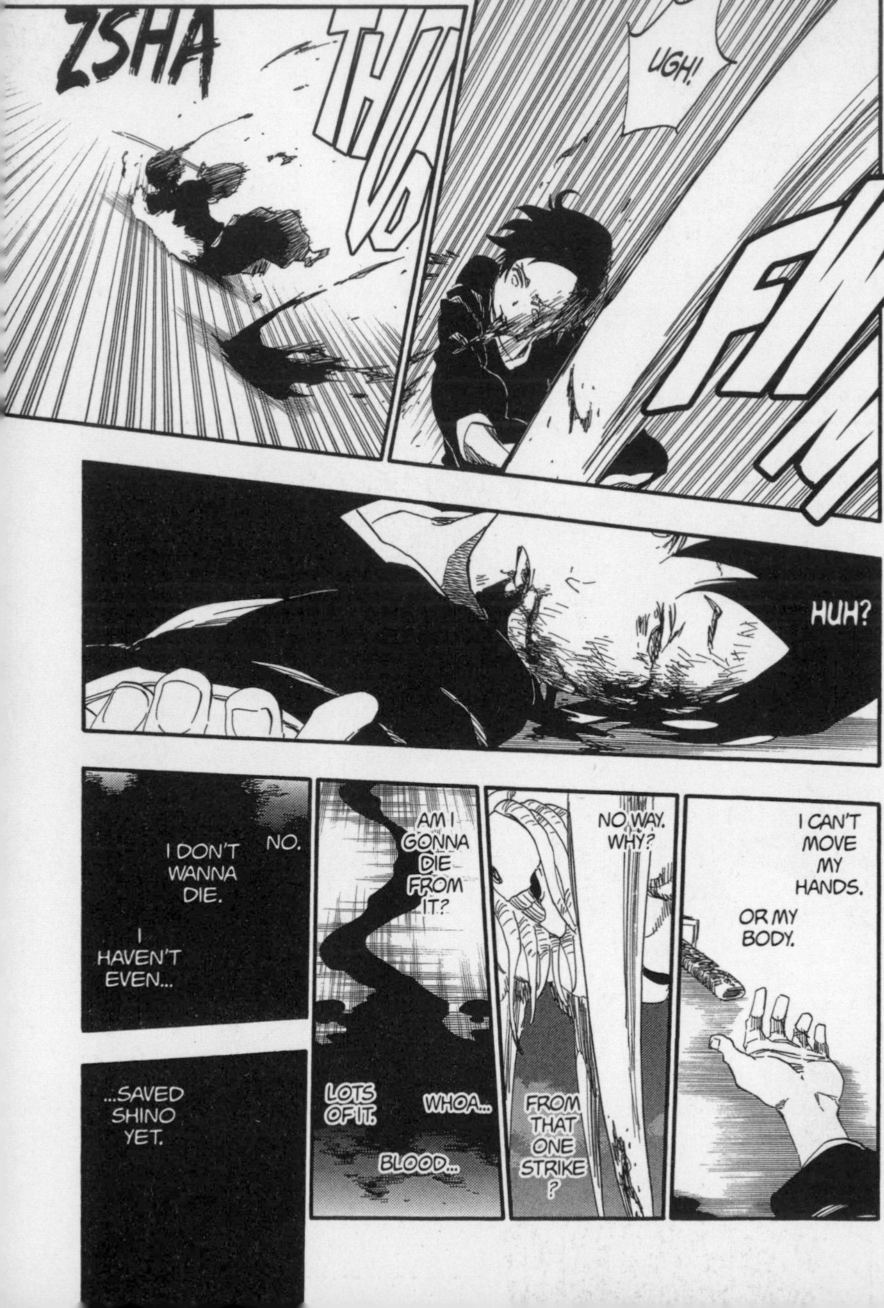
UGH!
FWM
THUD
ZSHA
HUH?
I CAN'T MOVE MY HANDS.
OR MY BODY.
NO WAY. WHY?
FROM THAT ONE STRIKE?
AM I GONNA DIE FROM IT?
WHOA...
BLOOD...
LOTS OF IT.
NO.
I DON'T WANNA DIE.
I HAVEN'T EVEN...
...SAVED SHINO YET.

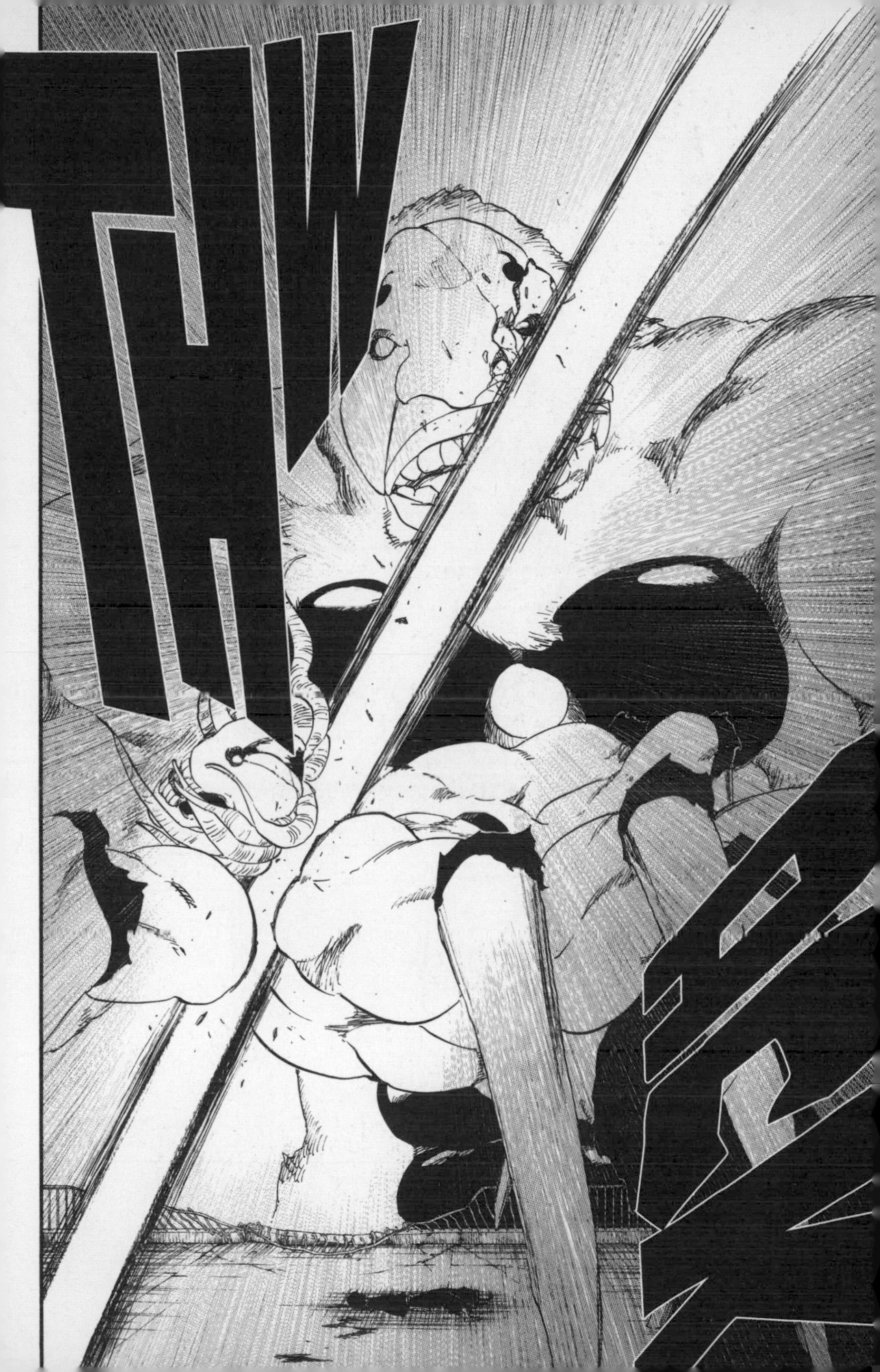

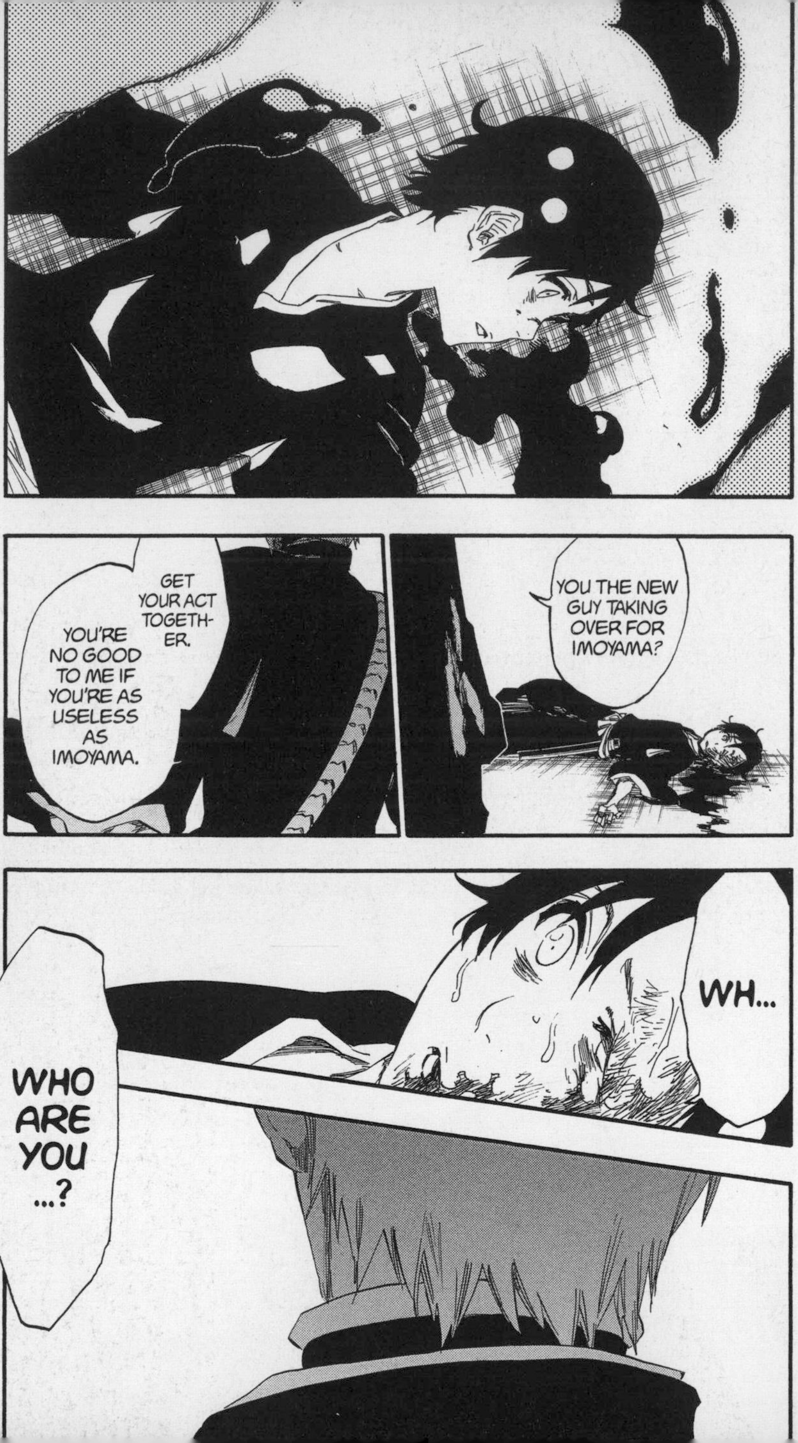
YOU THE NEW GUY TAKING OVER FOR IMOYAMA?
GET YOUR ACT TOGETH-ER.
YOU'RE NO GOOD TO ME IF YOU'RE AS USELESS AS IMOYAMA.
WH...
WHO ARE YOU ...?

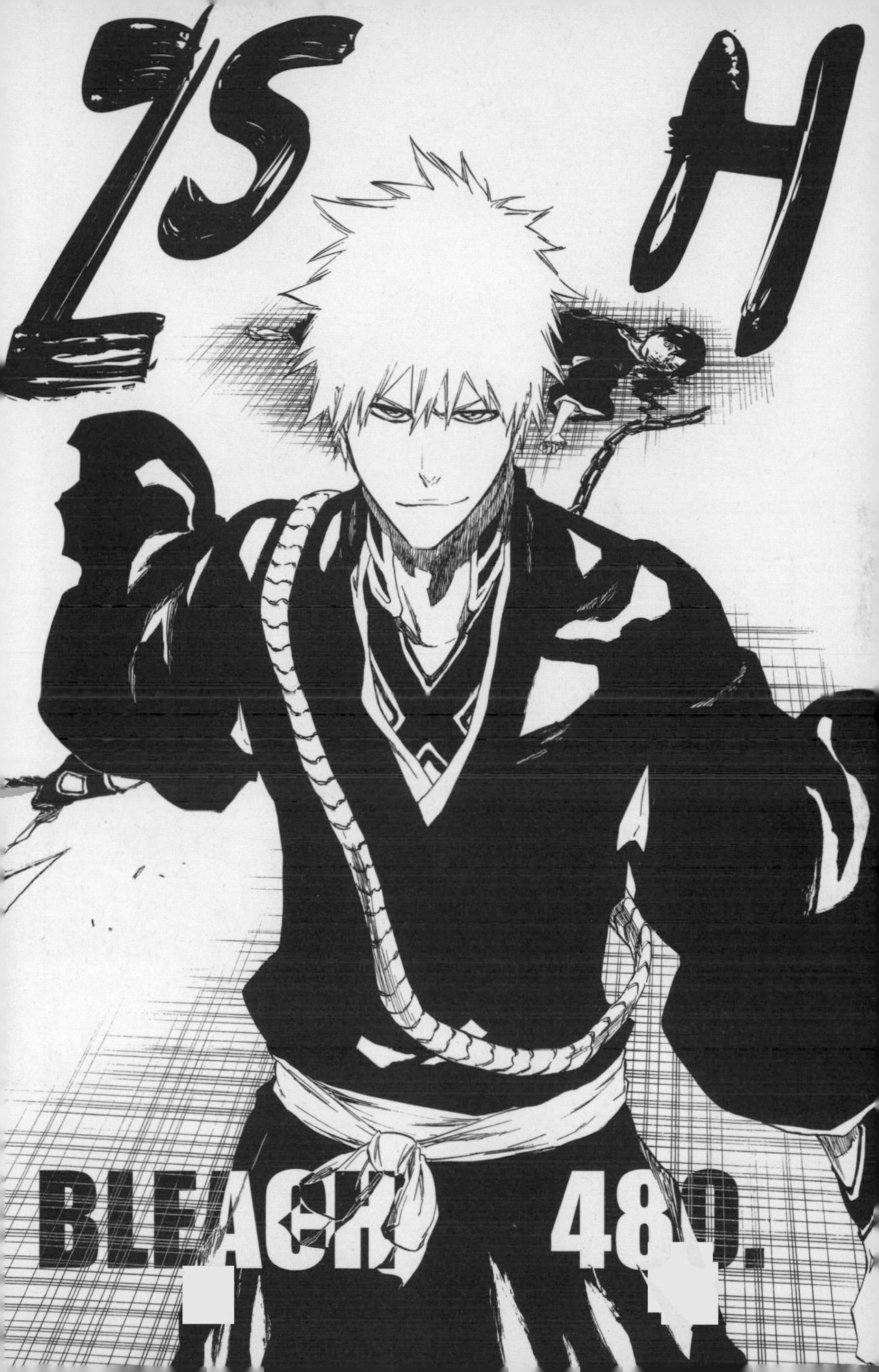
BLEACH
480.

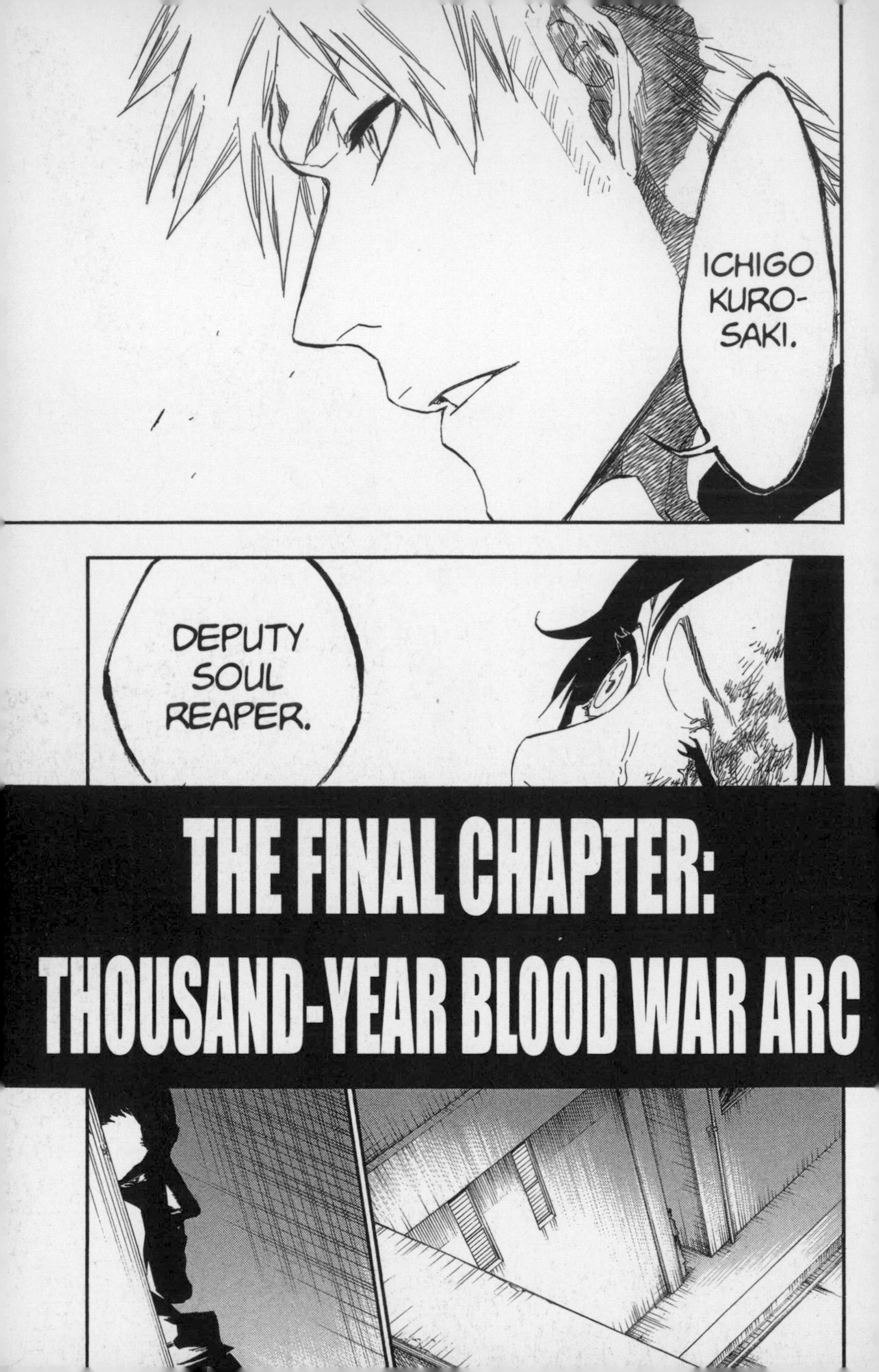
ICHIGO KURO-SAKI.
DEPUTY SOUL REAPER.
THE FINAL CHAPTER: THOUSAND-YEAR BLOOD WAR ARC

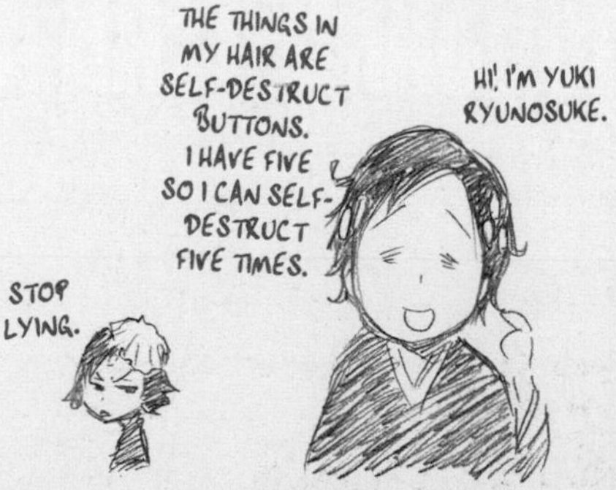
HI! I'M YUKI RYUNOSUKE.
THE THINGS IN MY HAIR ARE SELF-DESTRUCT BUTTONS. I HAVE FIVE SO I CAN SELF-DESTRUCT FIVE TIMES.
STOP LYING.

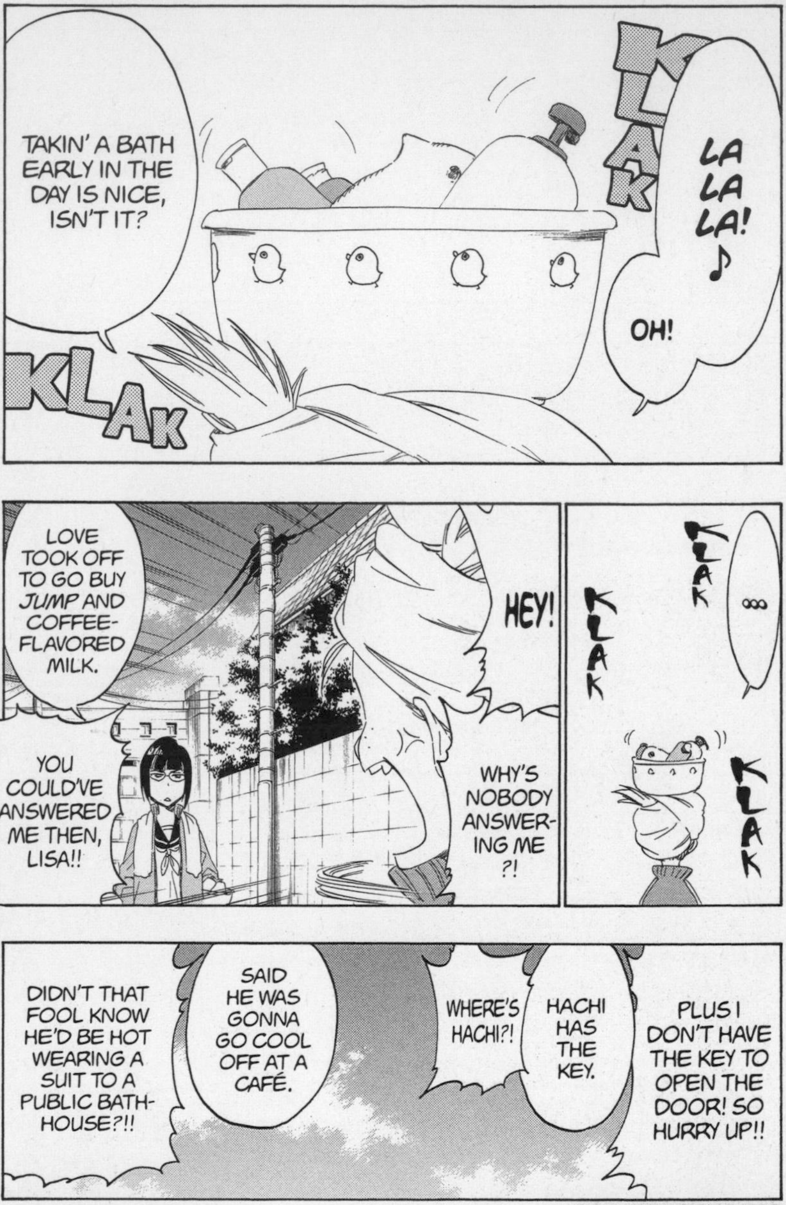
KLAK
LA LA LA! ♪
OH!
TAKIN' A BATH EARLY IN THE DAY IS NICE, ISN'T IT?
KLAK
KLAK
...
KLAK
KLAK
HEY!
WHY'S NOBODY ANSWERING ME?!
LOVE TOOK OFF TO GO BUY *JUMP* AND COFFEE-FLAVORED MILK.
YOU COULD'VE ANSWERED ME THEN, LISA!!
PLUS I DON'T HAVE THE KEY TO OPEN THE DOOR! SO HURRY UP!!
HACHI HAS THE KEY.
WHERE'S HACHI?!
SAID HE WAS GONNA GO COOL OFF AT A CAFÉ.
DIDN'T THAT FOOL KNOW HE'D BE HOT WEARING A SUIT TO A PUBLIC BATHHOUSE?!!

481. THE TEARING

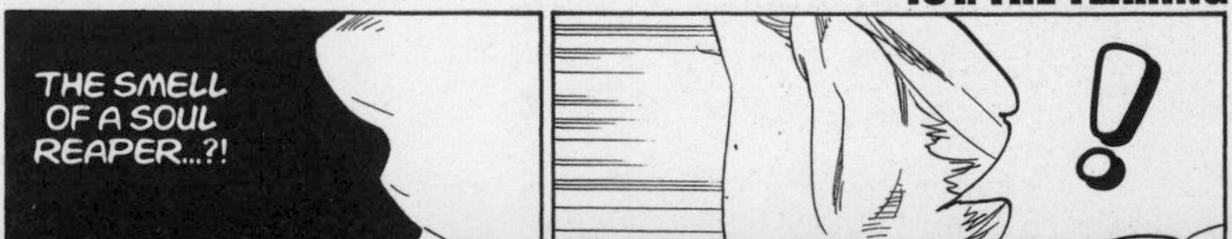
!
THE SMELL OF A SOUL REAPER...?!

BZZ...
BZZ...
...
WHAT THE HELL IS THAT...?

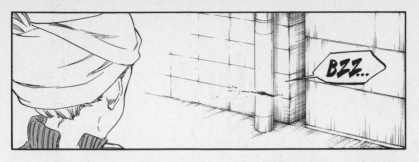

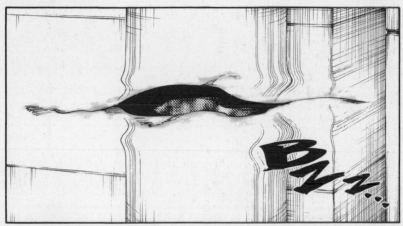

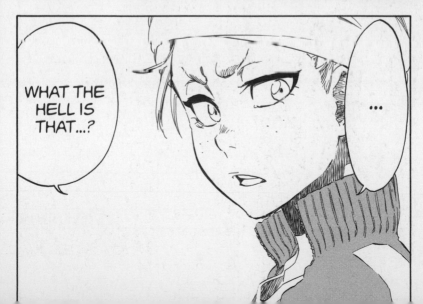

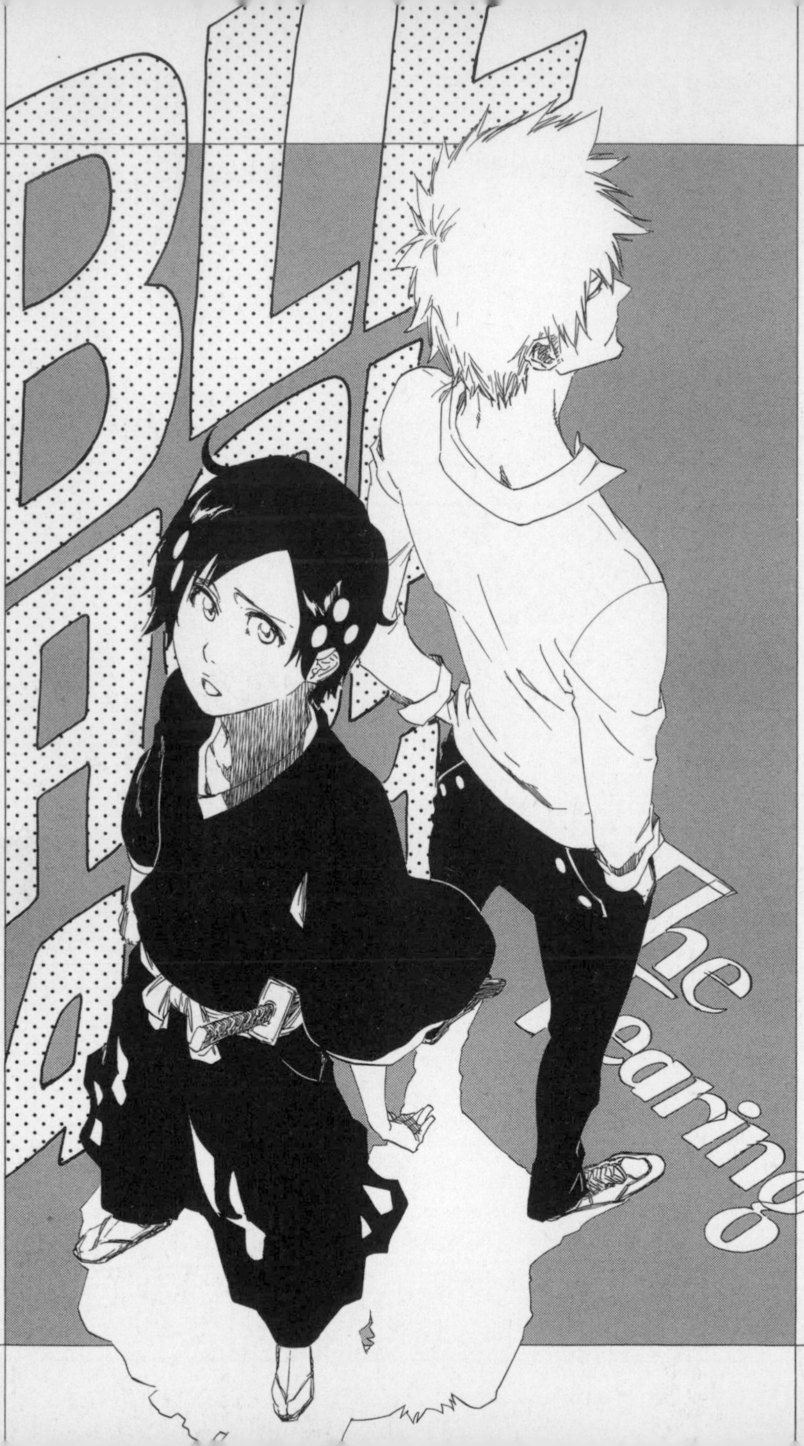

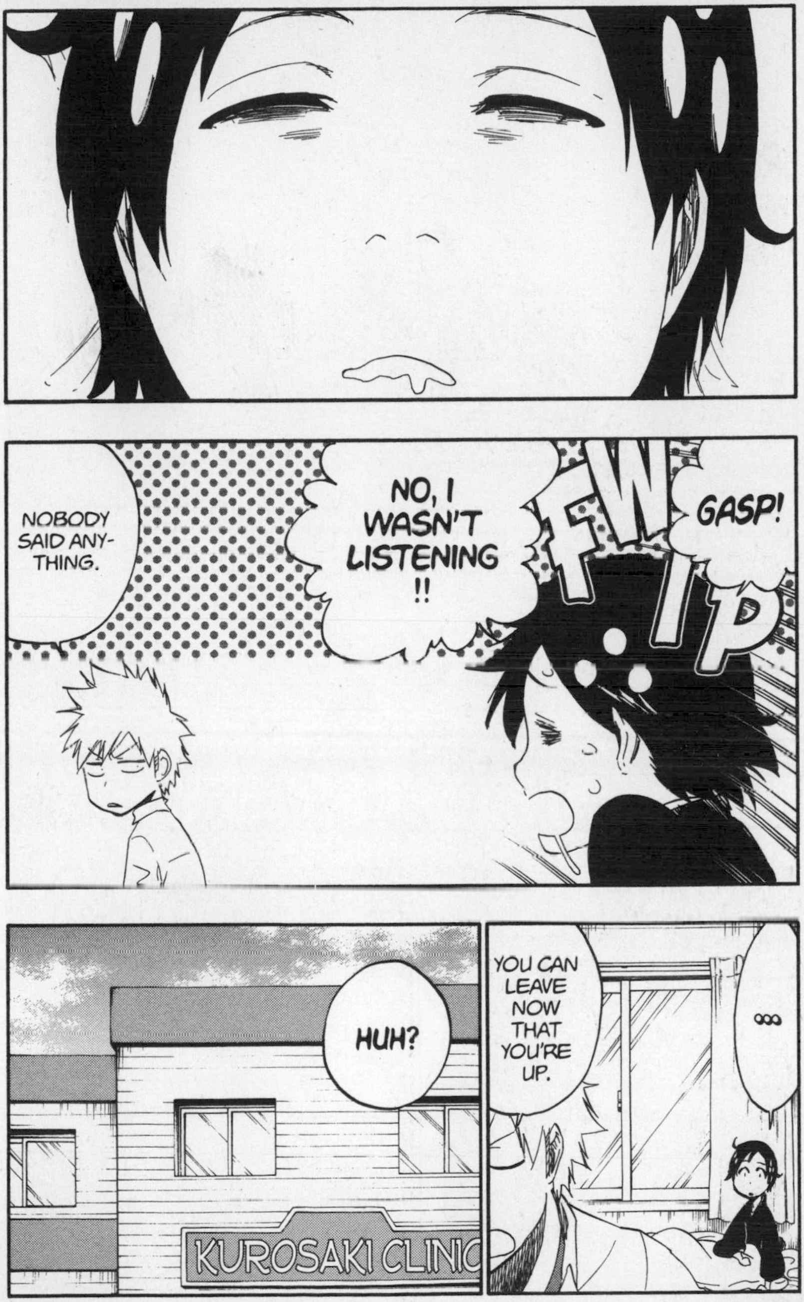
GASP!
FWIP
NO, I WASN'T LISTENING!!
NOBODY SAID ANYTHING.
...
YOU CAN LEAVE NOW THAT YOU'RE UP.
HUH?
KUROSAKI CLINIC

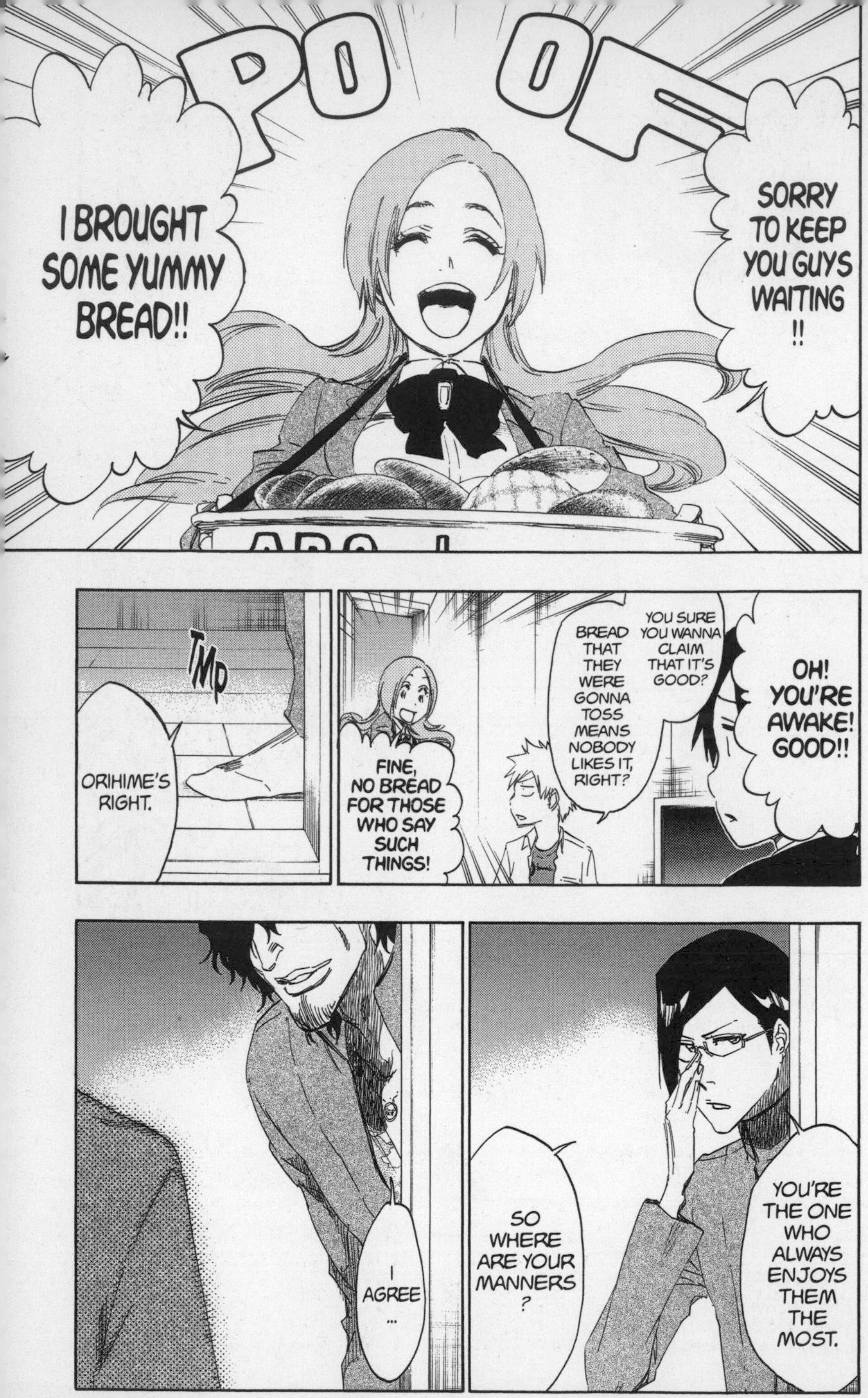
POOF
SORRY TO KEEP YOU GUYS WAITING!!
I BROUGHT SOME YUMMY BREAD!!
OH! YOU'RE AWAKE! GOOD!!
YOU SURE YOU WANNA CLAIM THAT IT'S GOOD?
BREAD THAT THEY WERE GONNA TOSS MEANS NOBODY LIKES IT, RIGHT?
FINE, NO BREAD FOR THOSE WHO SAY SUCH THINGS!
TMP
ORIHIME'S RIGHT.
YOU'RE THE ONE WHO ALWAYS ENJOYS THEM THE MOST.
SO WHERE ARE YOUR MANNERS?
I AGREE...

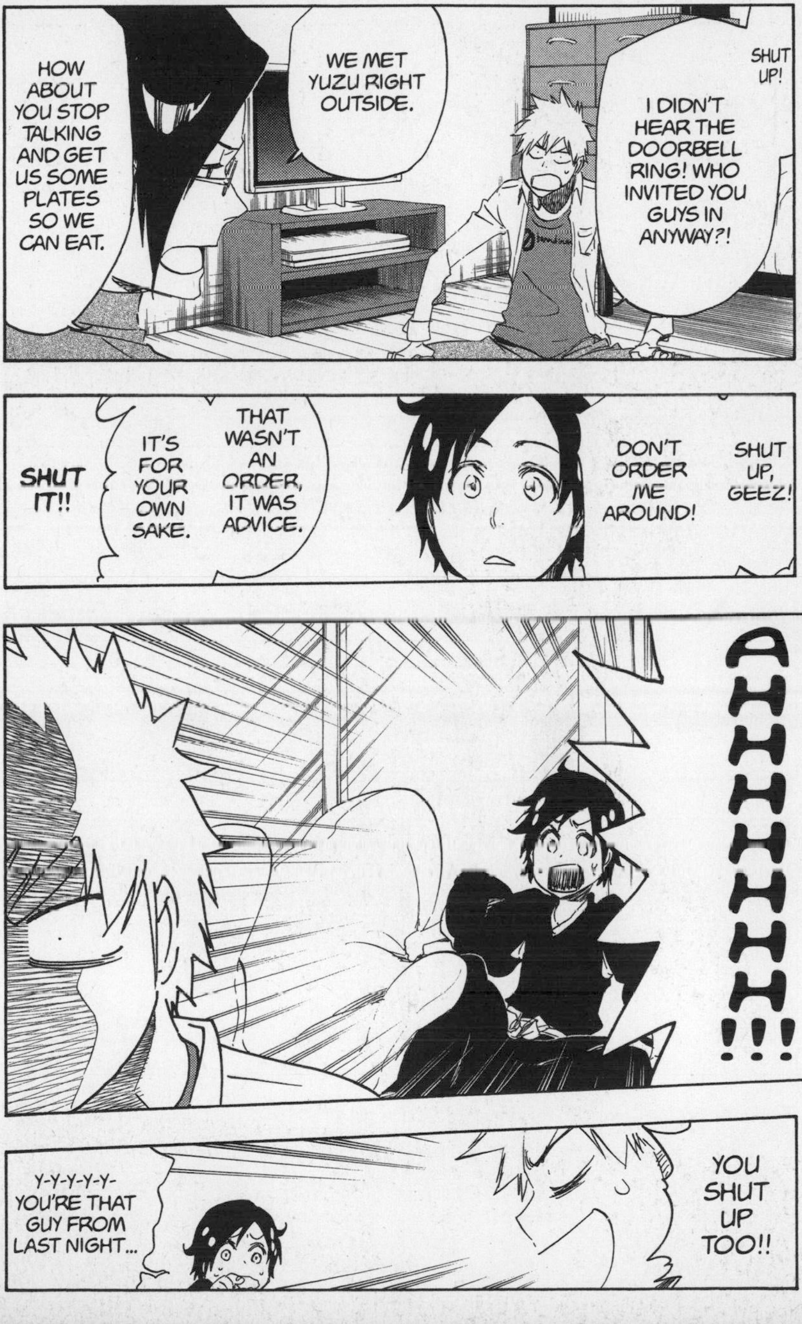
SHUT UP!
I DIDN'T HEAR THE DOORBELL RING! WHO INVITED YOU GUYS IN ANYWAY?!
WE MET YUZU RIGHT OUTSIDE.
HOW ABOUT YOU STOP TALKING AND GET US SOME PLATES SO WE CAN EAT.
SHUT UP, GEEZ!
DON'T ORDER ME AROUND!
THAT WASN'T AN ORDER, IT WAS ADVICE.
IT'S FOR YOUR OWN SAKE.
SHUT IT!!
AHHHHHHH!!!
YOU SHUT UP TOO!!
Y-Y-Y-Y-Y-YOU'RE THAT GUY FROM LAST NIGHT...

READ THIS WAY

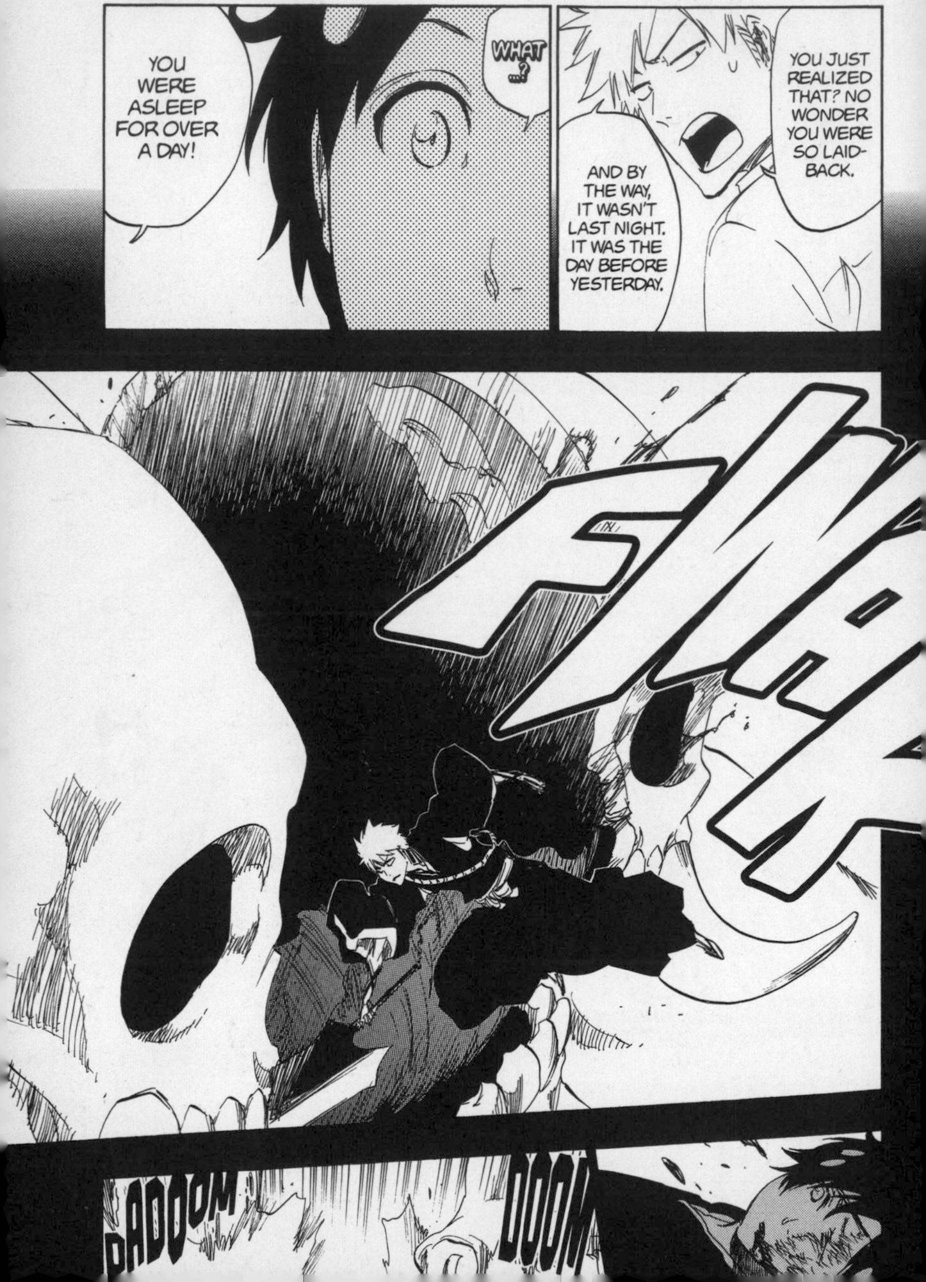
YOU JUST REALIZED THAT? NO WONDER YOU WERE SO LAID-BACK.
AND BY THE WAY, IT WASN'T LAST NIGHT. IT WAS THE DAY BEFORE YESTERDAY.
WHAT ...?
YOU WERE ASLEEP FOR OVER A DAY!
DOOM
PADOOM

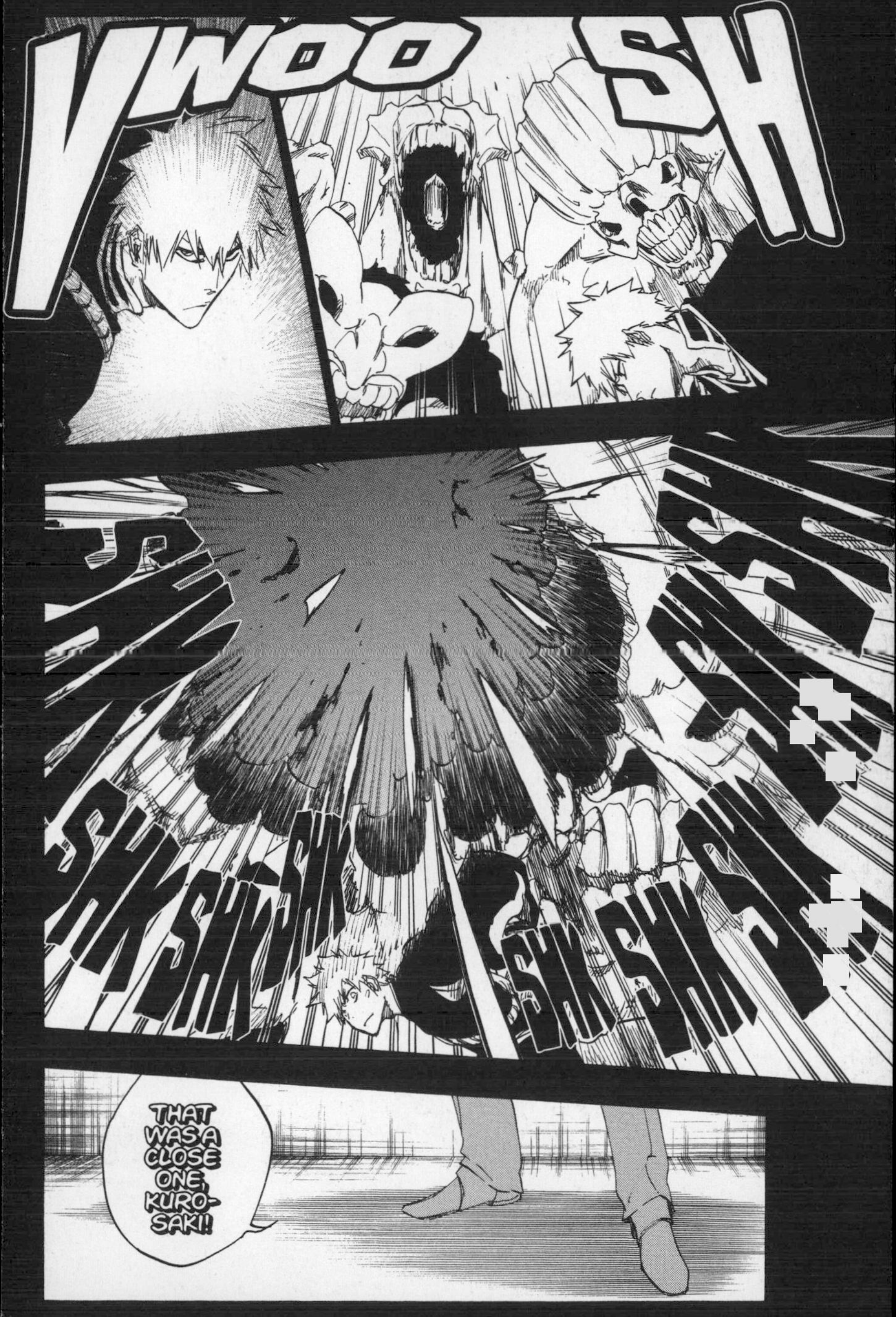
VWOOOSH
SHK SHK SHK
SHK SHK SHK
THAT WAS A CLOSE ONE, KURO-SAKI!!

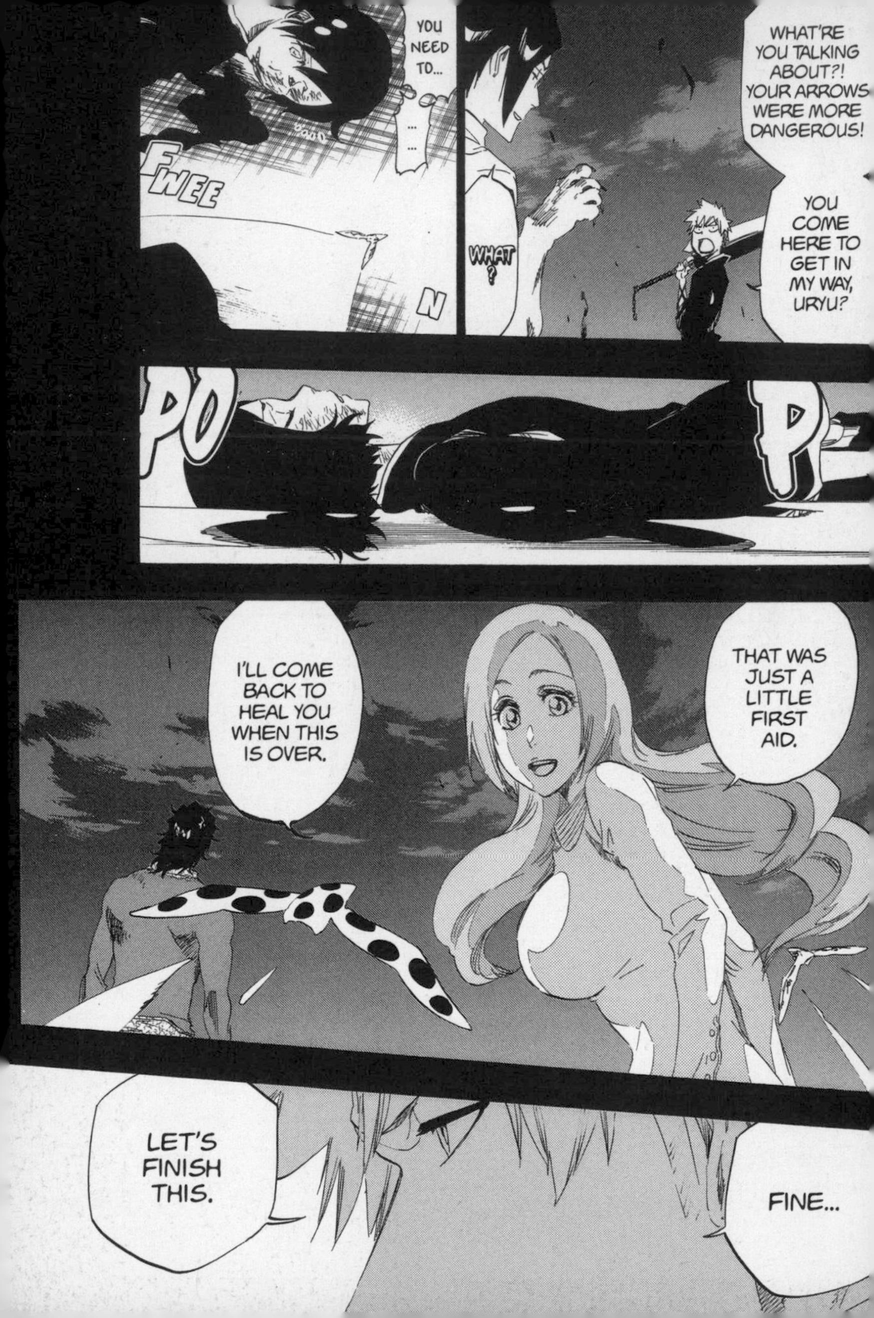
WHAT'RE YOU TALKING ABOUT?! YOUR ARROWS WERE MORE DANGEROUS!
YOU COME HERE TO GET IN MY WAY, URYU?
WHAT ?
YOU NEED TO...
...
...
FWEE
N
PO
P
THAT WAS JUST A LITTLE FIRST AID.
I'LL COME BACK TO HEAL YOU WHEN THIS IS OVER.
FINE...
LET'S FINISH THIS.

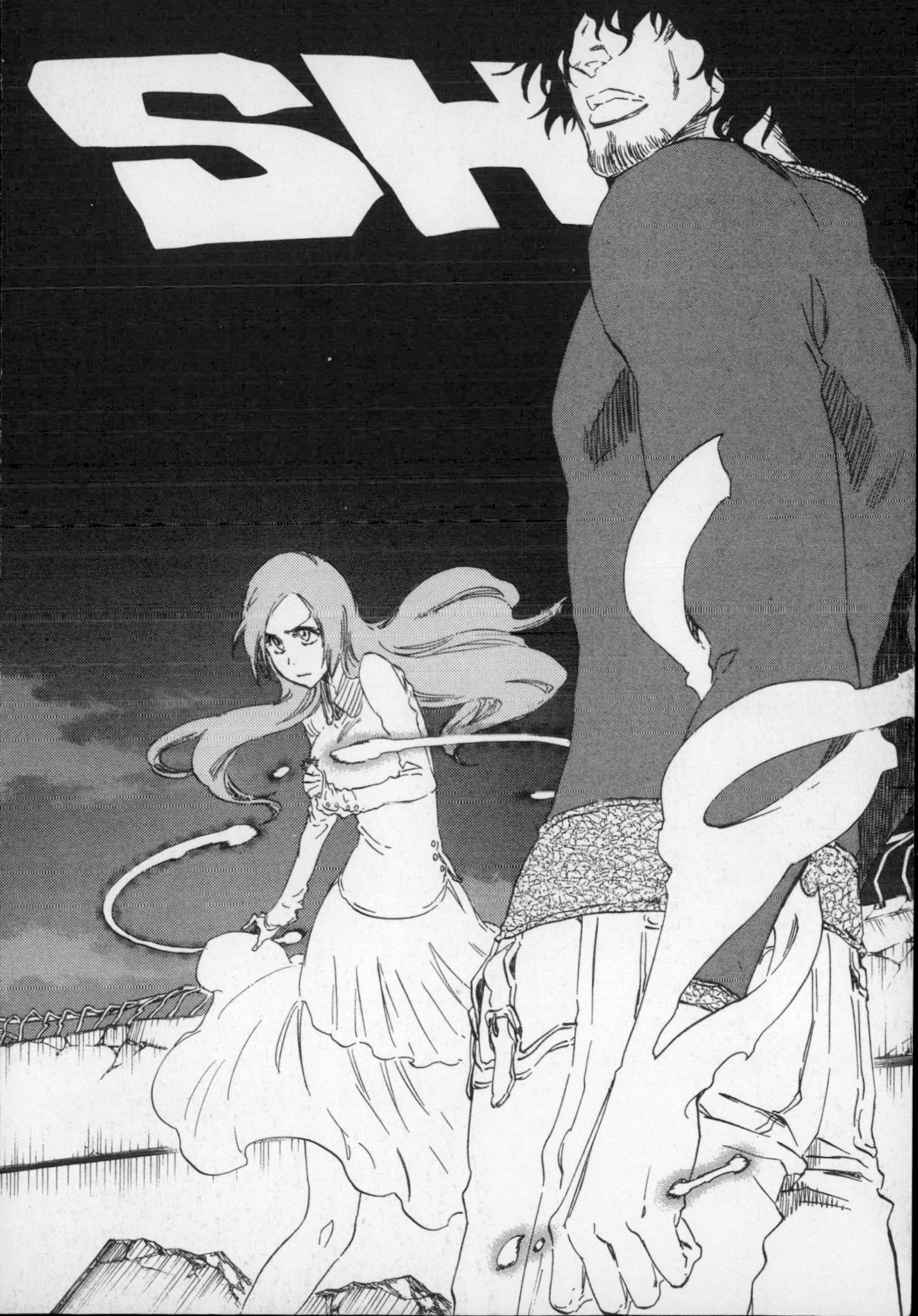
SH

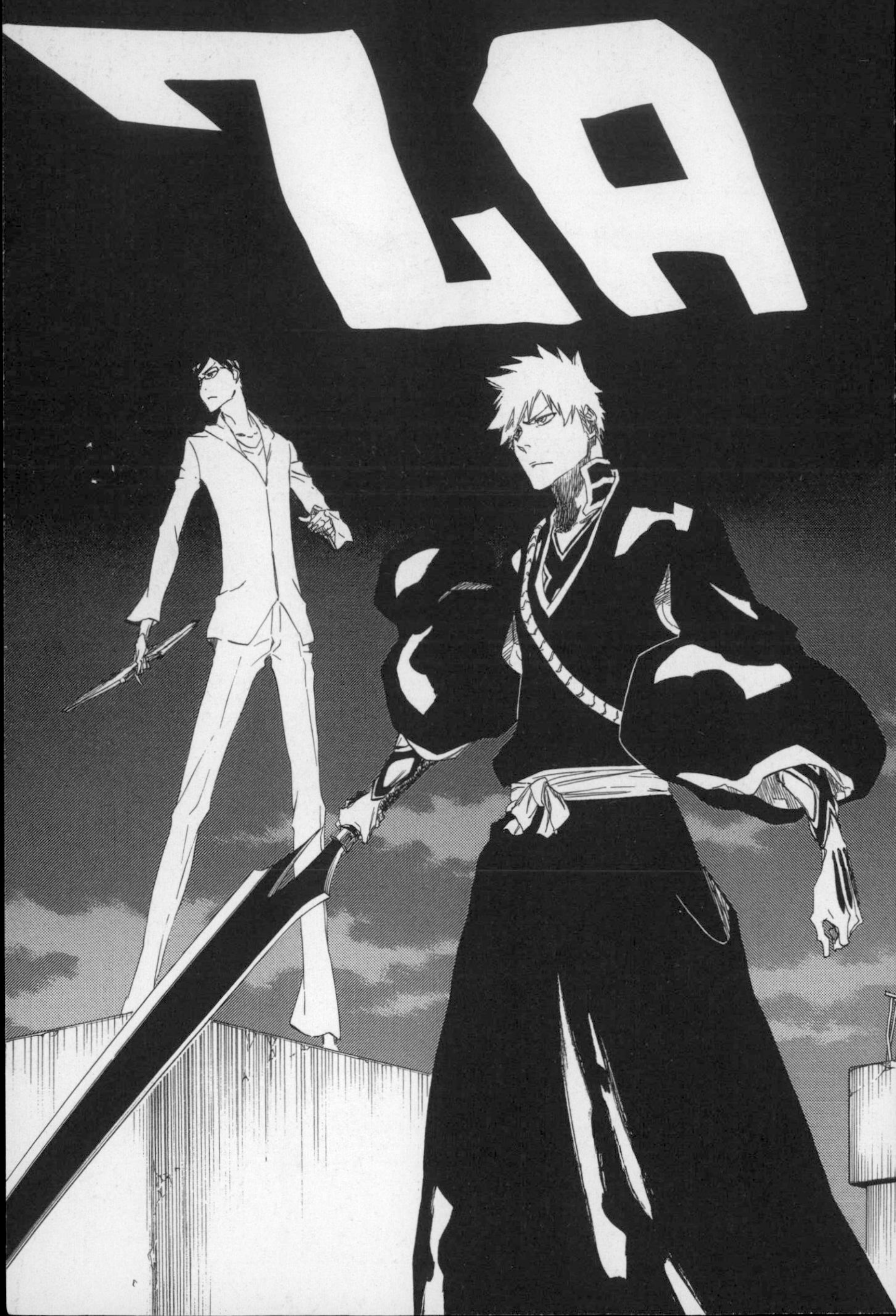

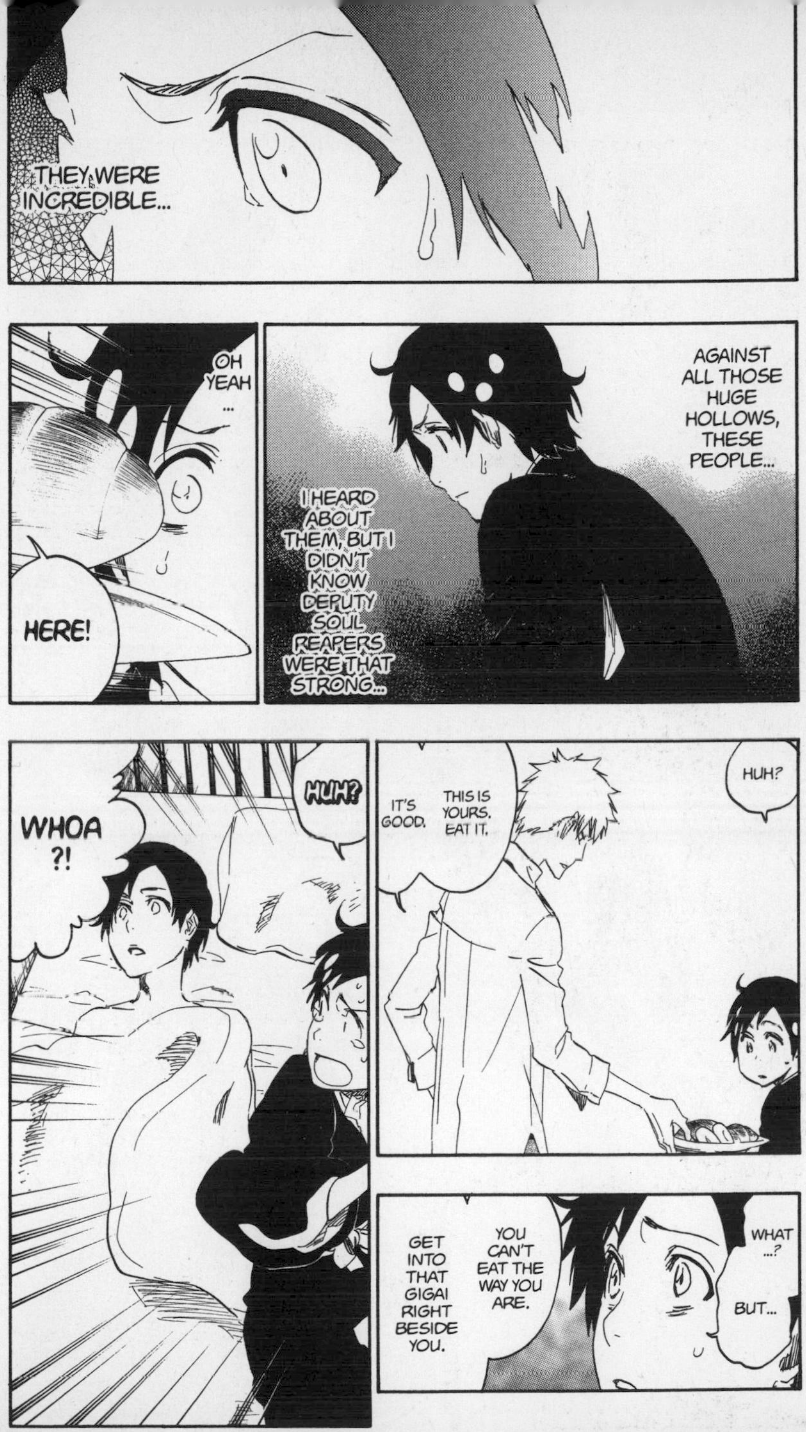
THEY WERE INCREDIBLE...
AGAINST ALL THOSE HUGE HOLLOWS, THESE PEOPLE...
I HEARD ABOUT THEM, BUT I DIDN'T KNOW DEPUTY SOUL REAPERS WERE THAT STRONG...
OH YEAH ...
HERE!
HUH?
THIS IS YOURS. EAT IT.
IT'S GOOD.
WHAT ...?
BUT...
YOU CAN'T EAT THE WAY YOU ARE.
GET INTO THAT GIGAI RIGHT BESIDE YOU.
HUH?
WHOA ?!

READ THIS WAY

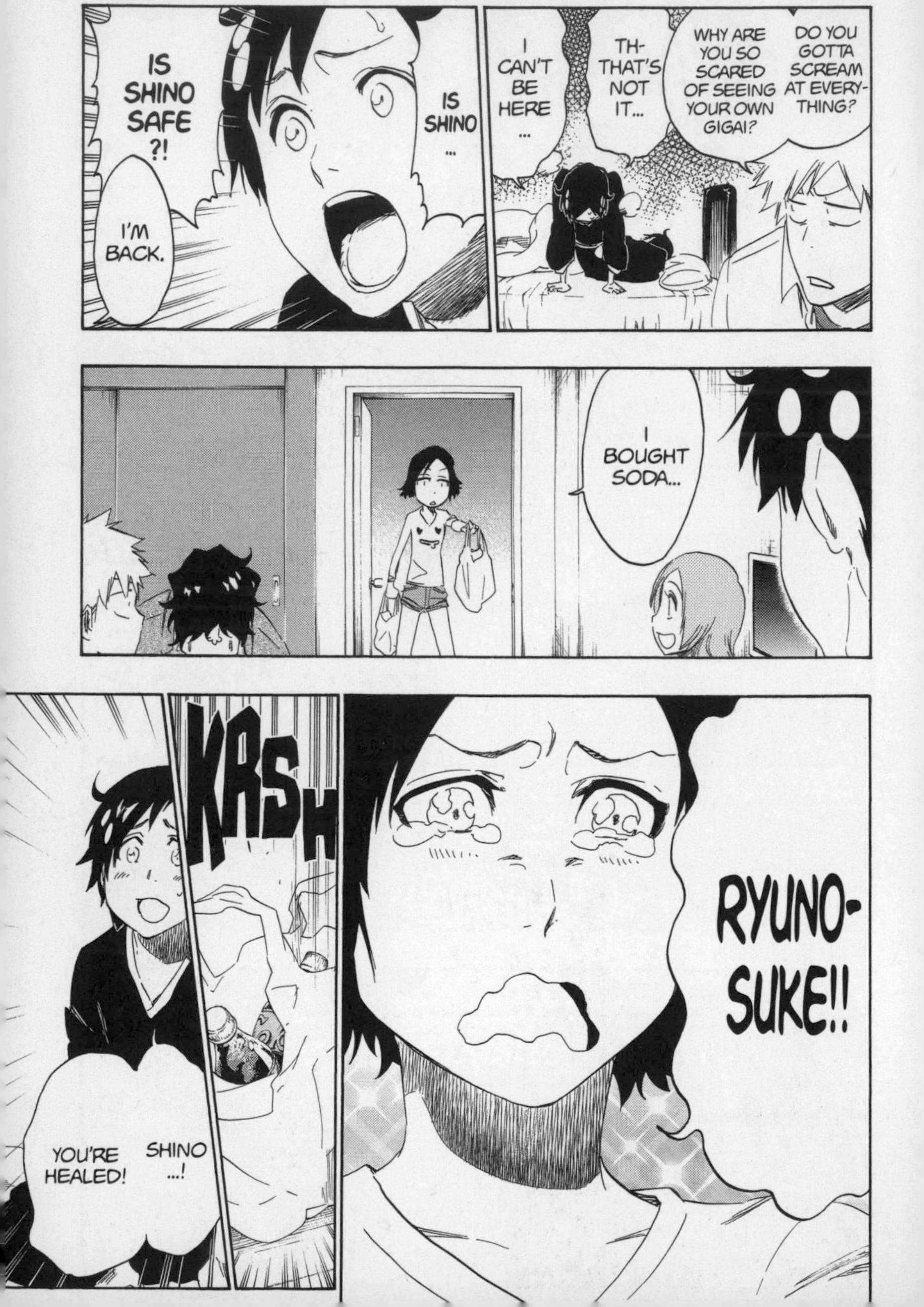
DO YOU GOTTA SCREAM AT EVERY-THING?
WHY ARE YOU SO SCARED OF SEEING YOUR OWN GIGAI?
TH-THAT'S NOT IT...
I CAN'T BE HERE ...
IS SHINO ...
IS SHINO SAFE ?!
I'M BACK.
I BOUGHT SODA...
RYUNO-SUKE!!
KRSH
SHINO ...!
YOU'RE HEALED!

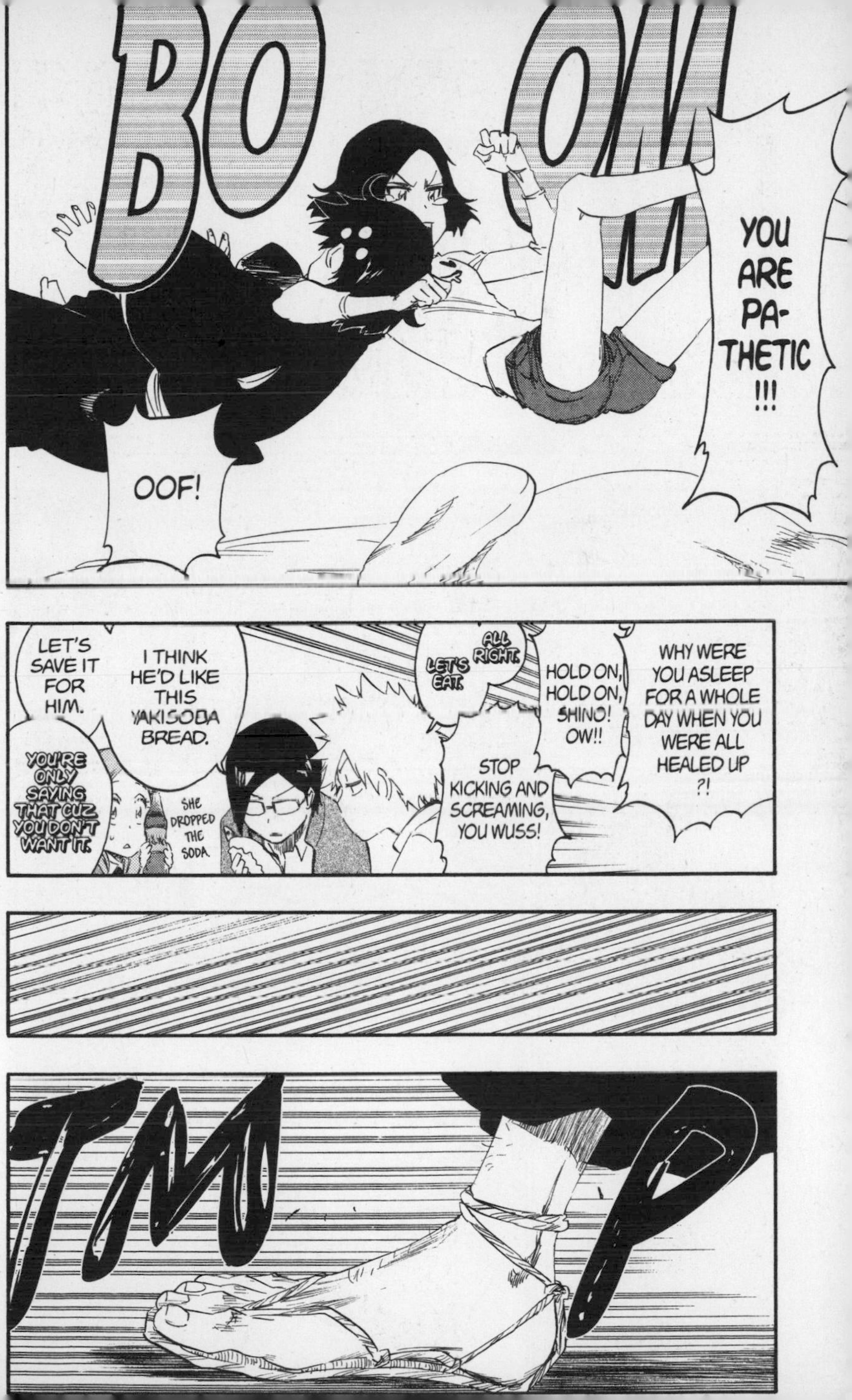
BOOM
YOU ARE PA-THETIC!!!
OOF!
WHY WERE YOU ASLEEP FOR A WHOLE DAY WHEN YOU WERE ALL HEALED UP?!
HOLD ON, HOLD ON, SHINO! OW!!
STOP KICKING AND SCREAMING, YOU WUSS!
ALL RIGHT.
LET'S EAT.
I THINK HE'D LIKE THIS YAKISODA BREAD.
SHE DROPPED THE SODA.
LET'S SAVE IT FOR HIM.
YOU'RE ONLY SAYING THAT CUZ YOU DON'T WANT IT.
TMP

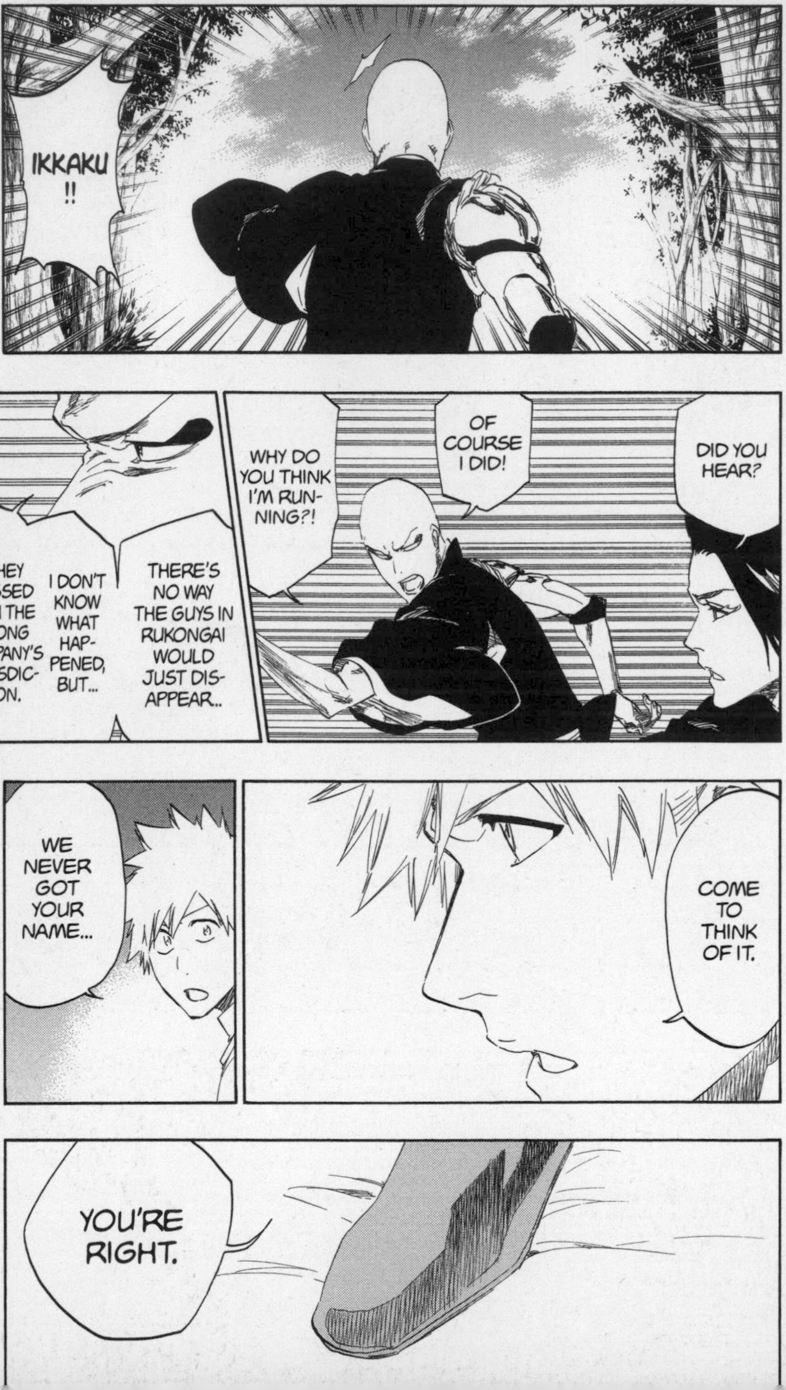
IKKAKU !!
DID YOU HEAR?
OF COURSE I DID!
WHY DO YOU THINK I'M RUNNING?!
THERE'S NO WAY THE GUYS IN RUKONGAI WOULD JUST DISAPPEAR..
I DON'T KNOW WHAT HAPPENED, BUT...
...THEY MESSED WITH THE WRONG COMPANY'S JURISDICTION.
COME TO THINK OF IT.
WE NEVER GOT YOUR NAME...
YOU'RE RIGHT.

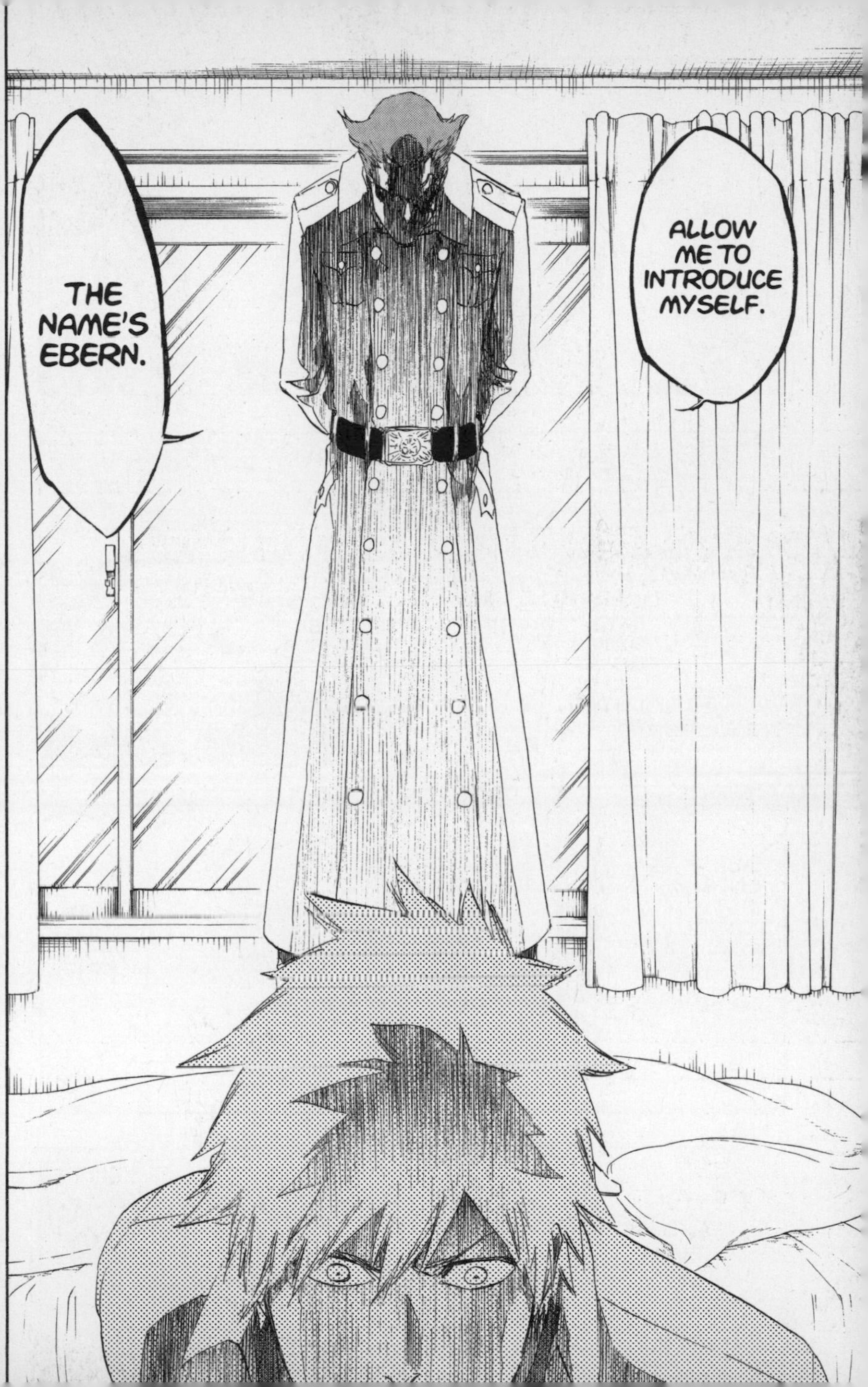
ALLOW ME TO INTRODUCE MYSELF.
THE NAME'S EBERN.

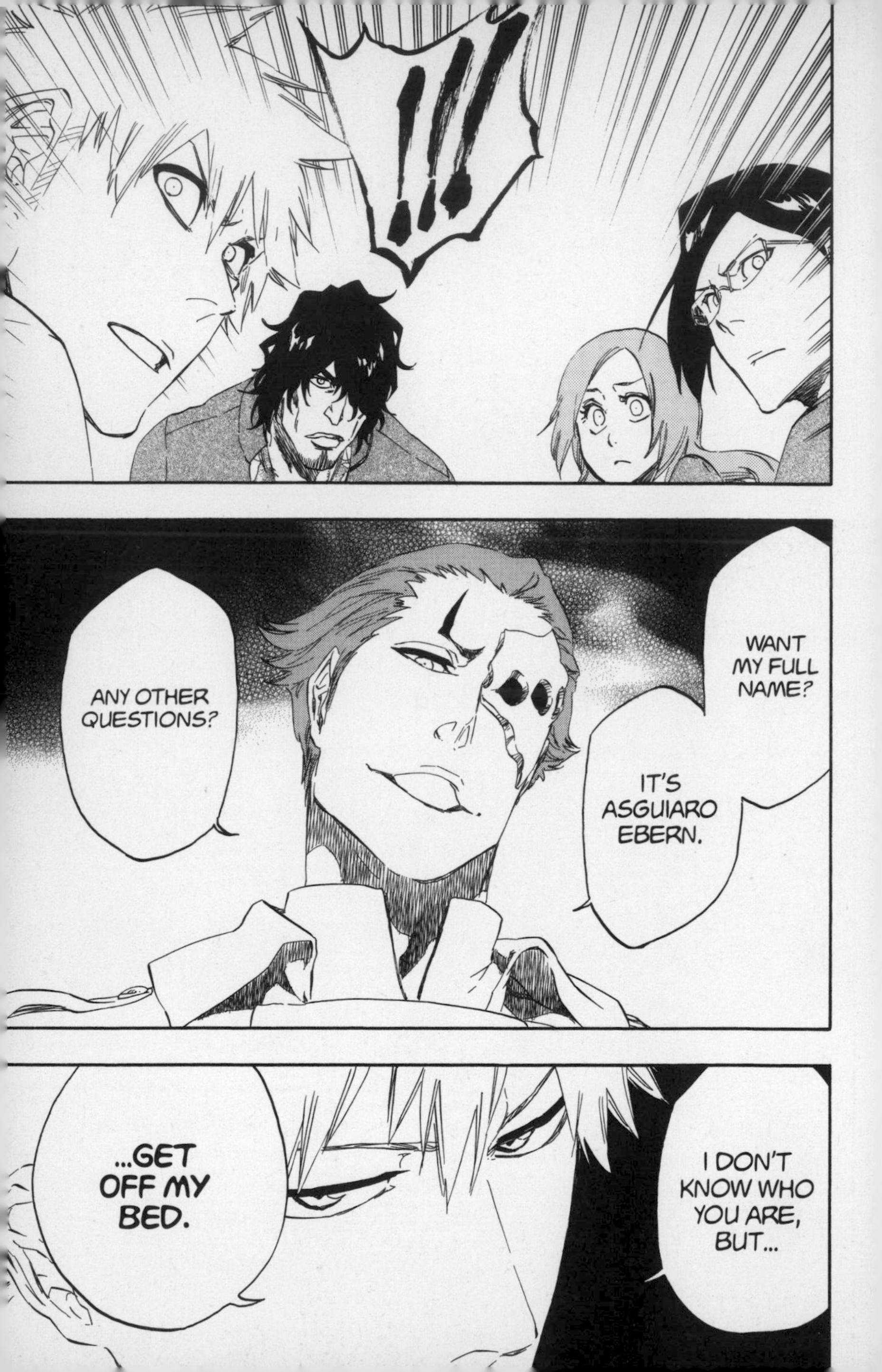

!!
WANT MY FULL NAME?
IT'S ASGUIARO EBERN.
ANY OTHER QUESTIONS?
I DON'T KNOW WHO YOU ARE, BUT...
...GET OFF MY BED.

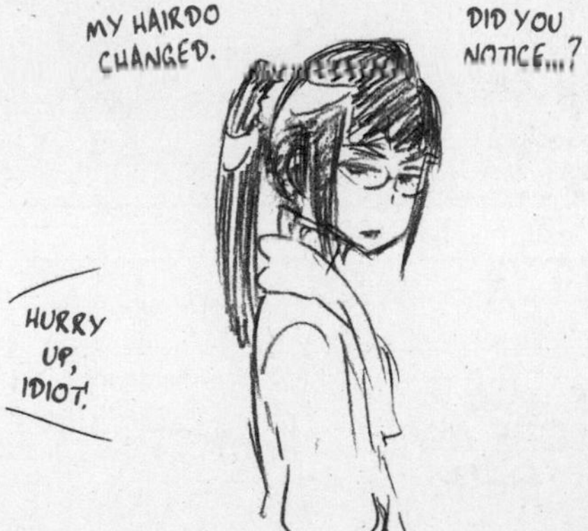
DID YOU NOTICE...?
MY HAIRDO CHANGED.
HURRY UP, IDIOT!

482. BAD RECOGNITION

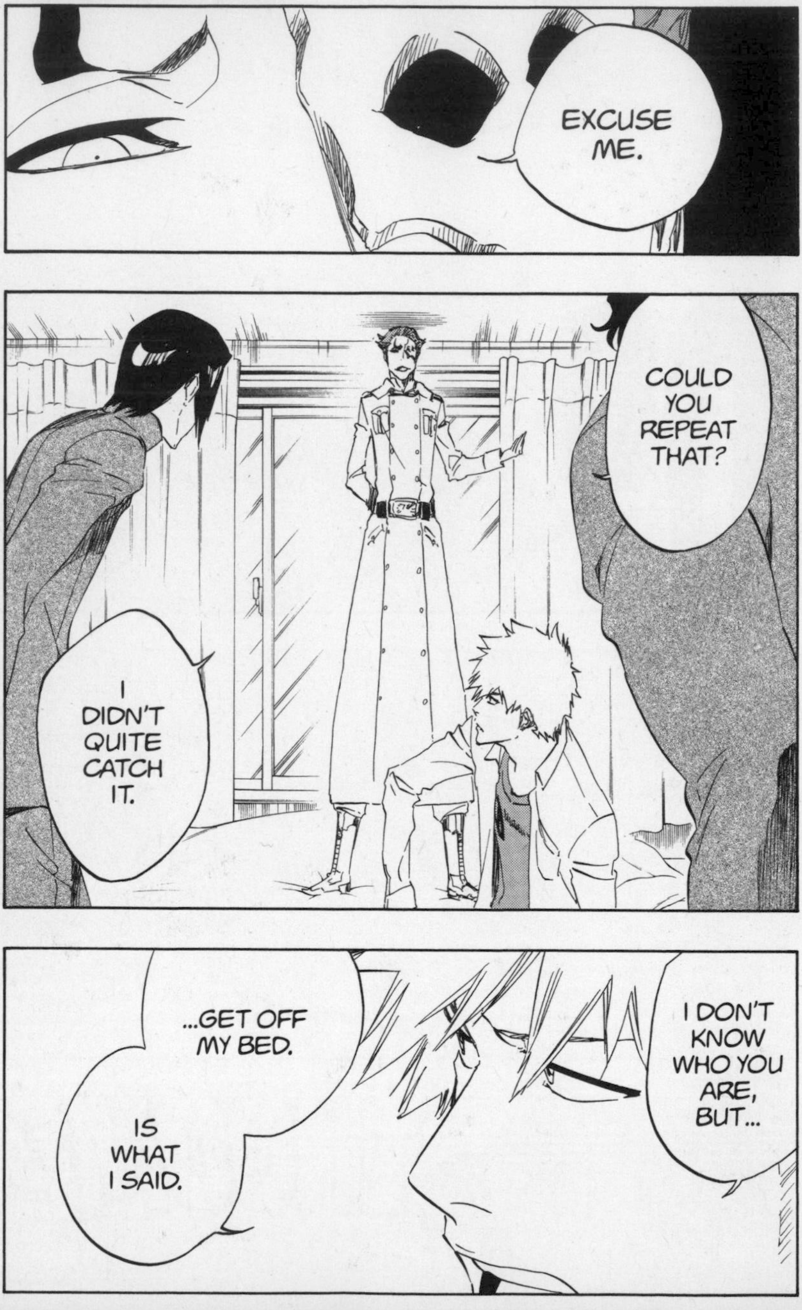
EXCUSE ME.
COULD YOU REPEAT THAT?
I DIDN'T QUITE CATCH IT.
I DON'T KNOW WHO YOU ARE, BUT...
...GET OFF MY BED.
IS WHAT I SAID.

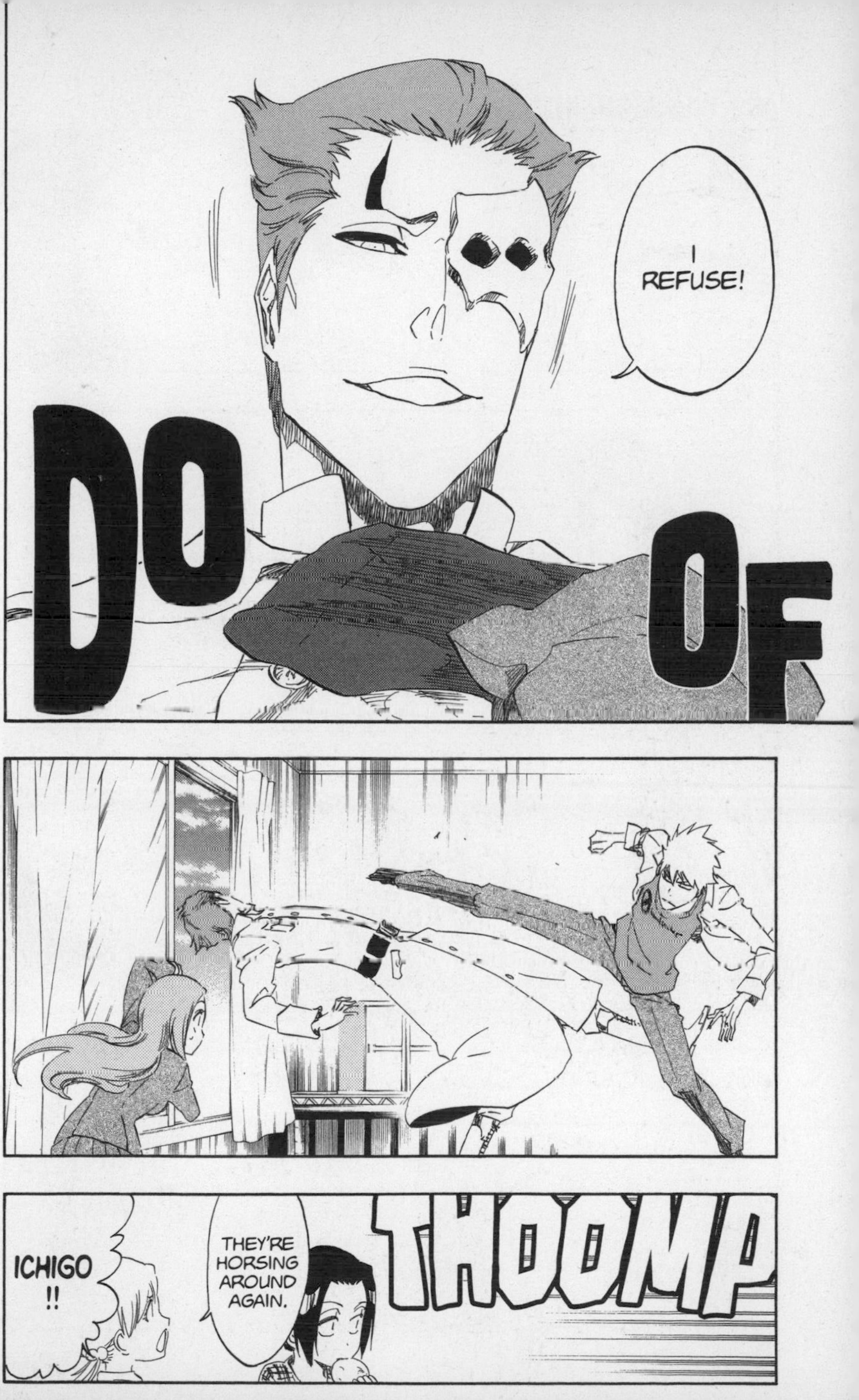
I REFUSE!
DOOF
THOOMP
THEY'RE HORSING AROUND AGAIN.
ICHIGO !!

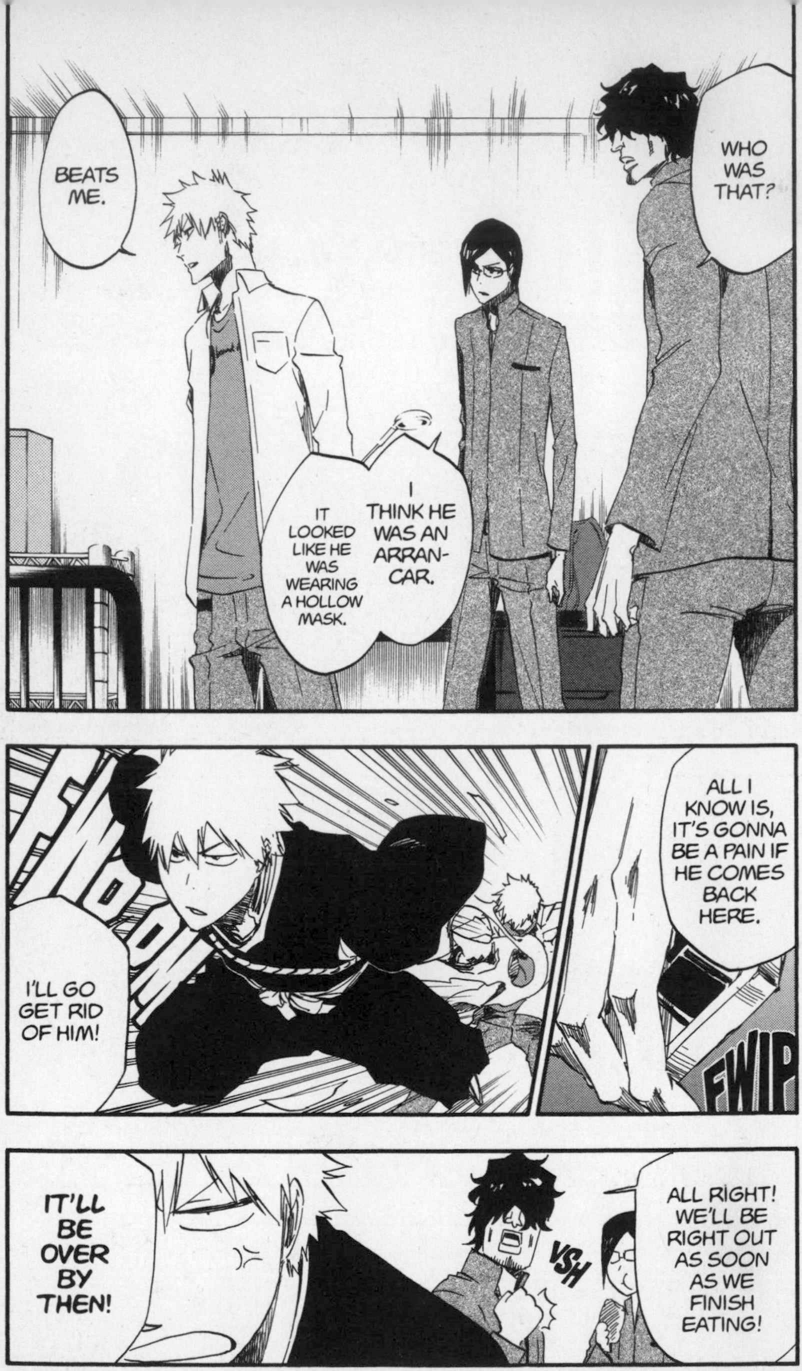
WHO WAS THAT?
BEATS ME.
I THINK HE WAS AN ARRAN-CAR.
IT LOOKED LIKE HE WAS WEARING A HOLLOW MASK.
ALL I KNOW IS, IT'S GONNA BE A PAIN IF HE COMES BACK HERE.
FWIP
I'LL GO GET RID OF HIM!
ALL RIGHT! WE'LL BE RIGHT OUT AS SOON AS WE FINISH EATING!
VSH
IT'LL BE OVER BY THEN!

BLEACH 482.

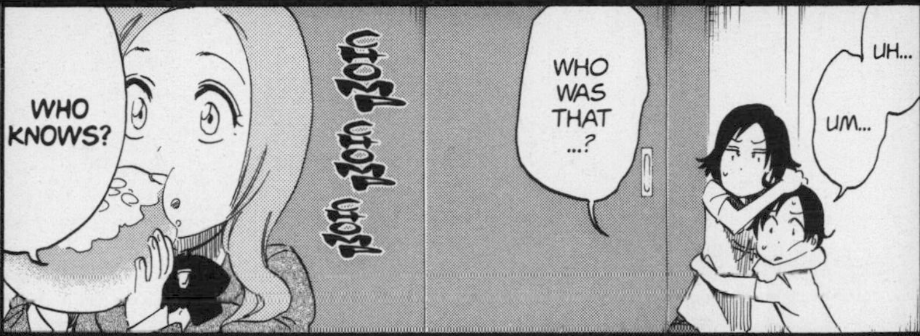
UH...
UM...
WHO WAS THAT ...?
CHOMP CHOMP CHOMP
WHO KNOWS?

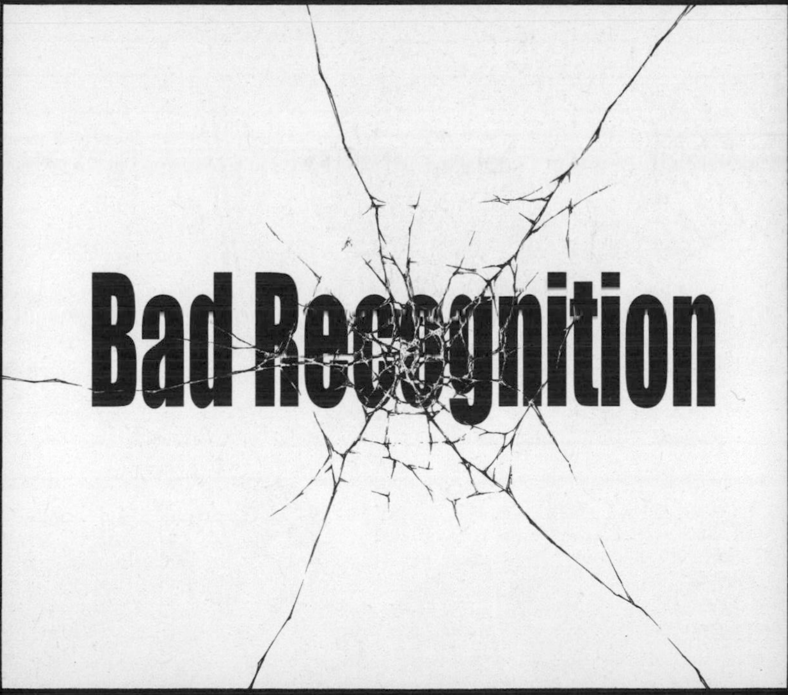
Bad Recognition

READ THIS WAY

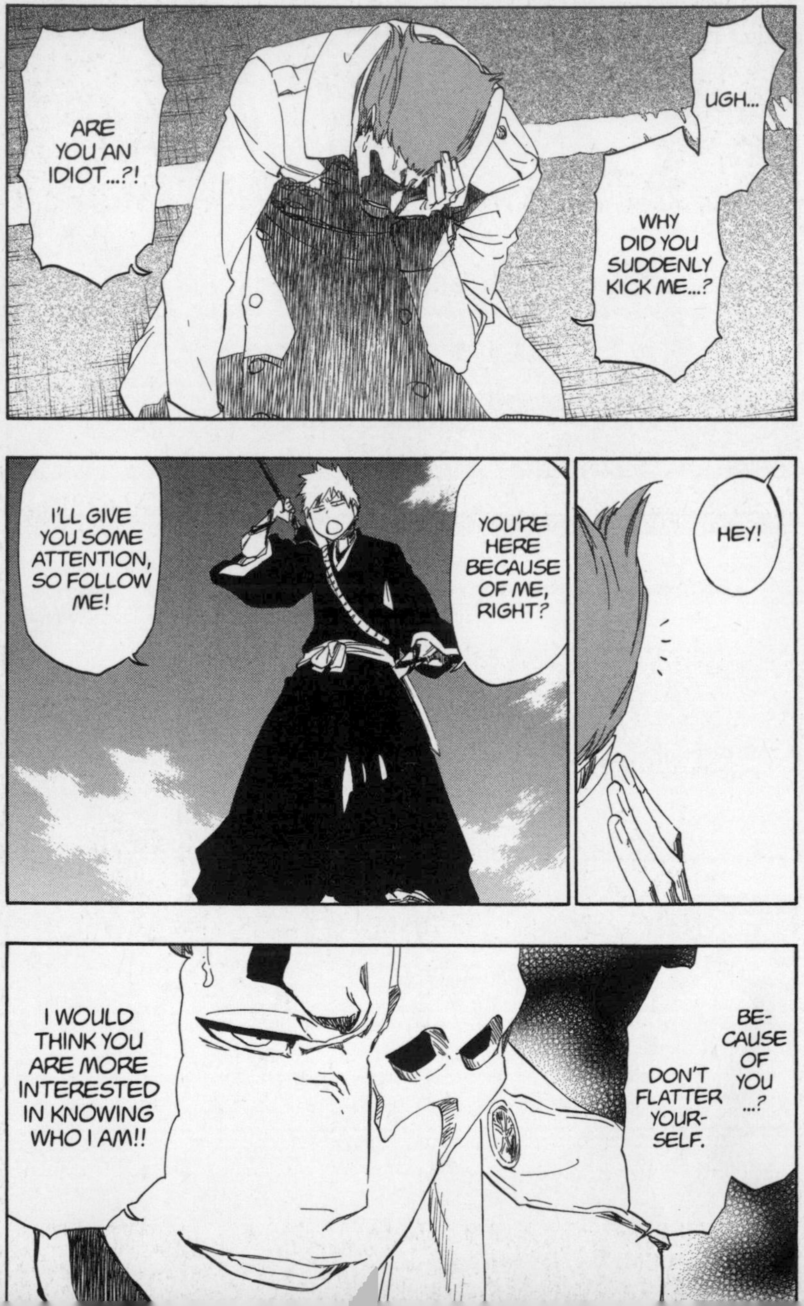
UGH...
WHY DID YOU SUDDENLY KICK ME...?
ARE YOU AN IDIOT...?!
HEY!
YOU'RE HERE BECAUSE OF ME, RIGHT?
I'LL GIVE YOU SOME ATTENTION, SO FOLLOW ME!
BE-CAUSE OF YOU ...?
DON'T FLATTER YOUR-SELF.
I WOULD THINK YOU ARE MORE INTERESTED IN KNOWING WHO I AM!!

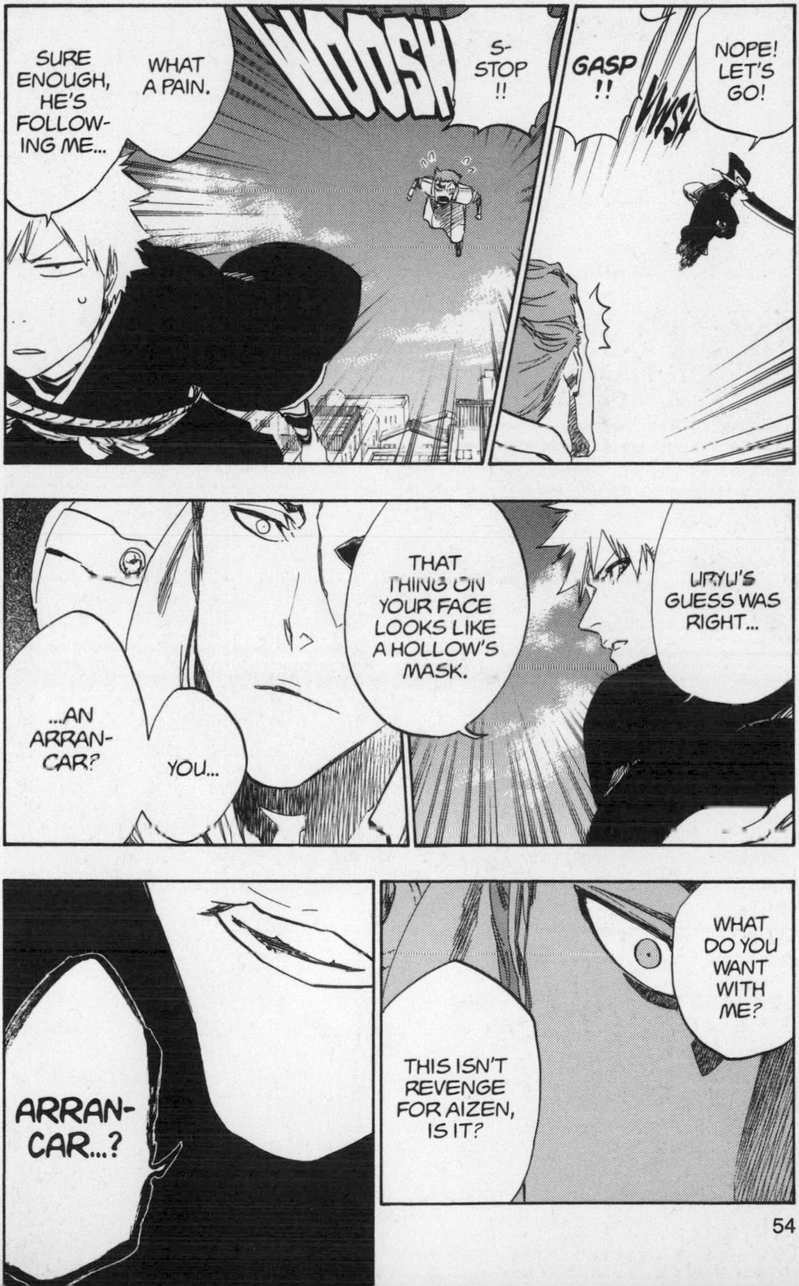
NOPE! LET'S GO!
VWSH
GASP !!
S-STOP !!
WOOSH
WHAT A PAIN.
SURE ENOUGH, HE'S FOLLOWING ME...
URYU'S GUESS WAS RIGHT...
THAT THING ON YOUR FACE LOOKS LIKE A HOLLOW'S MASK.
YOU...
...AN ARRANCAR?
WHAT DO YOU WANT WITH ME?
THIS ISN'T REVENGE FOR AIZEN, IS IT?
ARRANCAR...?

READ THIS WAY

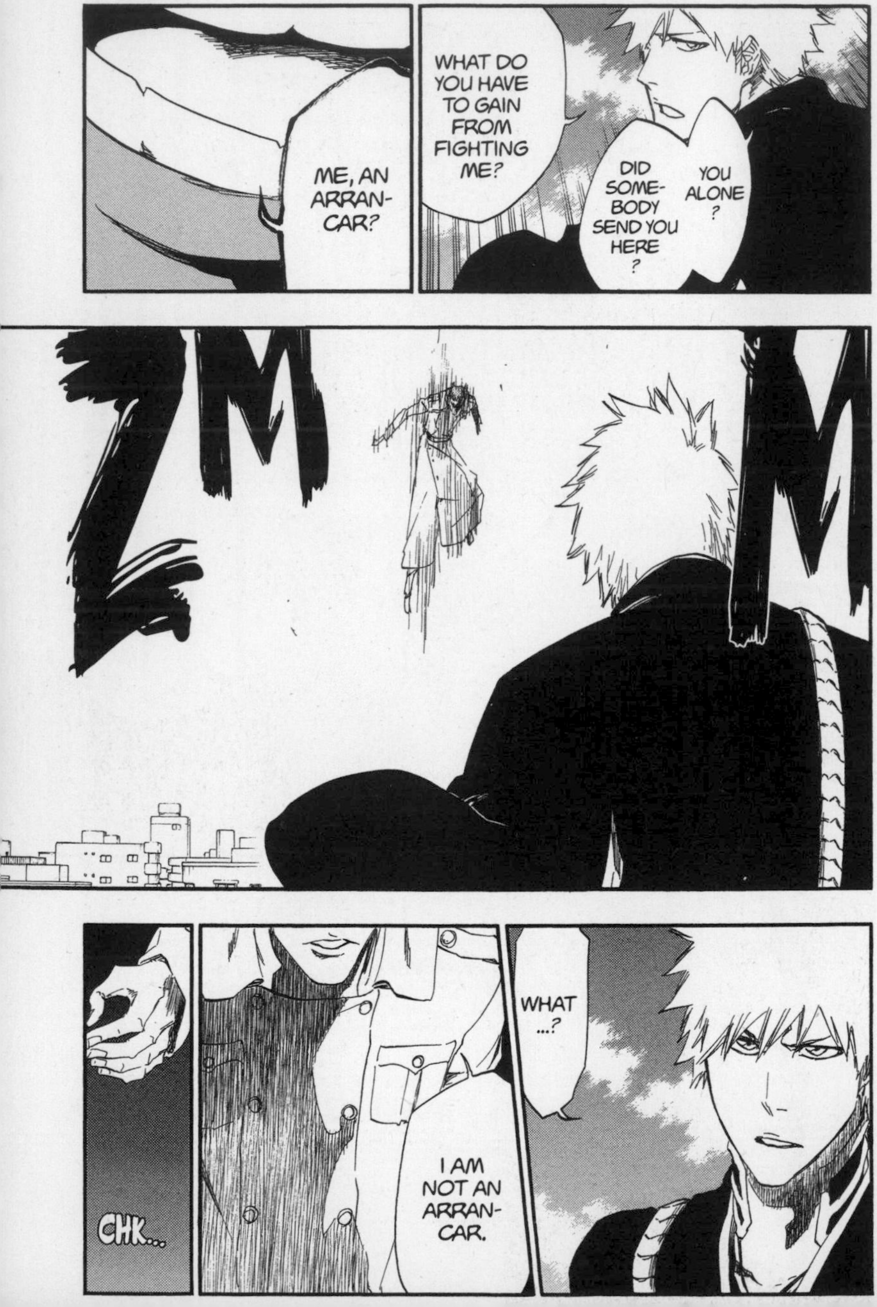
YOU ALONE?
DID SOMEBODY SEND YOU HERE?
WHAT DO YOU HAVE TO GAIN FROM FIGHTING ME?
ME, AN ARRANCAR?
WHAT...?
I AM NOT AN ARRANCAR.
CHK...

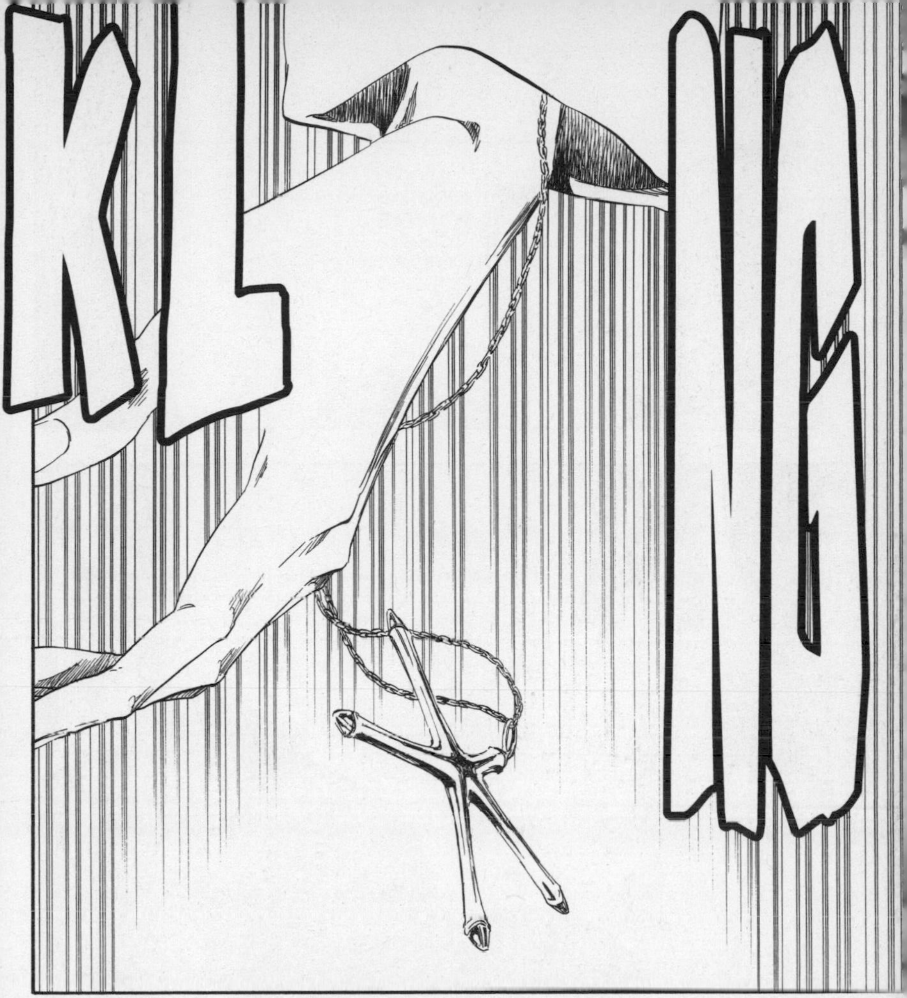
KL
NG
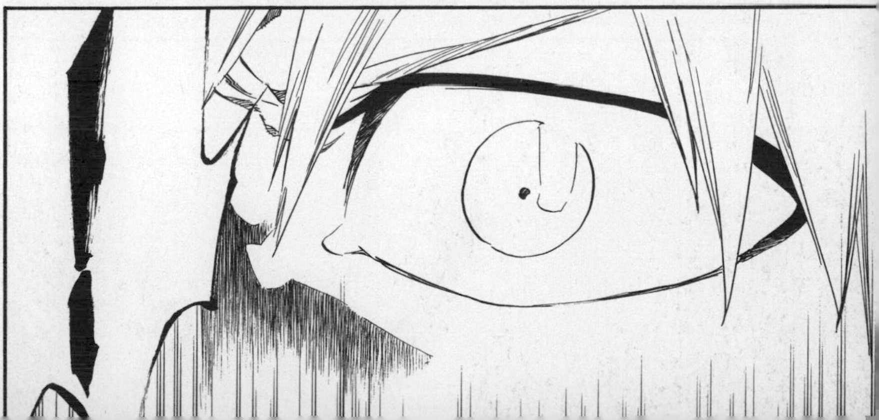

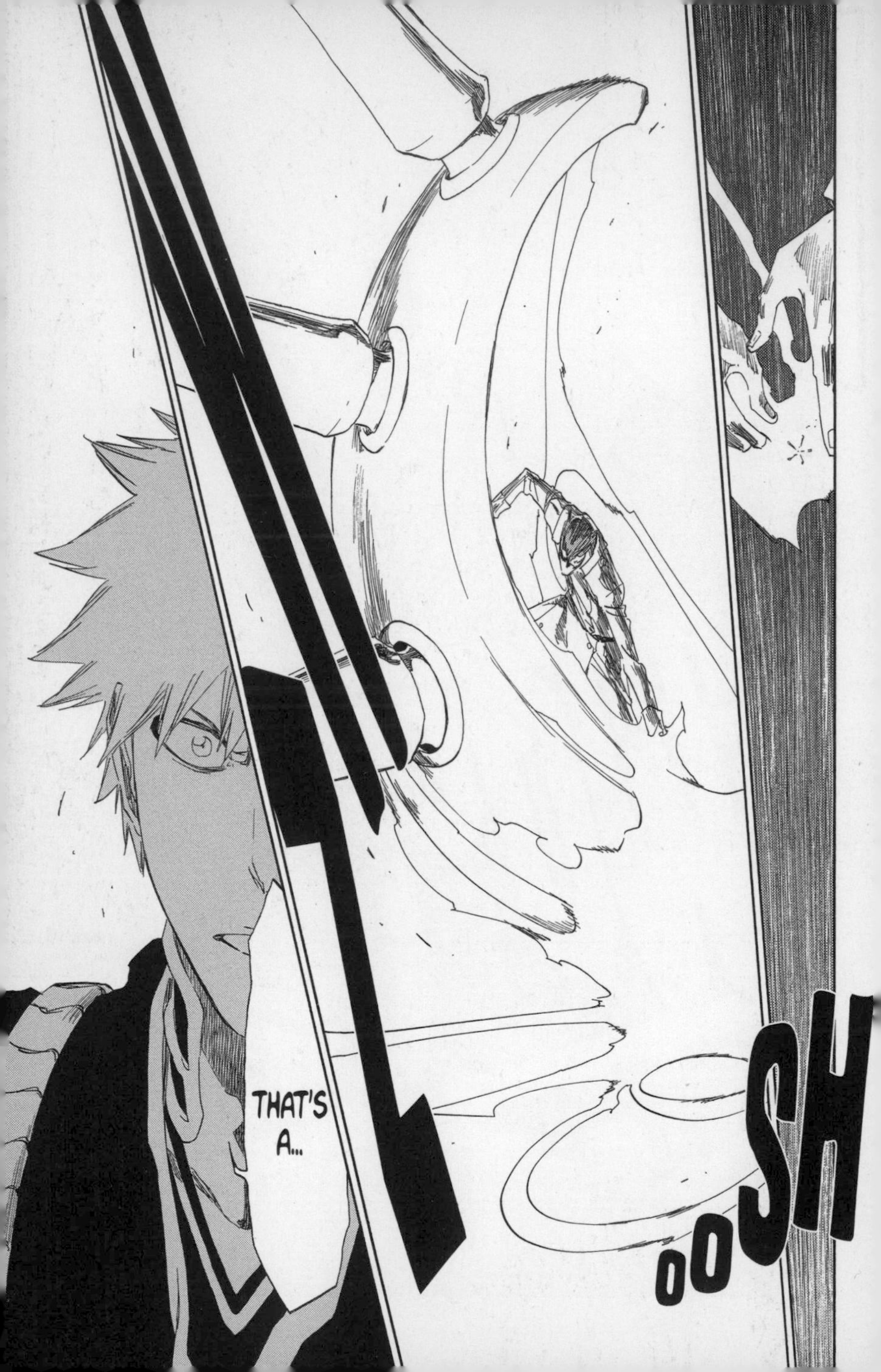

OOOSH
THAT'S A...

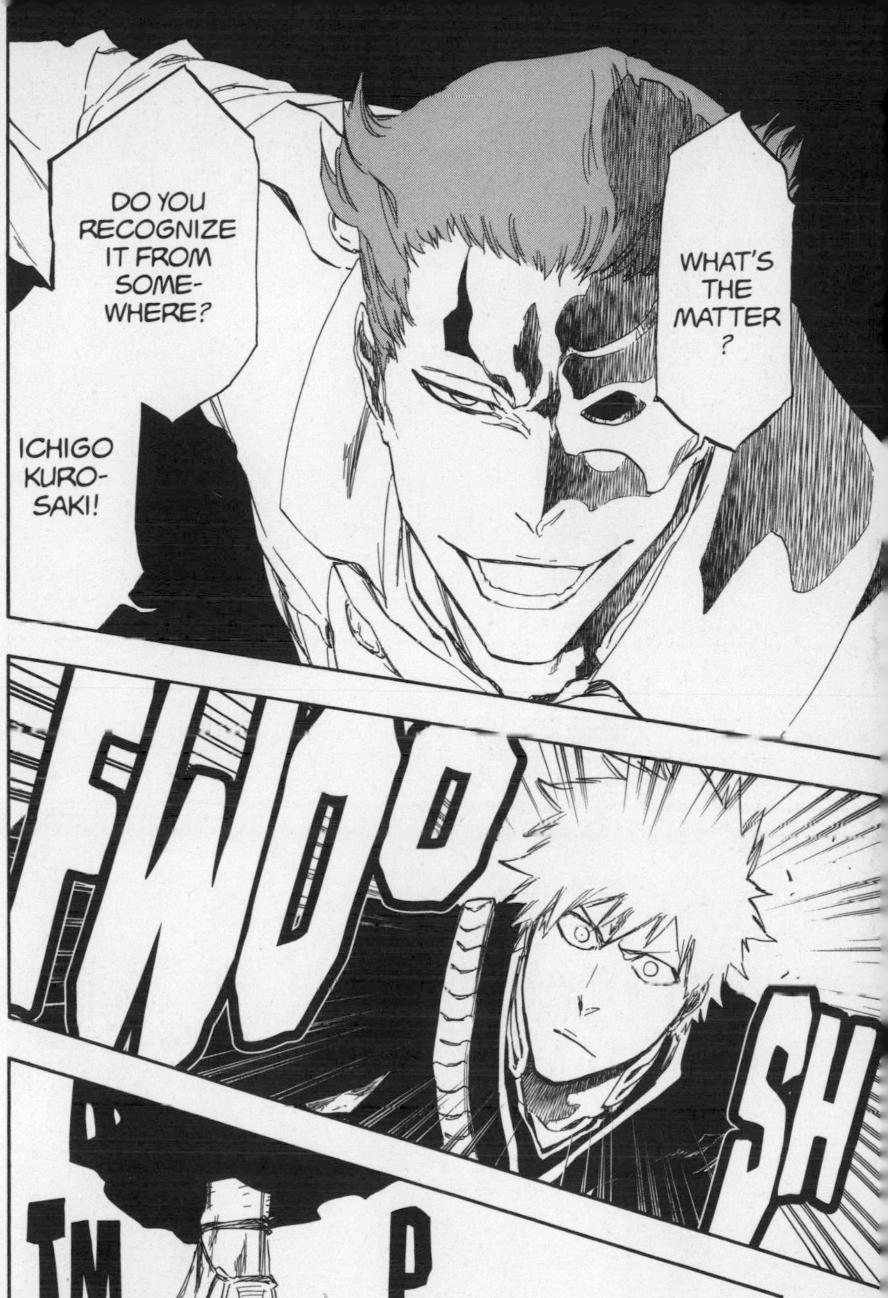
WHAT'S THE MATTER?
DO YOU RECOGNIZE IT FROM SOME-WHERE?
ICHIGO KURO-SAKI!
FWOP
SH
TM P

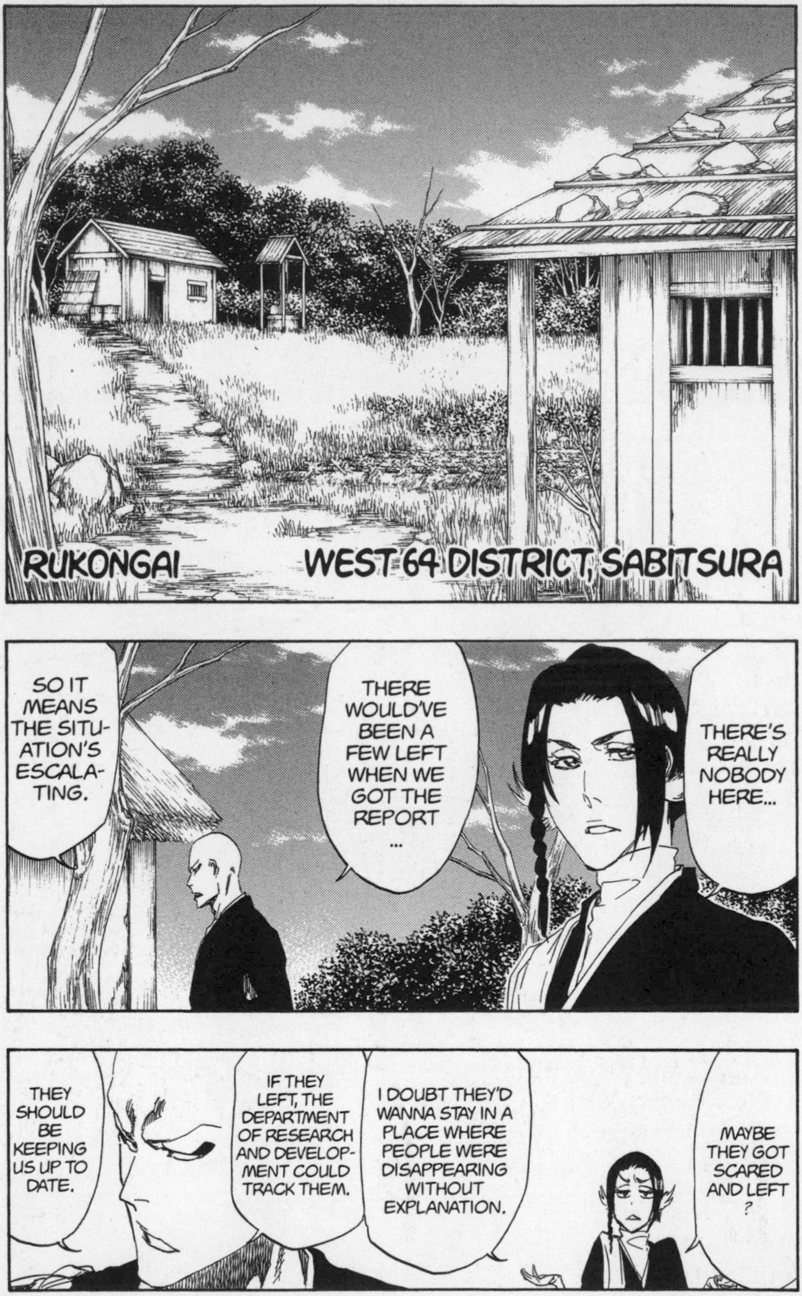
RUKONGAI
WEST 64 DISTRICT, SABITSURA
THERE'S REALLY NOBODY HERE...
THERE WOULD'VE BEEN A FEW LEFT WHEN WE GOT THE REPORT...
SO IT MEANS THE SITUATION'S ESCALATING.
MAYBE THEY GOT SCARED AND LEFT?
I DOUBT THEY'D WANNA STAY IN A PLACE WHERE PEOPLE WERE DISAPPEARING WITHOUT EXPLANATION.
IF THEY LEFT, THE DEPARTMENT OF RESEARCH AND DEVELOPMENT COULD TRACK THEM.
THEY SHOULD BE KEEPING US UP TO DATE.

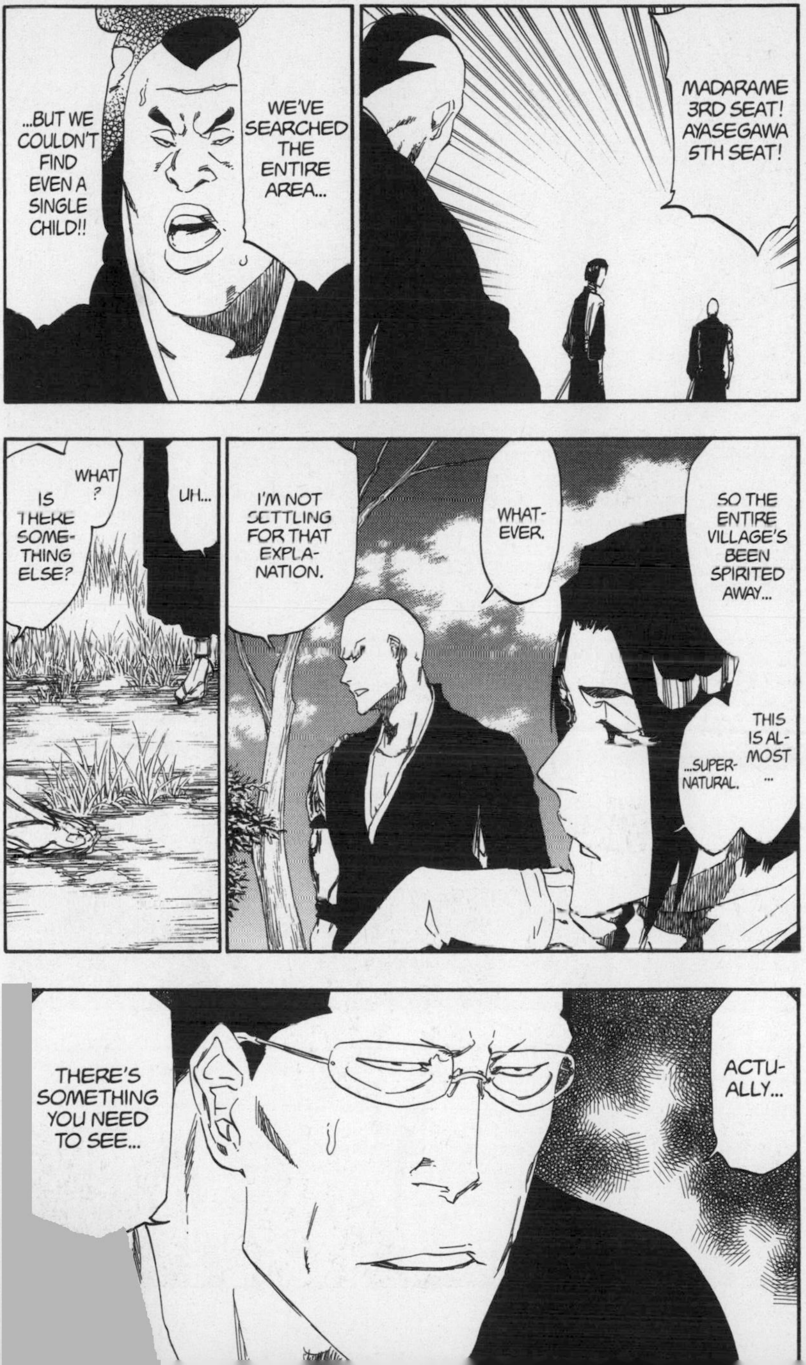
MADARAME 3RD SEAT! AYASEGAWA 5TH SEAT!
WE'VE SEARCHED THE ENTIRE AREA...
...BUT WE COULDN'T FIND EVEN A SINGLE CHILD!!
SO THE ENTIRE VILLAGE'S BEEN SPIRITED AWAY...
THIS IS ALMOST...
...SUPERNATURAL.
WHATEVER.
I'M NOT SETTLING FOR THAT EXPLANATION.
UH...
WHAT? IS THERE SOMETHING ELSE?
ACTUALLY...
THERE'S SOMETHING YOU NEED TO SEE...

READ THIS WAY

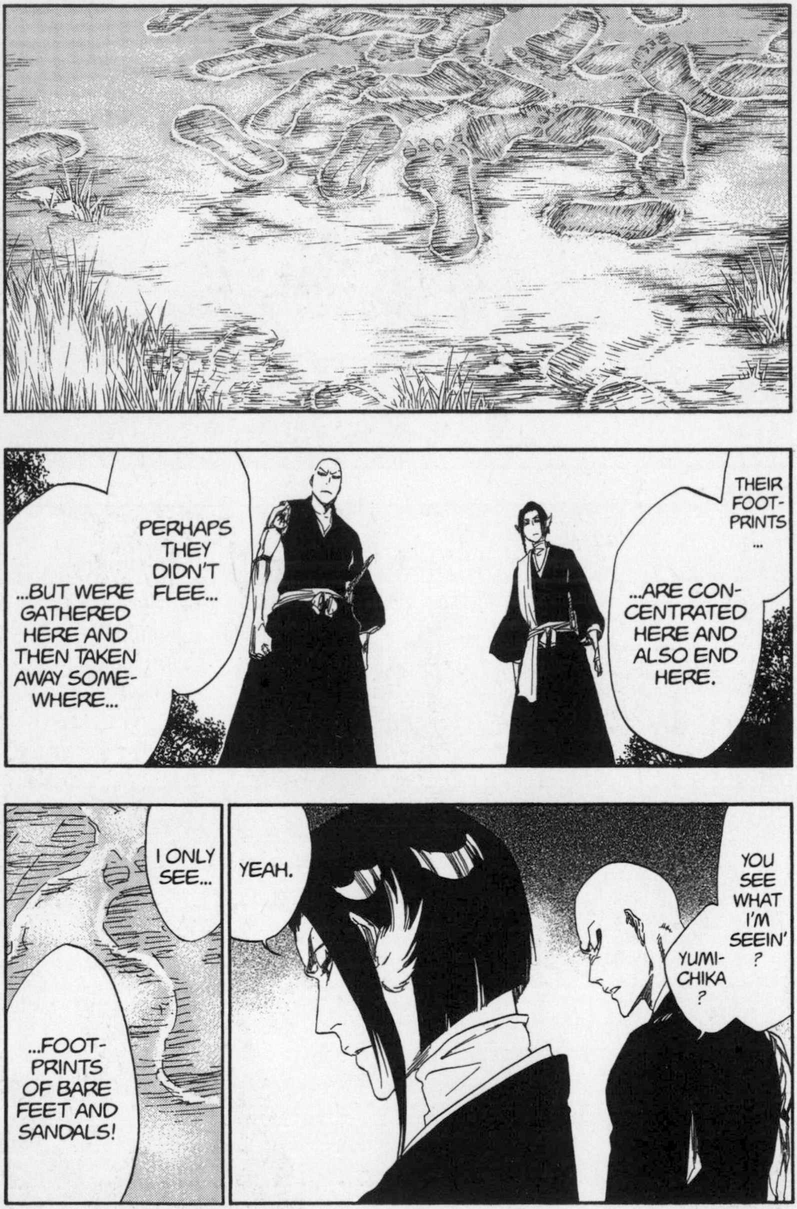
THEIR FOOTPRINTS...
...ARE CONCENTRATED HERE AND ALSO END HERE.
PERHAPS THEY DIDN'T FLEE...
...BUT WERE GATHERED HERE AND THEN TAKEN AWAY SOMEWHERE...
YOU SEE WHAT I'M SEEIN'?
YUMICHIKA?
YEAH.
I ONLY SEE...
...FOOTPRINTS OF BARE FEET AND SANDALS!

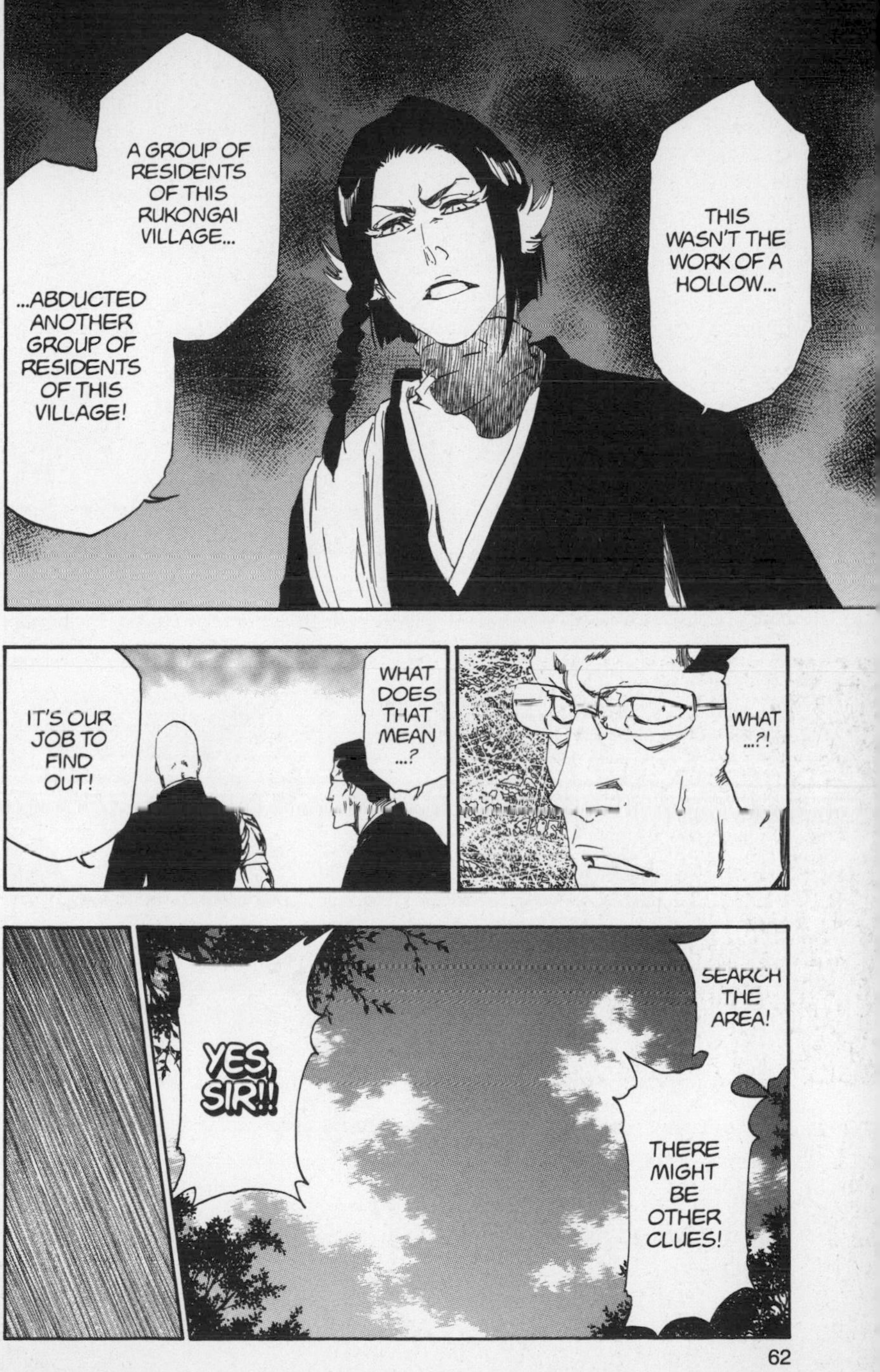
THIS WASN'T THE WORK OF A HOLLOW...
A GROUP OF RESIDENTS OF THIS RUKONGAI VILLAGE...
...ABDUCTED ANOTHER GROUP OF RESIDENTS OF THIS VILLAGE!
WHAT ...?!
WHAT DOES THAT MEAN ...?
IT'S OUR JOB TO FIND OUT!
SEARCH THE AREA!
THERE MIGHT BE OTHER CLUES!
YES, SIR!!

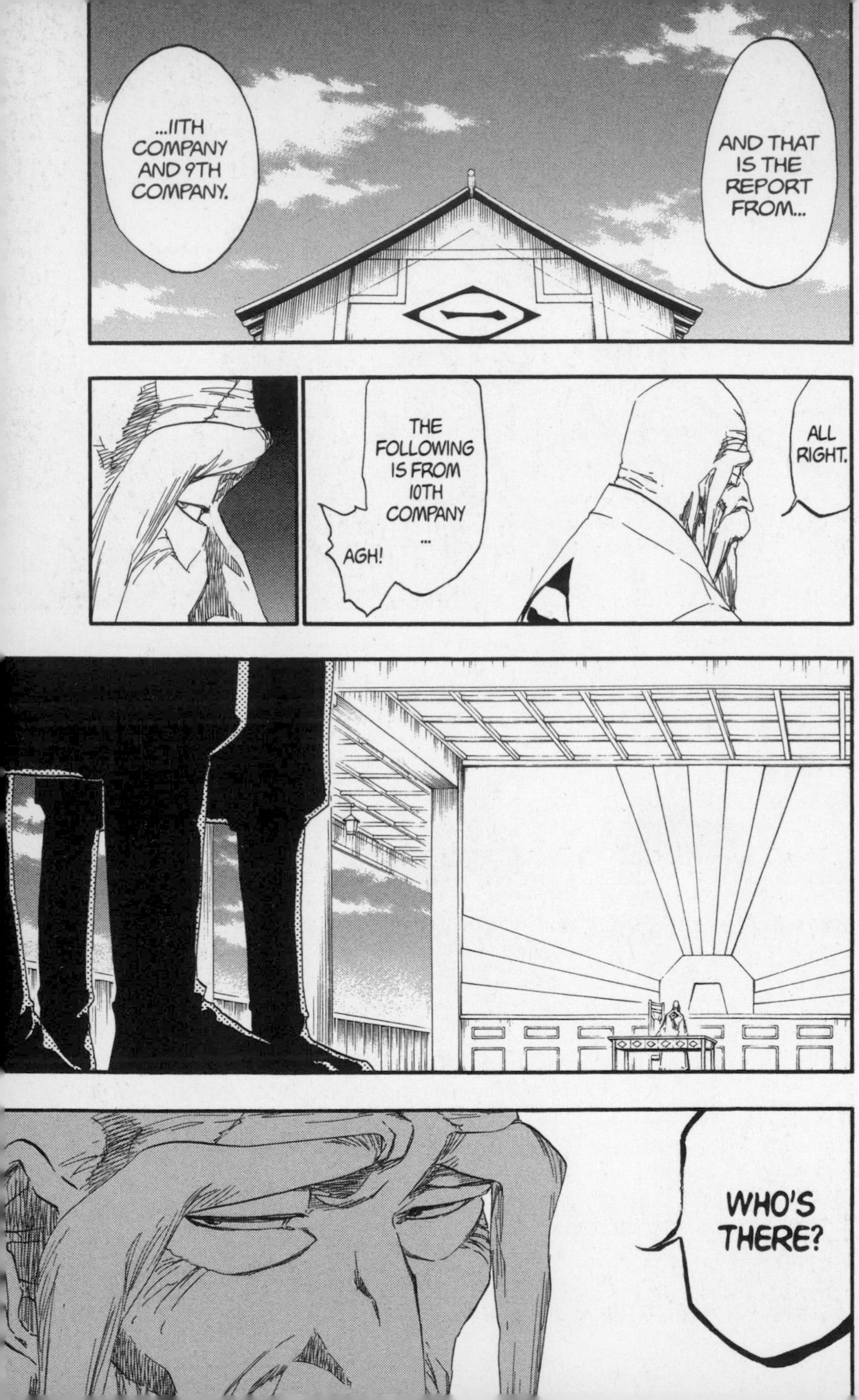
AND THAT IS THE REPORT FROM...
...11TH COMPANY AND 9TH COMPANY.
ALL RIGHT.
THE FOLLOWING IS FROM 10TH COMPANY ...
AGH!
WHO'S THERE?

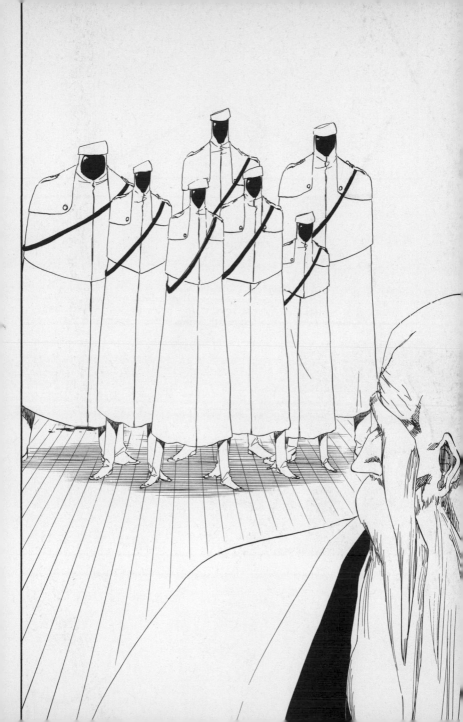

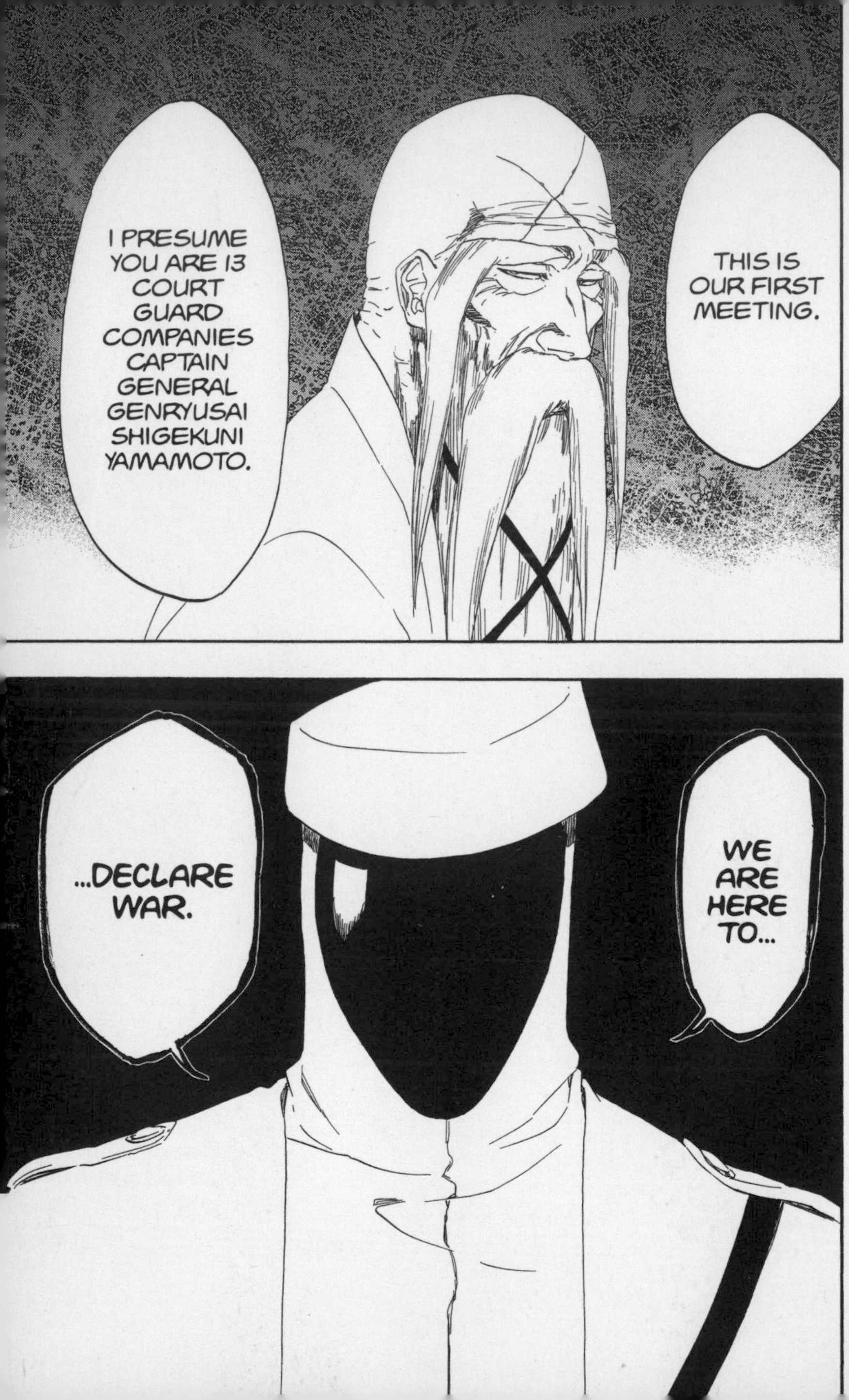
THIS IS OUR FIRST MEETING.
I PRESUME YOU ARE 13 COURT GUARD COMPANIES CAPTAIN GENERAL GENRYUSAI SHIGEKUNI YAMAMOTO.
WE ARE HERE TO...
...DECLARE WAR.

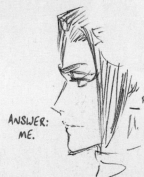

QUESTION: THERE'S A FASHIONABLE CHARACTER IN BLEACH WHO MADE HIMSELF EVEN MORE FASHIONABLE FOR THE NEW ARC. WHO IS THIS SUPREME KING OF FASHION?

ANSWER: ME.

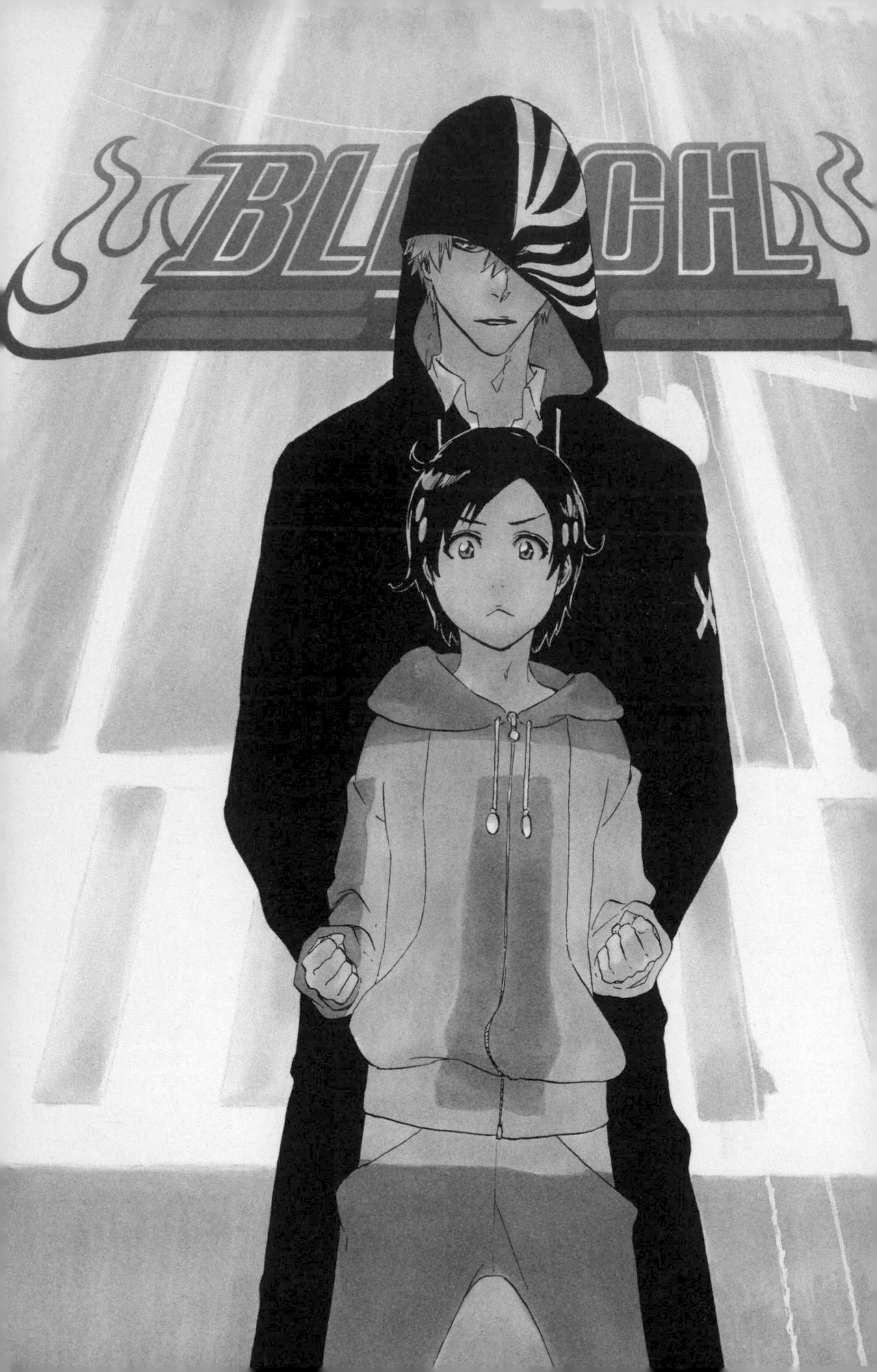

BLEACH
ブリーチ

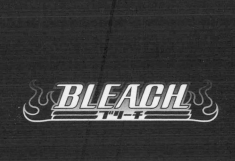

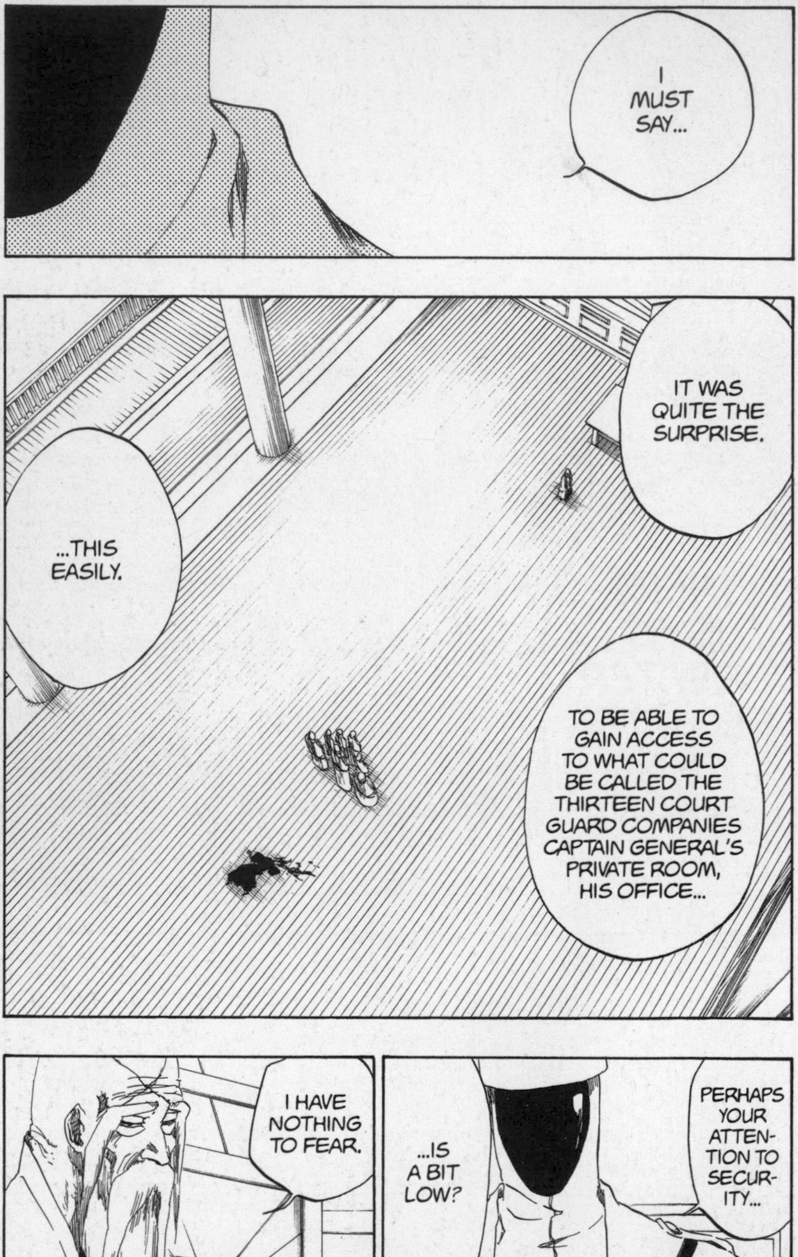
I MUST SAY...
IT WAS QUITE THE SURPRISE.
TO BE ABLE TO GAIN ACCESS TO WHAT COULD BE CALLED THE THIRTEEN COURT GUARD COMPANIES CAPTAIN GENERAL'S PRIVATE ROOM, HIS OFFICE...
...THIS EASILY.
PERHAPS YOUR ATTEN-TION TO SECUR-ITY...
...IS A BIT LOW?
I HAVE NOTHING TO FEAR.

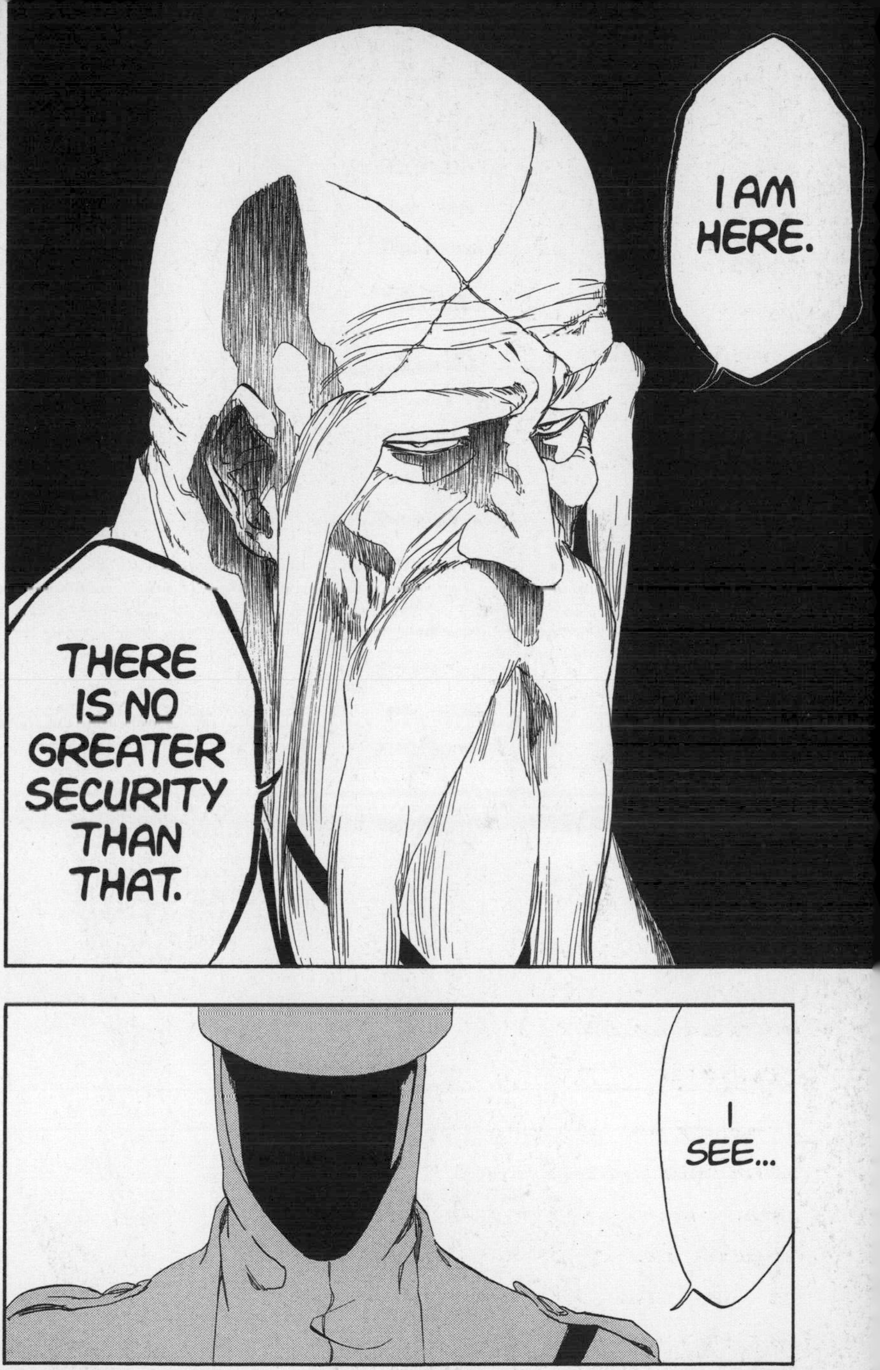
I AM HERE.
THERE IS NO GREATER SECURITY THAN THAT.
I SEE...

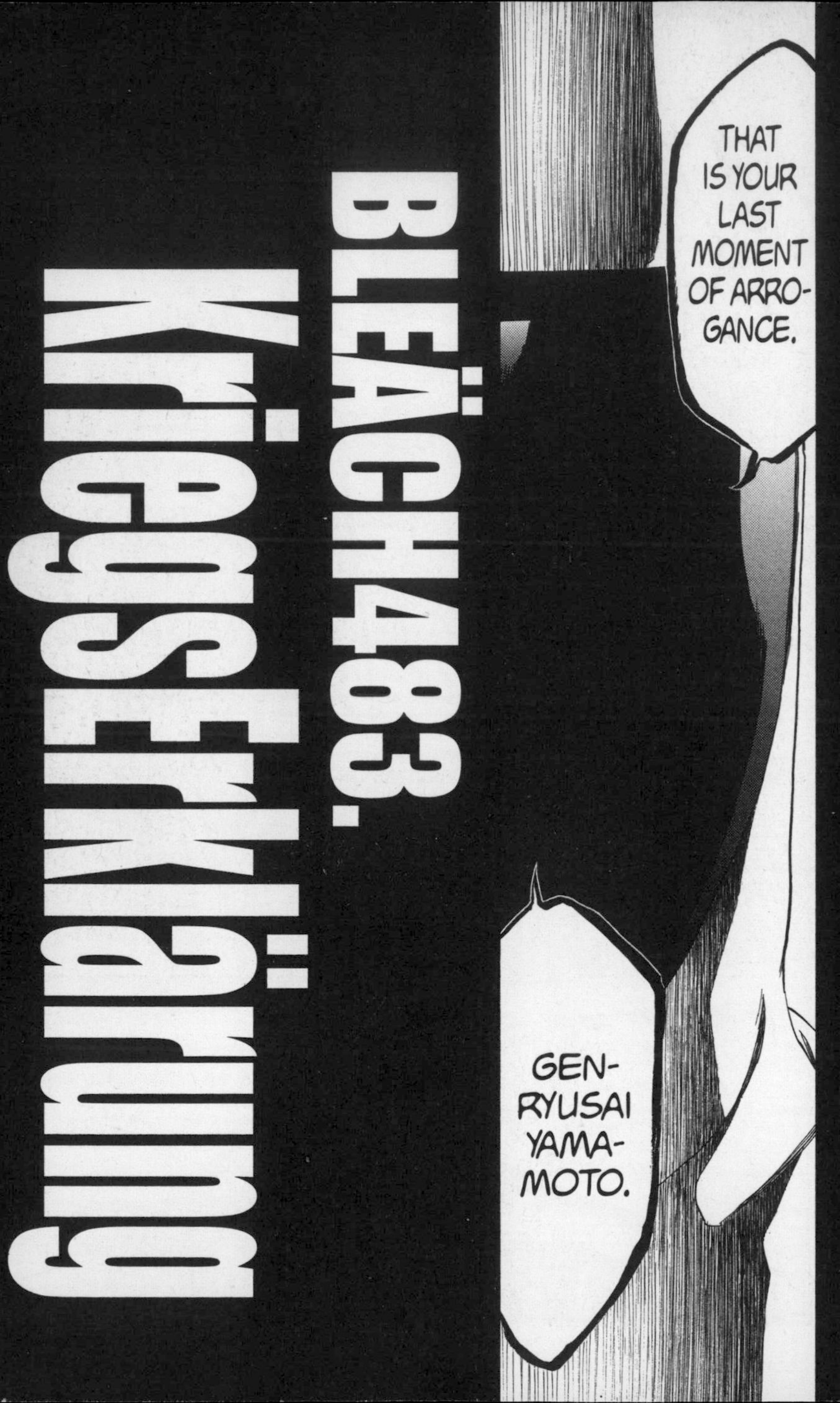
THAT IS YOUR LAST MOMENT OF ARRO-GANCE.
GEN-RYUSAI YAMA-MOTO.
BLEÄCH483.
Kriegserklärung

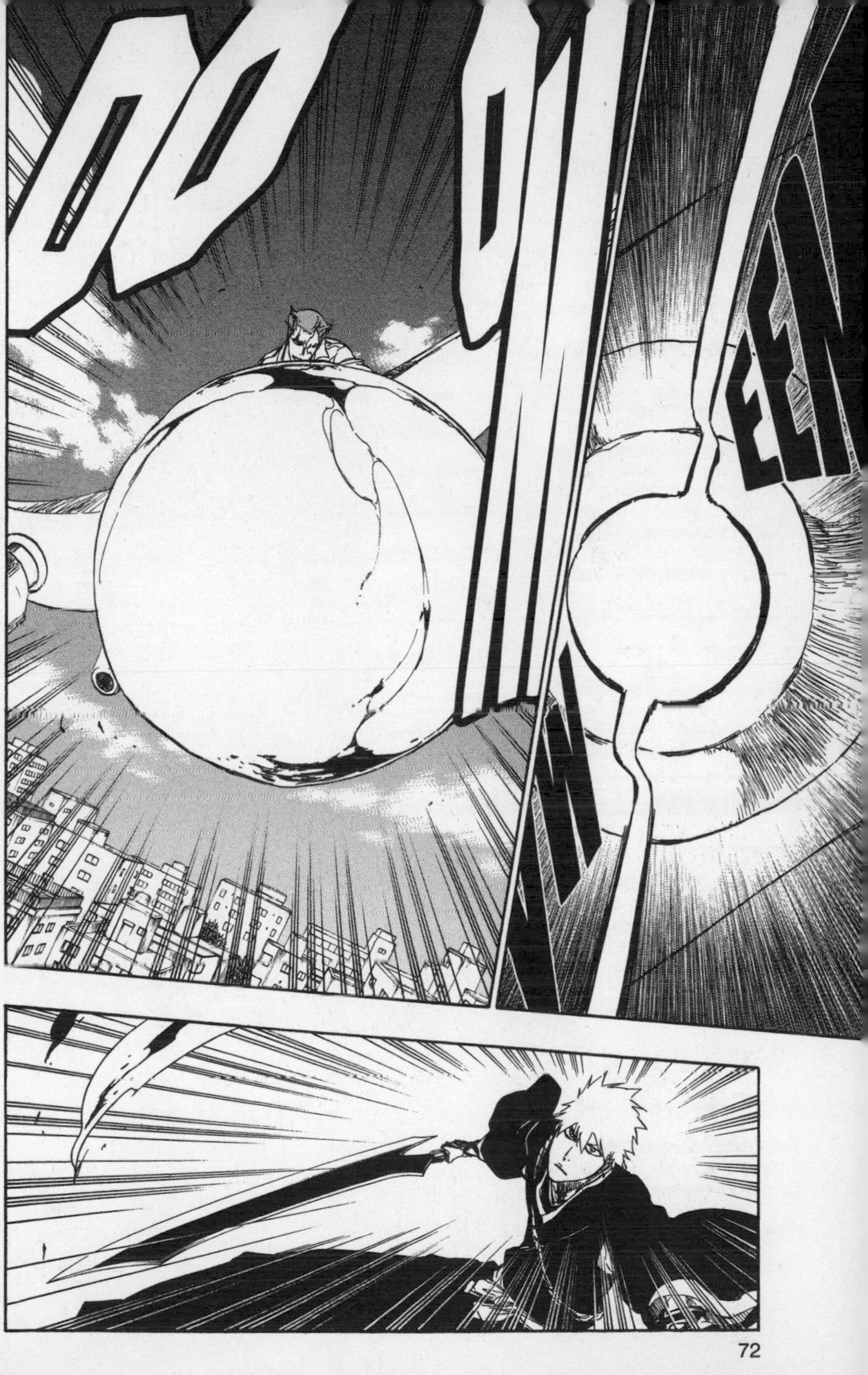

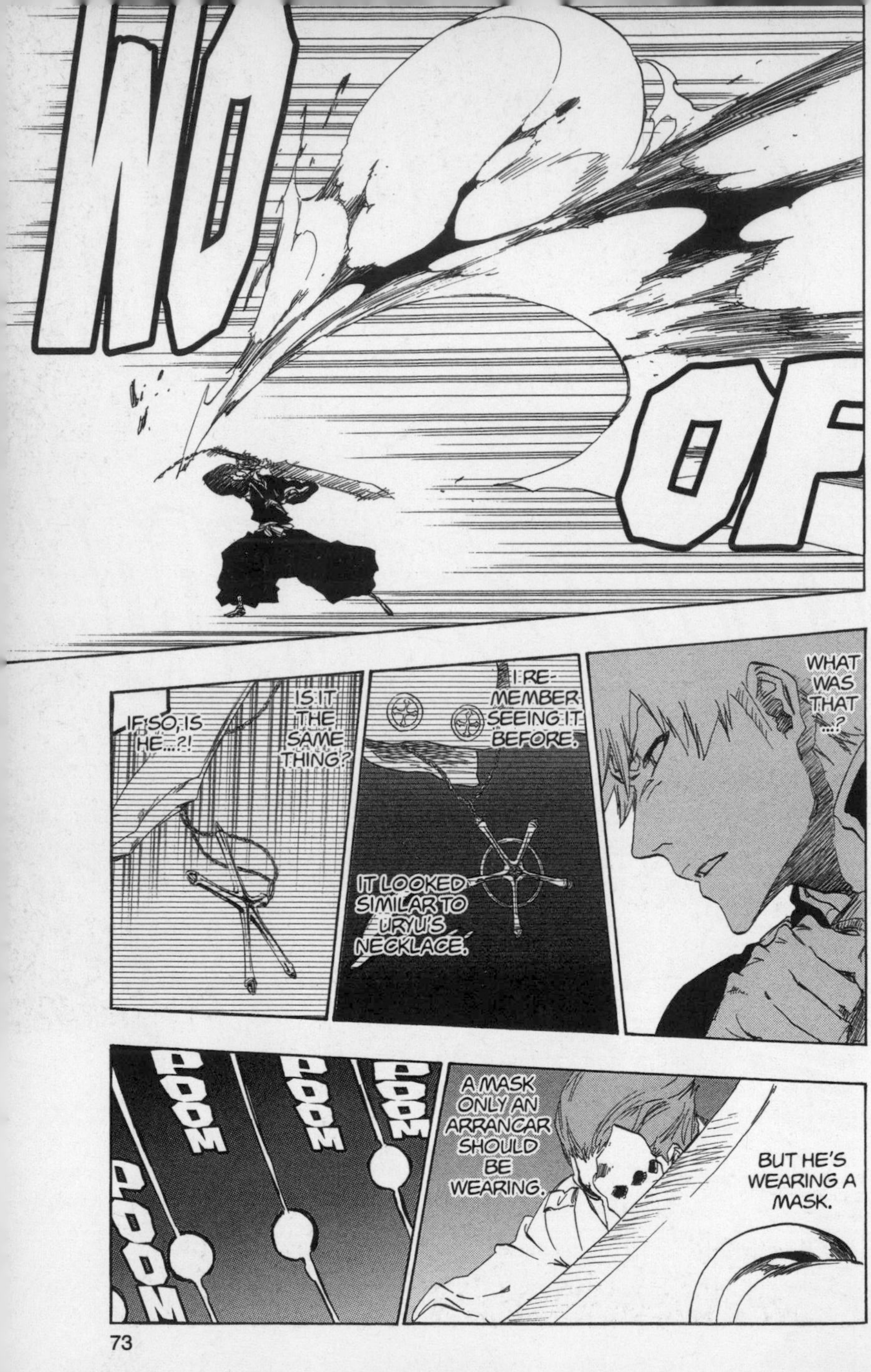
WHAT WAS THAT ...?
I REMEMBER SEEING IT BEFORE.
IT LOOKED SIMILAR TO URYU'S NECKLACE.
IS IT THE SAME THING?
IF SO, IS HE...?!
BUT HE'S WEARING A MASK.
A MASK ONLY AN ARRANCAR SHOULD BE WEARING.
DOOM
DOOM
DOOM
DOOM
DOOM

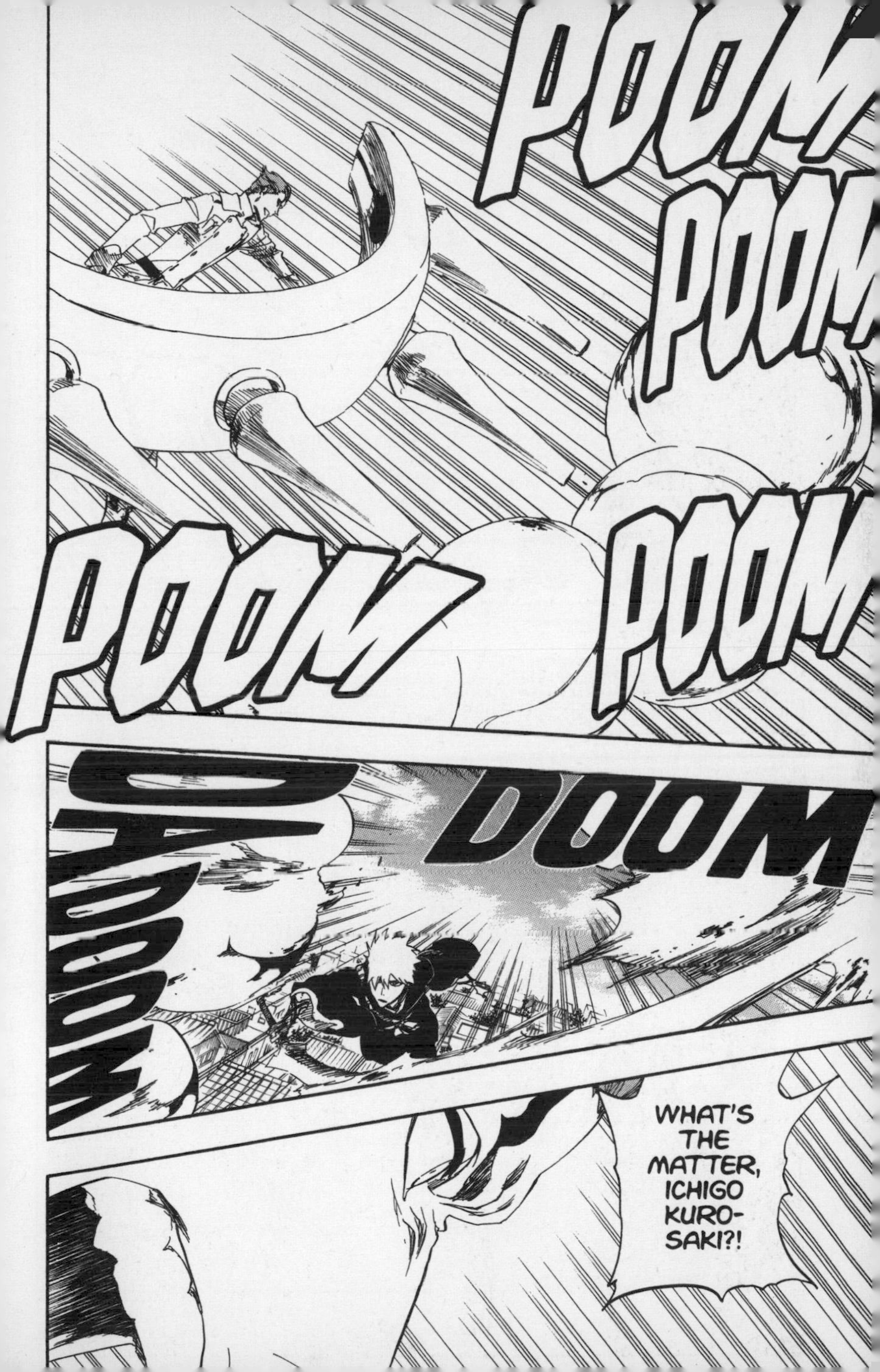
POOM
POOM
POOM
POOM
DOOM
DADOOM
WHAT'S THE MATTER, ICHIGO KURO-SAKI?!

READ THIS WAY

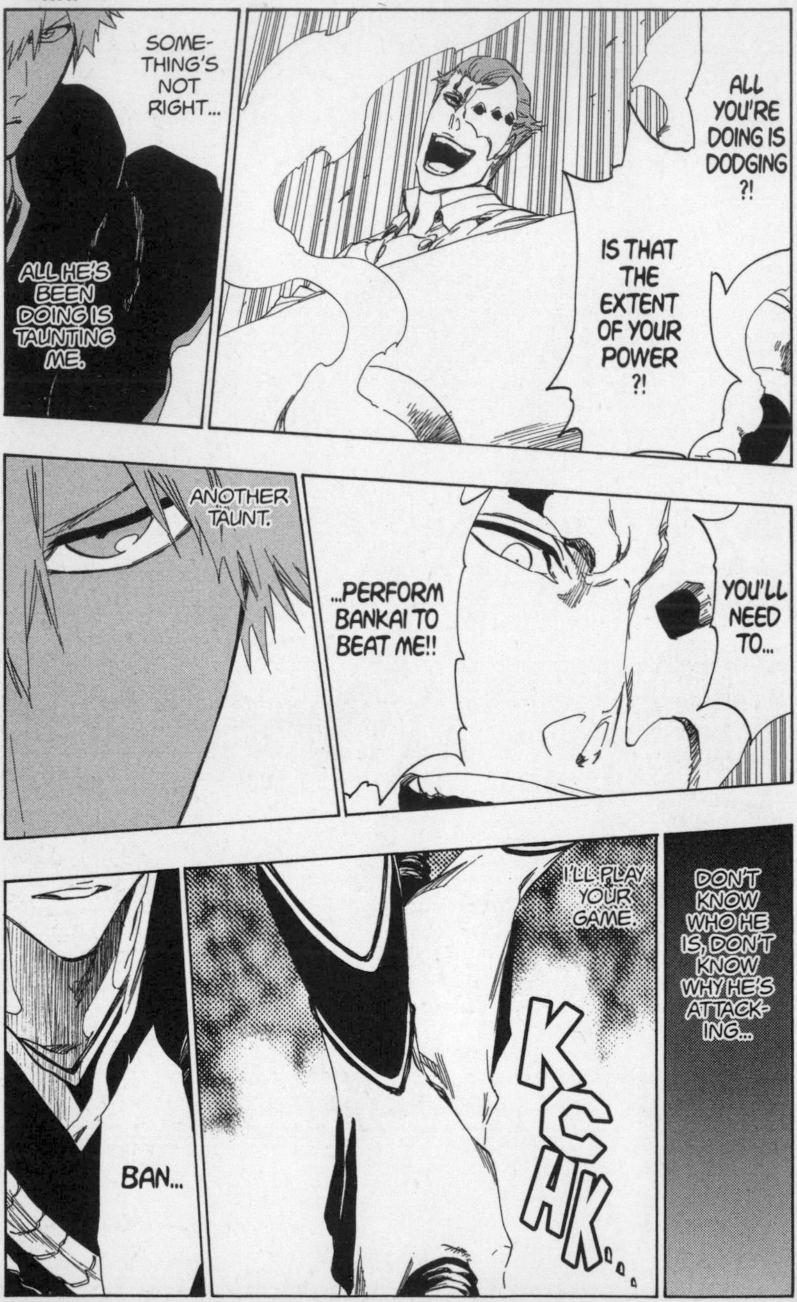
ALL YOU'RE DOING IS DODGING ?!
IS THAT THE EXTENT OF YOUR POWER ?!
SOME-THING'S NOT RIGHT...
ALL HE'S BEEN DOING IS TAUNTING ME.
YOU'LL NEED TO...
...PERFORM BANKAI TO BEAT ME!!
ANOTHER TAUNT.
DON'T KNOW WHO HE IS, DON'T KNOW WHY HE'S ATTACK-ING...
I'LL PLAY YOUR GAME.
KCHAK...
BAN...

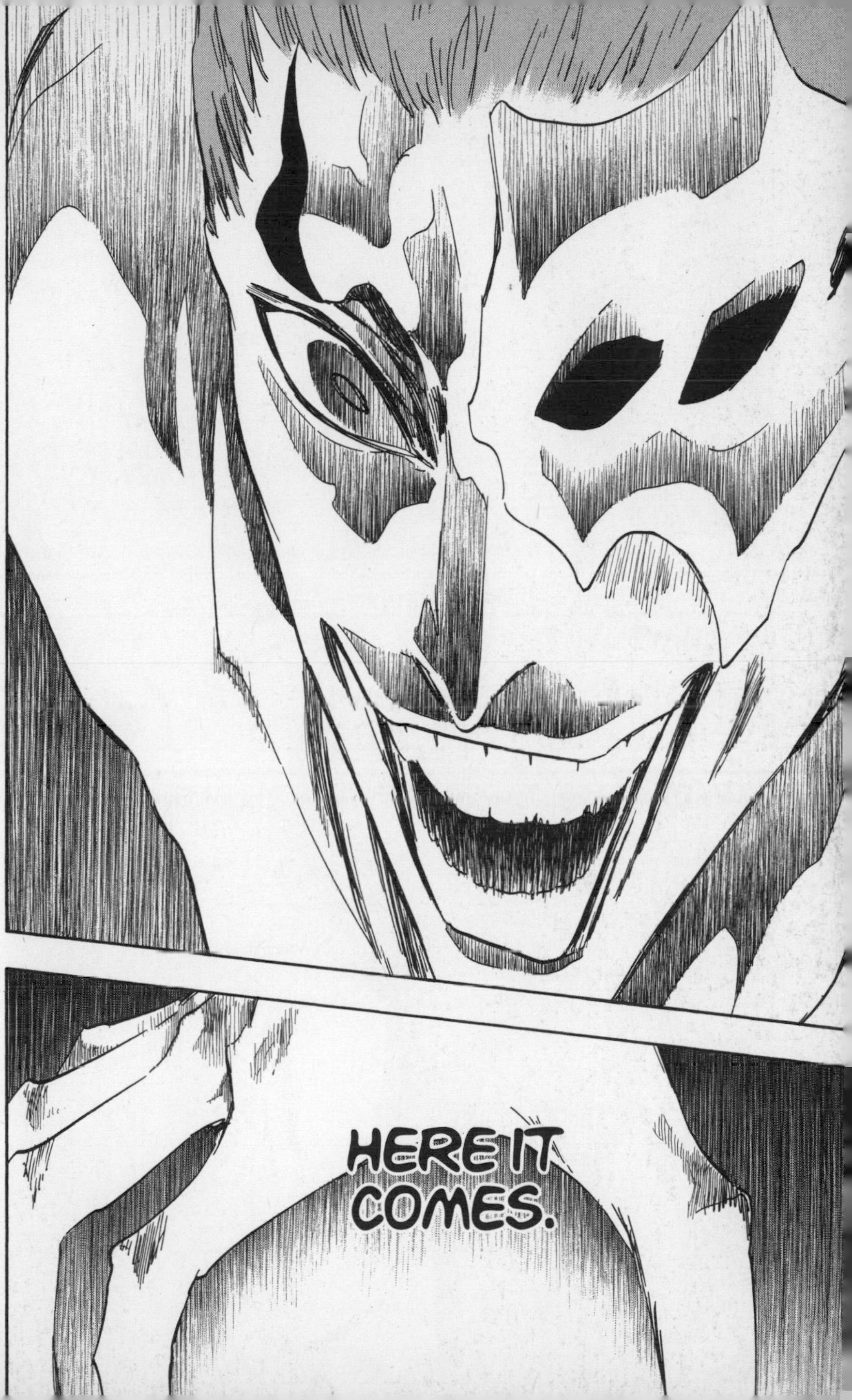
HERE IT COMES.

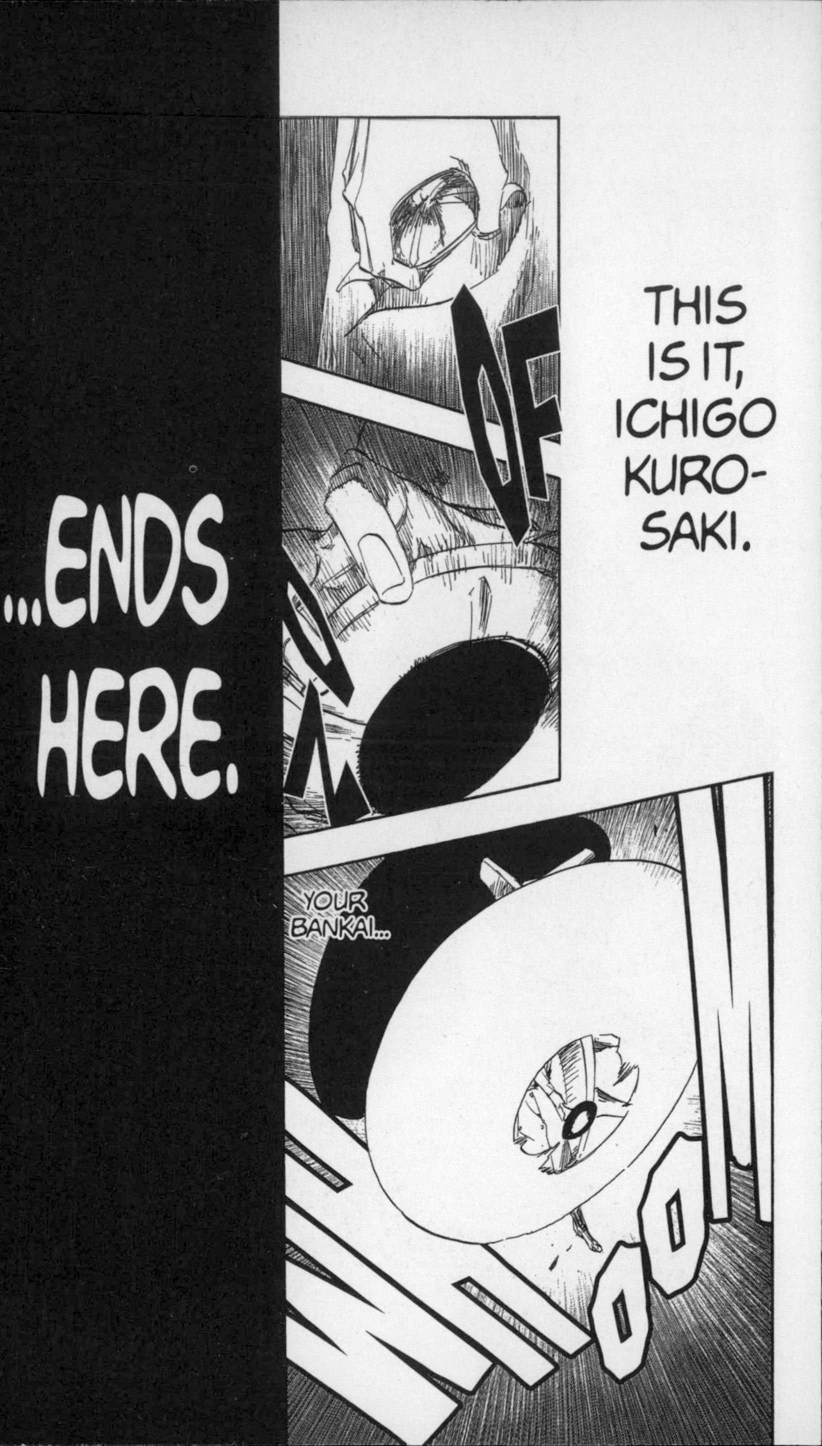

...ENDS HERE.

THIS IS IT, ICHIGO KURO-SAKI.

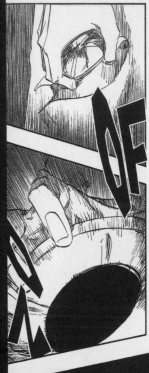

YOUR BANKAI...

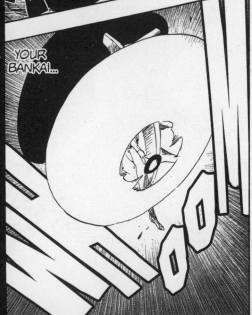

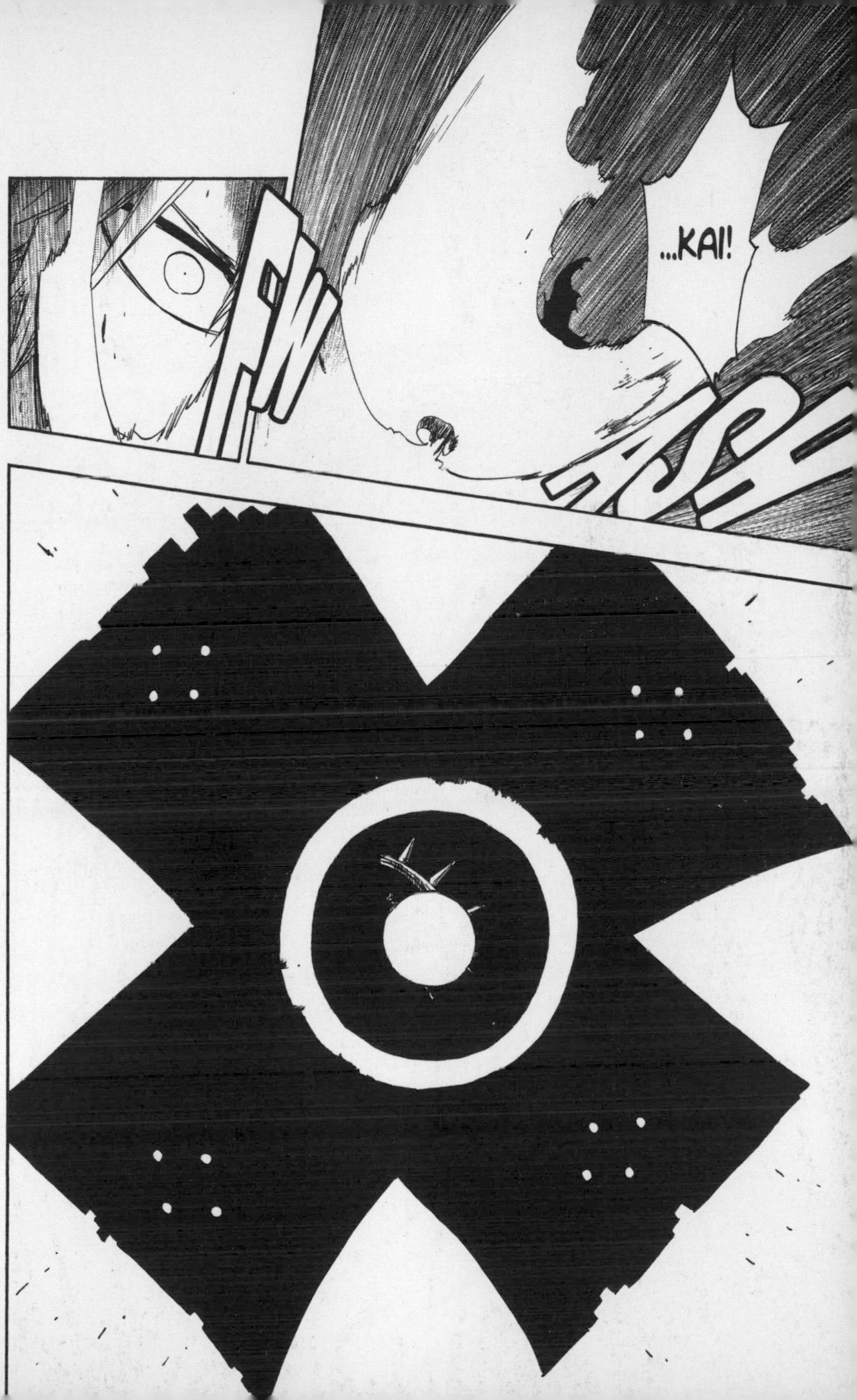
...KAI!
FWN

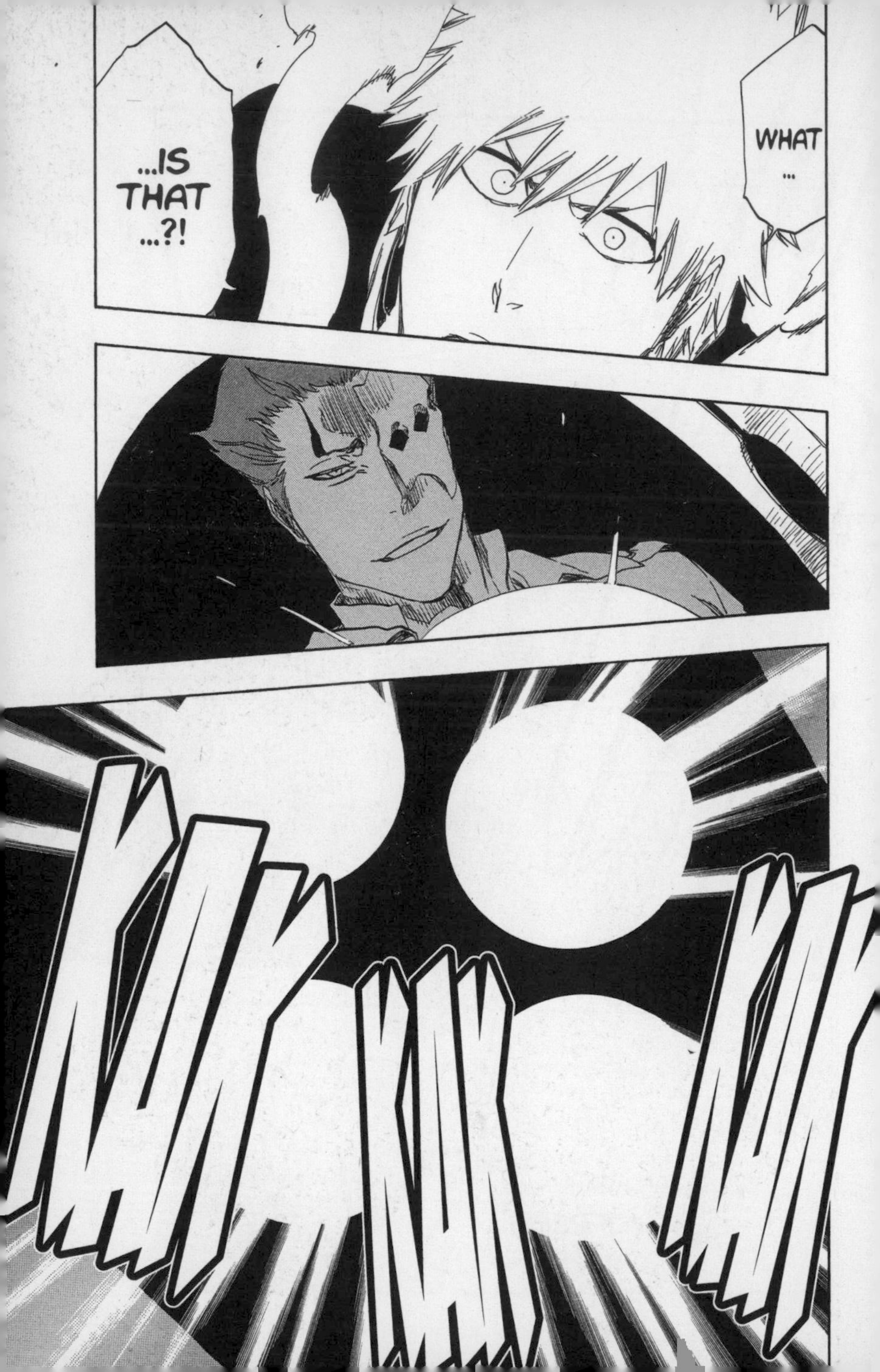
WHAT ...
...IS THAT ...?!

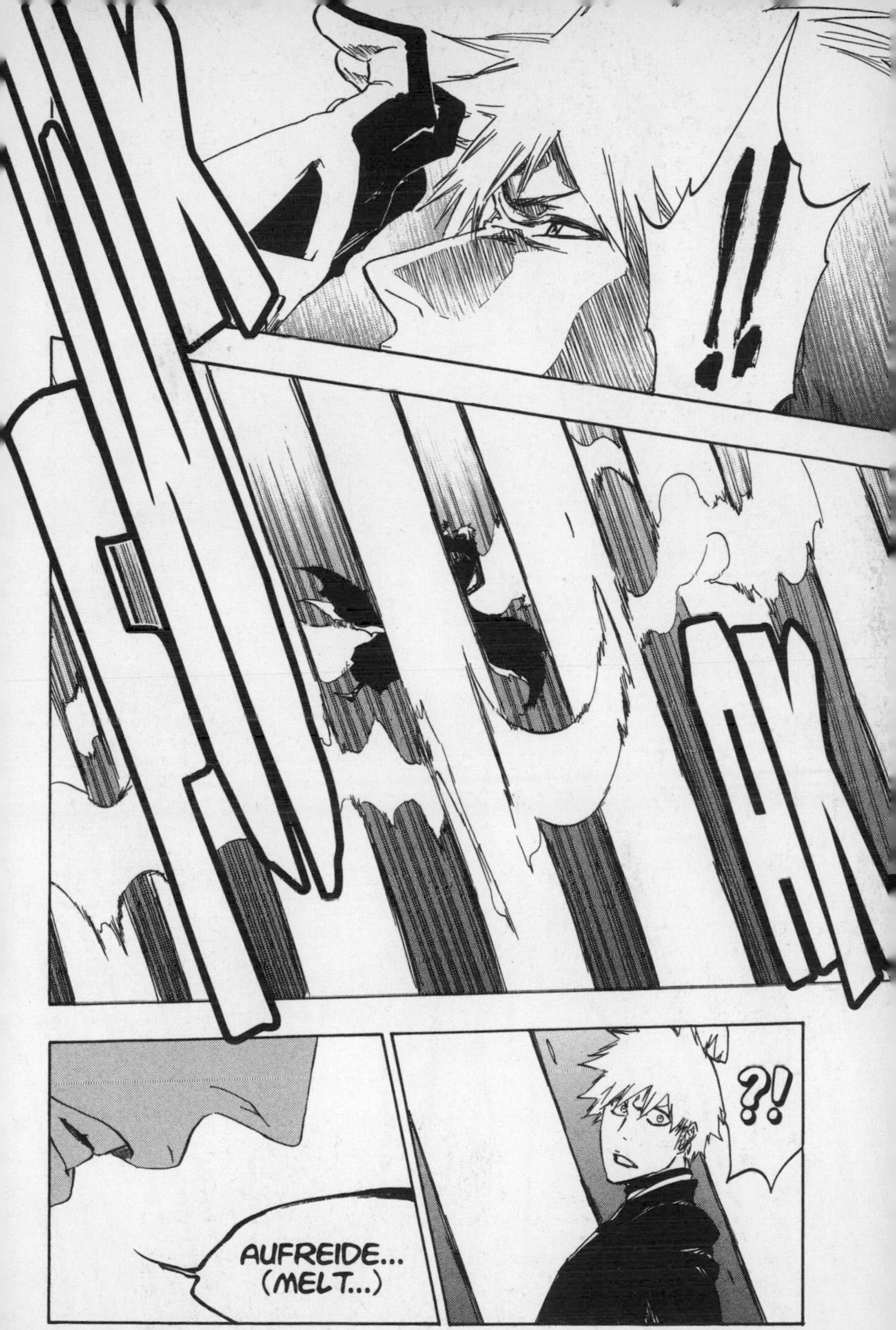
!!
?!
AUFREIDE...
(MELT...)

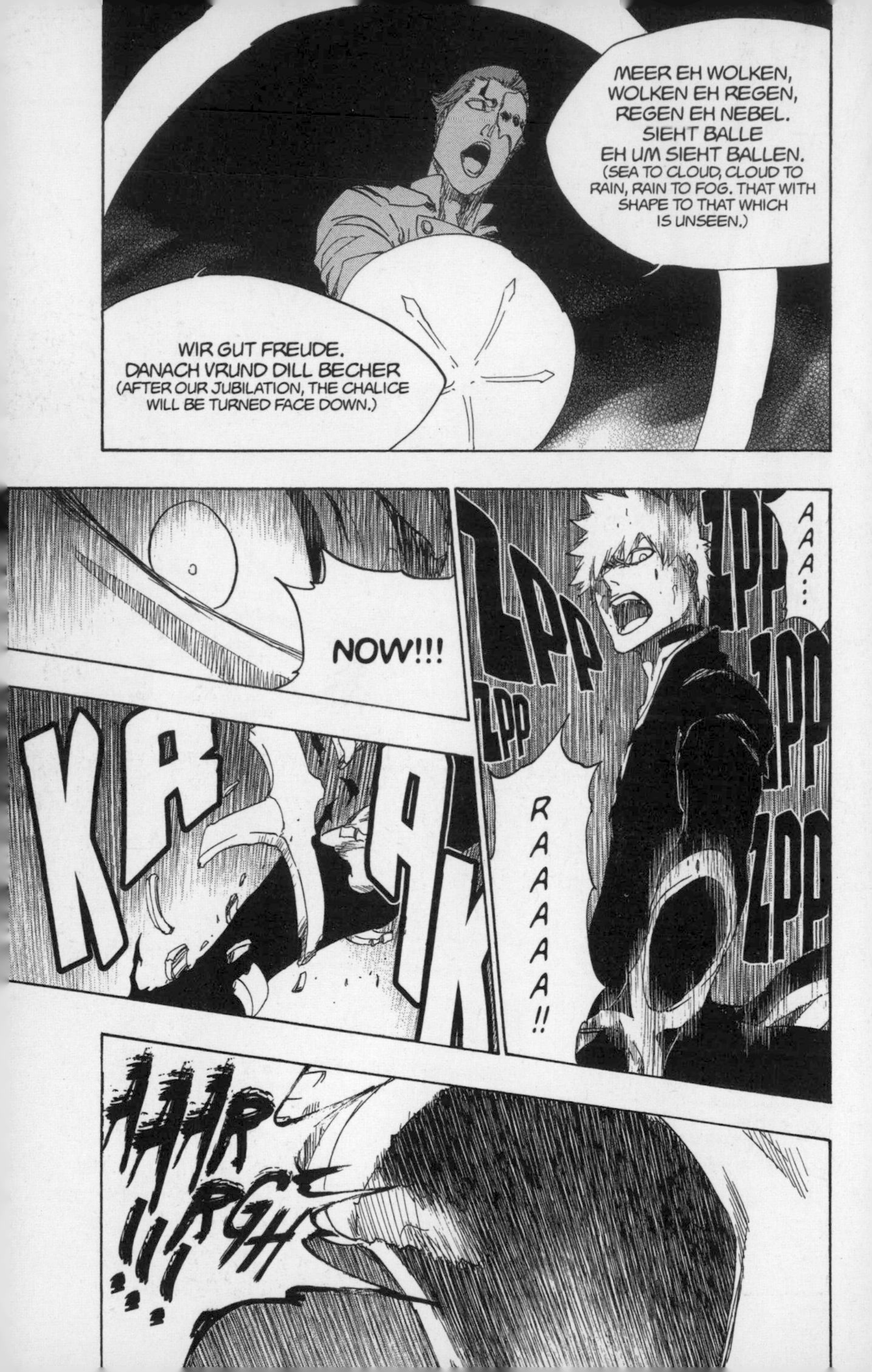
MEER EH WOLKEN, WOLKEN EH REGEN, REGEN EH NEBEL. SIEHT BALLE EH UM SIEHT BALLEN. (SEA TO CLOUD, CLOUD TO RAIN, RAIN TO FOG. THAT WITH SHAPE TO THAT WHICH IS UNSEEN.)
WIR GUT FREUDE. DANACH VRUND DILL BECHER (AFTER OUR JUBILATION, THE CHALICE WILL BE TURNED FACE DOWN.)
ZPP
AAA...
RAAAAAAA!!
NOW!!!
KRAK
AAAHRRGH!!!

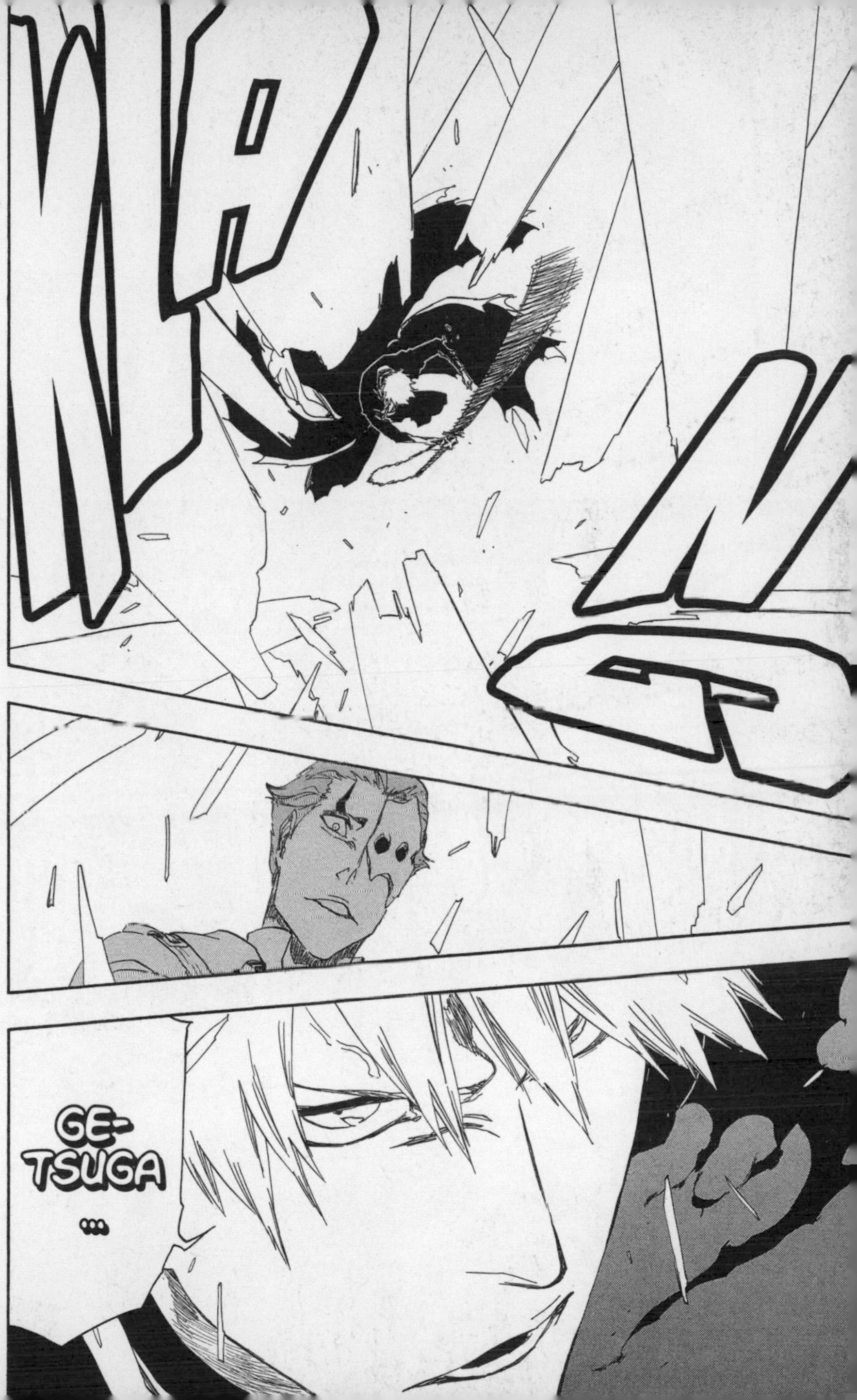
GE-
TSUGA
...

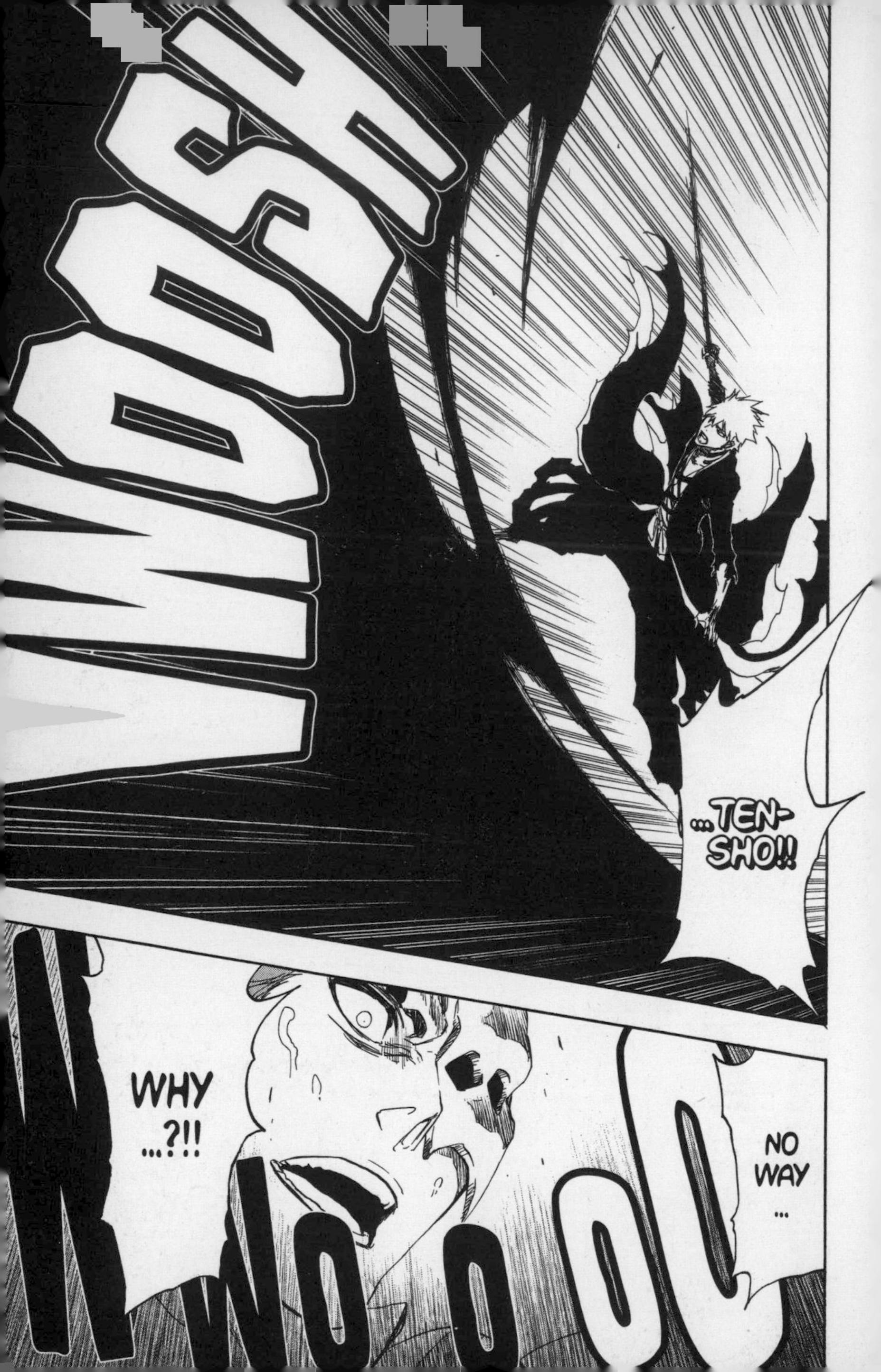
...TEN-
SHO!!
NO
WAY
...
WHY
...?!!

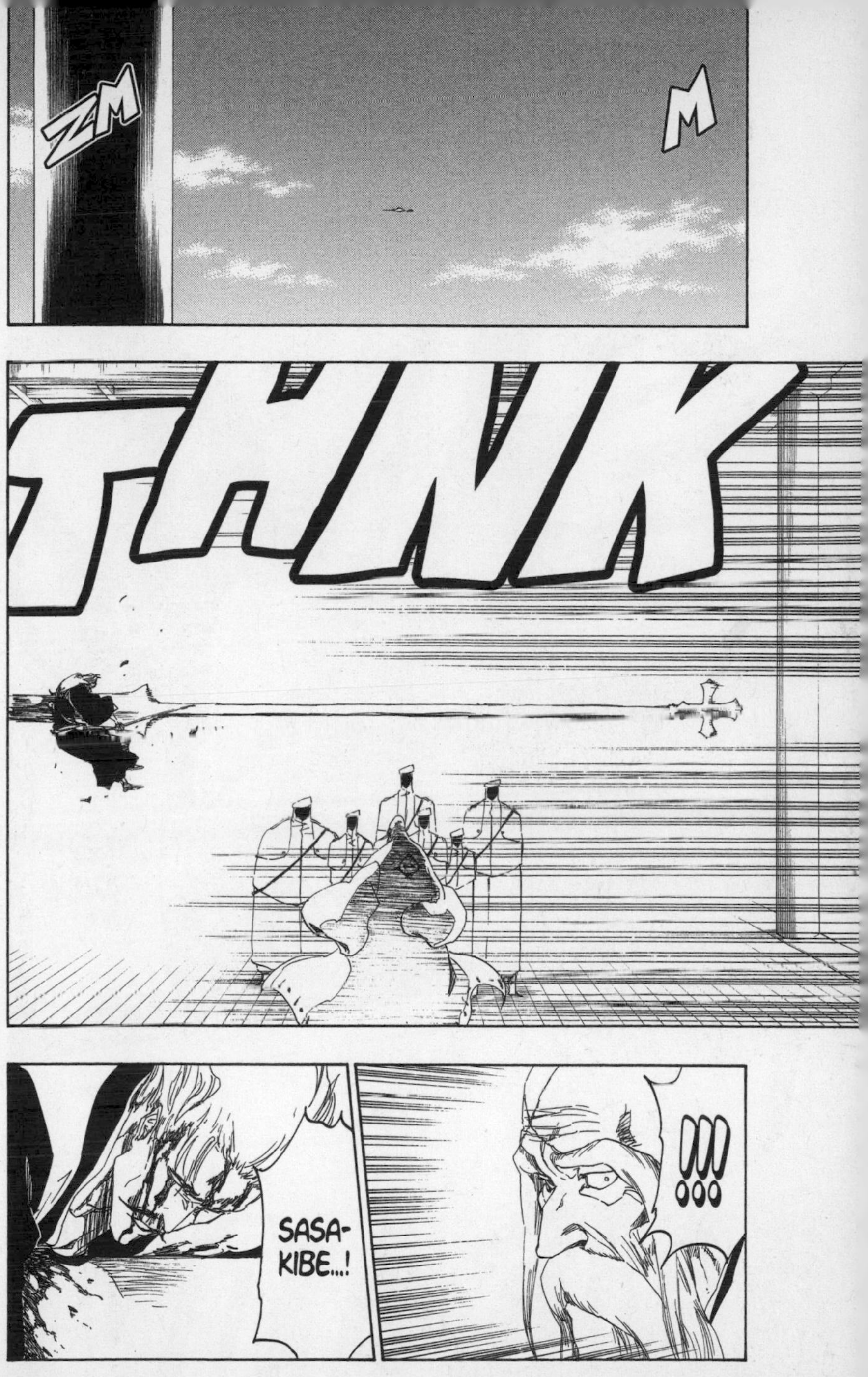
ZM
M
THNK
!!!
SASA-
KIBE...!

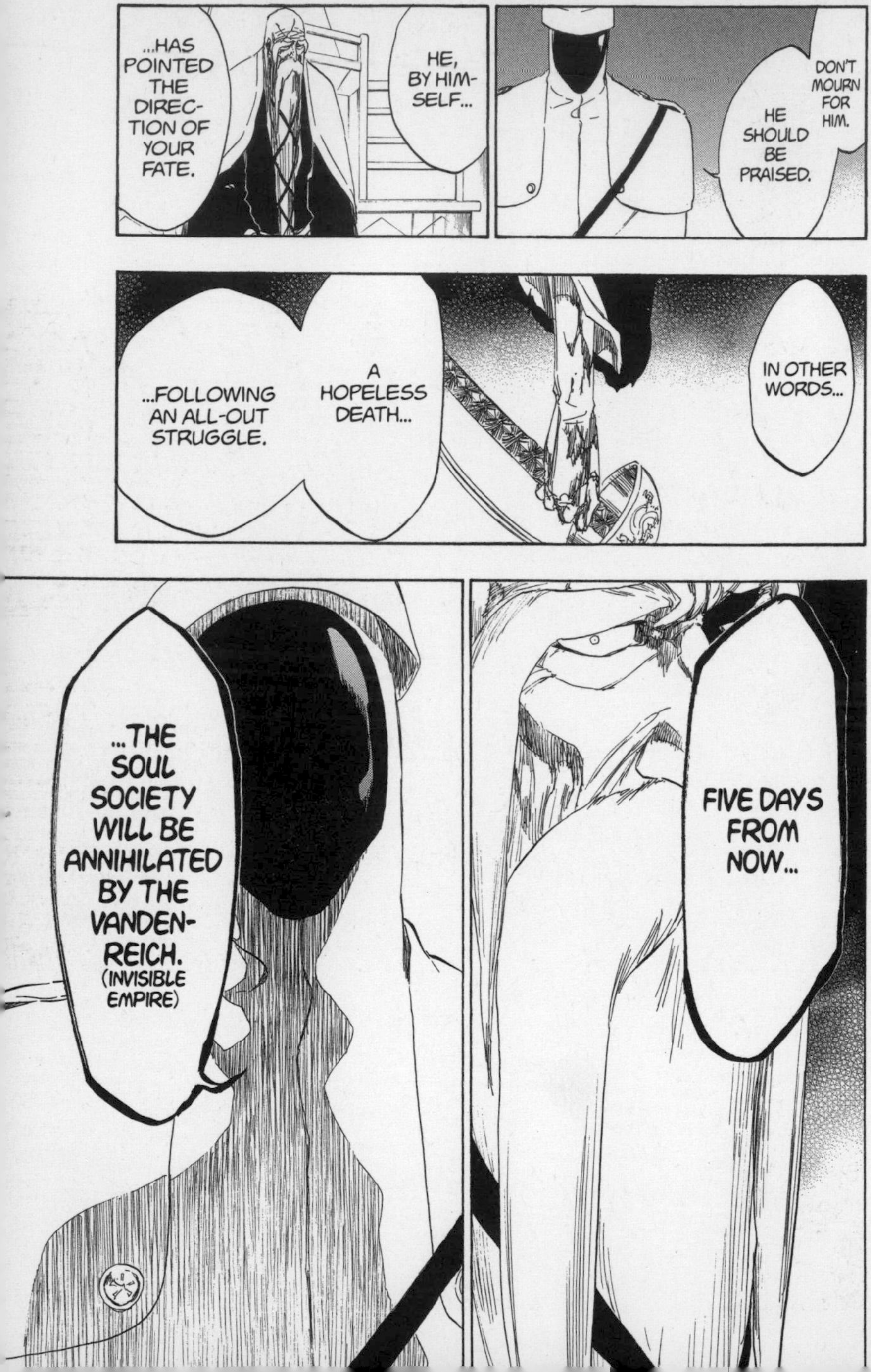
DON'T MOURN FOR HIM.
HE SHOULD BE PRAISED.
HE, BY HIMSELF...
...HAS POINTED THE DIRECTION OF YOUR FATE.
IN OTHER WORDS...
A HOPELESS DEATH...
...FOLLOWING AN ALL-OUT STRUGGLE.
FIVE DAYS FROM NOW...
...THE SOUL SOCIETY WILL BE ANNIHILATED BY THE VANDENREICH. (INVISIBLE EMPIRE)

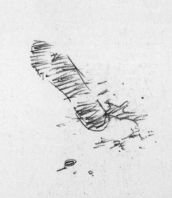

484. THE BUCKBEARD

FIVE DAYS FROM NOW...
...THE SOUL SOCIETY WILL BE ANNIHILATED BY THE VANDEN-REICH. (INVISIBLE EMPIRE)
FWP
KLAK

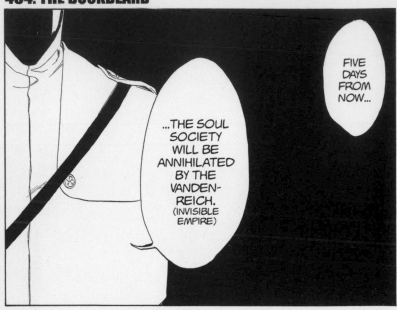

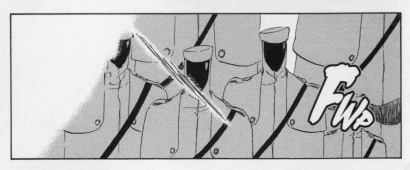

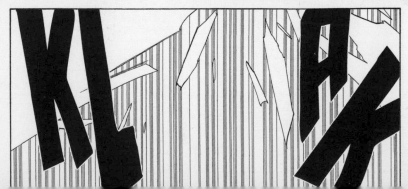

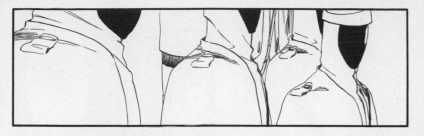

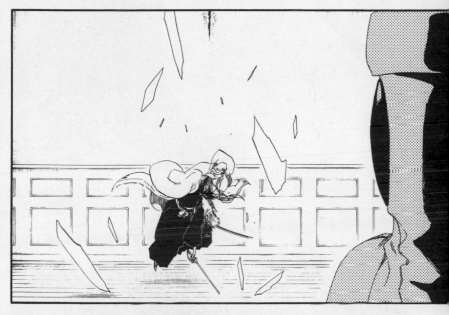

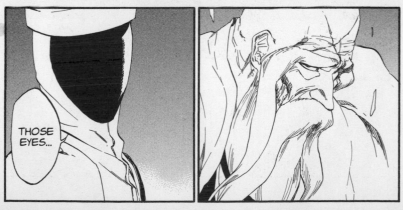

THOSE
EYES...

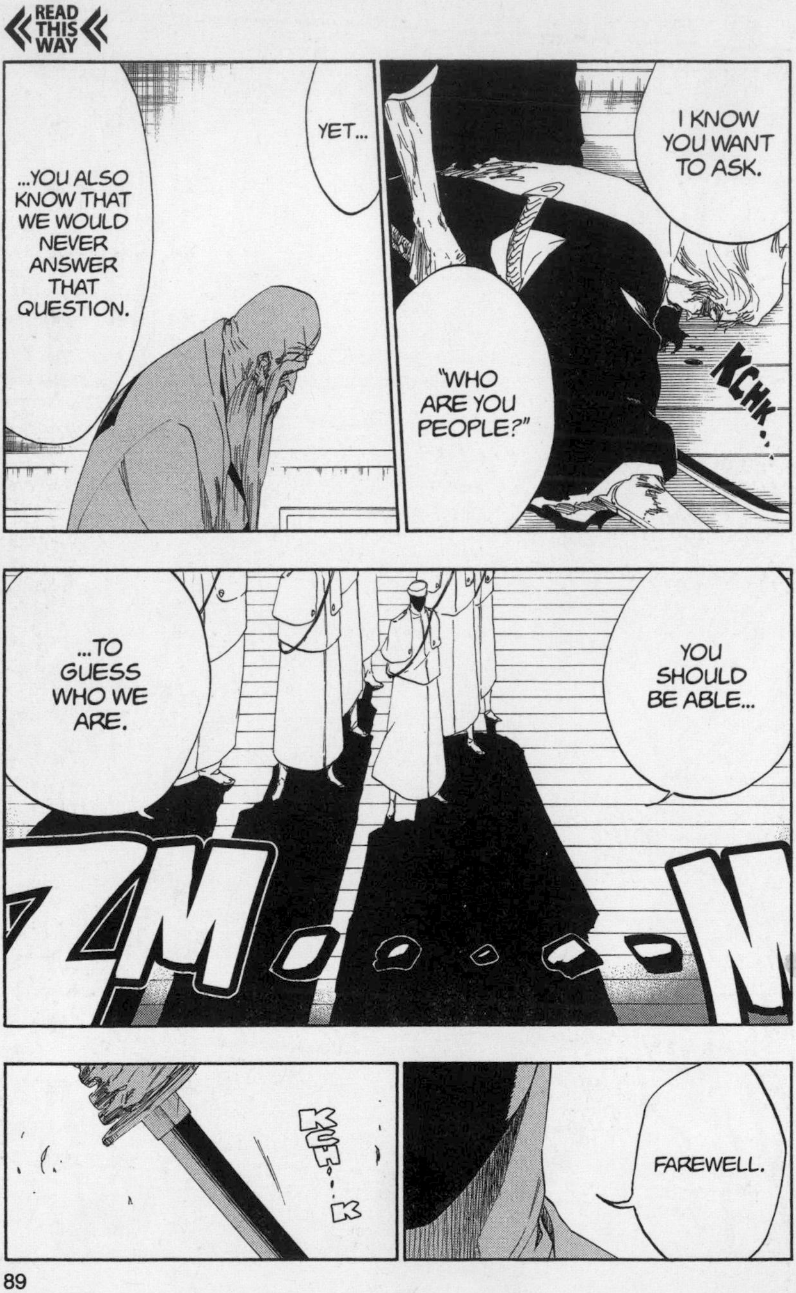
READ THIS WAY
I KNOW YOU WANT TO ASK.
"WHO ARE YOU PEOPLE?"
KCHK...
YET...
...YOU ALSO KNOW THAT WE WOULD NEVER ANSWER THAT QUESTION.
YOU SHOULD BE ABLE...
...TO GUESS WHO WE ARE.
ZM...M
FAREWELL.
KCH...K

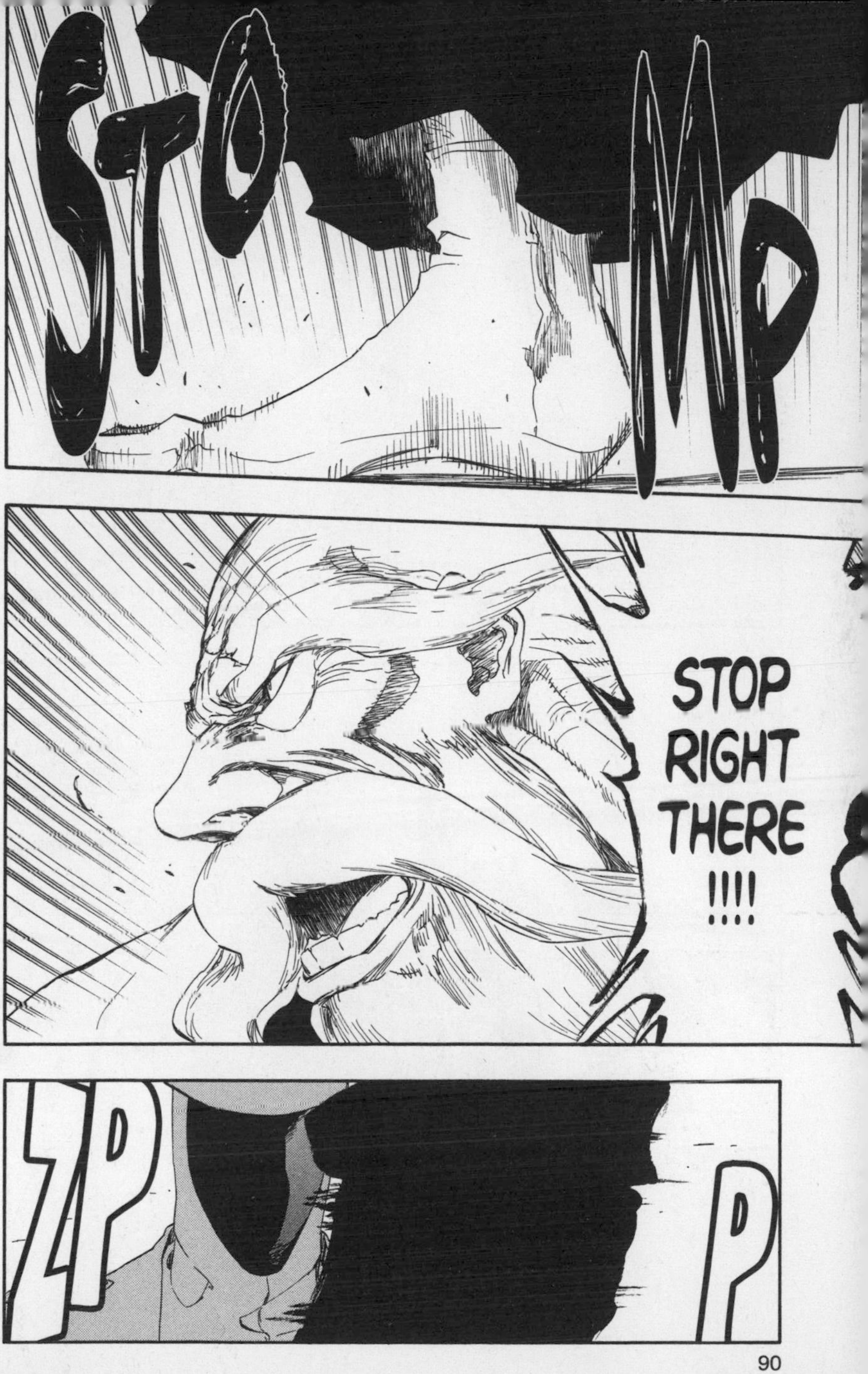
STOMP
STOP RIGHT THERE !!!!
ZPP

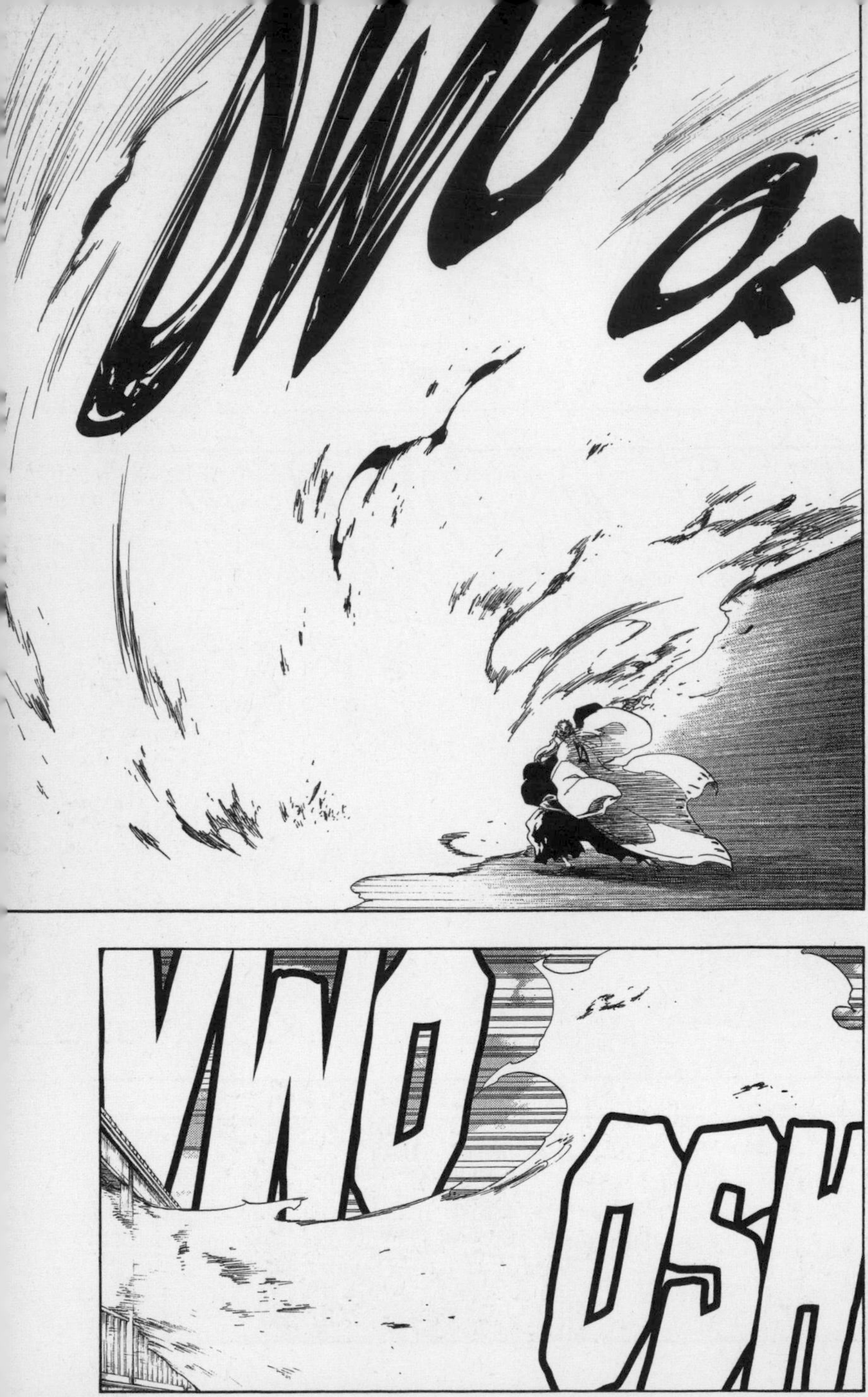
DWOOF
VWOOSH

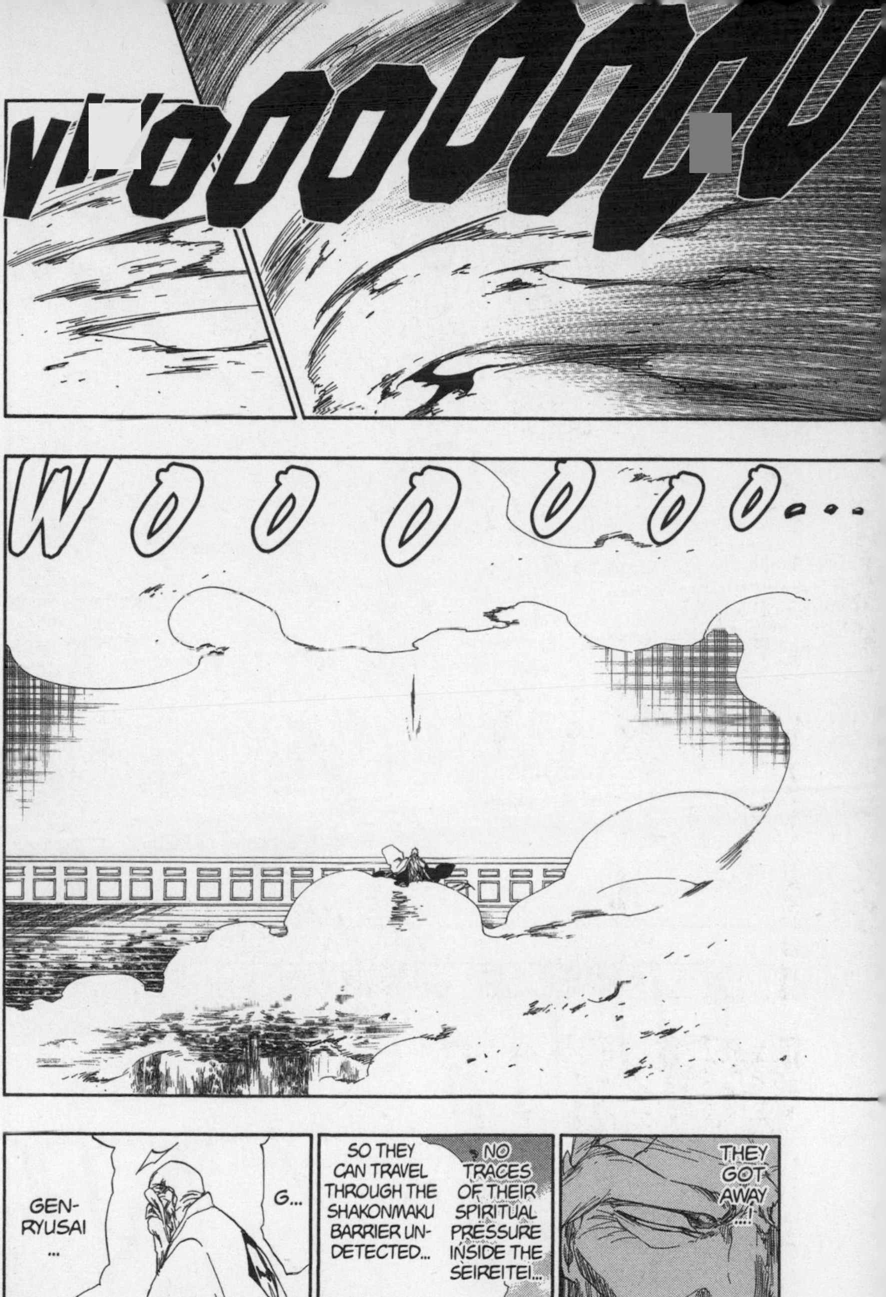
W O O O O O O...
THEY GOT AWAY...!!
NO TRACES OF THEIR SPIRITUAL PRESSURE INSIDE THE SEIREITEI...
SO THEY CAN TRAVEL THROUGH THE SHAKONMAKU BARRIER UN-DETECTED...
G...
GEN-RYUSAI ...

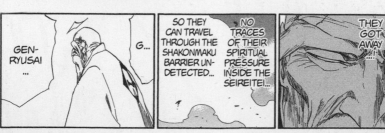

READ THIS WAY

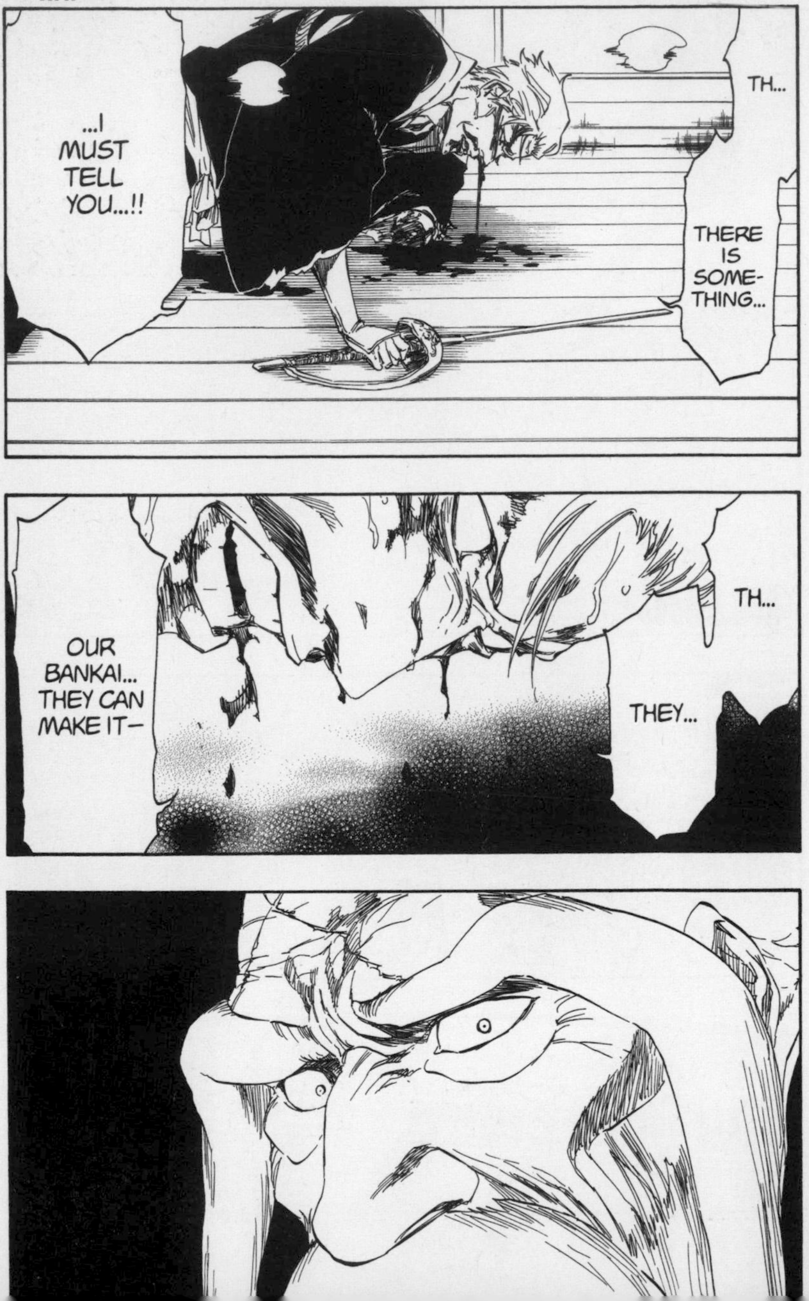

TH...
THERE IS SOMETHING...
...I MUST TELL YOU...!!
TH...
THEY...
OUR BANKAI... THEY CAN MAKE IT—

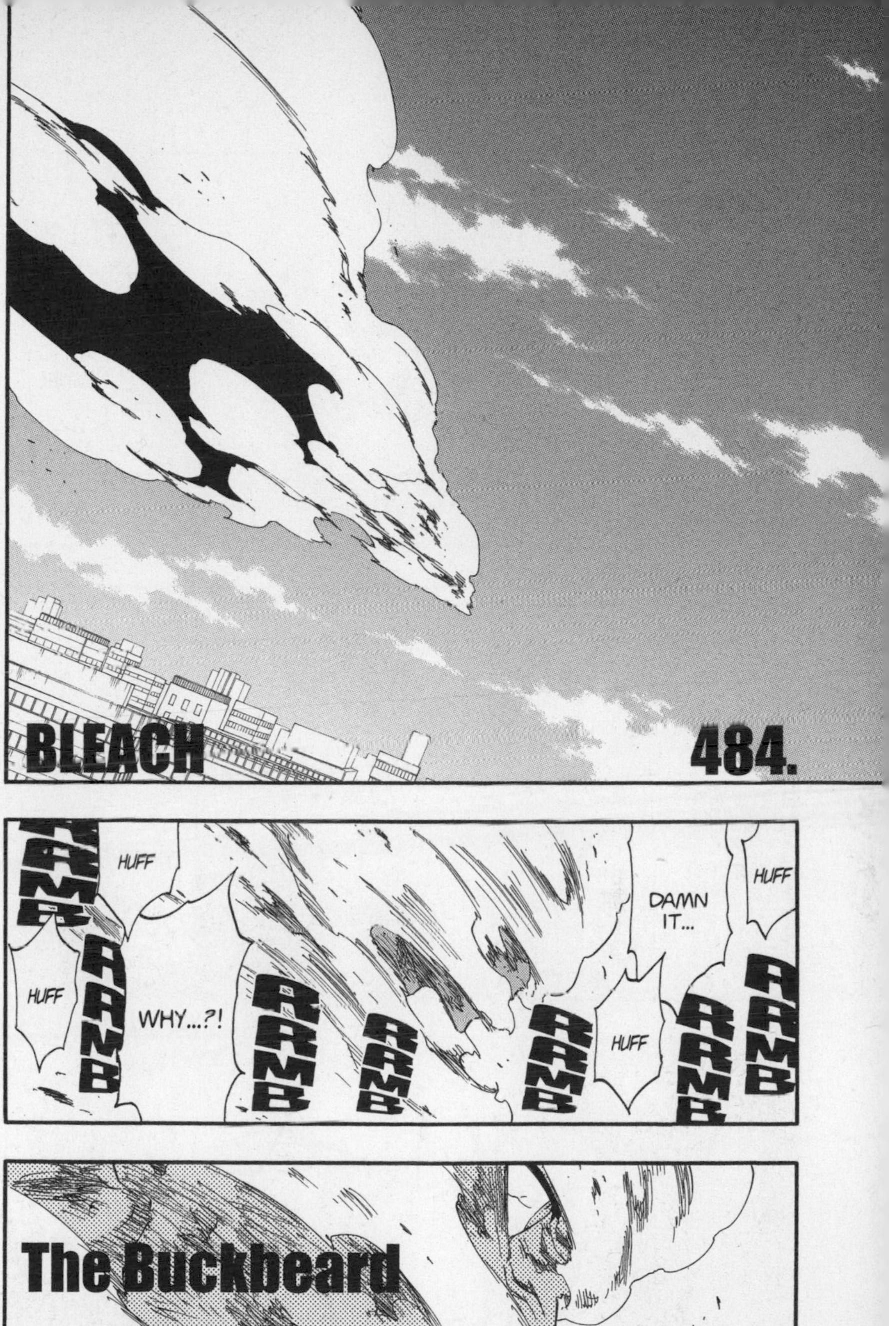
BLEACH
484.
HUFF
RRMB
RRMB
DAMN IT...
HUFF
RRMB
RRMB
RRMB
WHY...?!
RRMB
HUFF
HUFF
RRMB
The Buckbeard

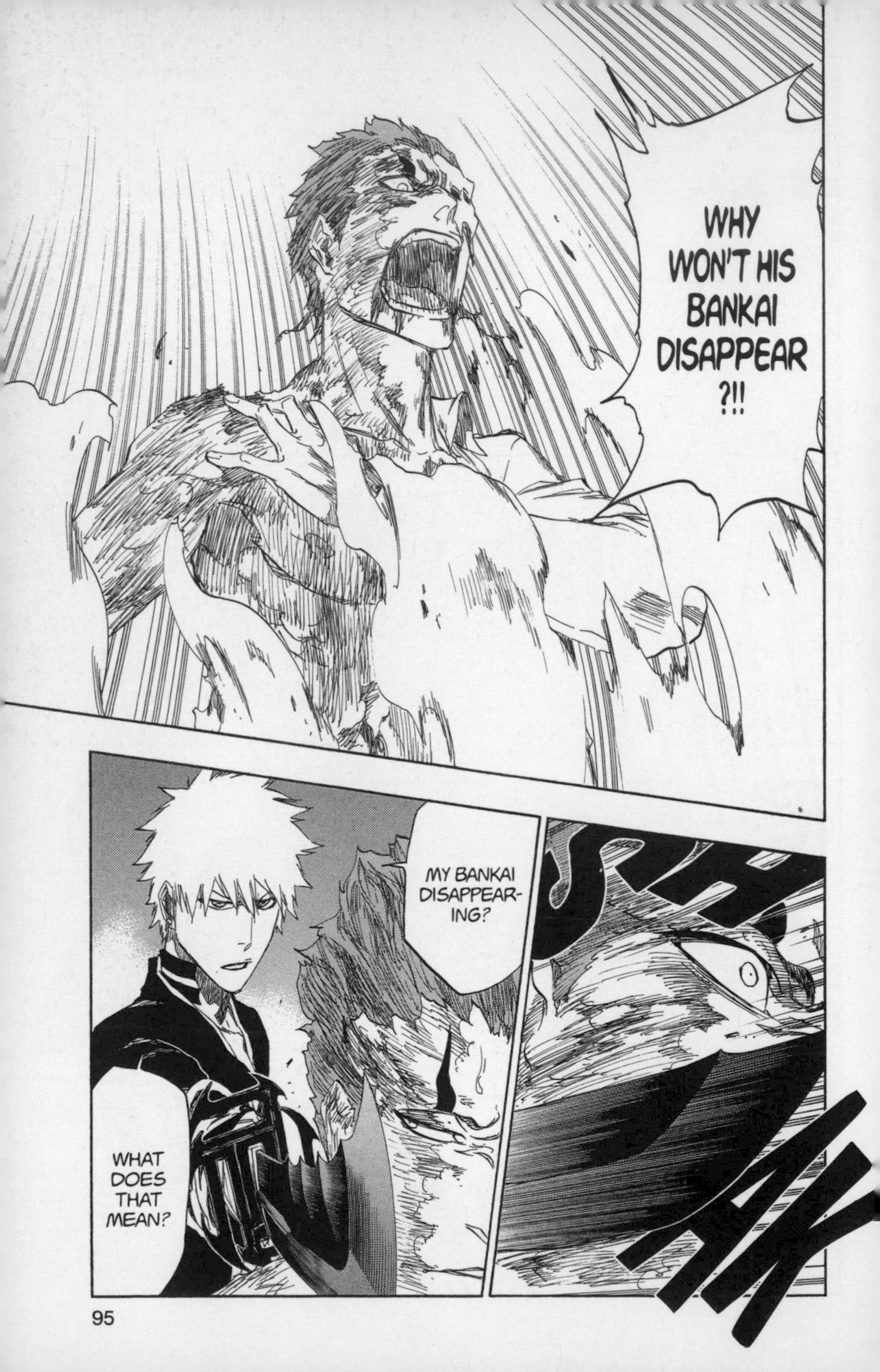
WHY WON'T HIS BANKAI DISAPPEAR ?!!
MY BANKAI DISAPPEAR-ING?
WHAT DOES THAT MEAN?

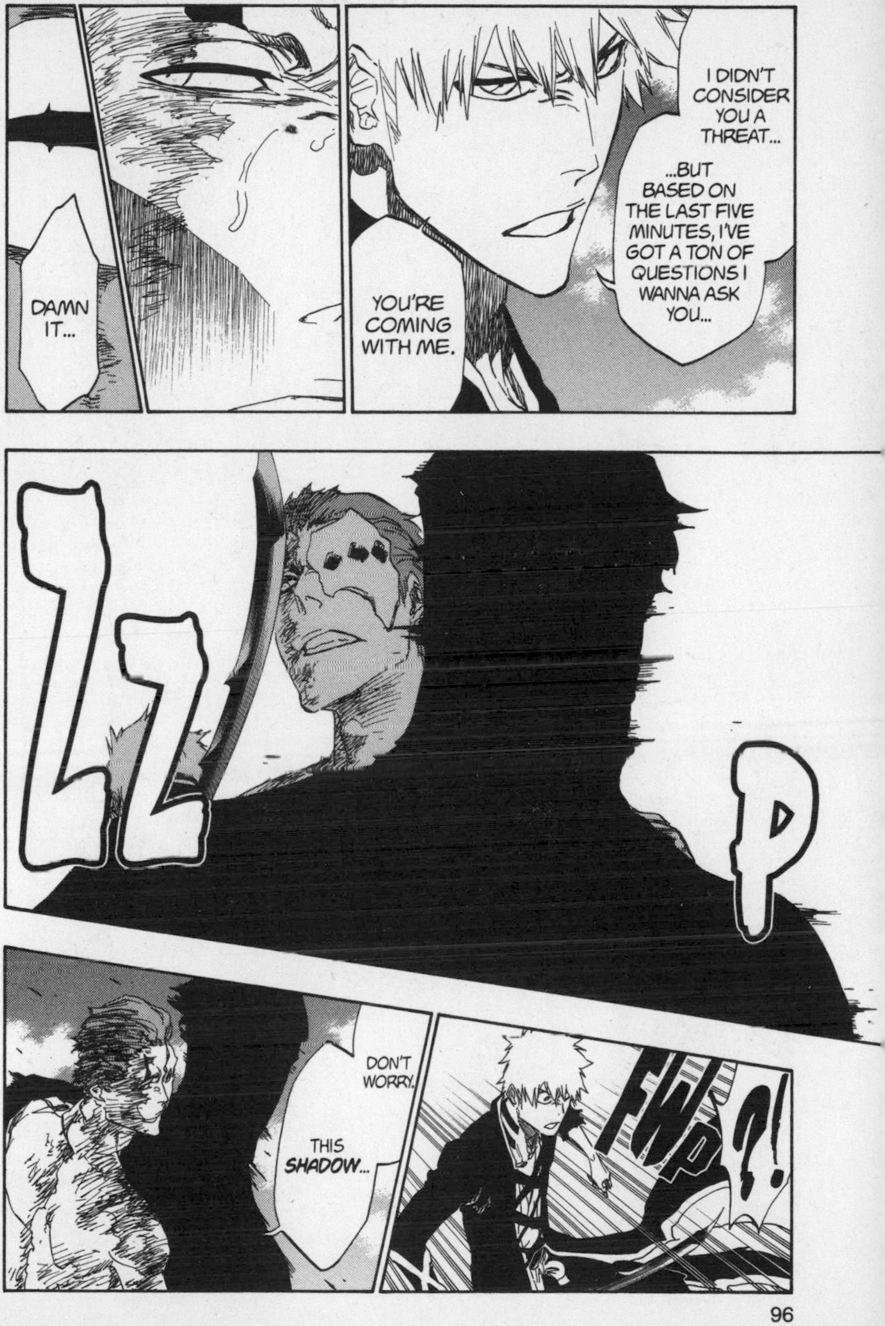
I DIDN'T CONSIDER YOU A THREAT...
...BUT BASED ON THE LAST FIVE MINUTES, I'VE GOT A TON OF QUESTIONS I WANNA ASK YOU...
YOU'RE COMING WITH ME.
DAMN IT...
ZZP
FWP
?!
DON'T WORRY.
THIS SHADOW...

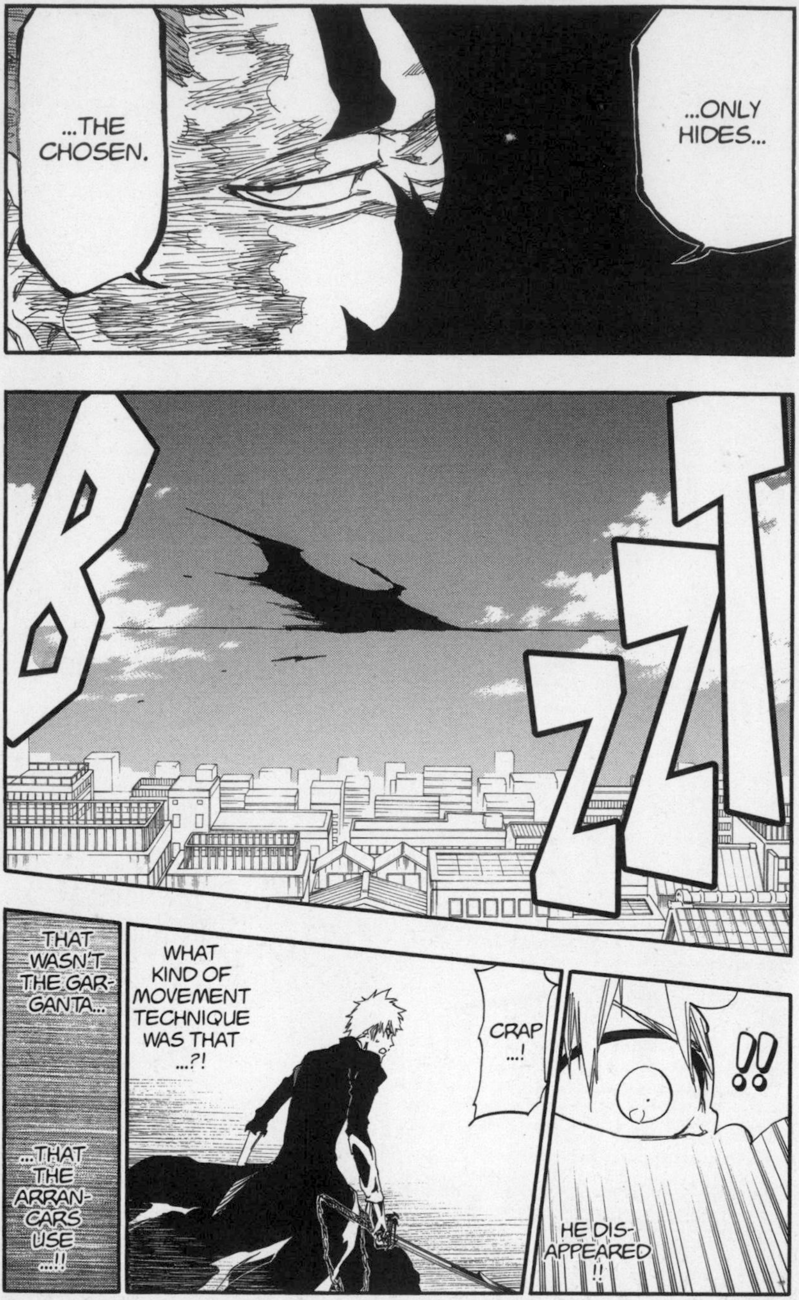
...ONLY HIDES...
...THE CHOSEN.
BZZT
!!
HE DIS-APPEARED !!
CRAP ...!
WHAT KIND OF MOVEMENT TECHNIQUE WAS THAT ...?!
THAT WASN'T THE GAR-GANTA...
...THAT THE ARRAN-CARS USE ...!!

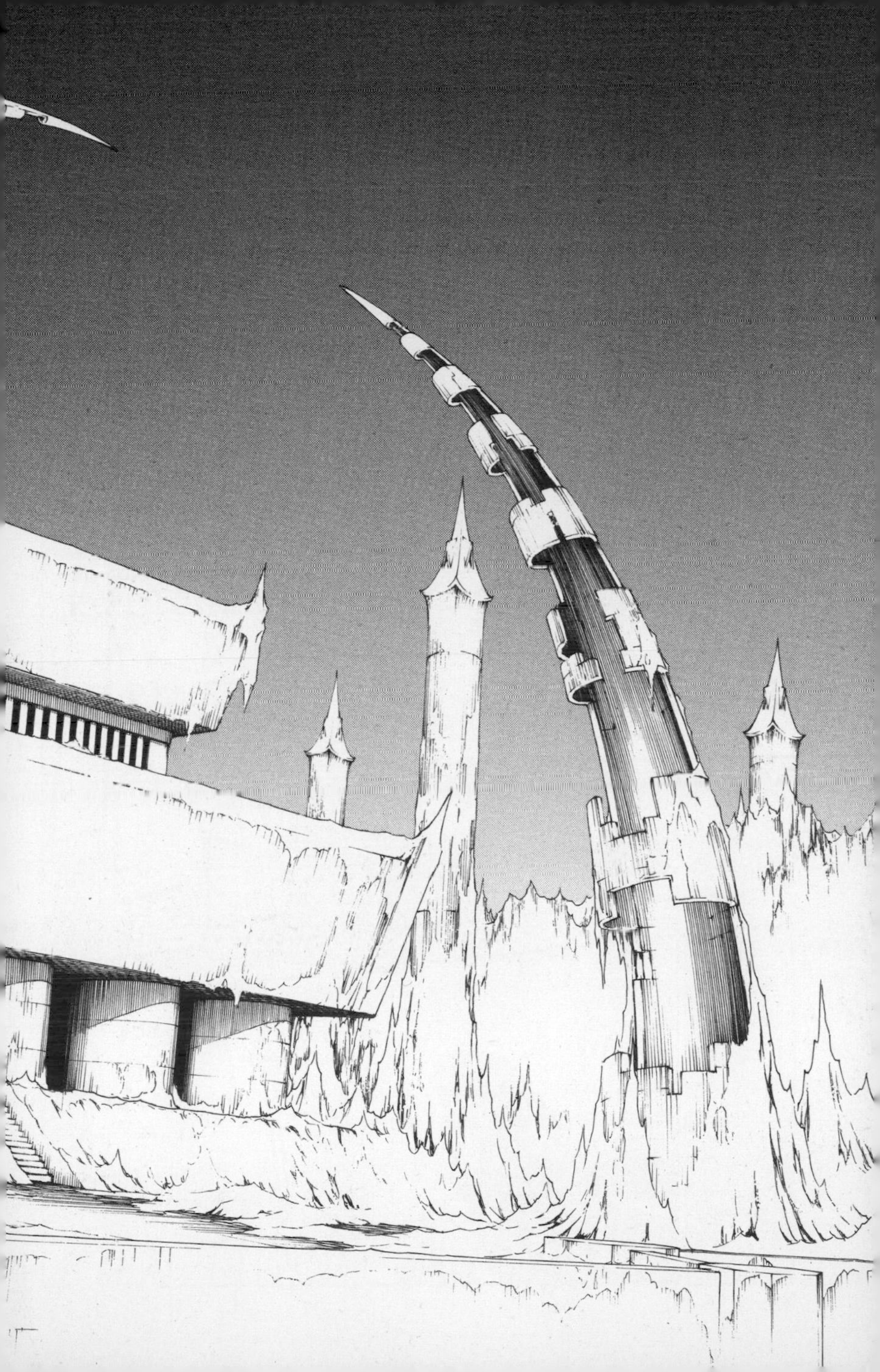

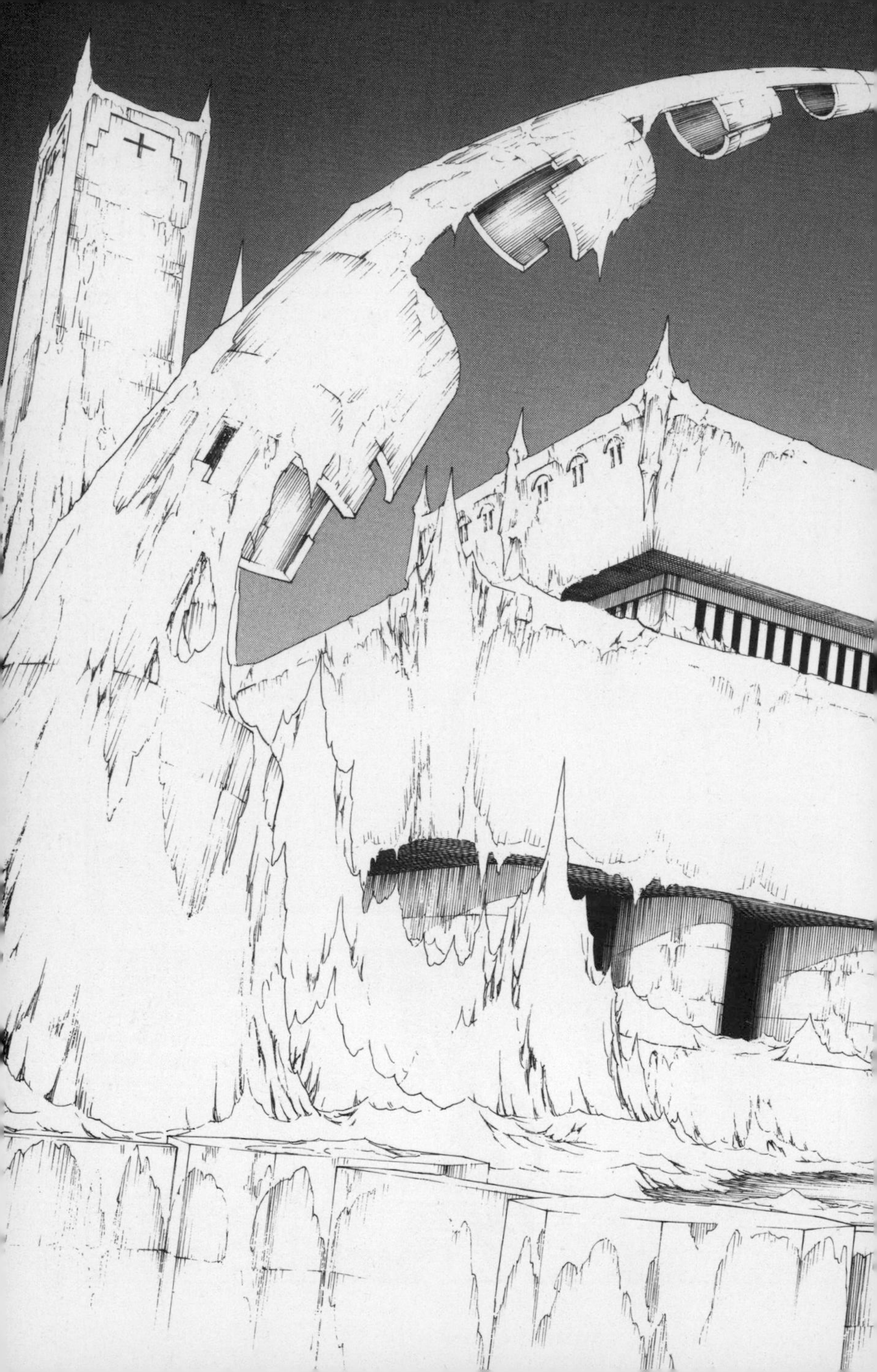

TMP
ZSH

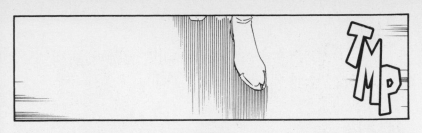

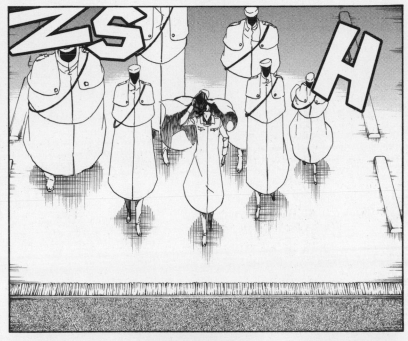

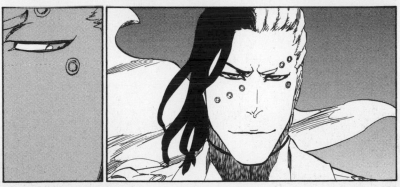

READ THIS WAY

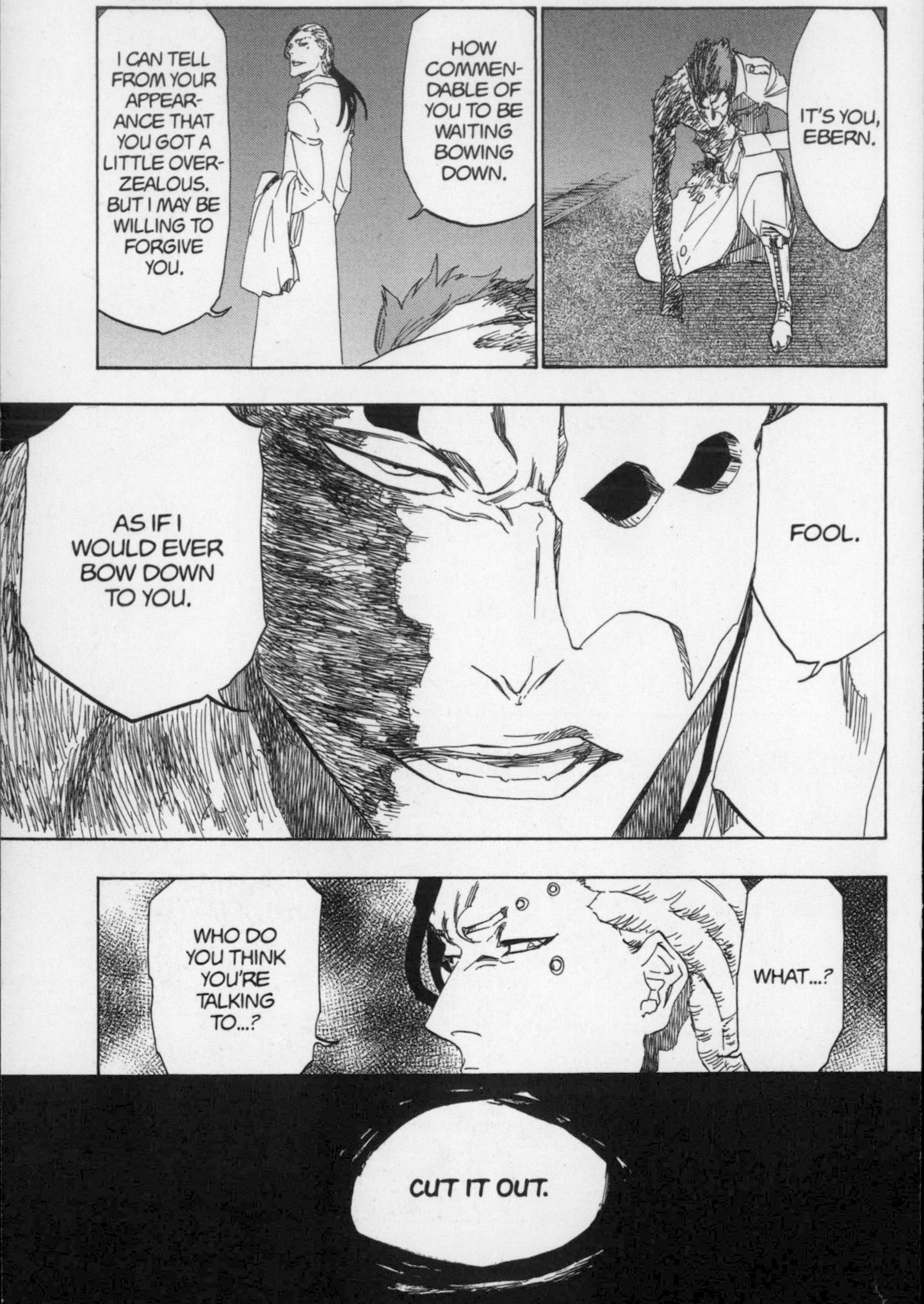
IT'S YOU, EBERN.
HOW COMMENDABLE OF YOU TO BE WAITING BOWING DOWN.
I CAN TELL FROM YOUR APPEARANCE THAT YOU GOT A LITTLE OVERZEALOUS. BUT I MAY BE WILLING TO FORGIVE YOU.
FOOL.
AS IF I WOULD EVER BOW DOWN TO YOU.
WHAT...?
WHO DO YOU THINK YOU'RE TALKING TO...?
CUT IT OUT.

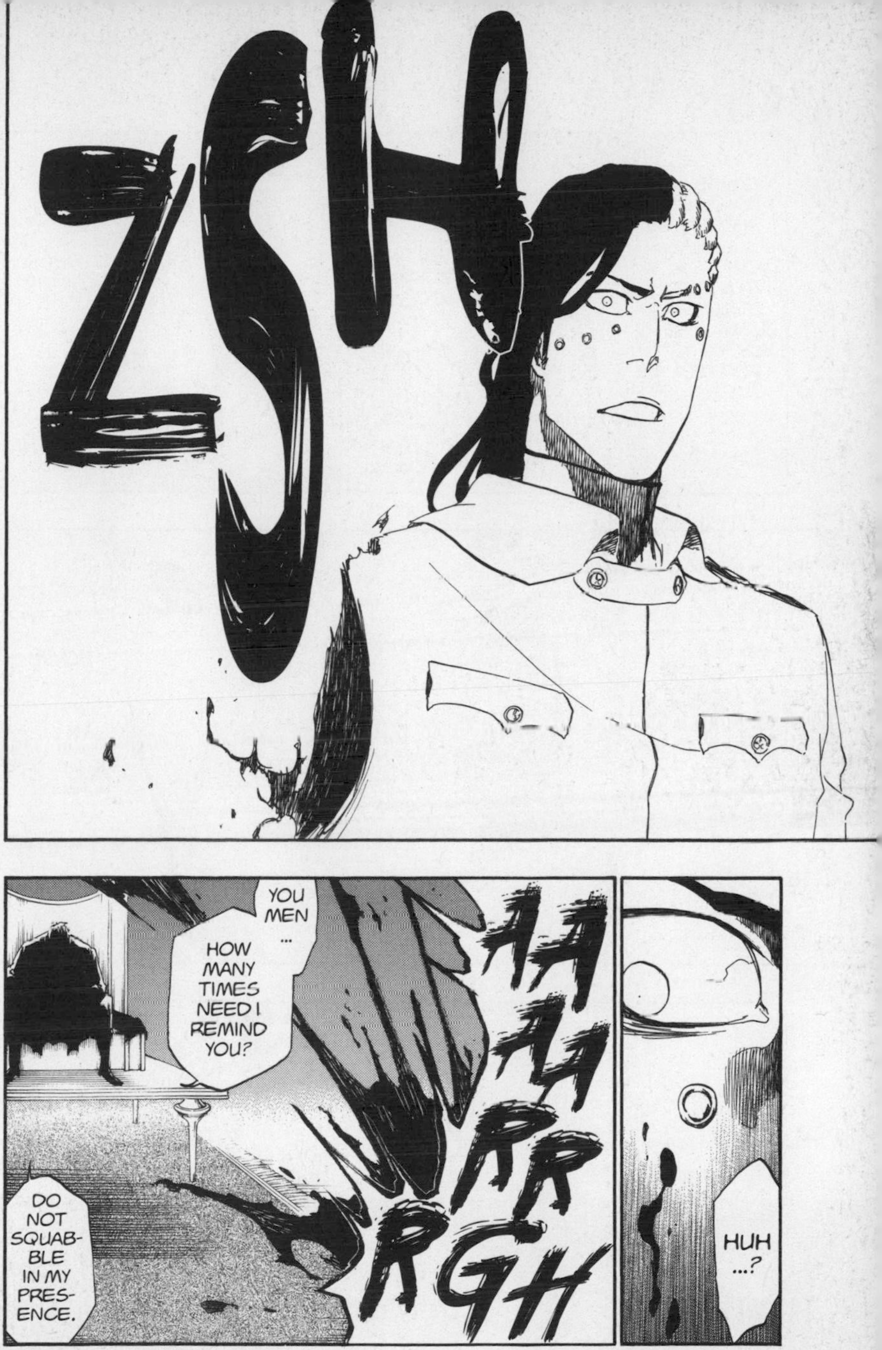
ZSHH
HUH ...?
AAAARRRRRGH
YOU MEN ...
HOW MANY TIMES NEED I REMIND YOU?
DO NOT SQUABBLE IN MY PRESENCE.

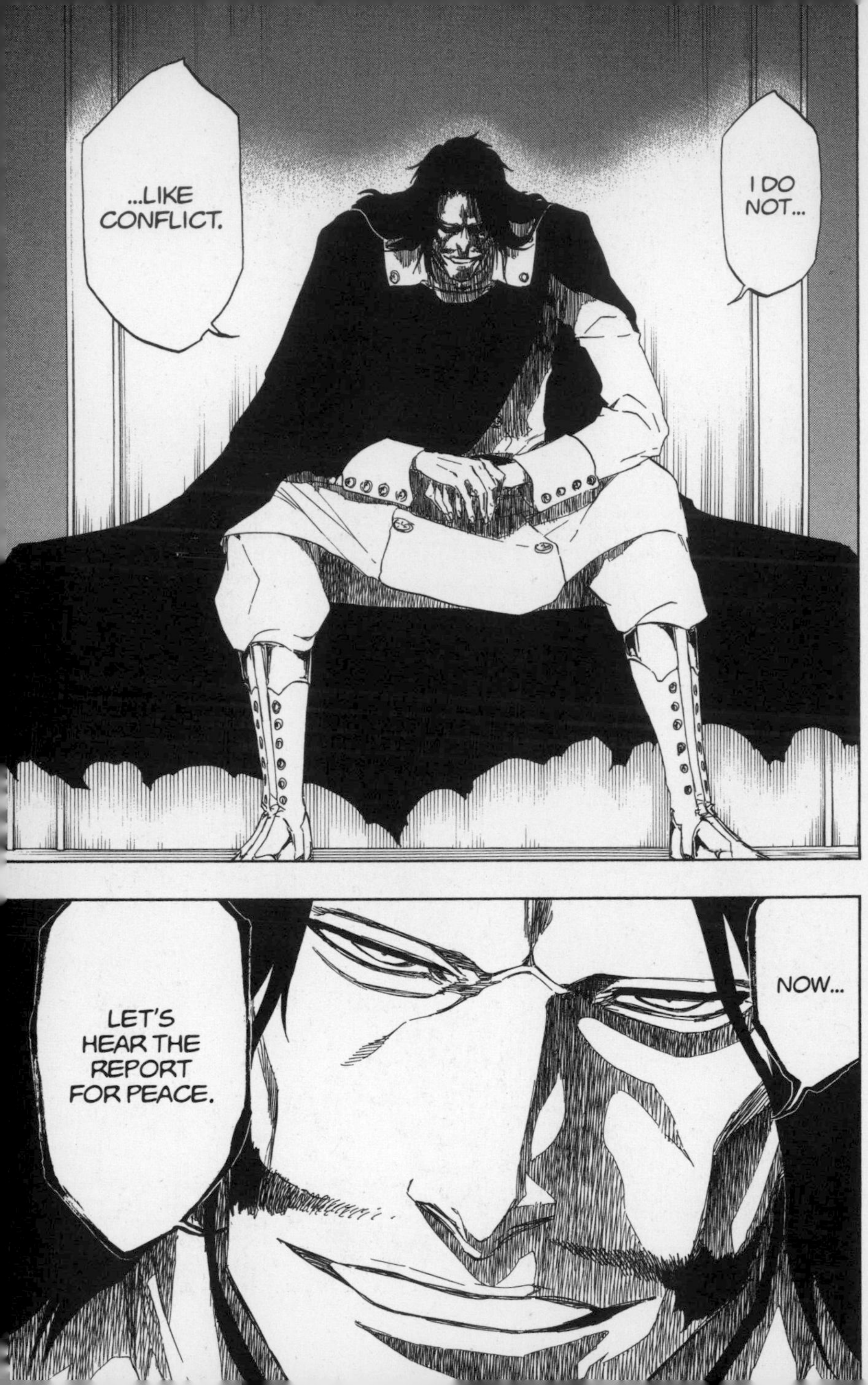
I DO NOT...
...LIKE CONFLICT.
NOW...
LET'S HEAR THE REPORT FOR PEACE.

Peace

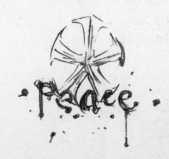

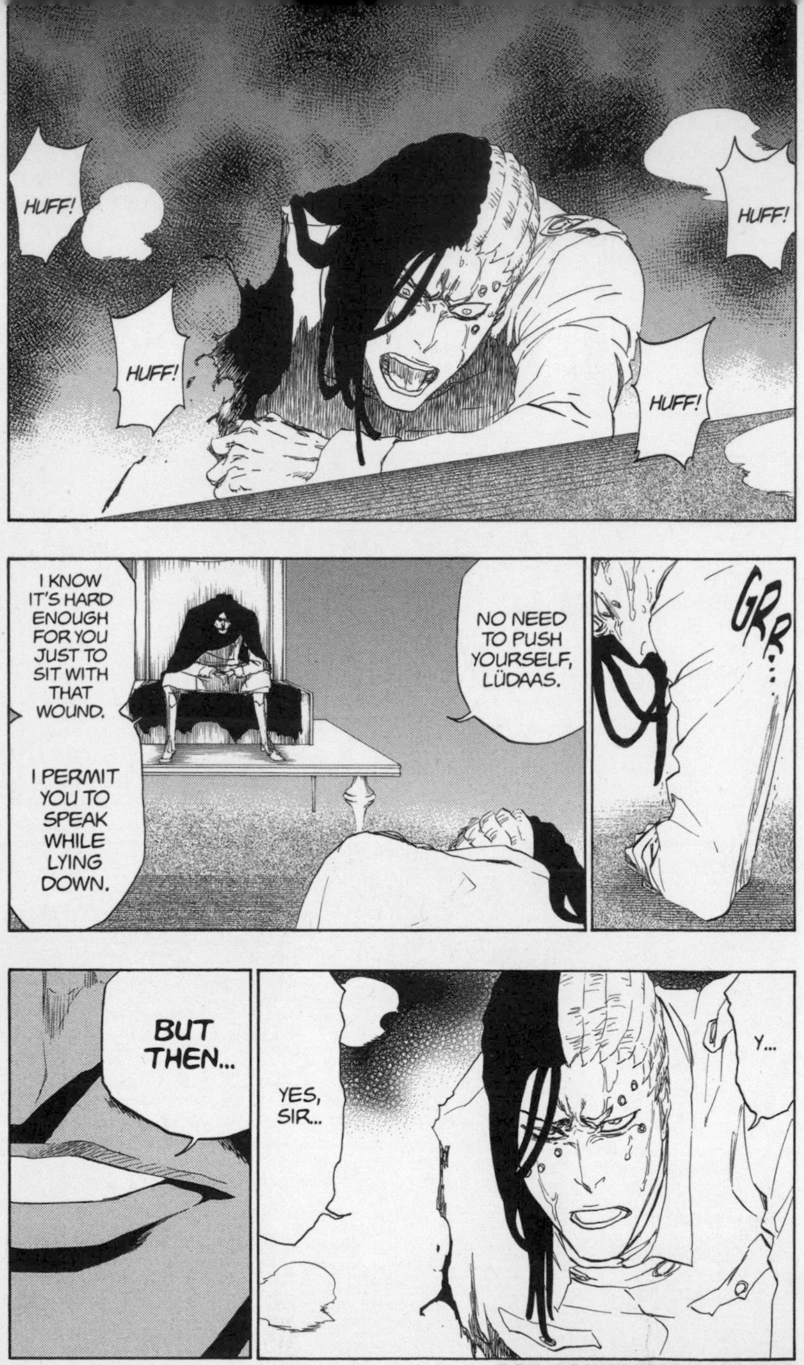
HUFF!
HUFF!
HUFF!
HUFF!
GRR...
NO NEED TO PUSH YOURSELF, LÜDAAS.
I KNOW IT'S HARD ENOUGH FOR YOU JUST TO SIT WITH THAT WOUND.
I PERMIT YOU TO SPEAK WHILE LYING DOWN.
Y...
YES, SIR...
BUT THEN...

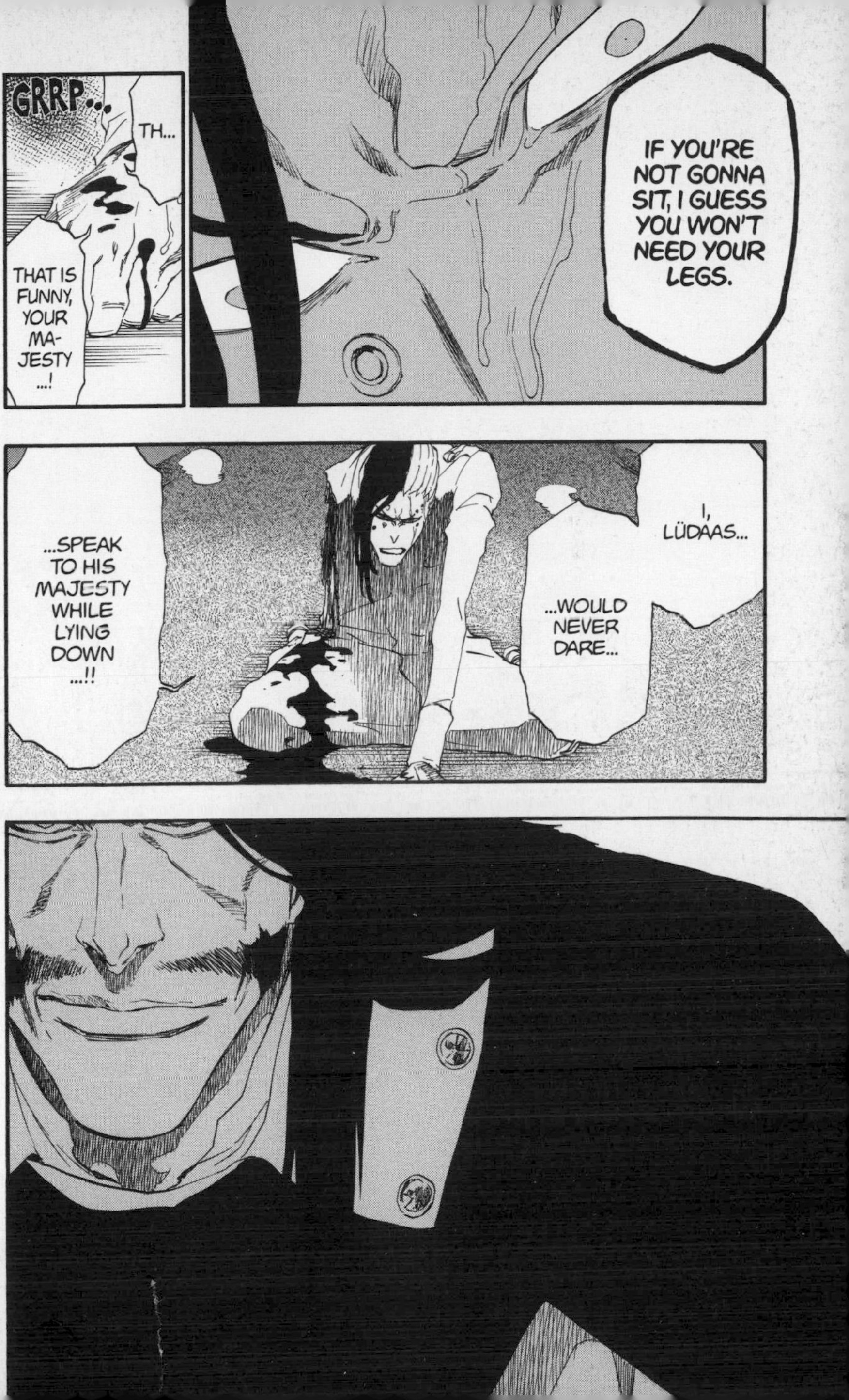

IF YOU'RE NOT GONNA SIT, I GUESS YOU WON'T NEED YOUR LEGS.
GRRP...
TH...
THAT IS FUNNY, YOUR MAJESTY ...!
I, LÜDAAS...
...WOULD NEVER DARE...
...SPEAK TO HIS MAJESTY WHILE LYING DOWN ...!!

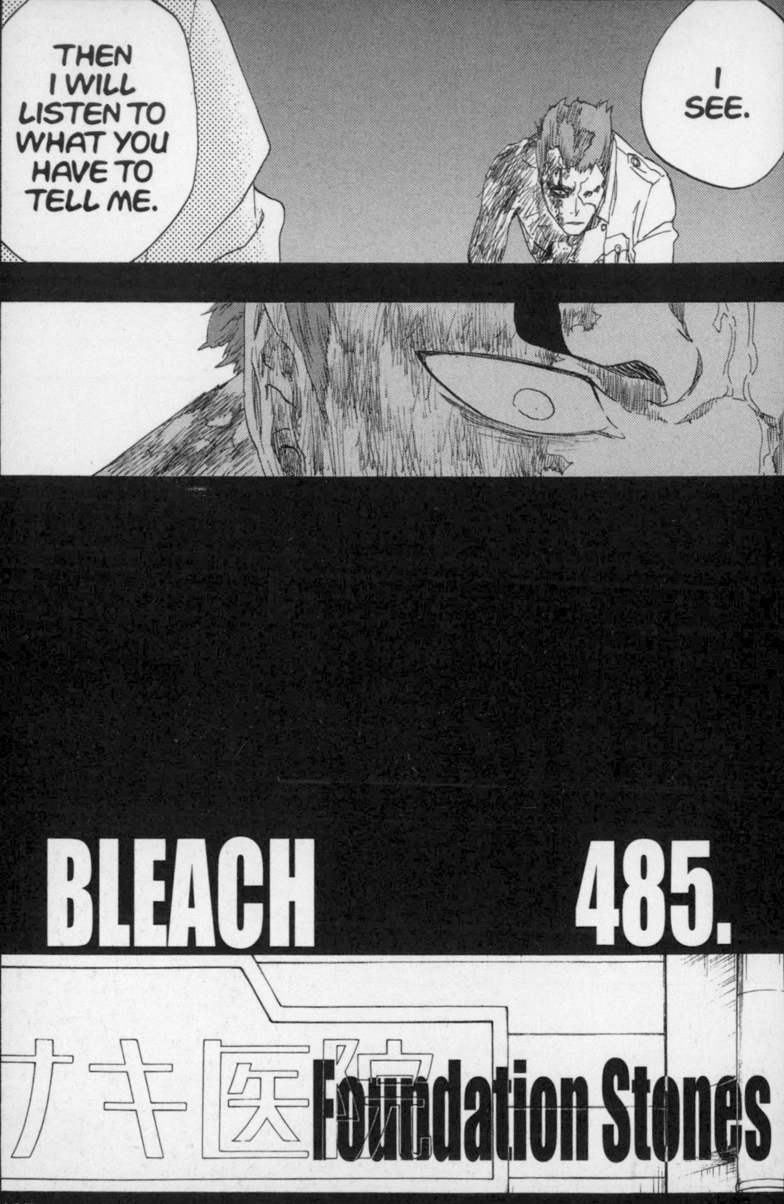
I SEE.
THEN I WILL LISTEN TO WHAT YOU HAVE TO TELL ME.
BLEACH
485.
Foundation Stones

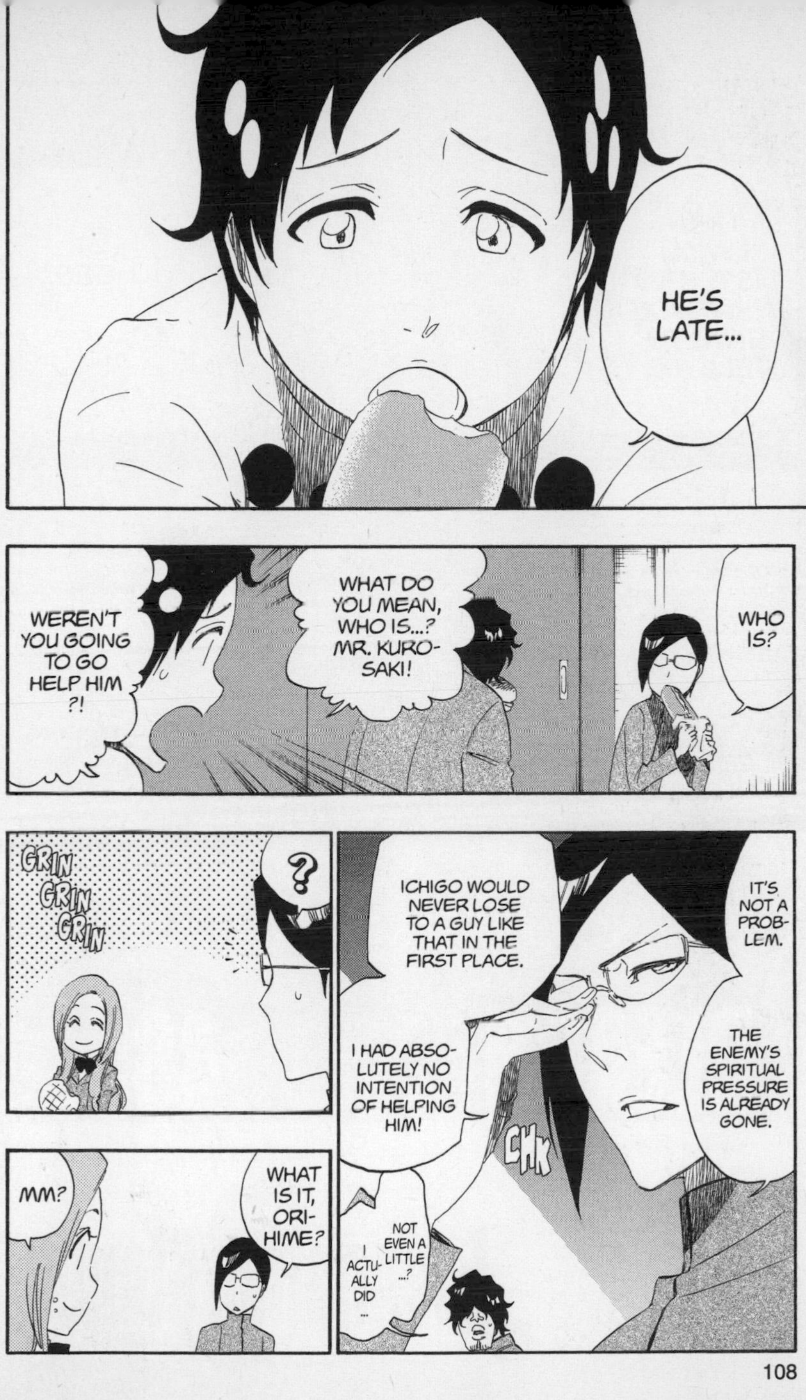
HE'S LATE...
WHO IS?
WHAT DO YOU MEAN, WHO IS...? MR. KURO-SAKI!
WEREN'T YOU GOING TO GO HELP HIM?!
IT'S NOT A PROB-LEM.
ICHIGO WOULD NEVER LOSE TO A GUY LIKE THAT IN THE FIRST PLACE.
THE ENEMY'S SPIRITUAL PRESSURE IS ALREADY GONE.
I HAD ABSO-LUTELY NO INTENTION OF HELPING HIM!
CHK
NOT EVEN A LITTLE...?
I ACTU-ALLY DID...
?
GRIN GRIN GRIN
WHAT IS IT, ORI-HIME?
MM?

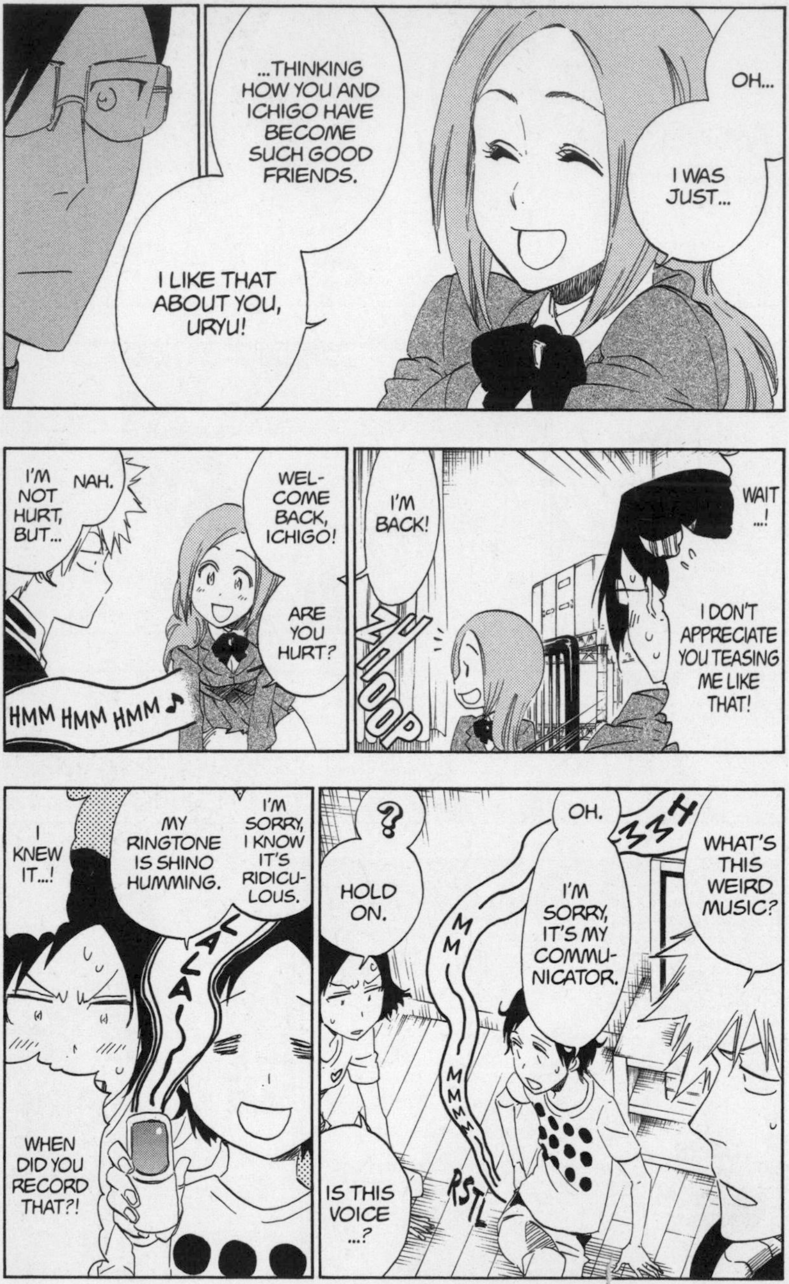
OH...
I WAS JUST...
...THINKING HOW YOU AND ICHIGO HAVE BECOME SUCH GOOD FRIENDS.
I LIKE THAT ABOUT YOU, URYU!
WAIT ...!
I DON'T APPRECIATE YOU TEASING ME LIKE THAT!
I'M BACK!
ZHOOOP
WEL-COME BACK, ICHIGO!
ARE YOU HURT?
NAH.
I'M NOT HURT, BUT...
HMM HMM HMM ♪
MMMH
WHAT'S THIS WEIRD MUSIC?
OH.
I'M SORRY, IT'S MY COMMU-NICATOR.
?
HOLD ON.
MM MMMM
RSTL
IS THIS VOICE ...?
I'M SORRY, I KNOW IT'S RIDICU-LOUS.
MY RINGTONE IS SHINO HUMMING.
LALALA
I KNEW IT...!
WHEN DID YOU RECORD THAT?!

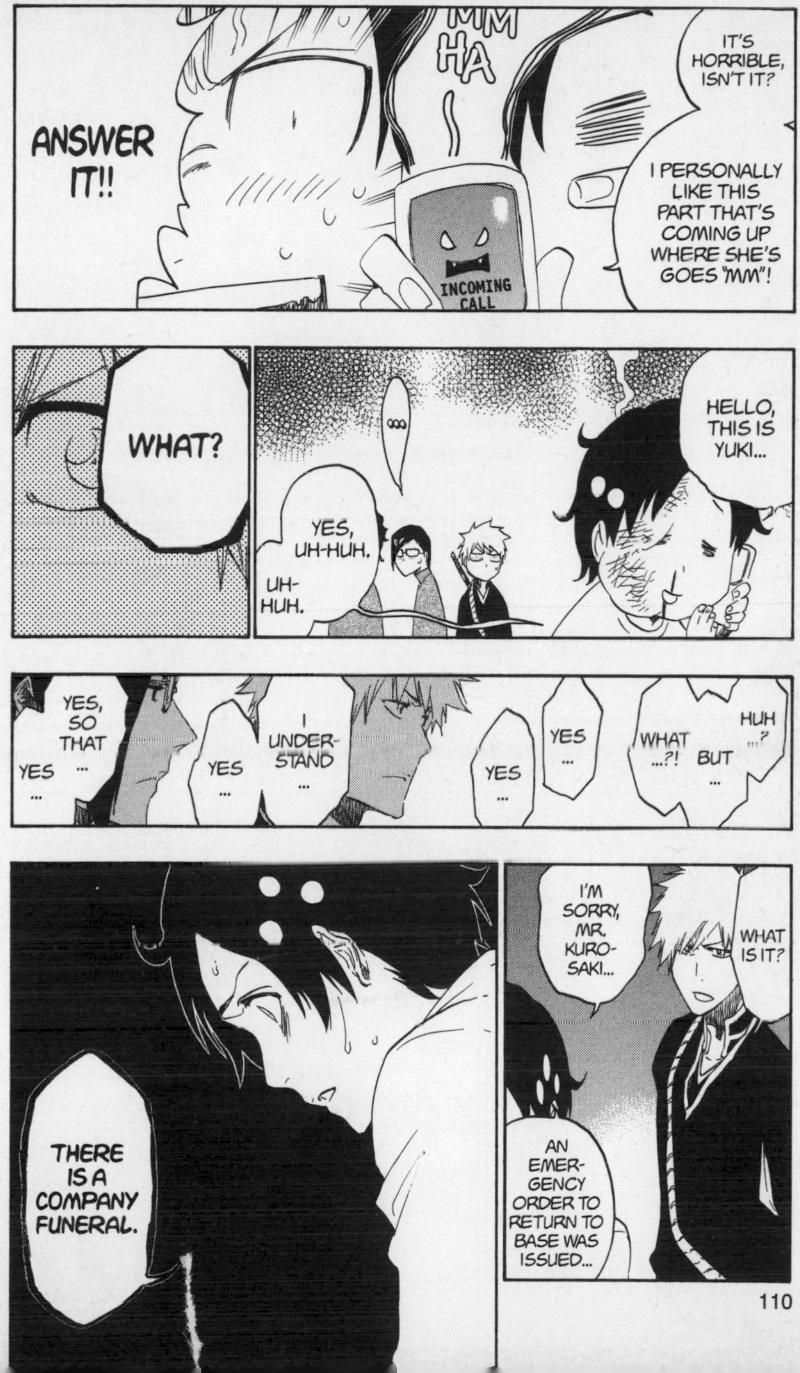
IT'S HORRIBLE, ISN'T IT?
MM HA
I PERSONALLY LIKE THIS PART THAT'S COMING UP WHERE SHE'S GOES "MM"!
INCOMING CALL
ANSWER IT!!
HELLO, THIS IS YUKI...
...
YES, UH-HUH.
UH-HUH.
WHAT?
HUH...?
WHAT...?! BUT...
YES...
YES...
I UNDERSTAND...
YES...
YES, SO THAT...
YES...
WHAT IS IT?
I'M SORRY, MR. KUROSAKI...
AN EMERGENCY ORDER TO RETURN TO BASE WAS ISSUED...
THERE IS A COMPANY FUNERAL.

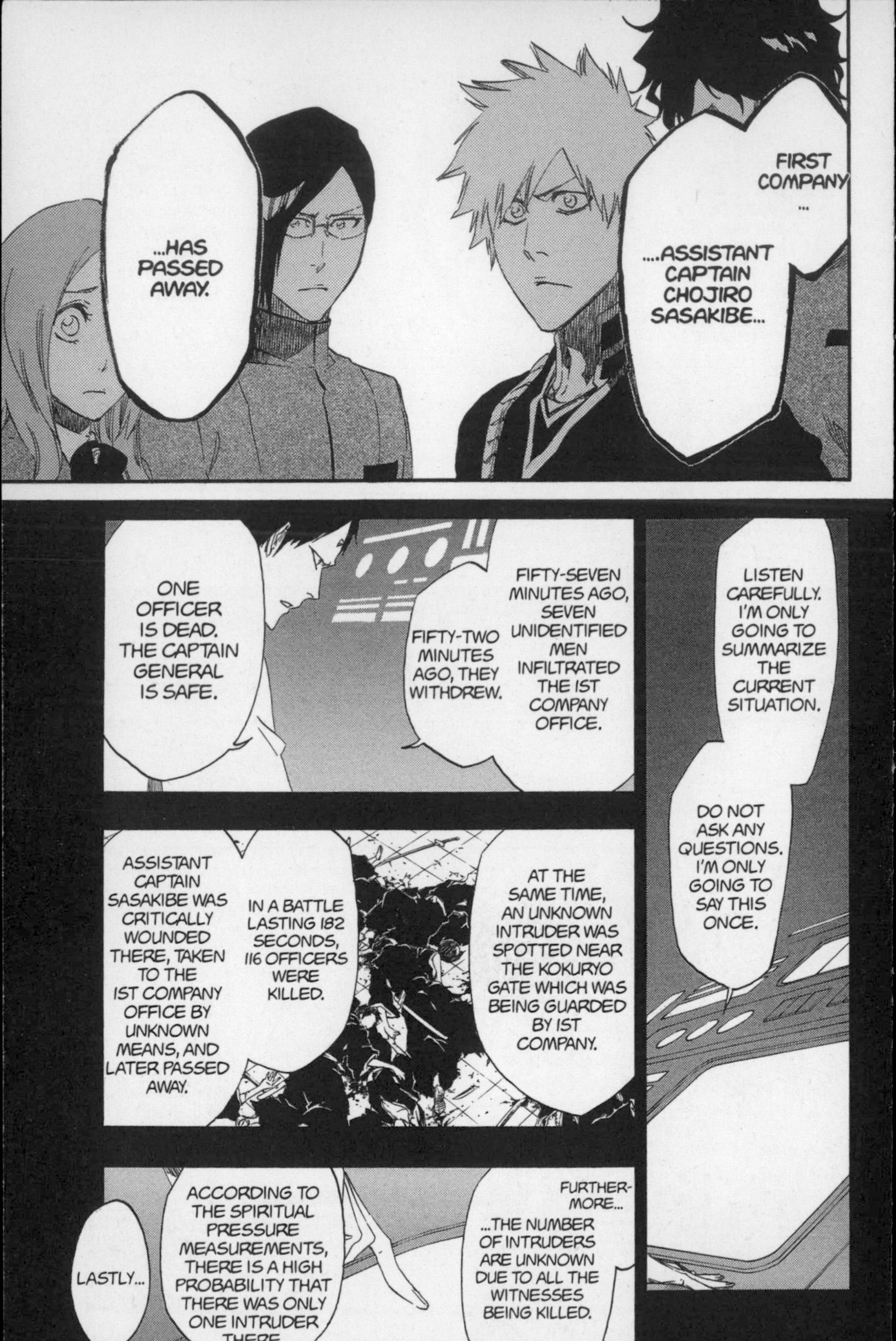
FIRST COMPANY ...
....ASSISTANT CAPTAIN CHOJIRO SASAKIBE...
...HAS PASSED AWAY.
LISTEN CAREFULLY. I'M ONLY GOING TO SUMMARIZE THE CURRENT SITUATION.
DO NOT ASK ANY QUESTIONS. I'M ONLY GOING TO SAY THIS ONCE.
FIFTY-SEVEN MINUTES AGO, SEVEN UNIDENTIFIED MEN INFILTRATED THE 1ST COMPANY OFFICE.
FIFTY-TWO MINUTES AGO, THEY WITHDREW.
ONE OFFICER IS DEAD. THE CAPTAIN GENERAL IS SAFE.
AT THE SAME TIME, AN UNKNOWN INTRUDER WAS SPOTTED NEAR THE KOKURYO GATE WHICH WAS BEING GUARDED BY 1ST COMPANY.
IN A BATTLE LASTING 182 SECONDS, 116 OFFICERS WERE KILLED.
ASSISTANT CAPTAIN SASAKIBE WAS CRITICALLY WOUNDED THERE, TAKEN TO THE 1ST COMPANY OFFICE BY UNKNOWN MEANS, AND LATER PASSED AWAY.
FURTHER-MORE...
...THE NUMBER OF INTRUDERS ARE UNKNOWN DUE TO ALL THE WITNESSES BEING KILLED.
ACCORDING TO THE SPIRITUAL PRESSURE MEASUREMENTS, THERE IS A HIGH PROBABILITY THAT THERE WAS ONLY ONE INTRUDER THERE.
LASTLY...

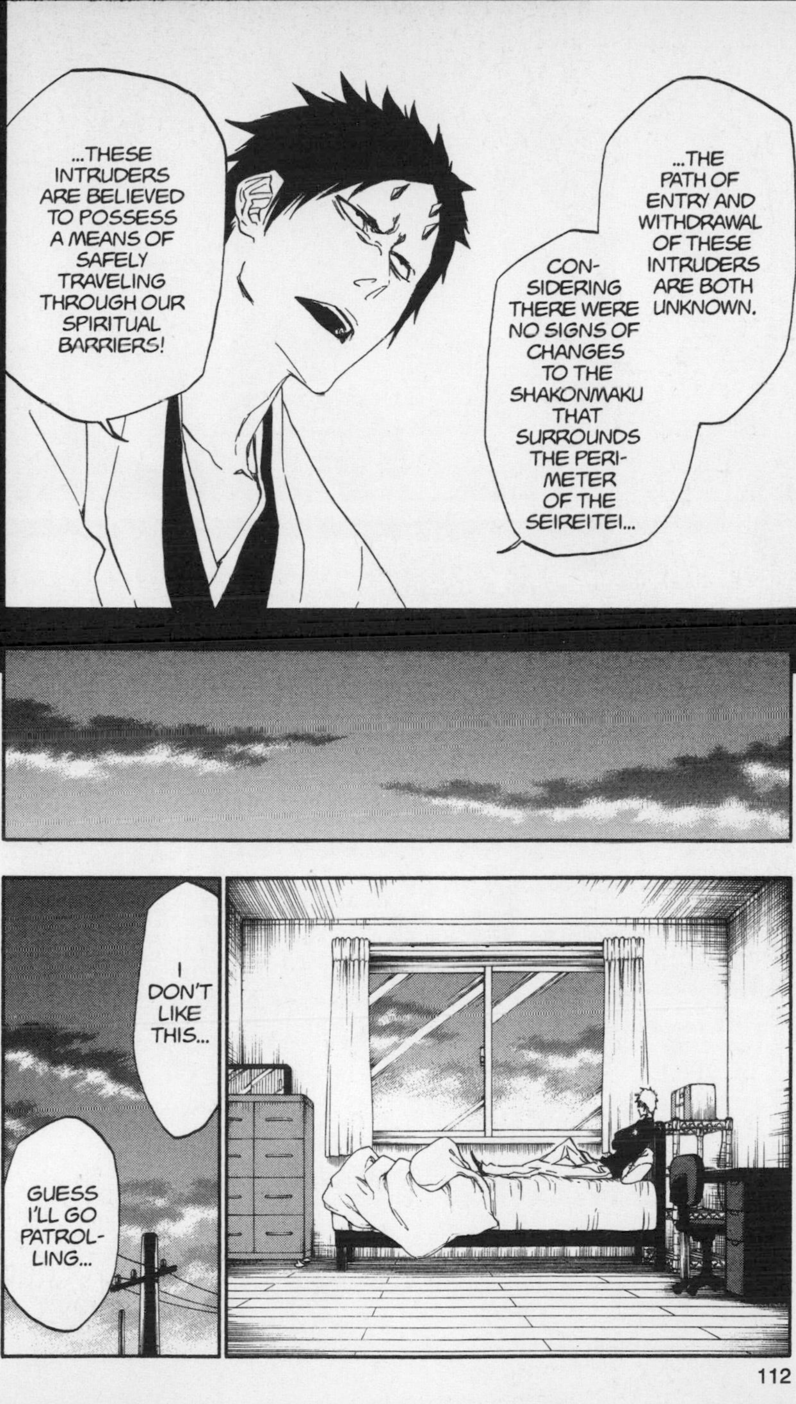
...THE PATH OF ENTRY AND WITHDRAWAL OF THESE INTRUDERS ARE BOTH UNKNOWN.
CON-SIDERING THERE WERE NO SIGNS OF CHANGES TO THE SHAKONMAKU THAT SURROUNDS THE PERI-METER OF THE SEIREITEI...
...THESE INTRUDERS ARE BELIEVED TO POSSESS A MEANS OF SAFELY TRAVELING THROUGH OUR SPIRITUAL BARRIERS!
I DON'T LIKE THIS...
GUESS I'LL GO PATROL-LING...

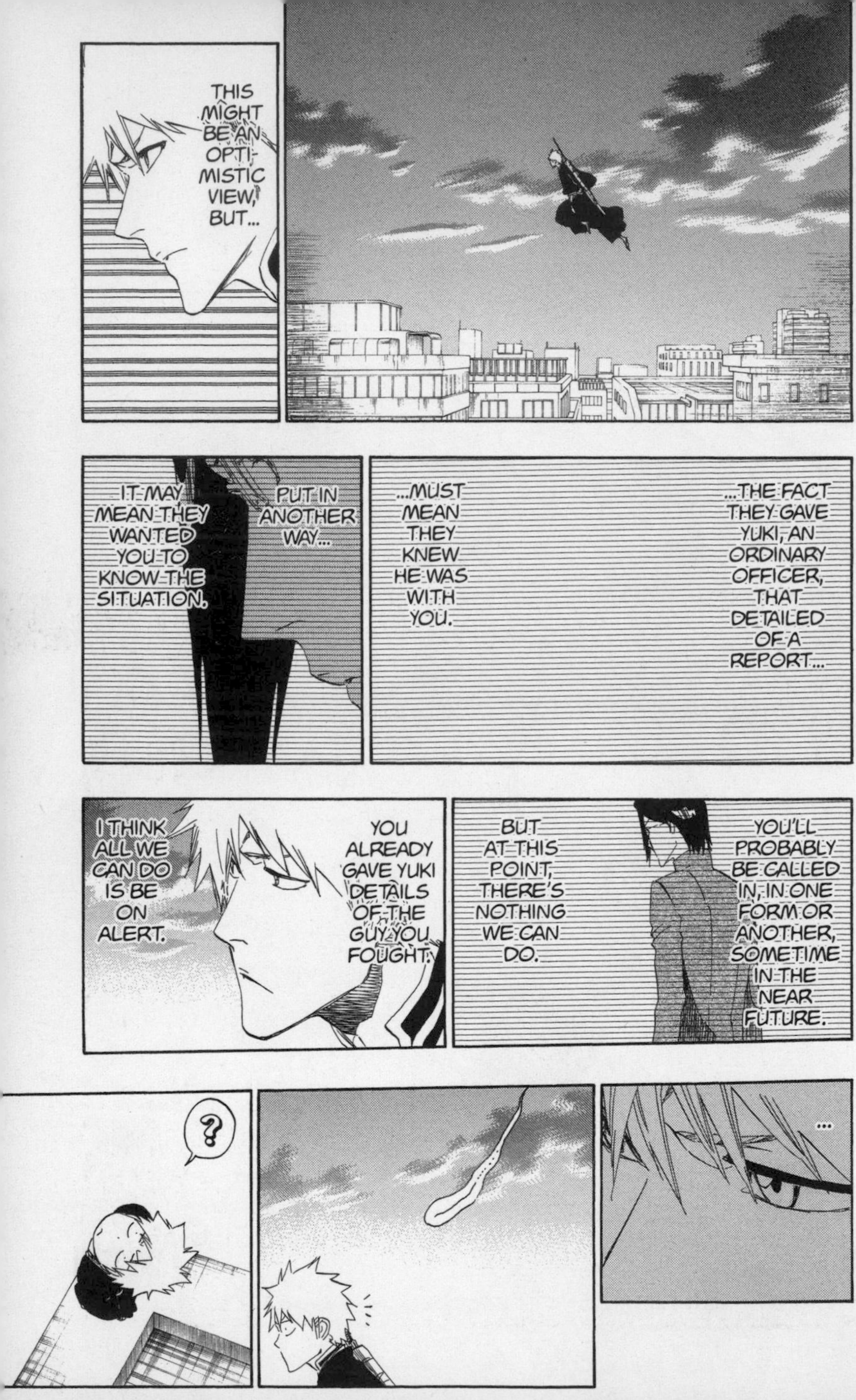
THIS MIGHT BE AN OPTI-MISTIC VIEW, BUT...
...THE FACT THEY GAVE YUKI, AN ORDINARY OFFICER, THAT DETAILED OF A REPORT...
...MUST MEAN THEY KNEW HE WAS WITH YOU.
PUT IN ANOTHER WAY...
IT MAY MEAN THEY WANTED YOU TO KNOW THE SITUATION.
YOU'LL PROBABLY BE CALLED IN, IN ONE FORM OR ANOTHER, SOMETIME IN THE NEAR FUTURE.
BUT AT THIS POINT, THERE'S NOTHING WE CAN DO.
YOU ALREADY GAVE YUKI DETAILS OF THE GUY YOU FOUGHT.
I THINK ALL WE CAN DO IS BE ON ALERT.
...
?

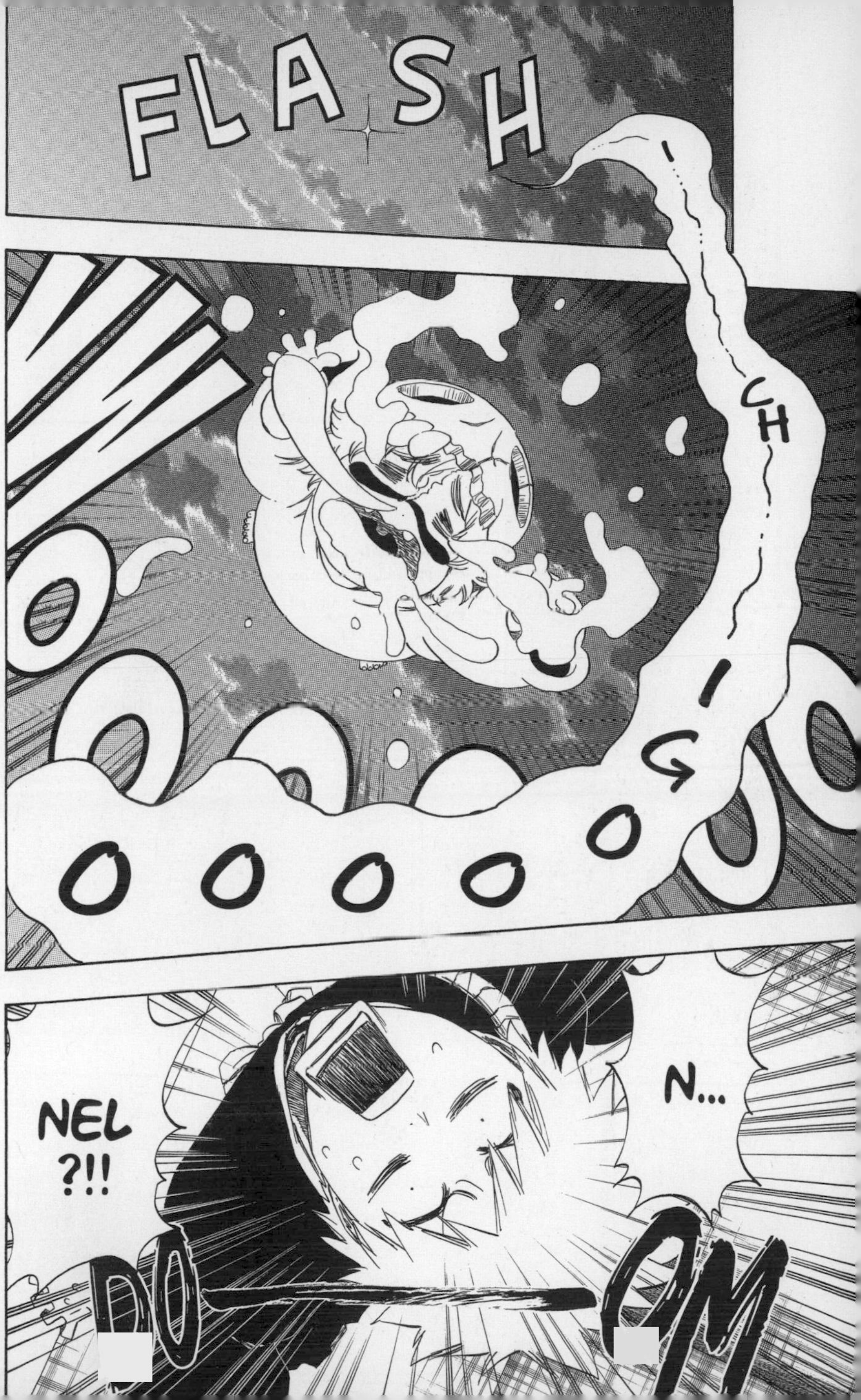

FLASH
WOOOOOOOOO
I... CH I G O
N...
NEL ?!!
DOOM

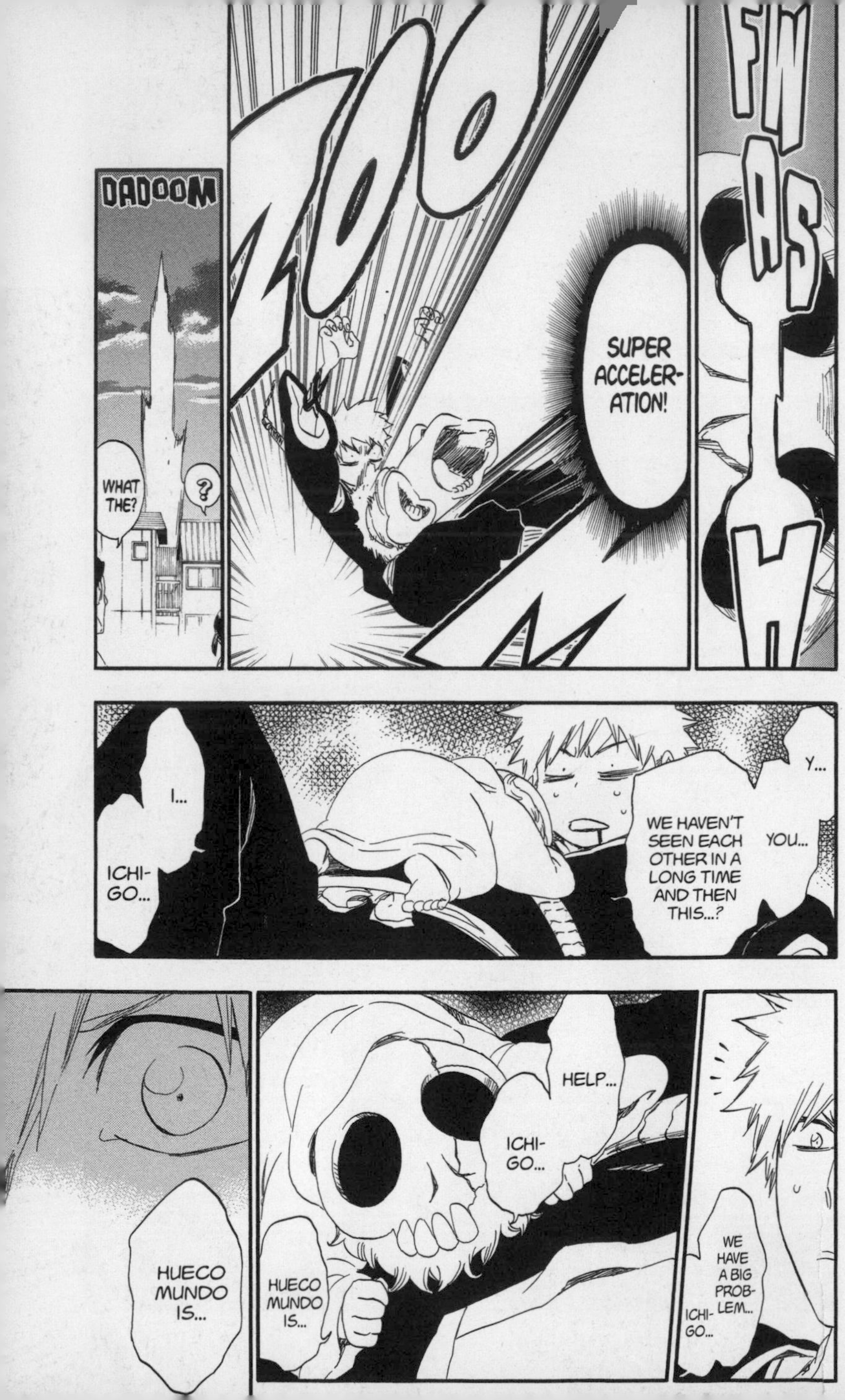
FWASH
ZOOOM
SUPER ACCELER-ATION!
DADOOM
WHAT THE?
?
Y...
YOU...
WE HAVEN'T SEEN EACH OTHER IN A LONG TIME AND THEN THIS...?
I...
ICHI-GO...
WE HAVE A BIG PROB-LEM...
ICHI-GO...
HELP...
ICHI-GO...
HUECO MUNDO IS...
HUECO MUNDO IS...

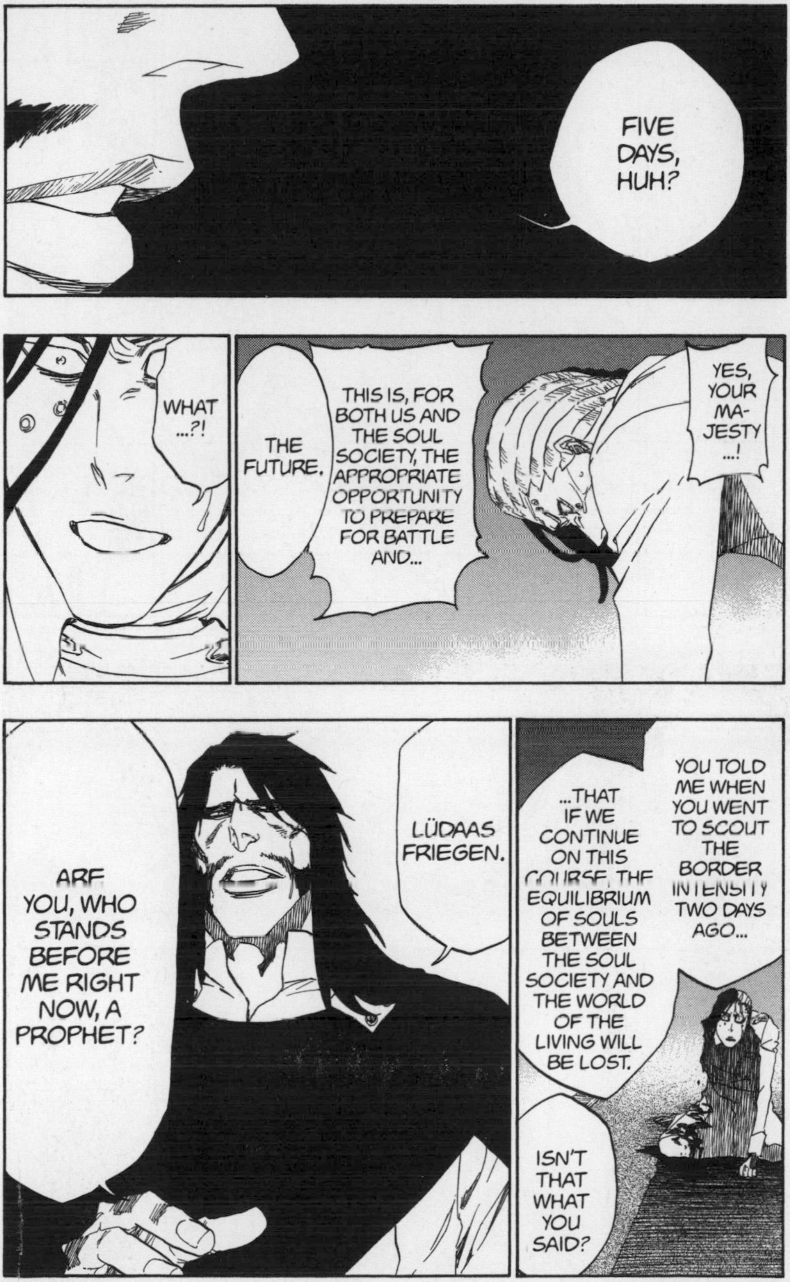
FIVE DAYS, HUH?
YES, YOUR MA-JESTY ...!
THIS IS, FOR BOTH US AND THE SOUL SOCIETY, THE APPROPRIATE OPPORTUNITY TO PREPARE FOR BATTLE AND...
THE FUTURE.
WHAT ...?!
YOU TOLD ME WHEN YOU WENT TO SCOUT THE BORDER INTENSITY TWO DAYS AGO...
...THAT IF WE CONTINUE ON THIS COURSE, THE EQUILIBRIUM OF SOULS BETWEEN THE SOUL SOCIETY AND THE WORLD OF THE LIVING WILL BE LOST.
ISN'T THAT WHAT YOU SAID?
LÜDAAS FRIEGEN.
ARE YOU, WHO STANDS BEFORE ME RIGHT NOW, A PROPHET?

READ THIS WAY

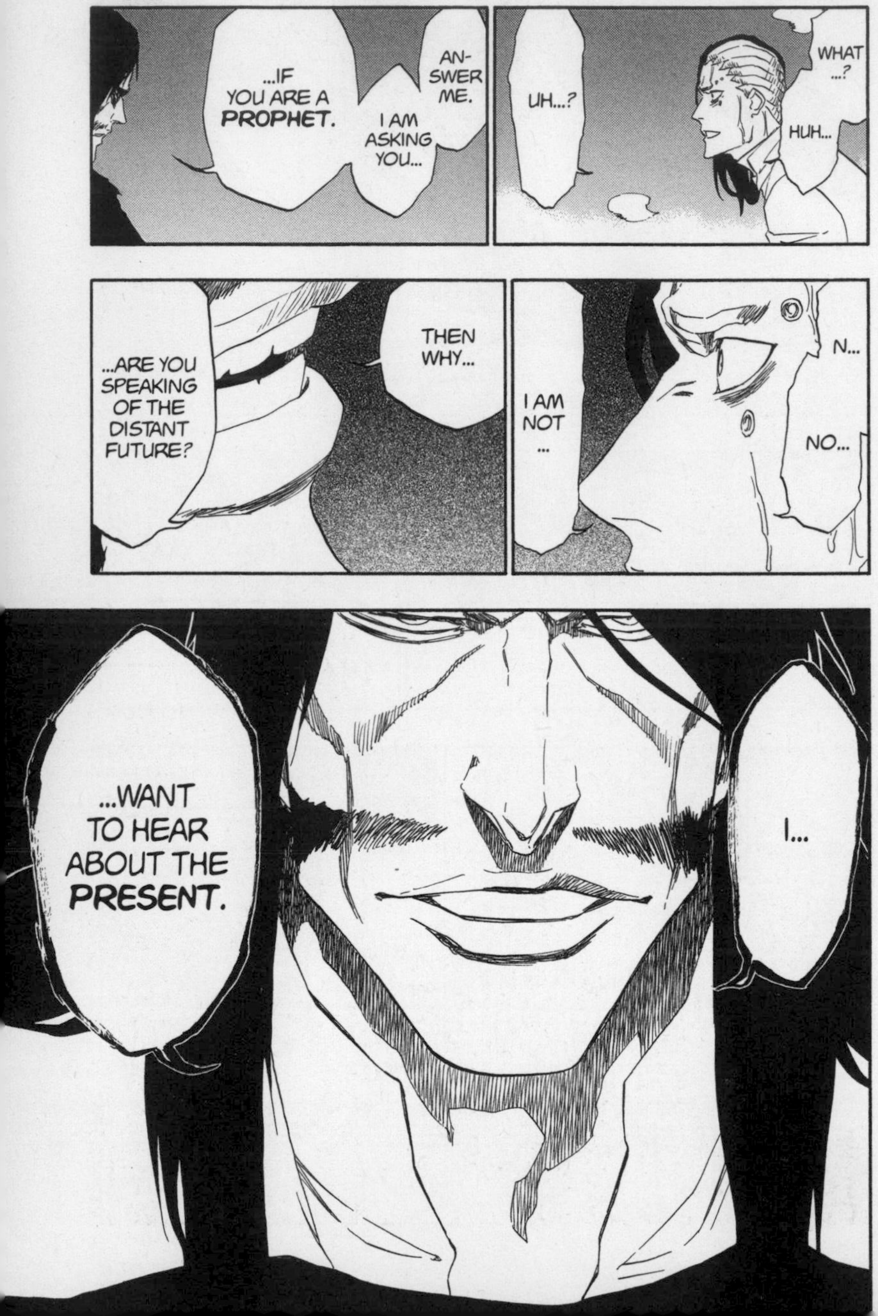
WHAT ...?
HUH...
UH...?
AN-SWER ME.
I AM ASKING YOU...
...IF YOU ARE A PROPHET.
N...
NO...
I AM NOT ...
THEN WHY...
...ARE YOU SPEAKING OF THE DISTANT FUTURE?
I...
...WANT TO HEAR ABOUT THE PRESENT.

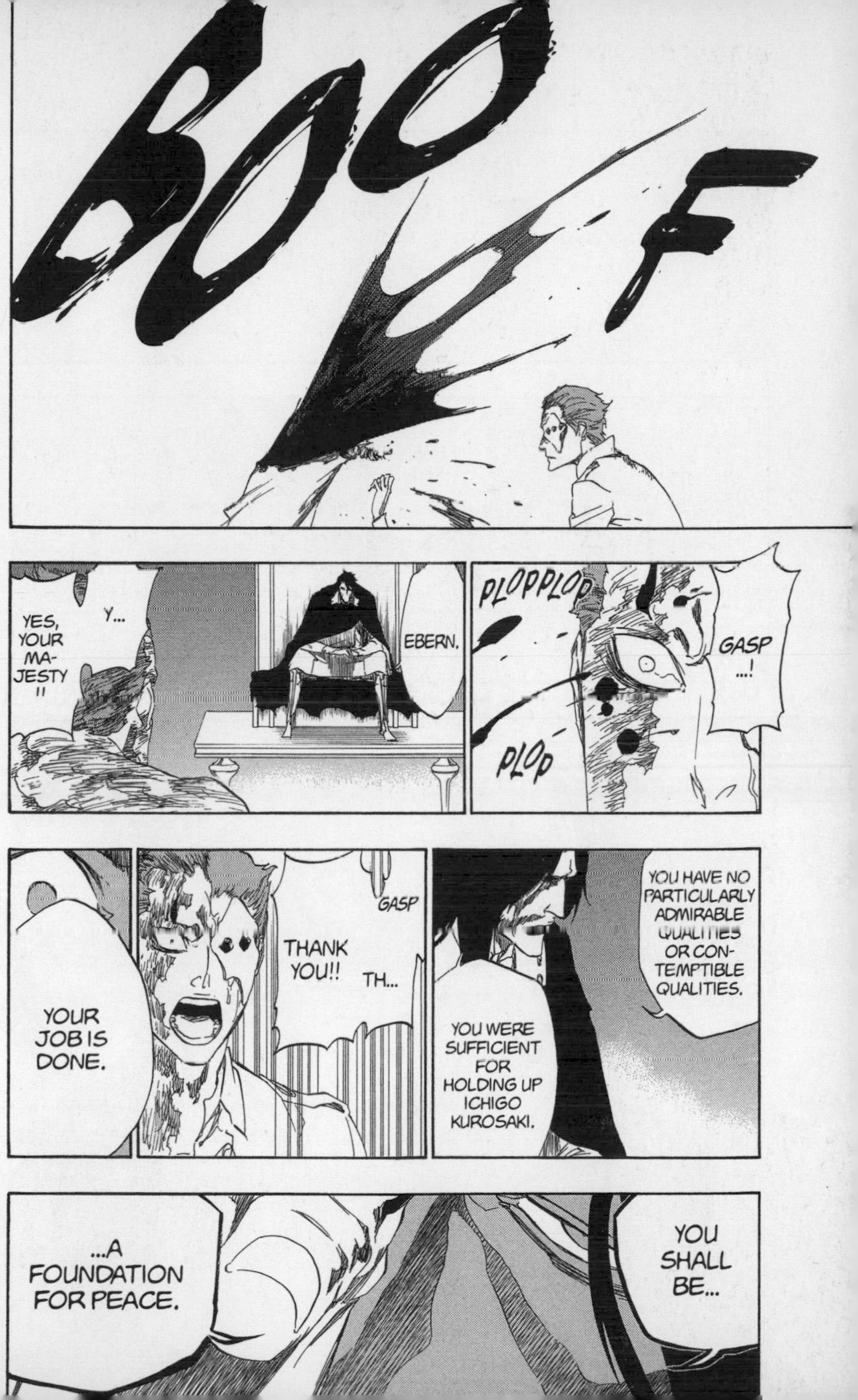
BOOUF
PLOPPLOP
GASP ...!
PLOP
EBERN.
Y...
YES, YOUR MAJESTY!!
YOU HAVE NO PARTICULARLY ADMIRABLE QUALITIES OR CONTEMPTIBLE QUALITIES.
YOU WERE SUFFICIENT FOR HOLDING UP ICHIGO KUROSAKI.
GASP
TH...
THANK YOU!!
YOUR JOB IS DONE.
YOU SHALL BE...
...A FOUNDATION FOR PEACE.

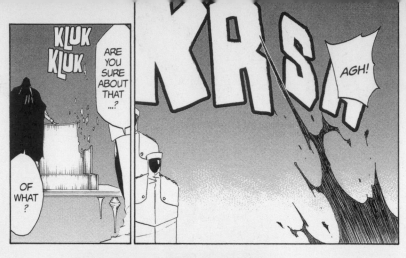

KLUK
KLUK

ARE YOU SURE ABOUT THAT...?

OF WHAT?

KRSH

AGH!

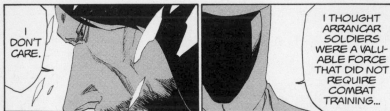

I DON'T CARE.

I THOUGHT ARRANCAR SOLDIERS WERE A VALUABLE FORCE THAT DID NOT REQUIRE COMBAT TRAINING...

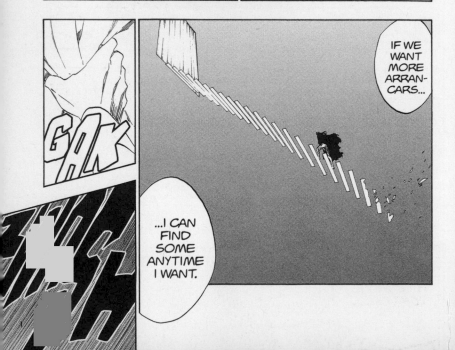

GAK

IF WE WANT MORE ARRAN-CARS...

...I CAN FIND SOME ANYTIME I WANT.

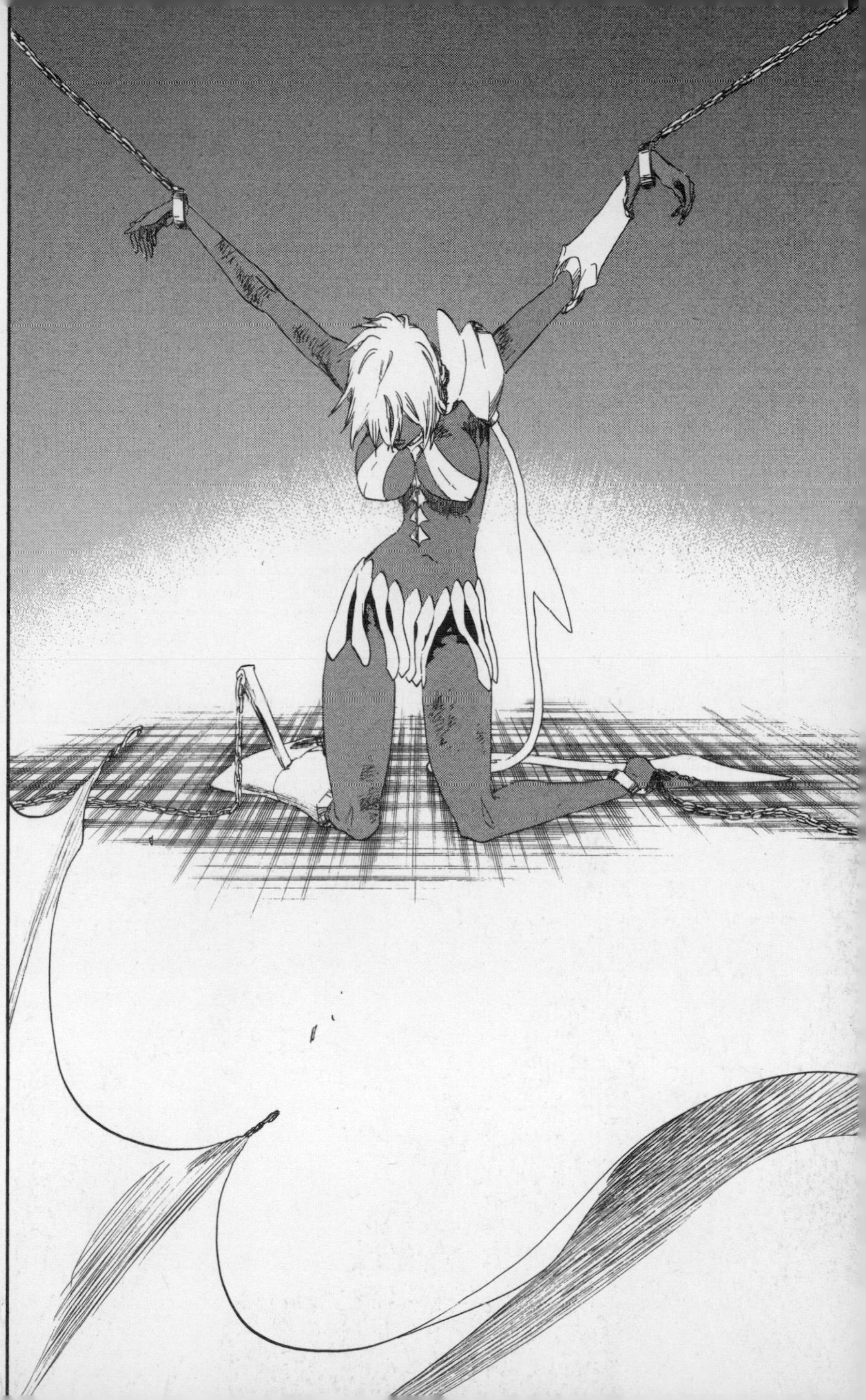

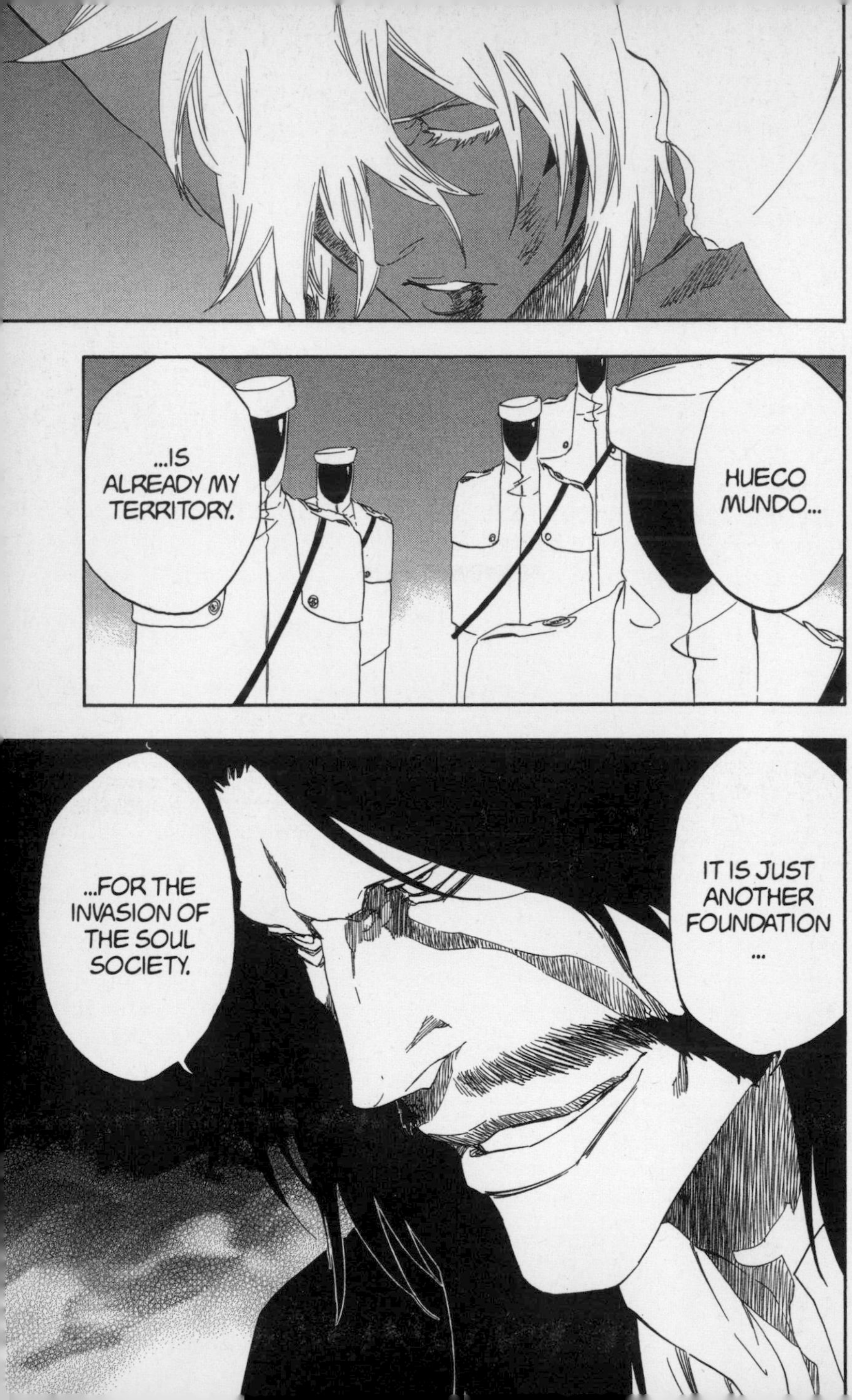
HUECO MUNDO...
...IS ALREADY MY TERRITORY.
IT IS JUST ANOTHER FOUNDATION ...
...FOR THE INVASION OF THE SOUL SOCIETY.

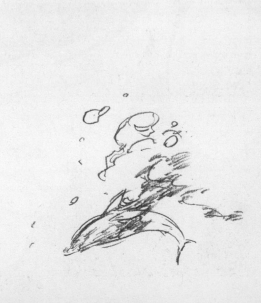

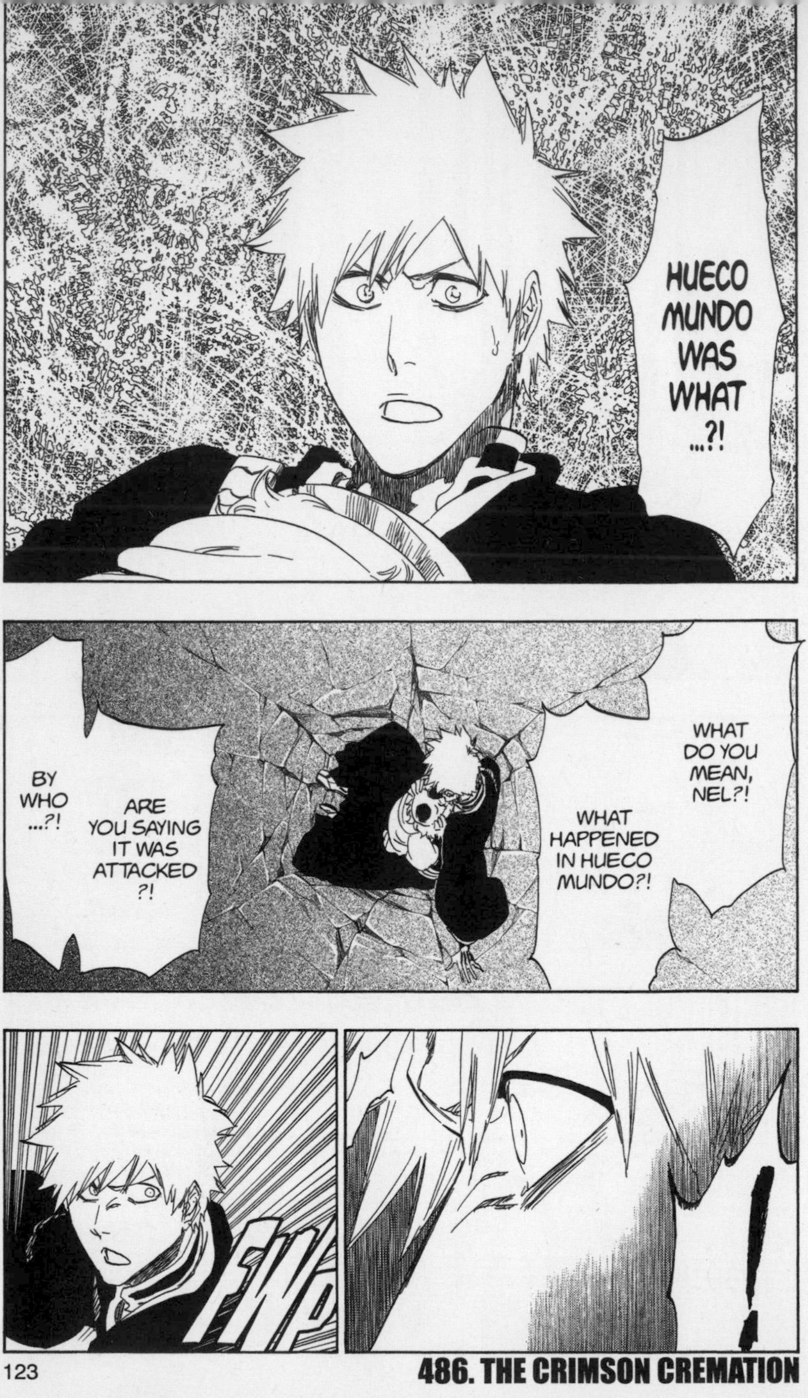
HUECO MUNDO WAS WHAT ...?!
WHAT DO YOU MEAN, NEL?!
WHAT HAPPENED IN HUECO MUNDO?!
ARE YOU SAYING IT WAS ATTACKED ?!
BY WHO ...?!
!
FWP

486. THE CRIMSON CREMATION

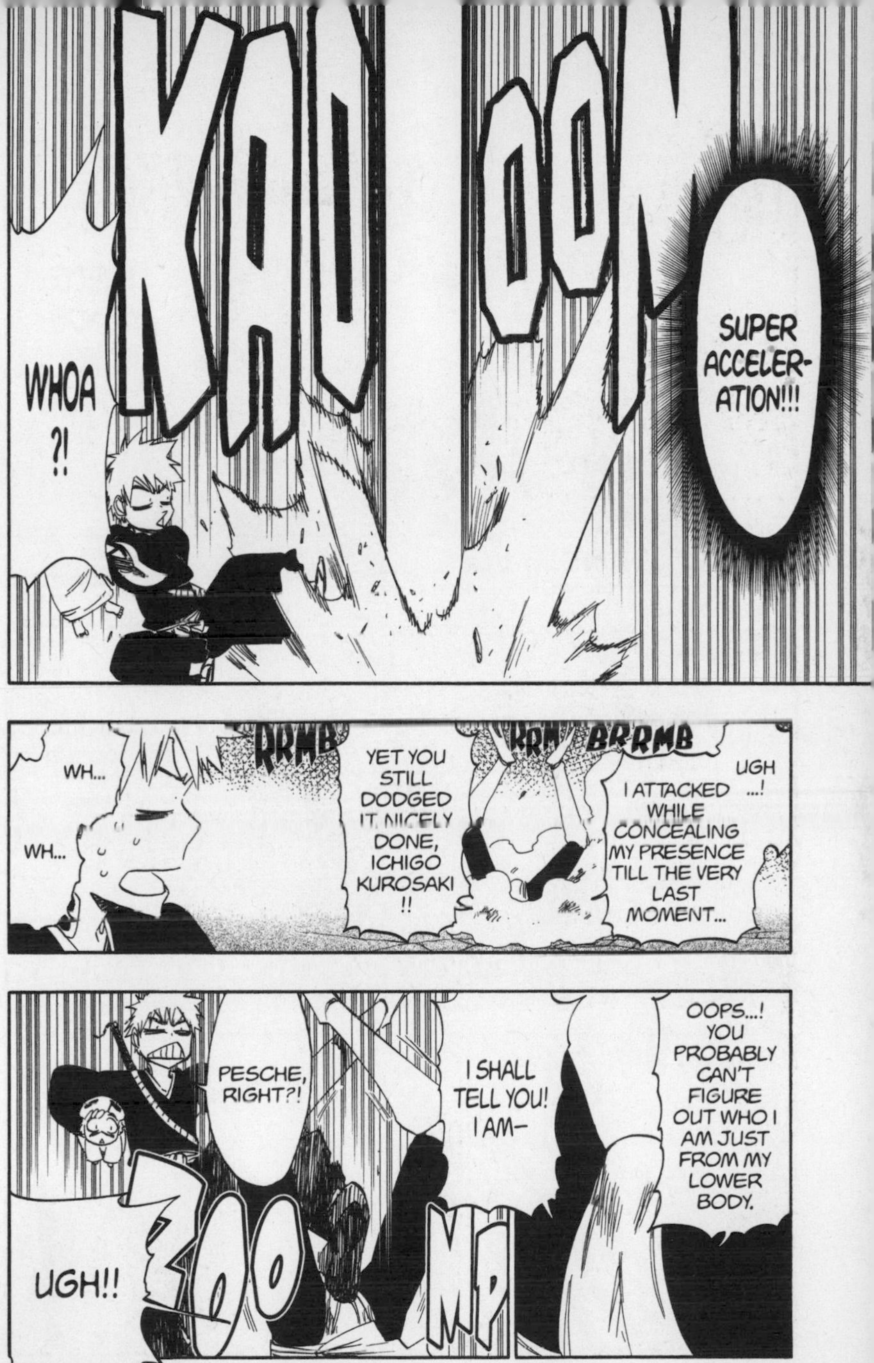
SUPER ACCELER-ATION!!!
KABOOM
WHOA ?!
UGH ...!
I ATTACKED WHILE CONCEALING MY PRESENCE TILL THE VERY LAST MOMENT...
BRRMB
RRM
YET YOU STILL DODGED IT. NICELY DONE, ICHIGO KUROSAKI !!
RRMB
WH...
WH...
OOPS...! YOU PROBABLY CAN'T FIGURE OUT WHO I AM JUST FROM MY LOWER BODY.
I SHALL TELL YOU! I AM—
PESCHE, RIGHT?!
ZOOMP
UGH!!

READ THIS WAY

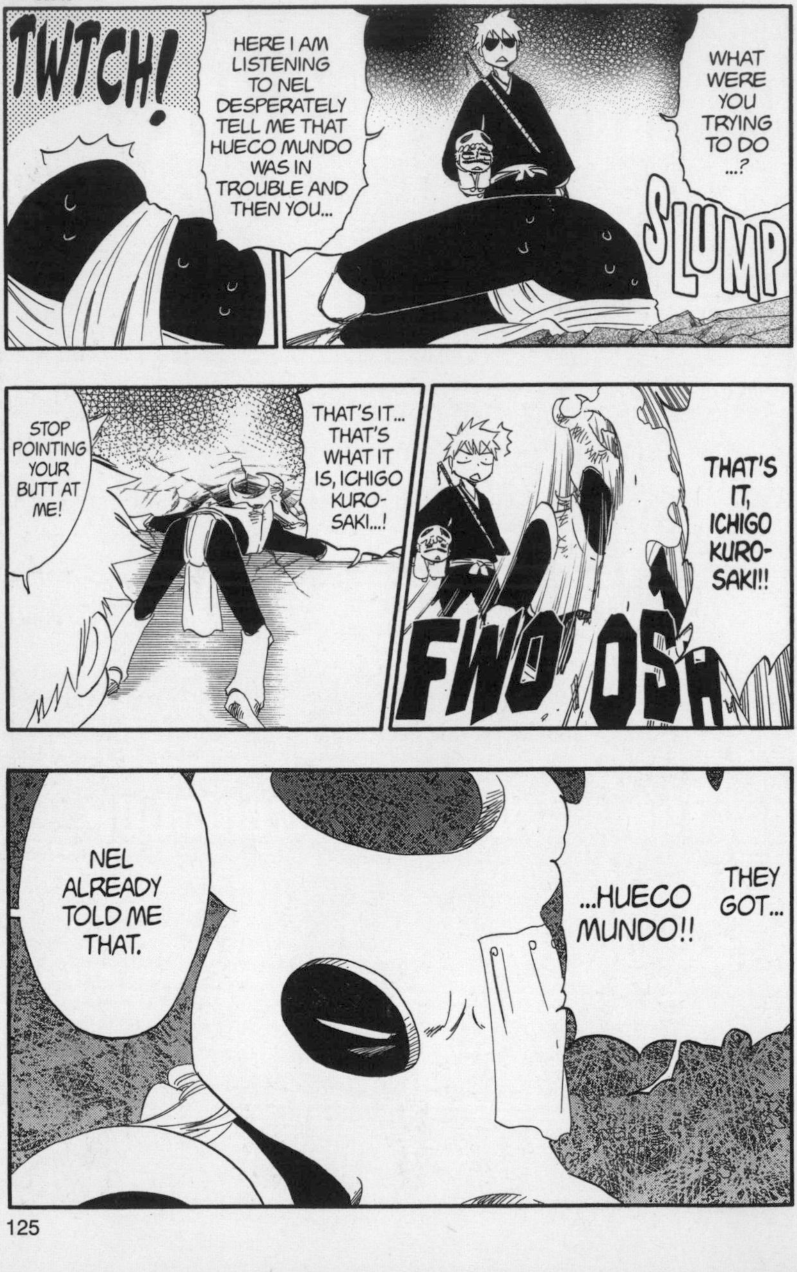
WHAT WERE YOU TRYING TO DO ...?
SLUMP
HERE I AM LISTENING TO NEL DESPERATELY TELL ME THAT HUECO MUNDO WAS IN TROUBLE AND THEN YOU...
TWTCH!
THAT'S IT, ICHIGO KURO-SAKI!!
FWOOSH
THAT'S IT... THAT'S WHAT IT IS, ICHIGO KURO-SAKI...!
STOP POINTING YOUR BUTT AT ME!
THEY GOT...
...HUECO MUNDO!!
NEL ALREADY TOLD ME THAT.

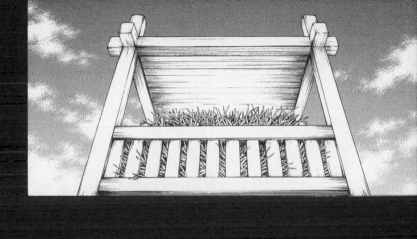

The Crimson Cremation

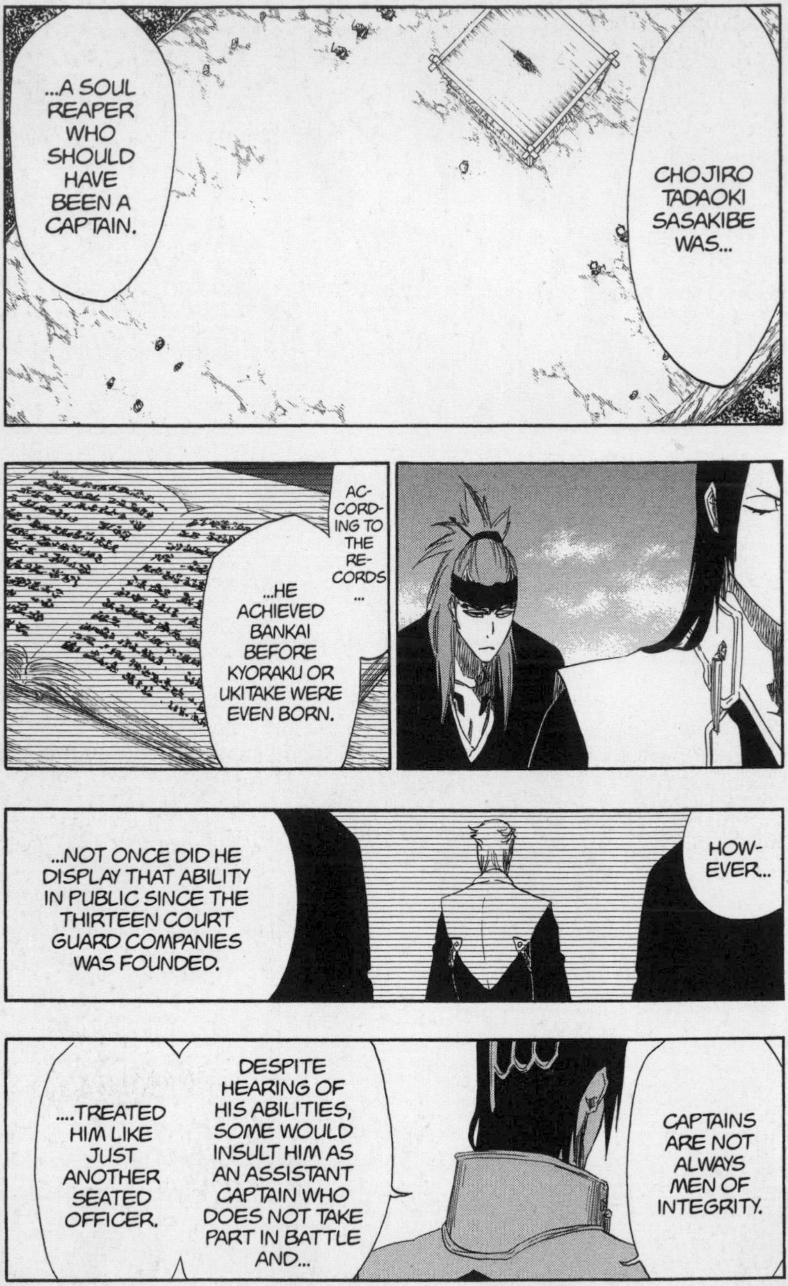
CHOJIRO TADAOKI SASAKIBE WAS...
...A SOUL REAPER WHO SHOULD HAVE BEEN A CAPTAIN.
ACCORDING TO THE RECORDS...
...HE ACHIEVED BANKAI BEFORE KYORAKU OR UKITAKE WERE EVEN BORN.
HOWEVER...
...NOT ONCE DID HE DISPLAY THAT ABILITY IN PUBLIC SINCE THE THIRTEEN COURT GUARD COMPANIES WAS FOUNDED.
CAPTAINS ARE NOT ALWAYS MEN OF INTEGRITY.
DESPITE HEARING OF HIS ABILITIES, SOME WOULD INSULT HIM AS AN ASSISTANT CAPTAIN WHO DOES NOT TAKE PART IN BATTLE AND...
....TREATED HIM LIKE JUST ANOTHER SEATED OFFICER.

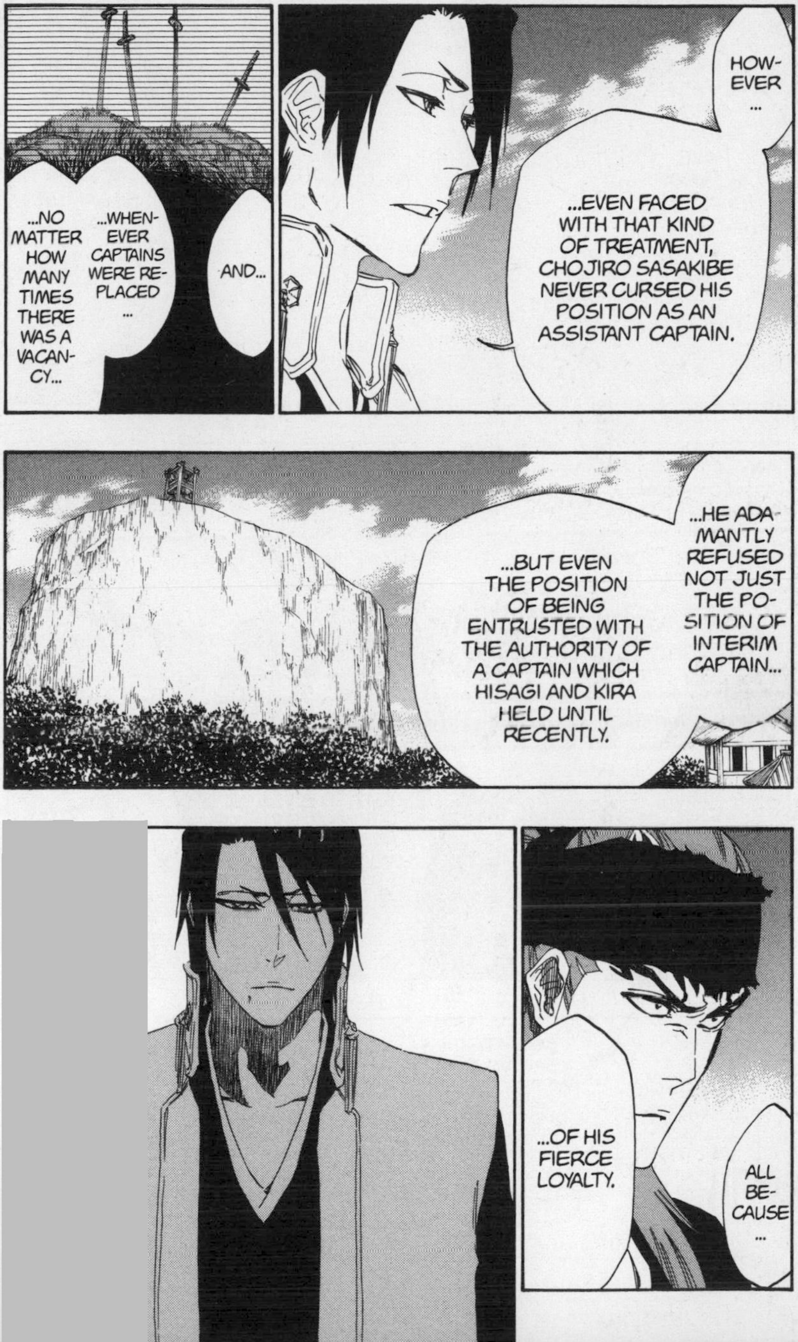
HOWEVER...
...EVEN FACED WITH THAT KIND OF TREATMENT, CHOJIRO SASAKIBE NEVER CURSED HIS POSITION AS AN ASSISTANT CAPTAIN.
AND...
...WHENEVER CAPTAINS WERE REPLACED...
...NO MATTER HOW MANY TIMES THERE WAS A VACANCY...
...HE ADAMANTLY REFUSED NOT JUST THE POSITION OF INTERIM CAPTAIN...
...BUT EVEN THE POSITION OF BEING ENTRUSTED WITH THE AUTHORITY OF A CAPTAIN WHICH HISAGI AND KIRA HELD UNTIL RECENTLY.
ALL BECAUSE...
...OF HIS FIERCE LOYALTY.

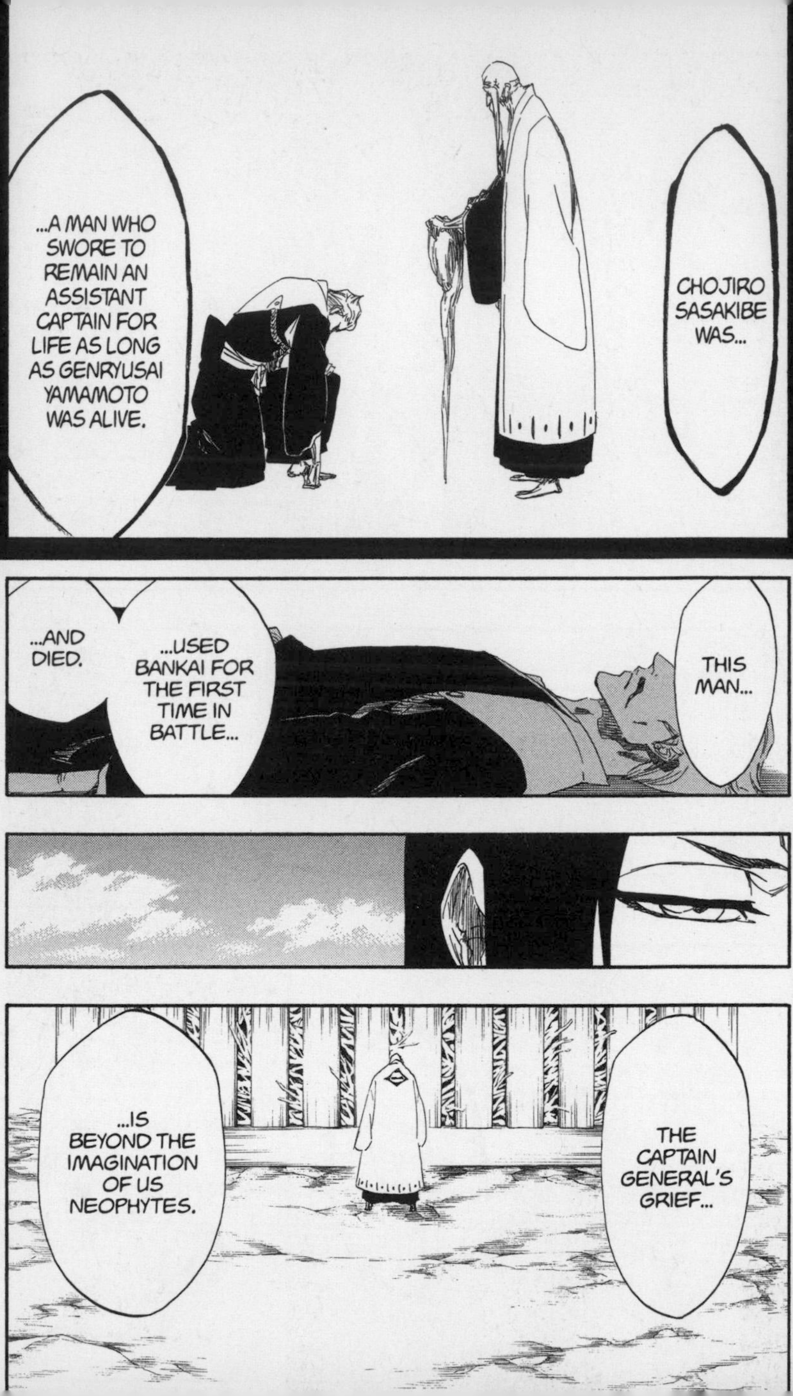
CHOJIRO SASAKIBE WAS...
...A MAN WHO SWORE TO REMAIN AN ASSISTANT CAPTAIN FOR LIFE AS LONG AS GENRYUSAI YAMAMOTO WAS ALIVE.
THIS MAN...
...USED BANKAI FOR THE FIRST TIME IN BATTLE...
...AND DIED.
THE CAPTAIN GENERAL'S GRIEF...
...IS BEYOND THE IMAGINATION OF US NEOPHYTES.

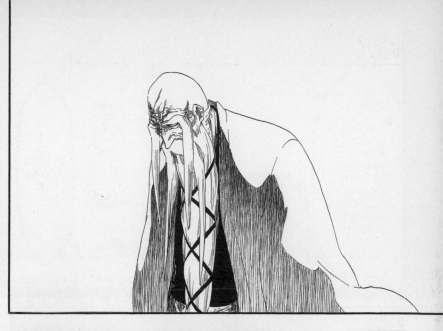

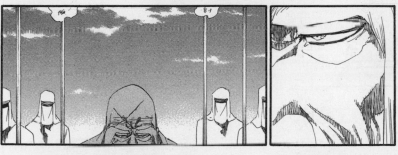

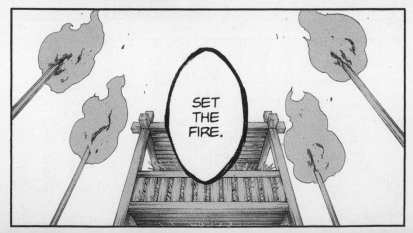

SET
THE
FIRE.

READ THIS WAY

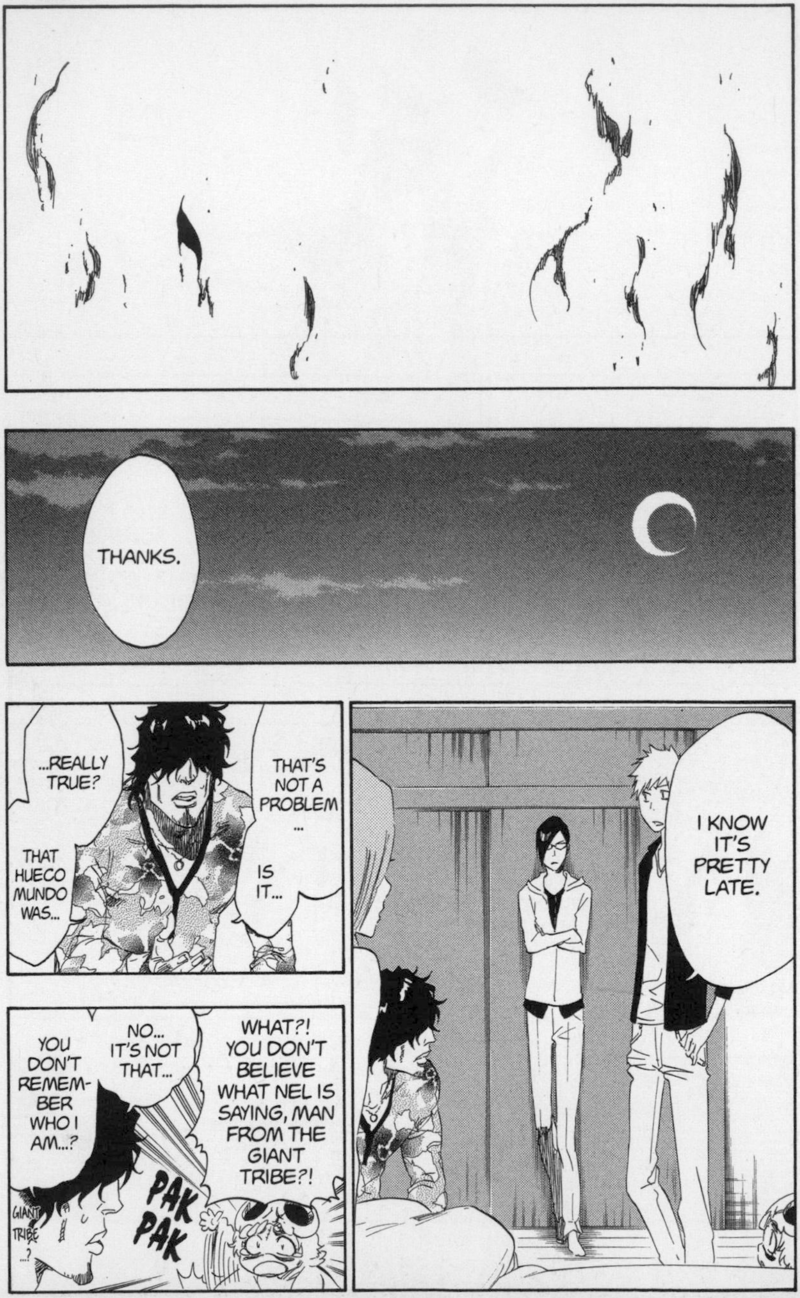
THANKS.
I KNOW IT'S PRETTY LATE.
THAT'S NOT A PROBLEM ... IS IT...
...REALLY TRUE?
THAT HUECO MUNDO WAS...
WHAT?! YOU DON'T BELIEVE WHAT NEL IS SAYING, MAN FROM THE GIANT TRIBE?!
NO... IT'S NOT THAT...
YOU DON'T REMEM-BER WHO I AM...?
PAK PAK
GIANT TRIBE ...?

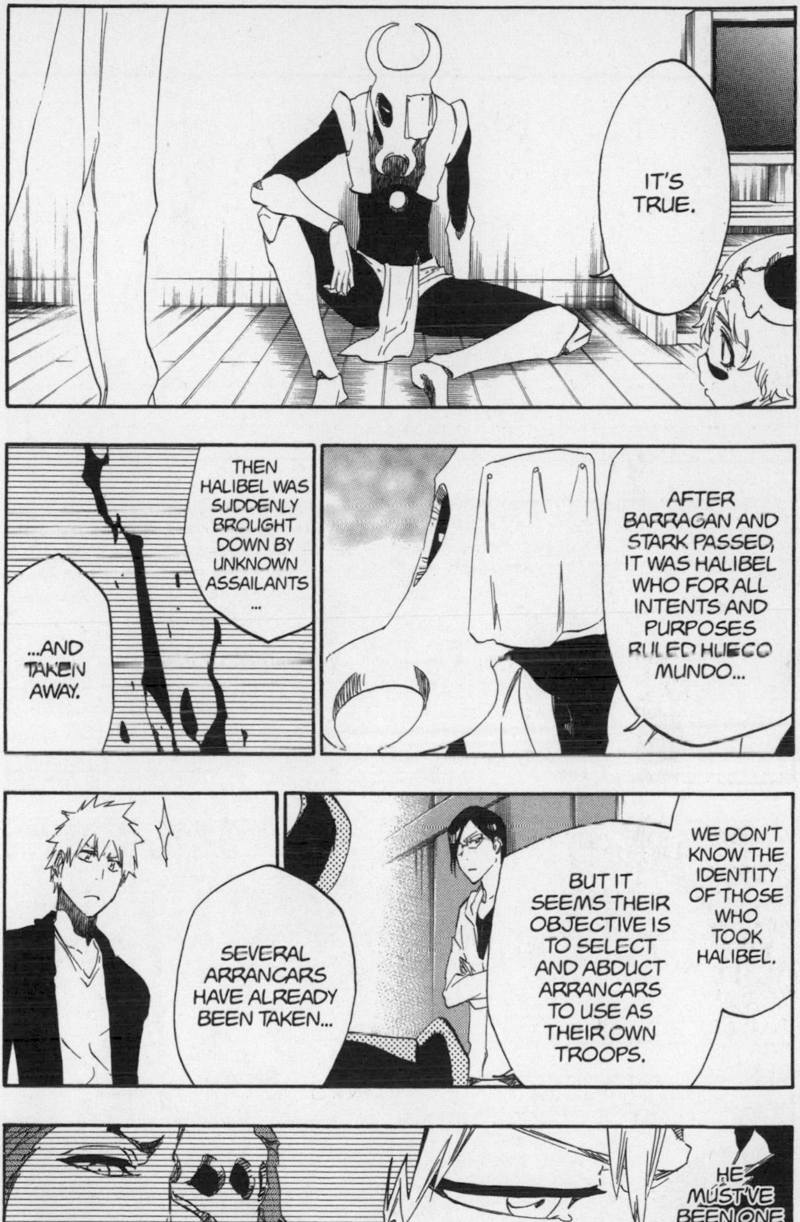
IT'S TRUE.
AFTER BARRAGAN AND STARK PASSED, IT WAS HALIBEL WHO FOR ALL INTENTS AND PURPOSES RULED HUECO MUNDO...
THEN HALIBEL WAS SUDDENLY BROUGHT DOWN BY UNKNOWN ASSAILANTS...
...AND TAKEN AWAY.
WE DON'T KNOW THE IDENTITY OF THOSE WHO TOOK HALIBEL.
BUT IT SEEMS THEIR OBJECTIVE IS TO SELECT AND ABDUCT ARRANCARS TO USE AS THEIR OWN TROOPS.
SEVERAL ARRANCARS HAVE ALREADY BEEN TAKEN...
HE MUST'VE BEEN ONE OF THEM...

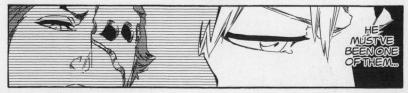

READ THIS WAY

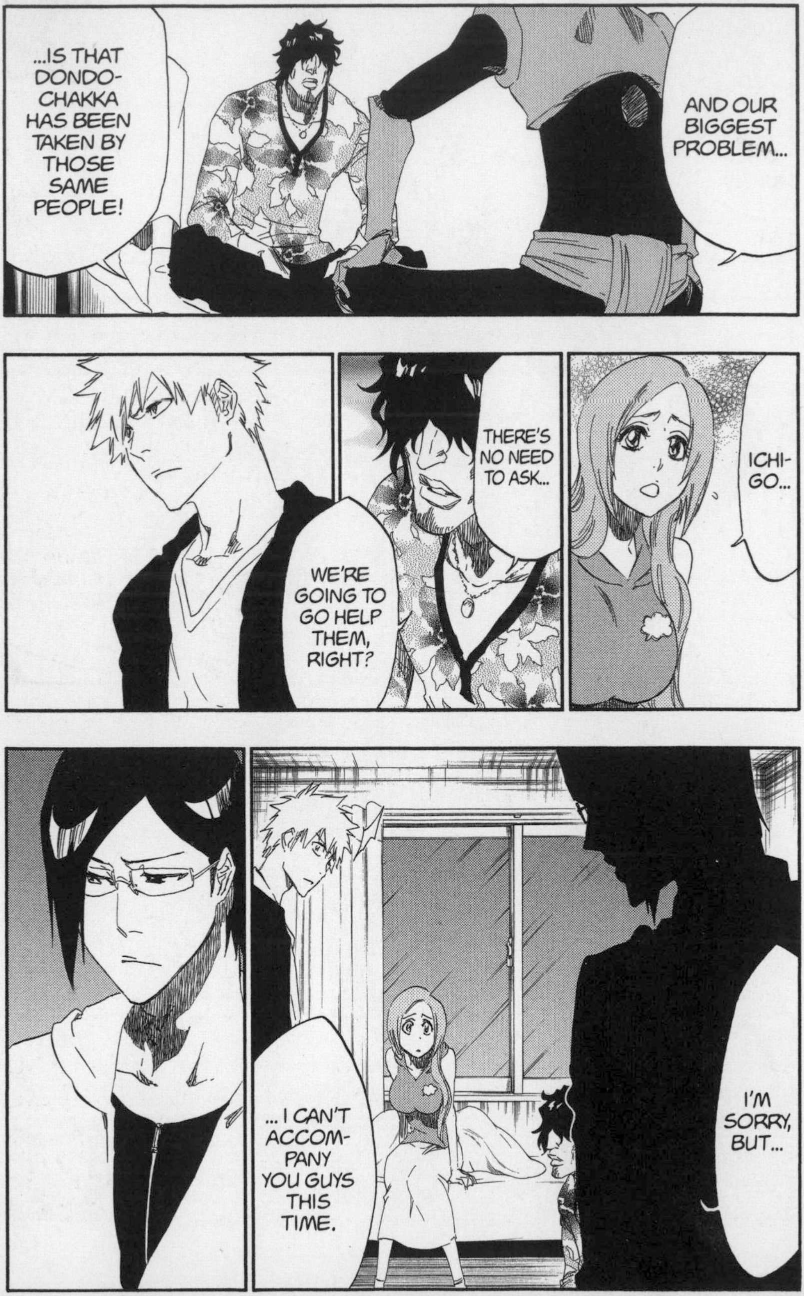
AND OUR BIGGEST PROBLEM...
...IS THAT DONDO-CHAKKA HAS BEEN TAKEN BY THOSE SAME PEOPLE!
ICHI-GO...
THERE'S NO NEED TO ASK...
WE'RE GOING TO GO HELP THEM, RIGHT?
I'M SORRY, BUT...
...I CAN'T ACCOMPANY YOU GUYS THIS TIME.

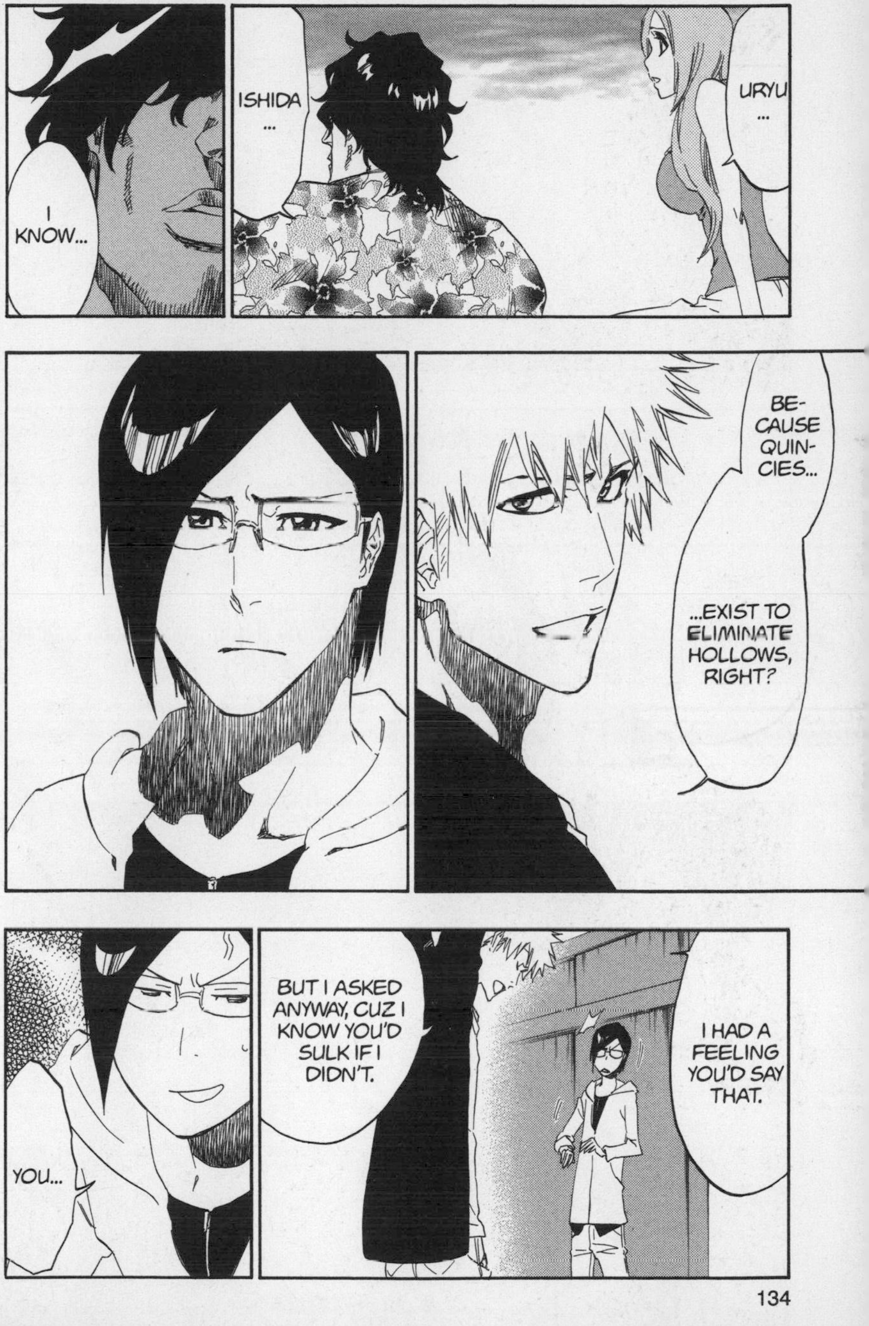
URYU ...
ISHIDA ...
I KNOW...
BE-CAUSE QUIN-CIES...
...EXIST TO ELIMINATE HOLLOWS, RIGHT?
I HAD A FEELING YOU'D SAY THAT.
BUT I ASKED ANYWAY, CUZ I KNOW YOU'D SULK IF I DIDN'T.
YOU...

READ THIS WAY

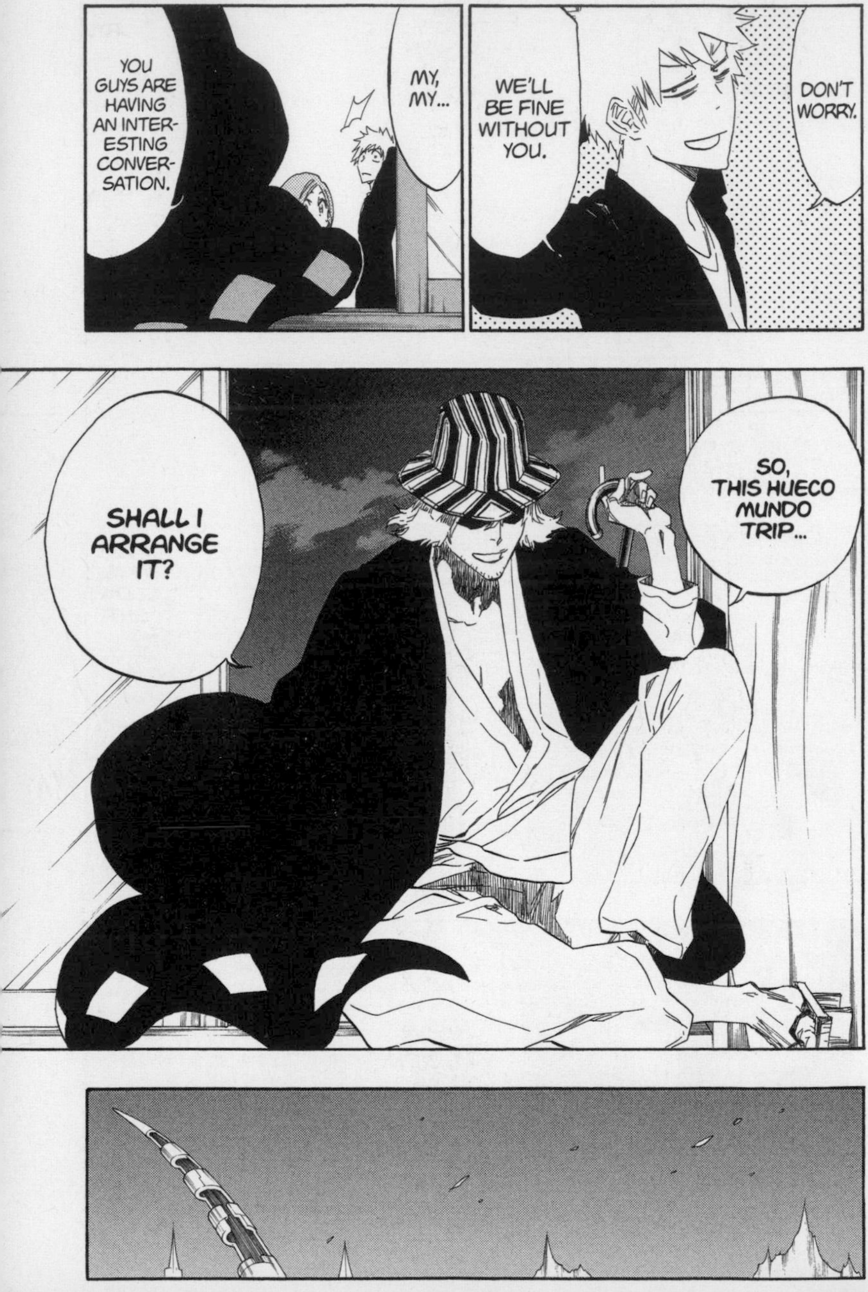
DON'T WORRY.
WE'LL BE FINE WITHOUT YOU.
MY, MY...
YOU GUYS ARE HAVING AN INTER-ESTING CONVER-SATION.
SO, THIS HUECO MUNDO TRIP...
SHALL I ARRANGE IT?

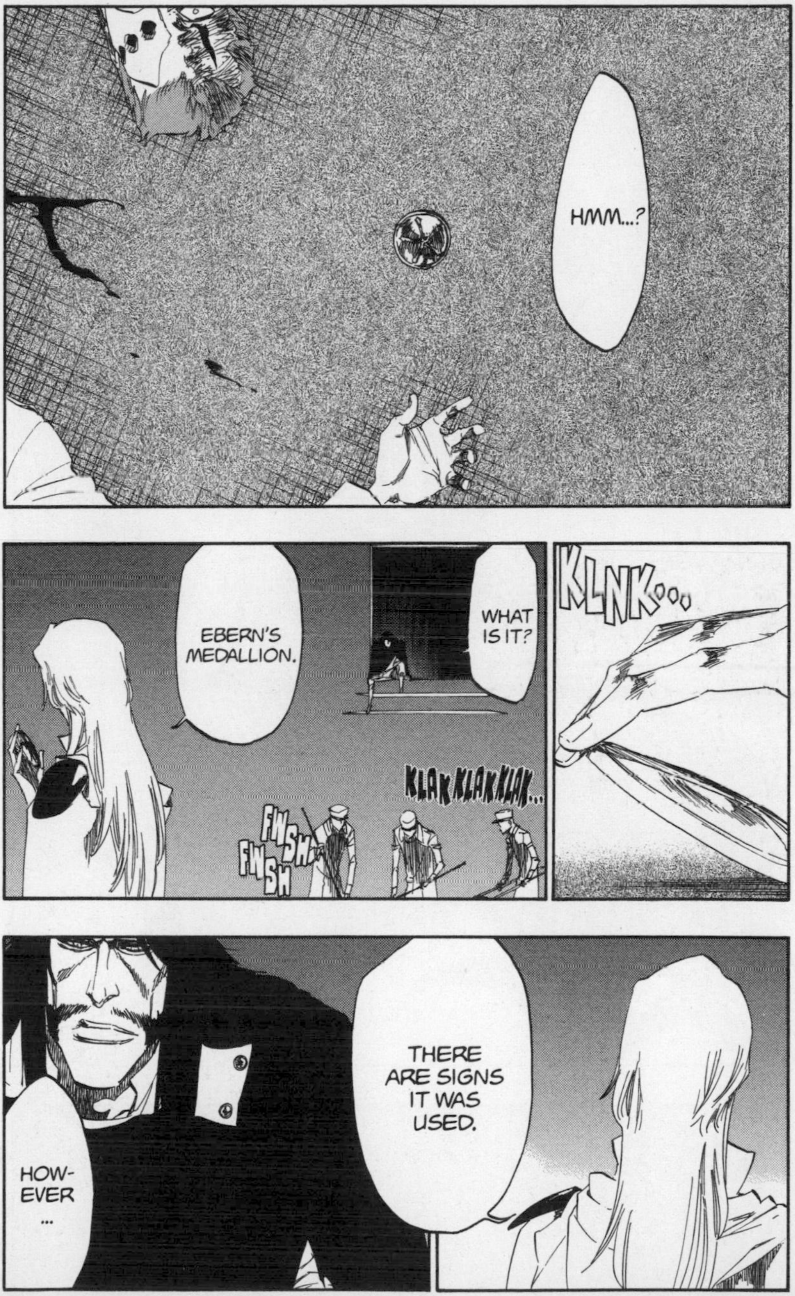
HMM...?
KLNK...
WHAT IS IT?
EBERN'S MEDALLION.
KLAK KLAK KLAK...
FWSH FWSH
THERE ARE SIGNS IT WAS USED.
HOW-EVER ...

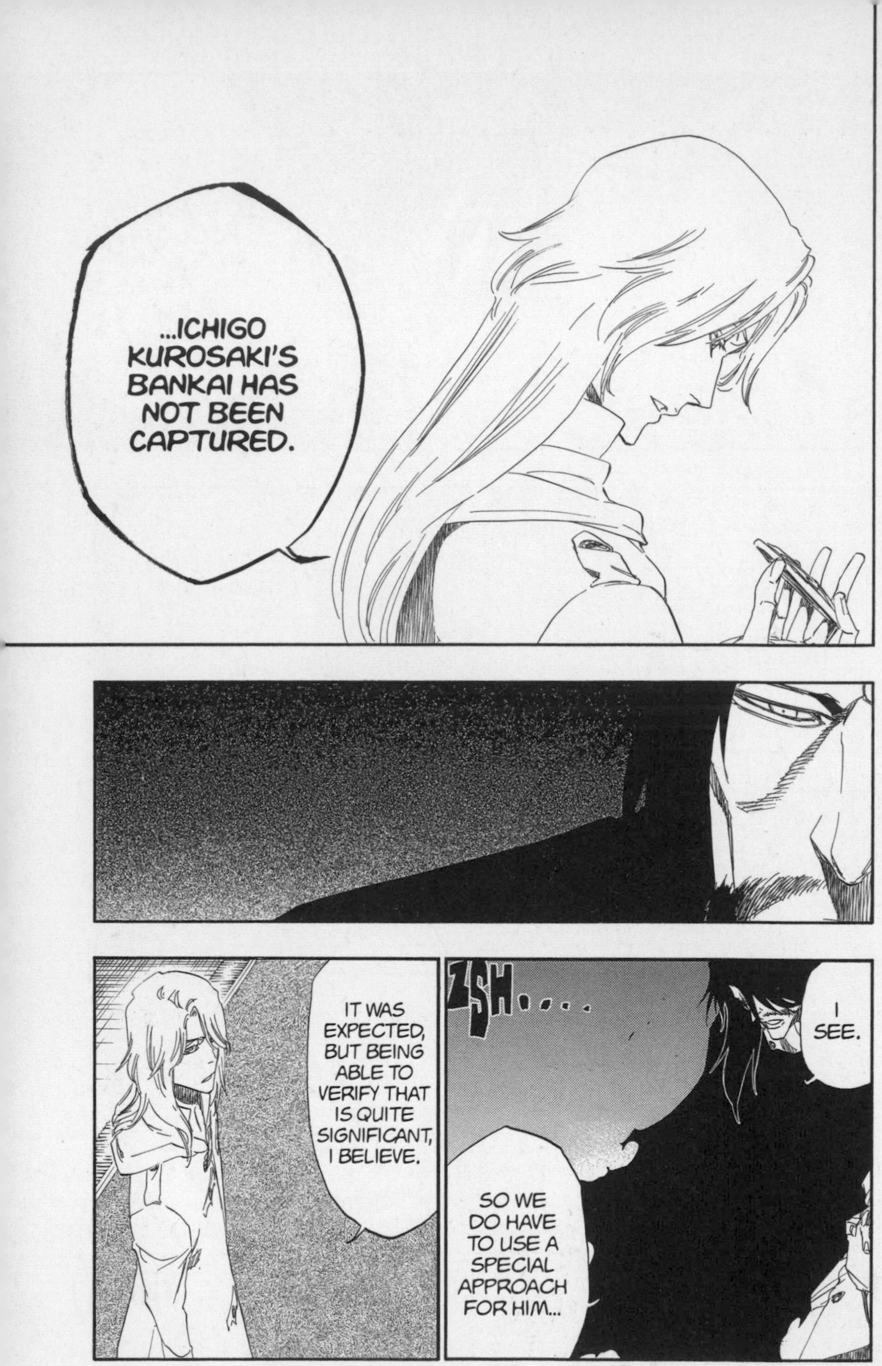
...ICHIGO KUROSAKI'S BANKAI HAS NOT BEEN CAPTURED.
I SEE.
ZSH...
SO WE DO HAVE TO USE A SPECIAL APPROACH FOR HIM...
IT WAS EXPECTED, BUT BEING ABLE TO VERIFY THAT IS QUITE SIGNIFICANT, I BELIEVE.

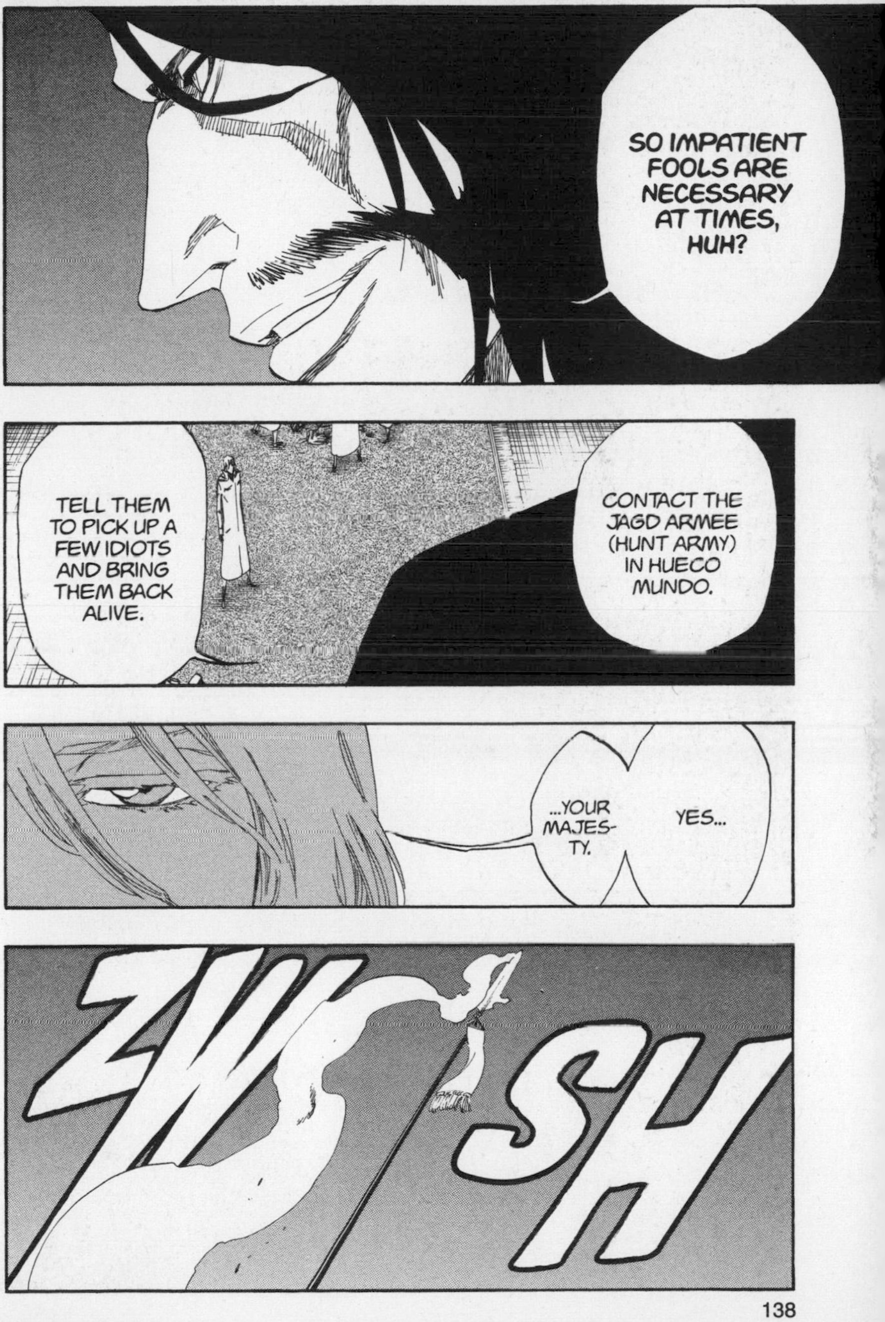
SO IMPATIENT FOOLS ARE NECESSARY AT TIMES, HUH?
CONTACT THE JAGD ARMEE (HUNT ARMY) IN HUECO MUNDO.
TELL THEM TO PICK UP A FEW IDIOTS AND BRING THEM BACK ALIVE.
YES...
...YOUR MAJES-TY.
ZWSH

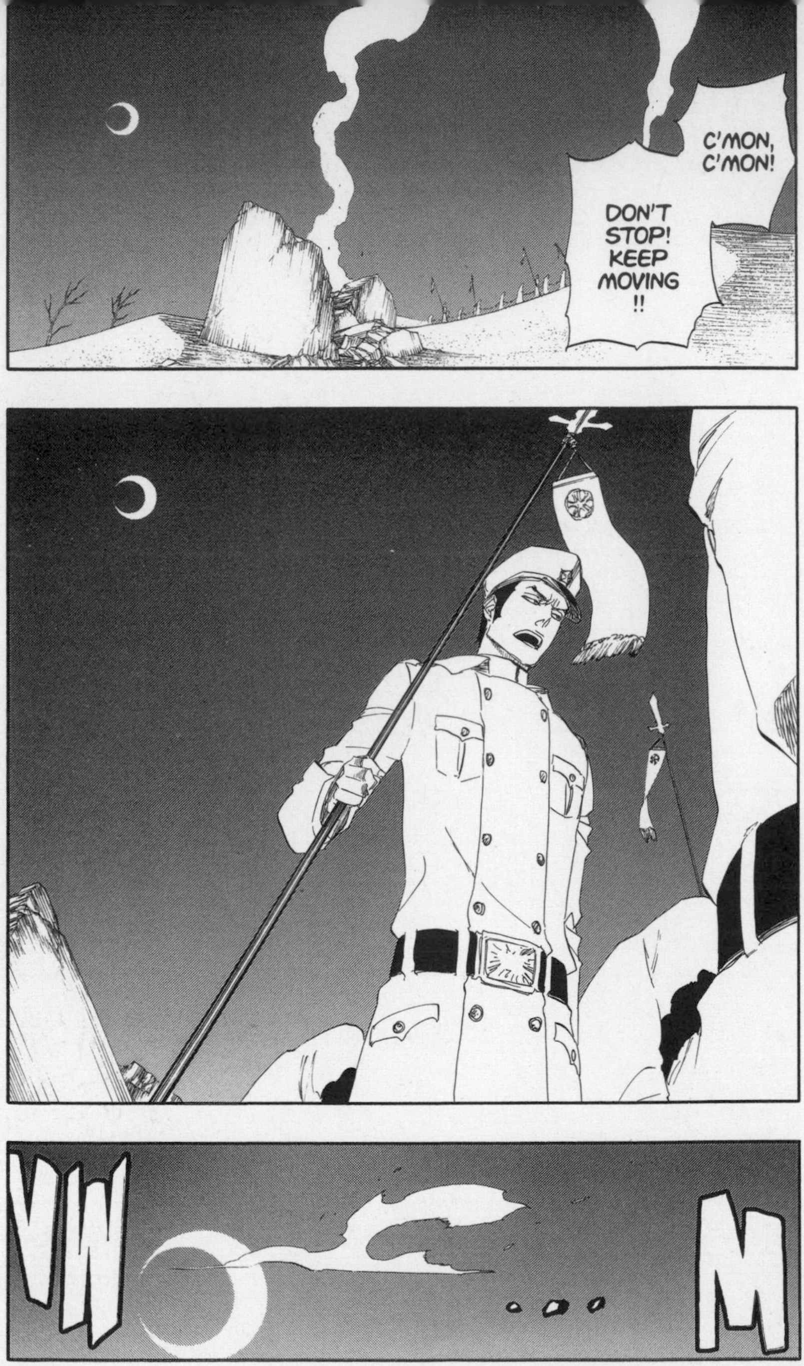
C'MON, C'MON!
DON'T STOP! KEEP MOVING !!
VWM...

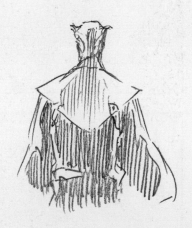

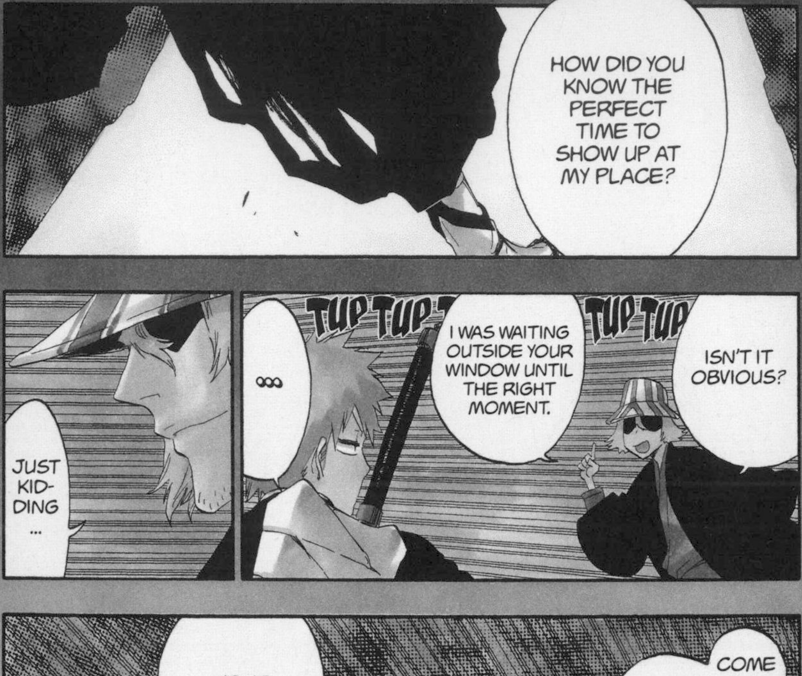
HOW DID YOU KNOW THE PERFECT TIME TO SHOW UP AT MY PLACE?
ISN'T IT OBVIOUS?
TUP TUP
I WAS WAITING OUTSIDE YOUR WINDOW UNTIL THE RIGHT MOMENT.
TUP TUP
...
JUST KID-DING ...
COME ON...
...I'LL NOTICE IF TWO ARRANCARS COME FALLING DOWN FROM HUECO MUNDO.
YOUR BATTLE EARLIER...
THE ABNOR-MALITIES IN THE SOUL SOCIETY...
THOSE WERE MORE THAN ENOUGH REASONS TO TAKE CAUTION.

487. BREATHE BUT BLIND

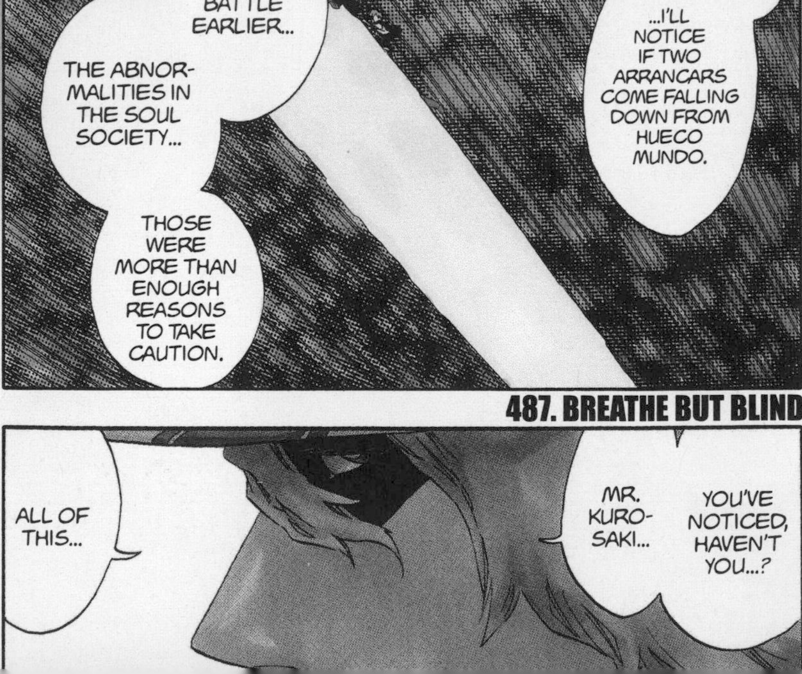
YOU'VE NOTICED, HAVEN'T YOU...?
MR. KURO-SAKI...
ALL OF THIS...

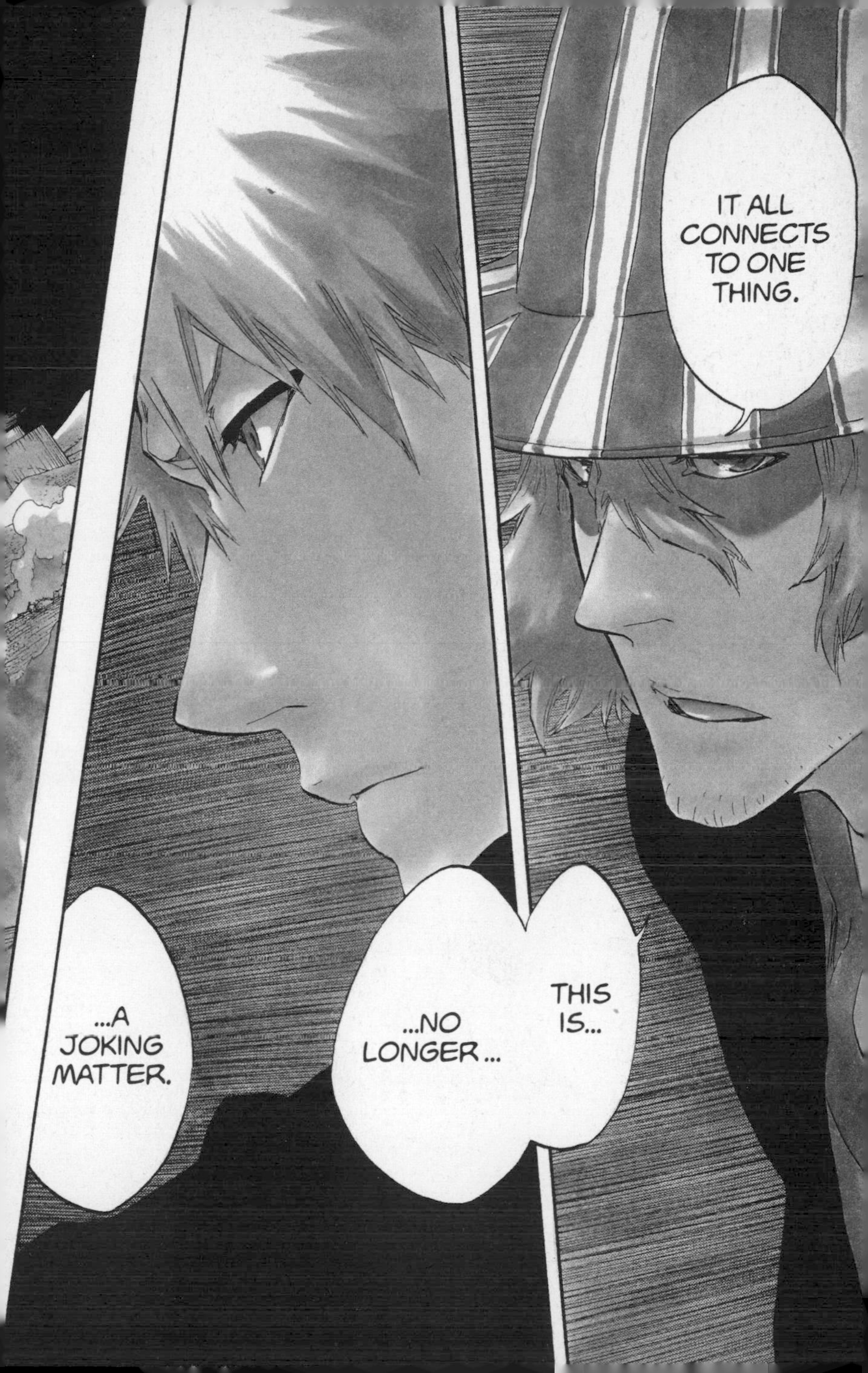
IT ALL CONNECTS TO ONE THING.
THIS IS...
...NO LONGER...
...A JOKING MATTER.

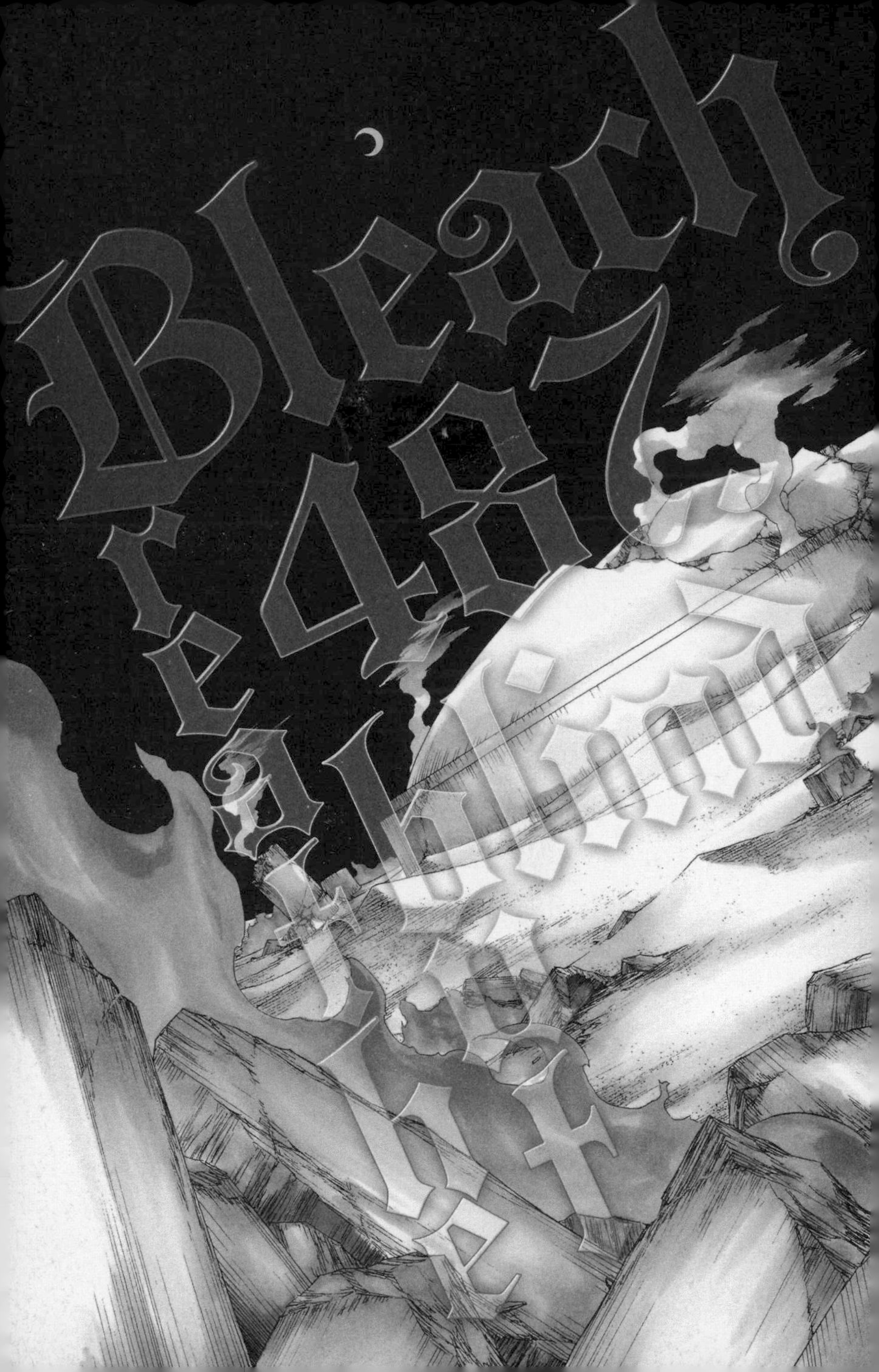
Bleach
427.

BLEACH
ブリーチ

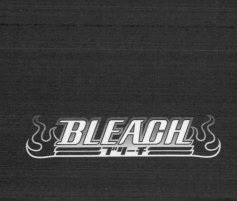

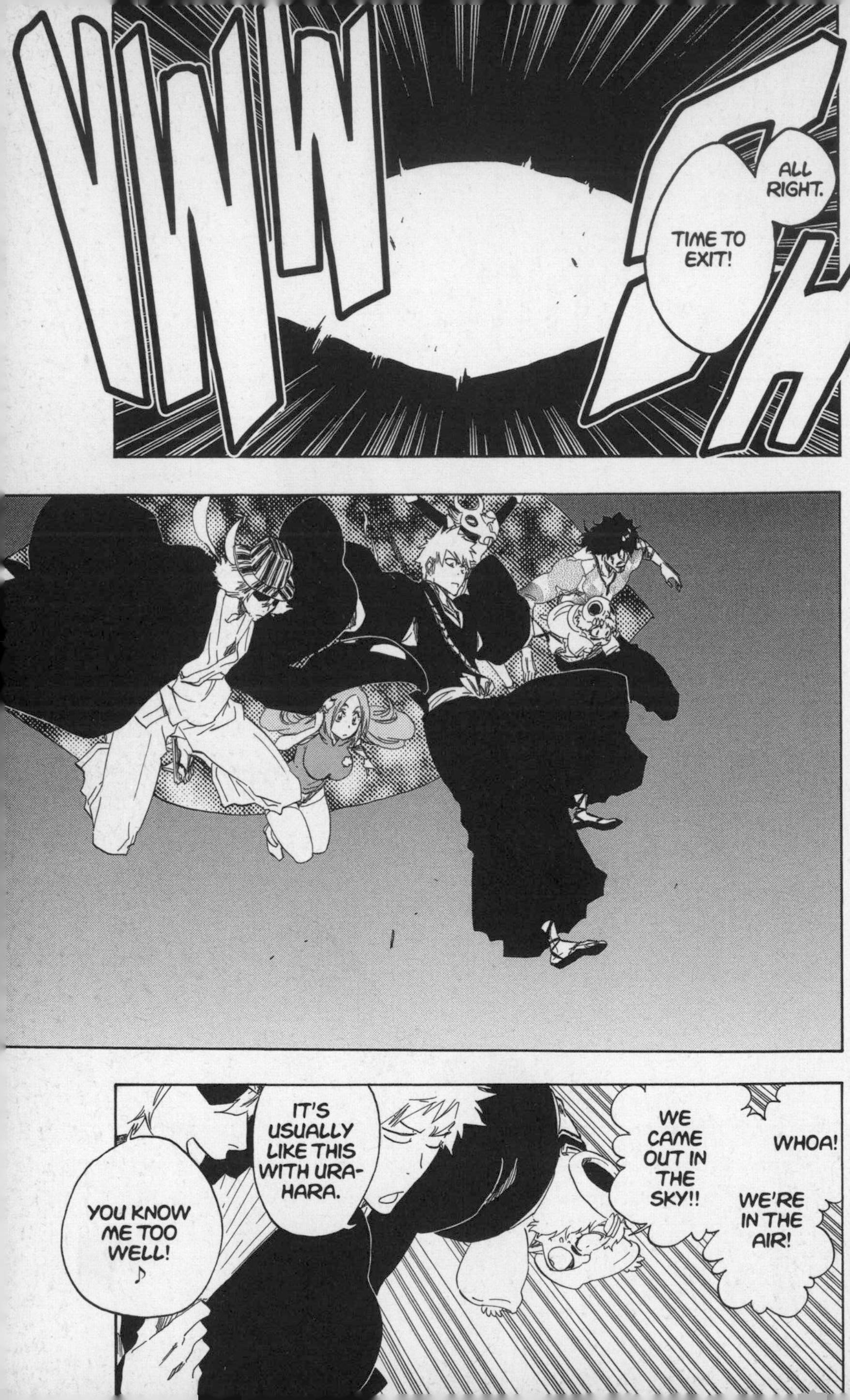
ALL RIGHT.
TIME TO EXIT!
WHOA!
WE'RE IN THE AIR!
WE CAME OUT IN THE SKY!!
IT'S USUALLY LIKE THIS WITH URA-HARA.
YOU KNOW ME TOO WELL! ♪

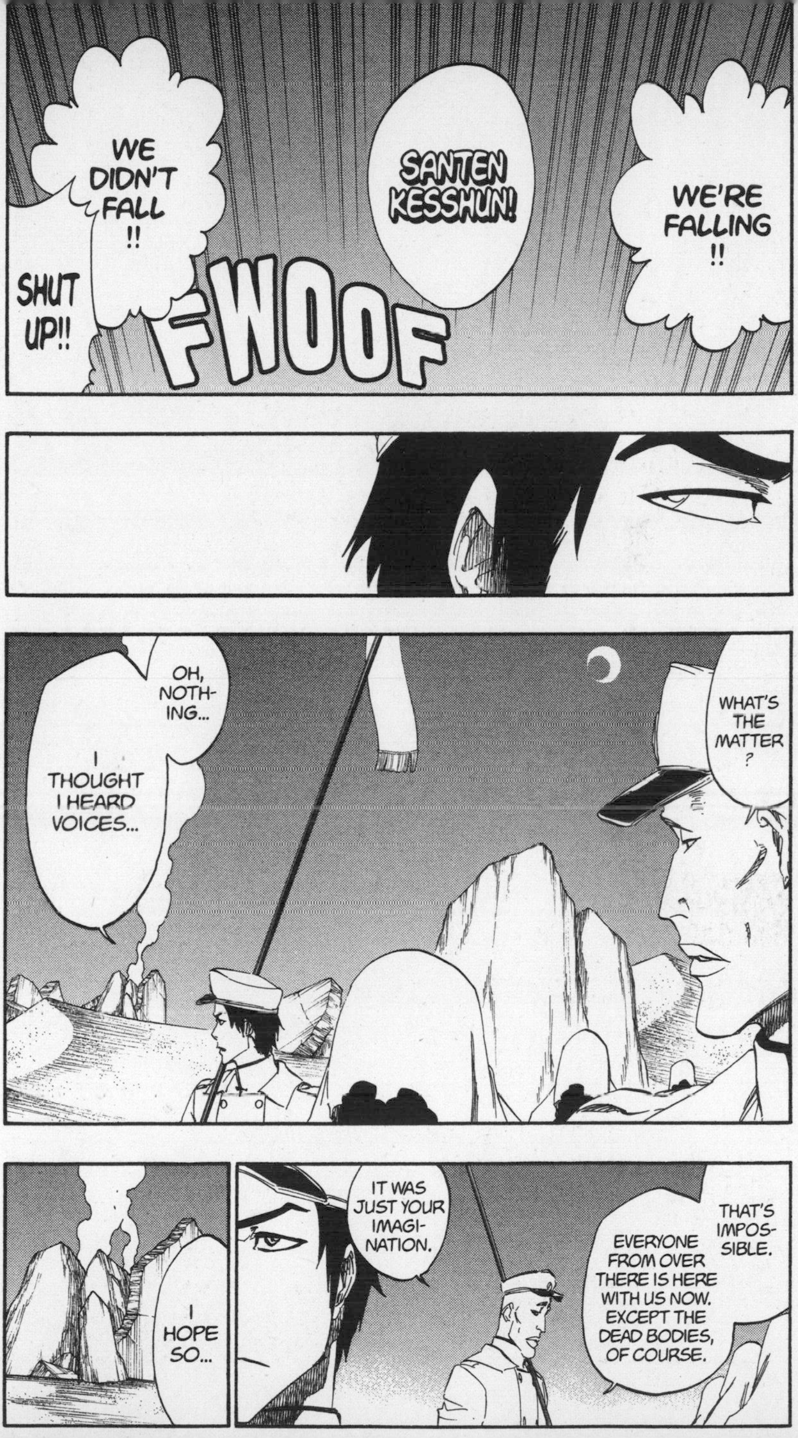
WE'RE FALLING !!
SANTEN KESSHUN!
WE DIDN'T FALL !!
SHUT UP!!
FWOOF
WHAT'S THE MATTER?
OH, NOTHING...
I THOUGHT I HEARD VOICES...
THAT'S IMPOSSIBLE.
EVERYONE FROM OVER THERE IS HERE WITH US NOW. EXCEPT THE DEAD BODIES, OF COURSE.
IT WAS JUST YOUR IMAGINATION.
I HOPE SO...

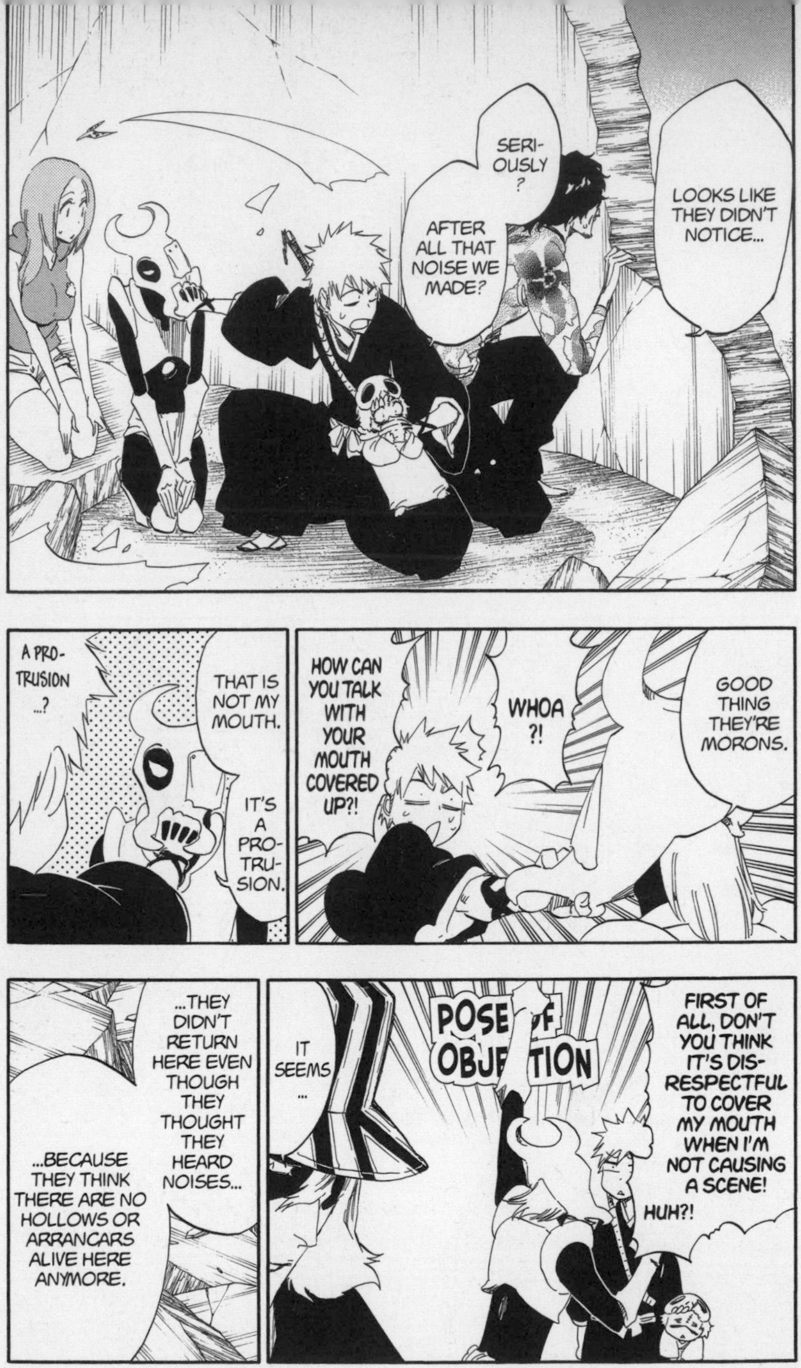
LOOKS LIKE THEY DIDN'T NOTICE...
SERI-OUSLY?
AFTER ALL THAT NOISE WE MADE?
GOOD THING THEY'RE MORONS.
WHOA?!
HOW CAN YOU TALK WITH YOUR MOUTH COVERED UP?!
THAT IS NOT MY MOUTH.
A PRO-TRUSION...?
IT'S A PRO-TRU-SION.
FIRST OF ALL, DON'T YOU THINK IT'S DIS-RESPECTFUL TO COVER MY MOUTH WHEN I'M NOT CAUSING A SCENE!
POSE OF OBJECTION
HUH?!
IT SEEMS...
...THEY DIDN'T RETURN HERE EVEN THOUGH THEY THOUGHT THEY HEARD NOISES...
...BECAUSE THEY THINK THERE ARE NO HOLLOWS OR ARRANCARS ALIVE HERE ANYMORE.

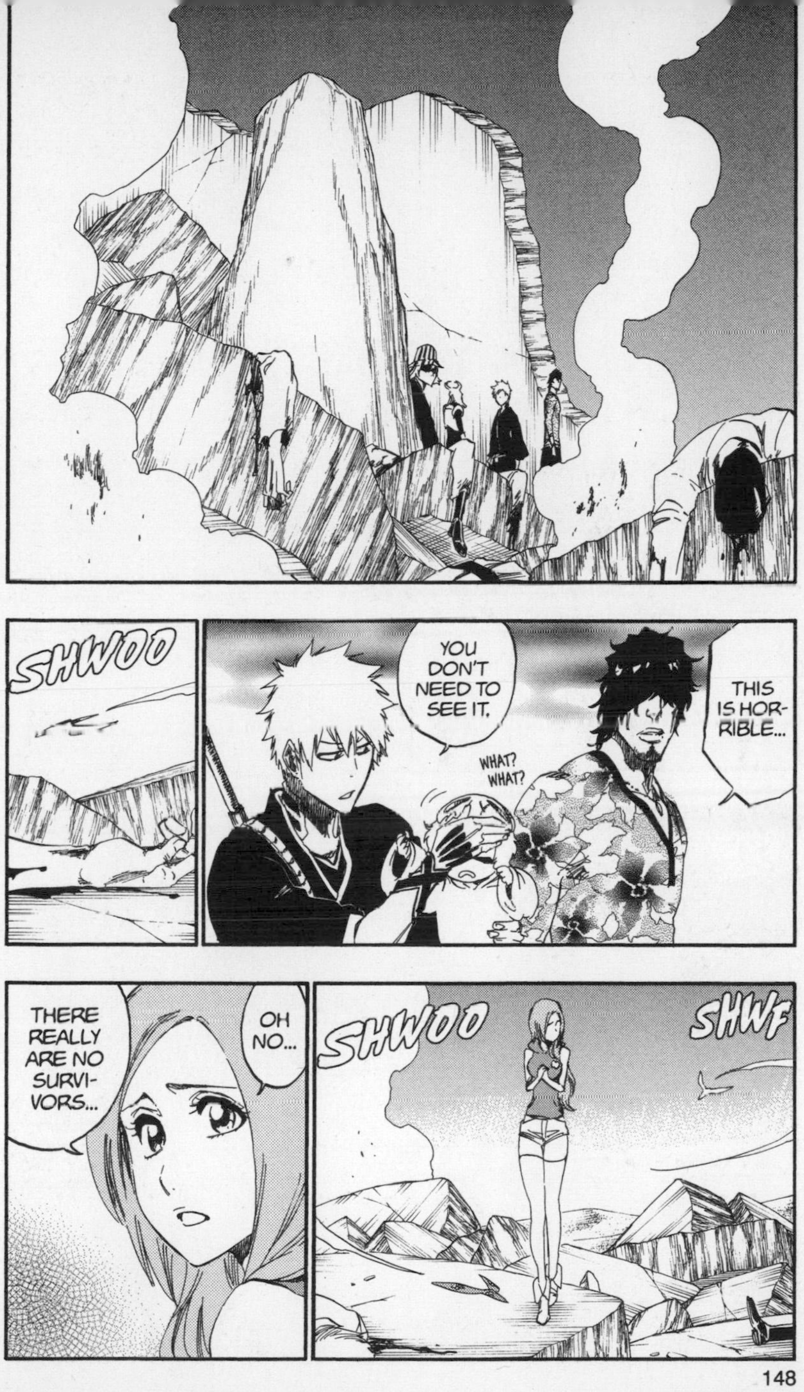
THIS IS HOR-RIBLE...
YOU DON'T NEED TO SEE IT.
WHAT? WHAT?
SHWOO
SHWF
SHWOO
OH NO...
THERE REALLY ARE NO SURVI-VORS...

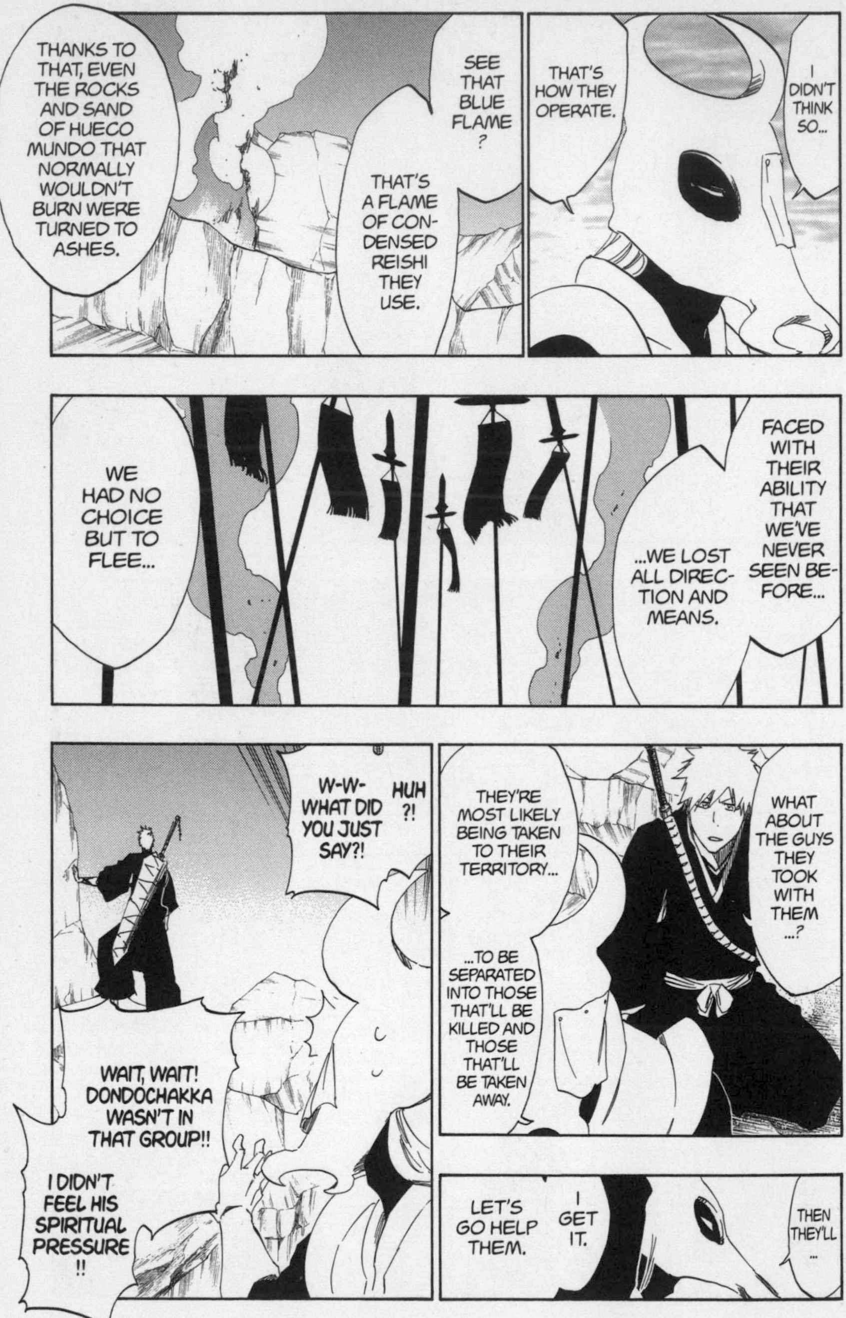
I DIDN'T THINK SO...
THAT'S HOW THEY OPERATE.
SEE THAT BLUE FLAME?
THAT'S A FLAME OF CONDENSED REISHI THEY USE.
THANKS TO THAT, EVEN THE ROCKS AND SAND OF HUECO MUNDO THAT NORMALLY WOULDN'T BURN WERE TURNED TO ASHES.
FACED WITH THEIR ABILITY THAT WE'VE NEVER SEEN BEFORE...
...WE LOST ALL DIRECTION AND MEANS.
WE HAD NO CHOICE BUT TO FLEE...
WHAT ABOUT THE GUYS THEY TOOK WITH THEM...?
THEY'RE MOST LIKELY BEING TAKEN TO THEIR TERRITORY...
...TO BE SEPARATED INTO THOSE THAT'LL BE KILLED AND THOSE THAT'LL BE TAKEN AWAY.
THEN THEY'LL...
I GET IT.
LET'S GO HELP THEM.
HUH?!
W-W-WHAT DID YOU JUST SAY?!
WAIT, WAIT! DONDOCHAKKA WASN'T IN THAT GROUP!!
I DIDN'T FEEL HIS SPIRITUAL PRESSURE!!

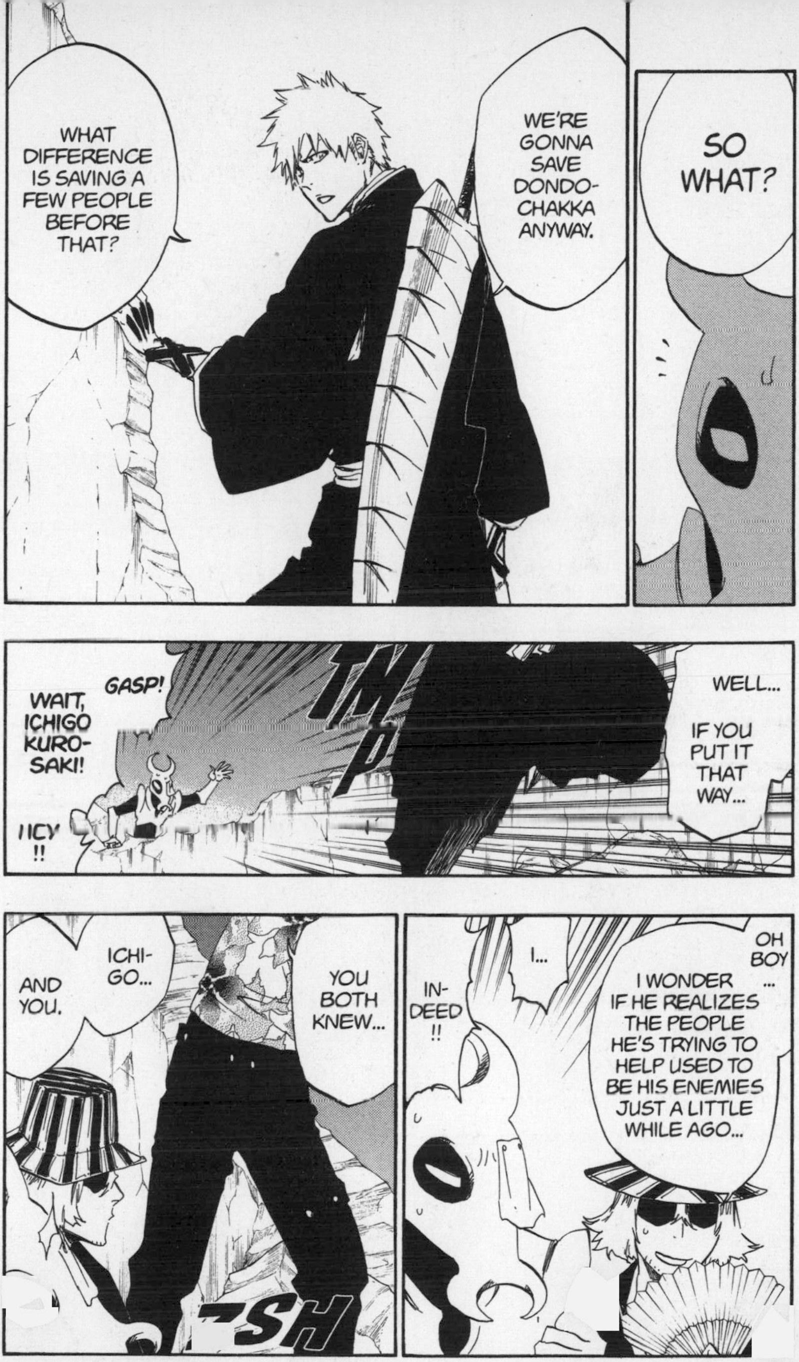
SO WHAT?
WE'RE GONNA SAVE DONDO-CHAKKA ANYWAY.
WHAT DIFFERENCE IS SAVING A FEW PEOPLE BEFORE THAT?
WELL... IF YOU PUT IT THAT WAY...
TMP
GASP!
WAIT, ICHIGO KURO-SAKI!
OH BOY ...
I WONDER IF HE REALIZES THE PEOPLE HE'S TRYING TO HELP USED TO BE HIS ENEMIES JUST A LITTLE WHILE AGO...
I...
IN-DEED !!
YOU BOTH KNEW...
ICHI-GO...
AND YOU.
ZSH

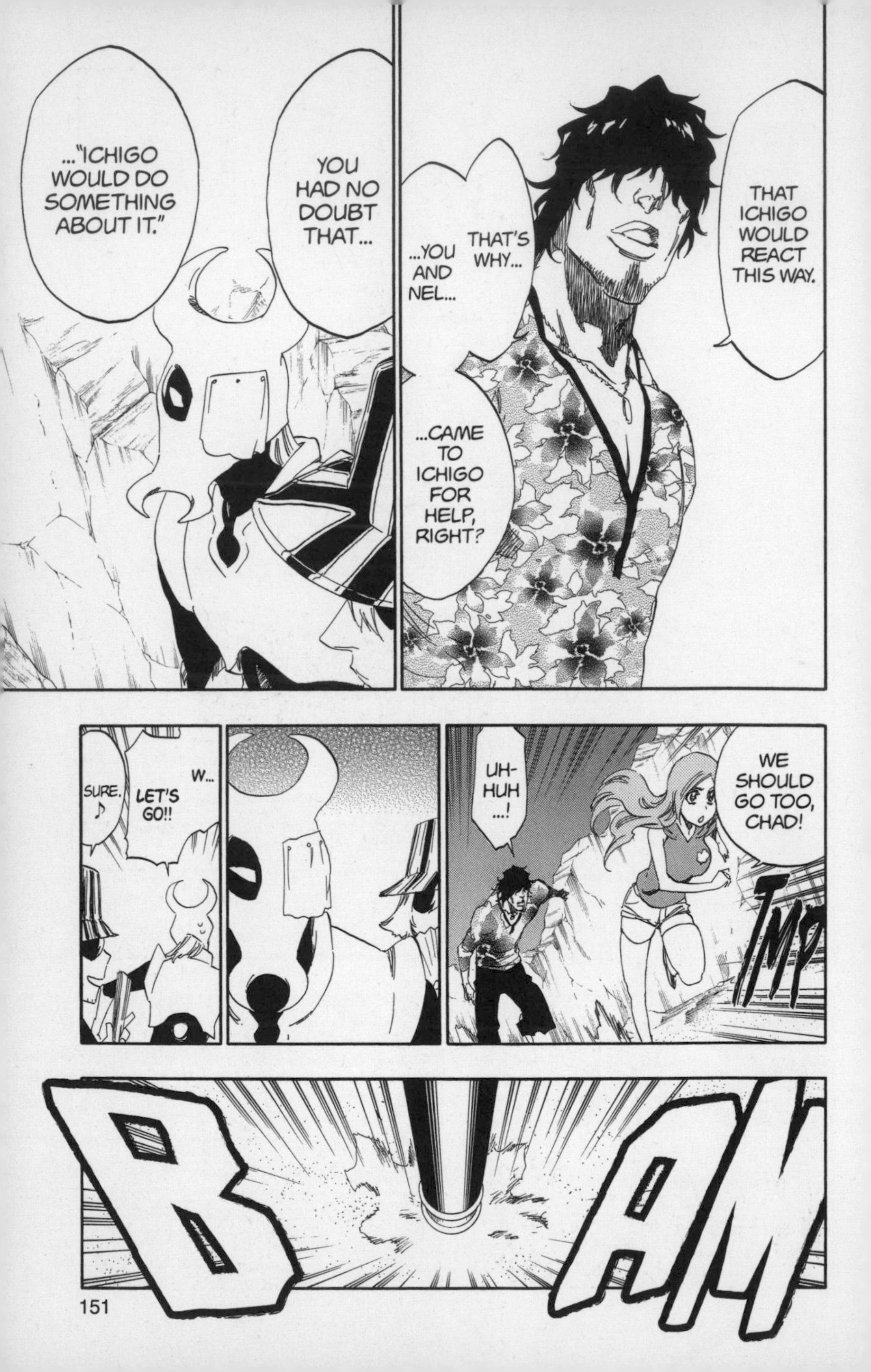
THAT ICHIGO WOULD REACT THIS WAY.
THAT'S WHY...
...YOU AND NEL...
...CAME TO ICHIGO FOR HELP, RIGHT?
YOU HAD NO DOUBT THAT...
..."ICHIGO WOULD DO SOMETHING ABOUT IT."
WE SHOULD GO TOO, CHAD!
UH-HUH...!
TMP
W...
LET'S GO!!
SURE. ♪
BAM

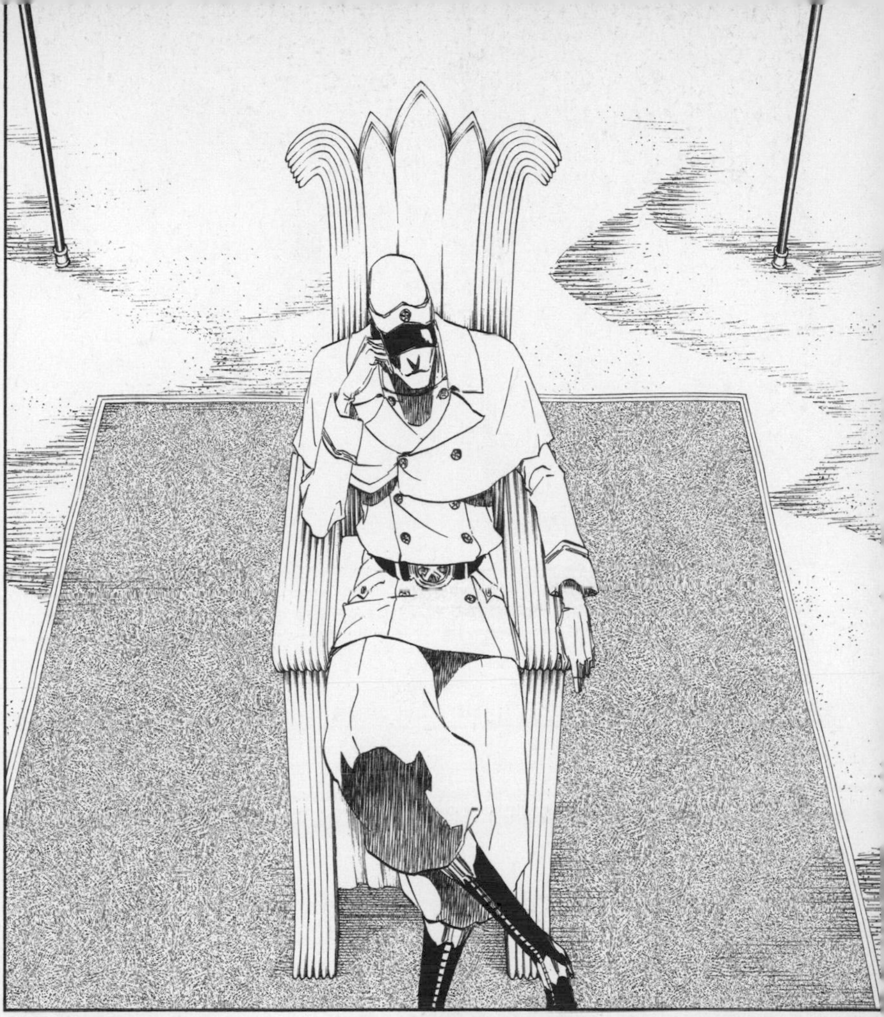
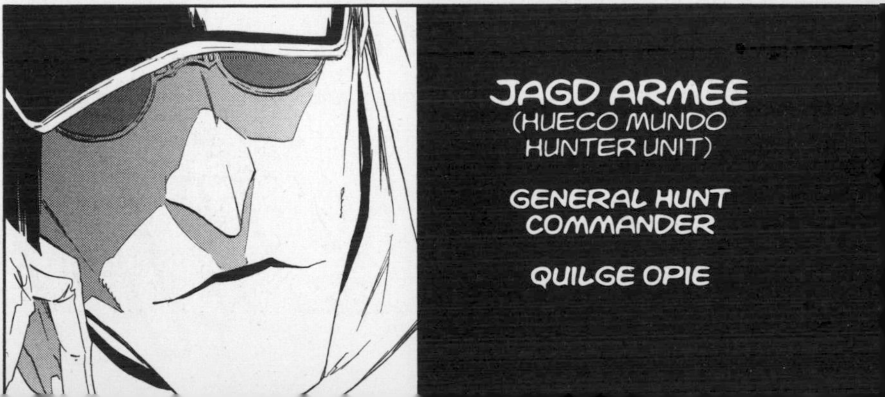
JAGD ARMEE
(HUECO MUNDO
HUNTER UNIT)
GENERAL HUNT
COMMANDER
QUILGE OPIE

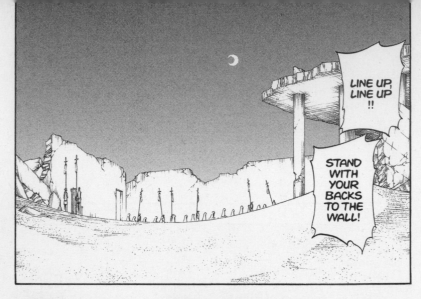

LINE UP, LINE UP !!

STAND WITH YOUR BACKS TO THE WALL!

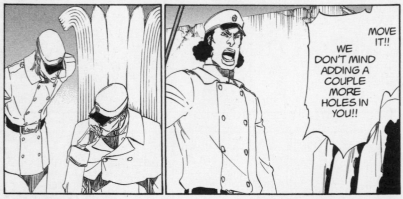

MOVE IT!!

WE DON'T MIND ADDING A COUPLE MORE HOLES IN YOU!!

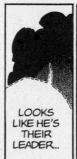

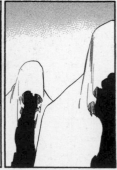

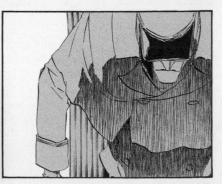

LOOKS LIKE HE'S THEIR LEADER..

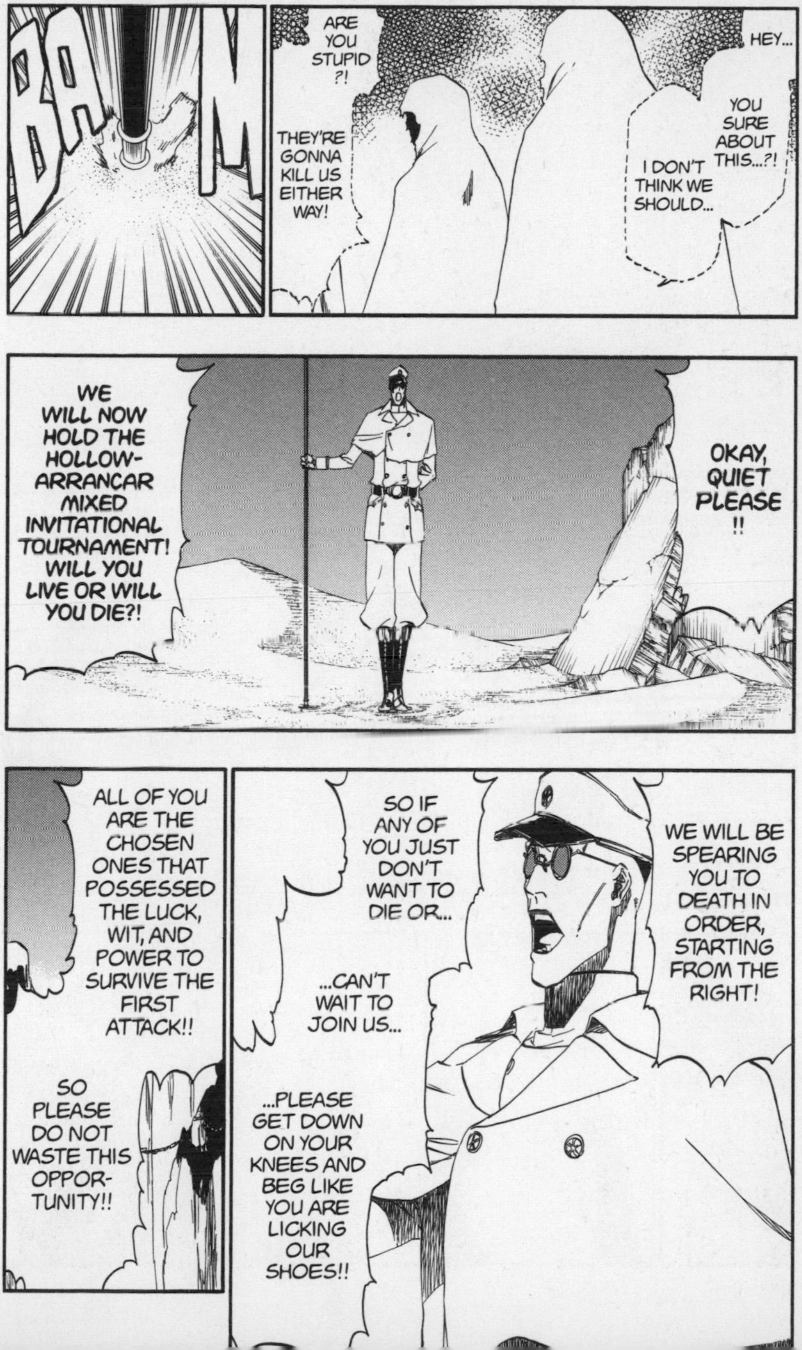
HEY...
YOU SURE ABOUT THIS...?!
I DON'T THINK WE SHOULD...
ARE YOU STUPID?!
THEY'RE GONNA KILL US EITHER WAY!
BAM
OKAY, QUIET PLEASE!!
WE WILL NOW HOLD THE HOLLOW-ARRANCAR MIXED INVITATIONAL TOURNAMENT! WILL YOU LIVE OR WILL YOU DIE?!
WE WILL BE SPEARING YOU TO DEATH IN ORDER, STARTING FROM THE RIGHT!
SO IF ANY OF YOU JUST DON'T WANT TO DIE OR...
...CAN'T WAIT TO JOIN US...
...PLEASE GET DOWN ON YOUR KNEES AND BEG LIKE YOU ARE LICKING OUR SHOES!!
ALL OF YOU ARE THE CHOSEN ONES THAT POSSESSED THE LUCK, WIT, AND POWER TO SURVIVE THE FIRST ATTACK!!
SO PLEASE DO NOT WASTE THIS OPPOR-TUNITY!!

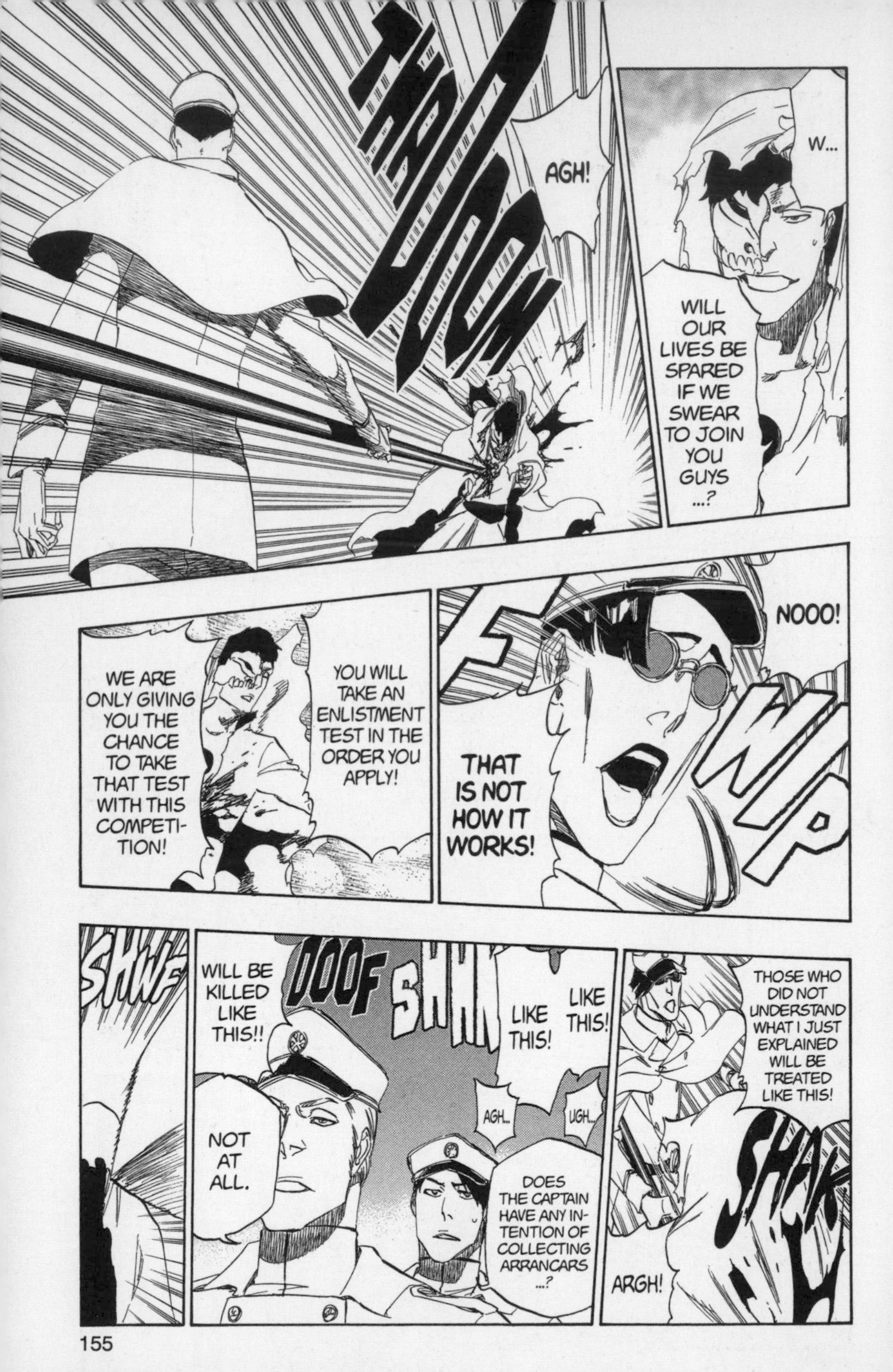
W...
WILL OUR LIVES BE SPARED IF WE SWEAR TO JOIN YOU GUYS ...?
AGH!
NOOO!
THAT IS NOT HOW IT WORKS!
YOU WILL TAKE AN ENLISTMENT TEST IN THE ORDER YOU APPLY!
WE ARE ONLY GIVING YOU THE CHANCE TO TAKE THAT TEST WITH THIS COMPETITION!
THOSE WHO DID NOT UNDERSTAND WHAT I JUST EXPLAINED WILL BE TREATED LIKE THIS!
ARGH!
LIKE THIS!
LIKE THIS!
DOOF
UGH...
AGH...
WILL BE KILLED LIKE THIS!!
DOES THE CAPTAIN HAVE ANY INTENTION OF COLLECTING ARRANCARS ...?
NOT AT ALL.

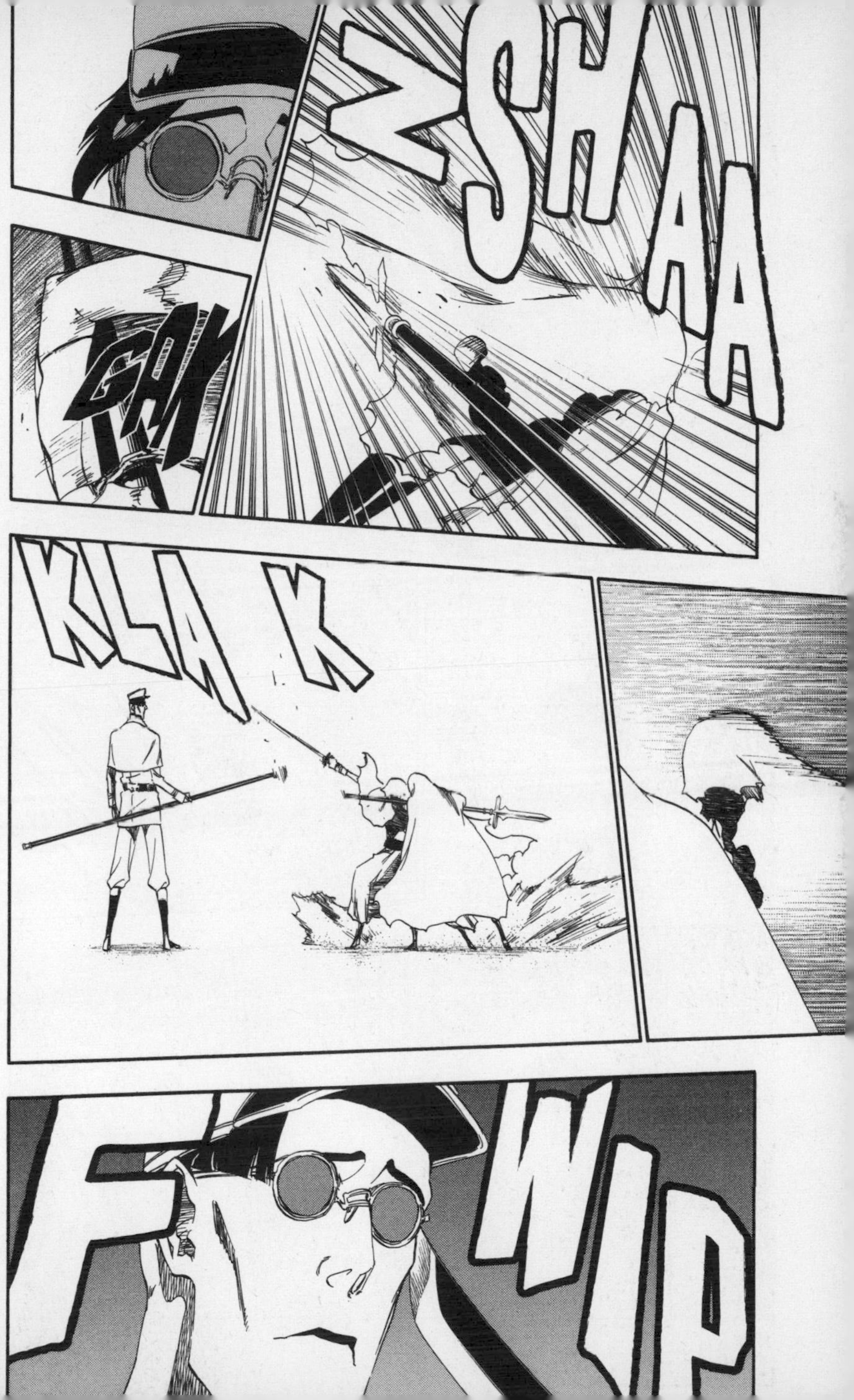
ZSHAA
GAN
KLAK
FWHIP

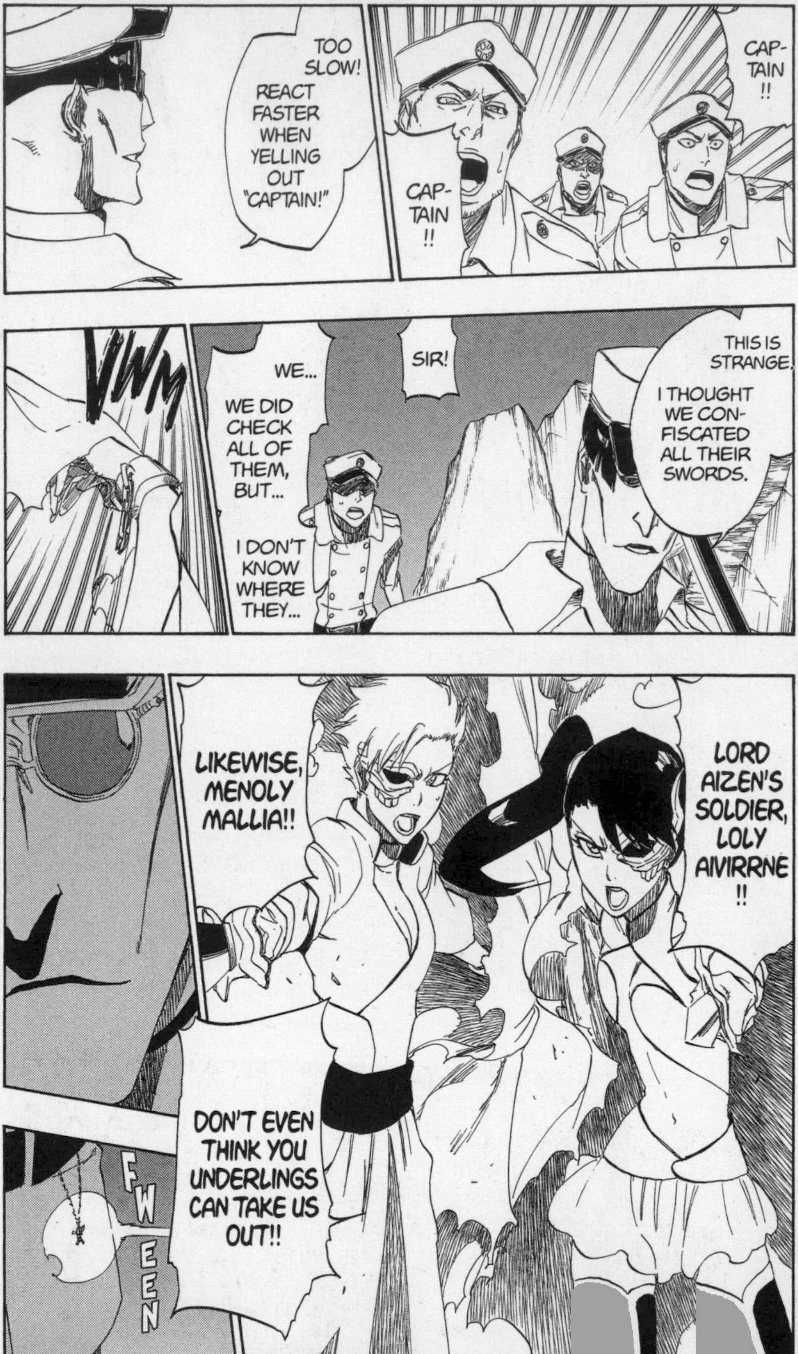

CAP-TAIN!!
CAP-TAIN!!
TOO SLOW! REACT FASTER WHEN YELLING OUT "CAPTAIN!"
THIS IS STRANGE. I THOUGHT WE CONFISCATED ALL THEIR SWORDS.
SIR!
WE... WE DID CHECK ALL OF THEM, BUT... I DON'T KNOW WHERE THEY...
VWM
LORD AIZEN'S SOLDIER, LOLY AIVIRRNE!!
LIKEWISE, MENOLY MALLIA!!
DON'T EVEN THINK YOU UNDERLINGS CAN TAKE US OUT!!
FWEEN

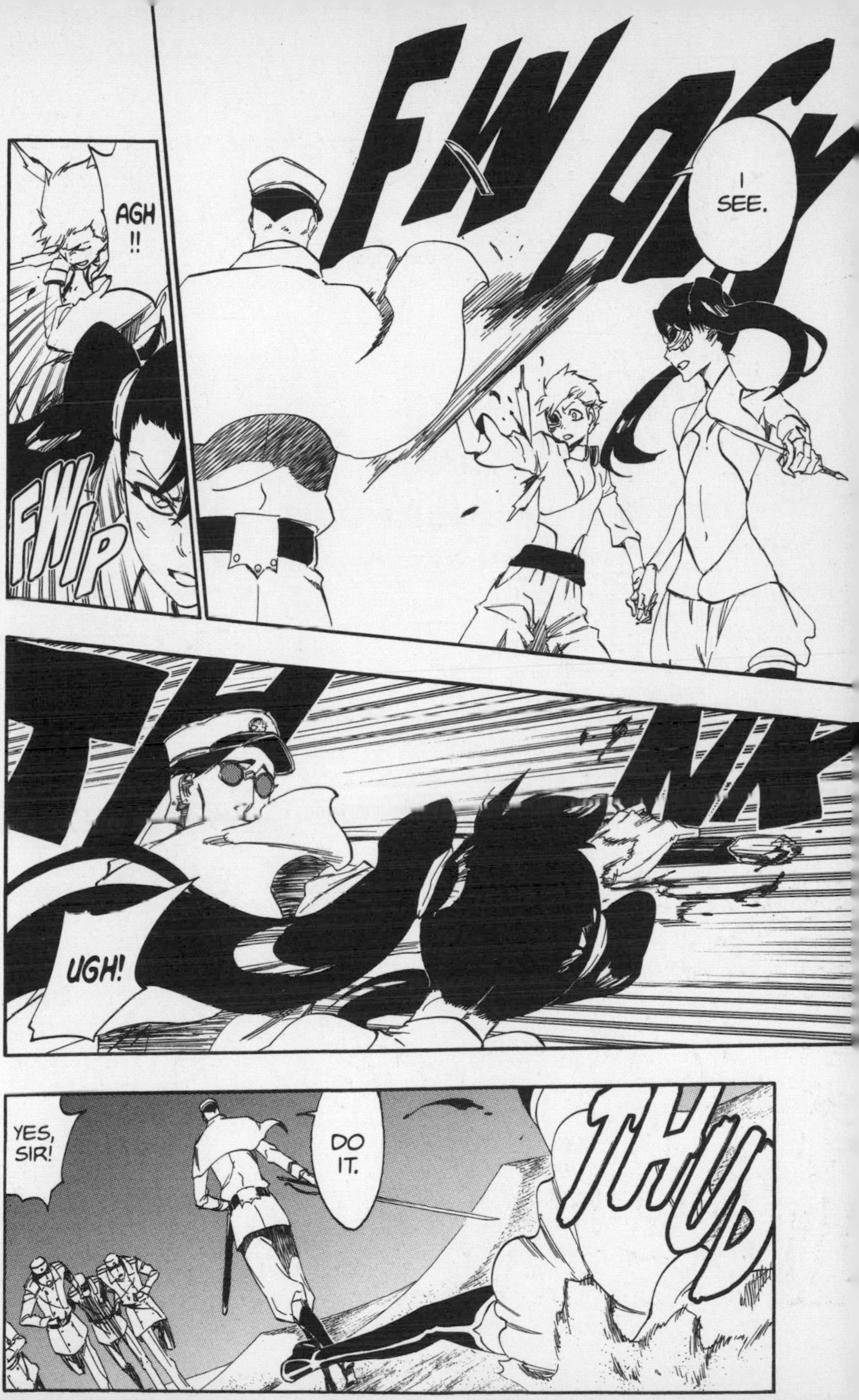
I SEE.
AGH !!
FWIP
UGH!
DO IT.
YES, SIR!

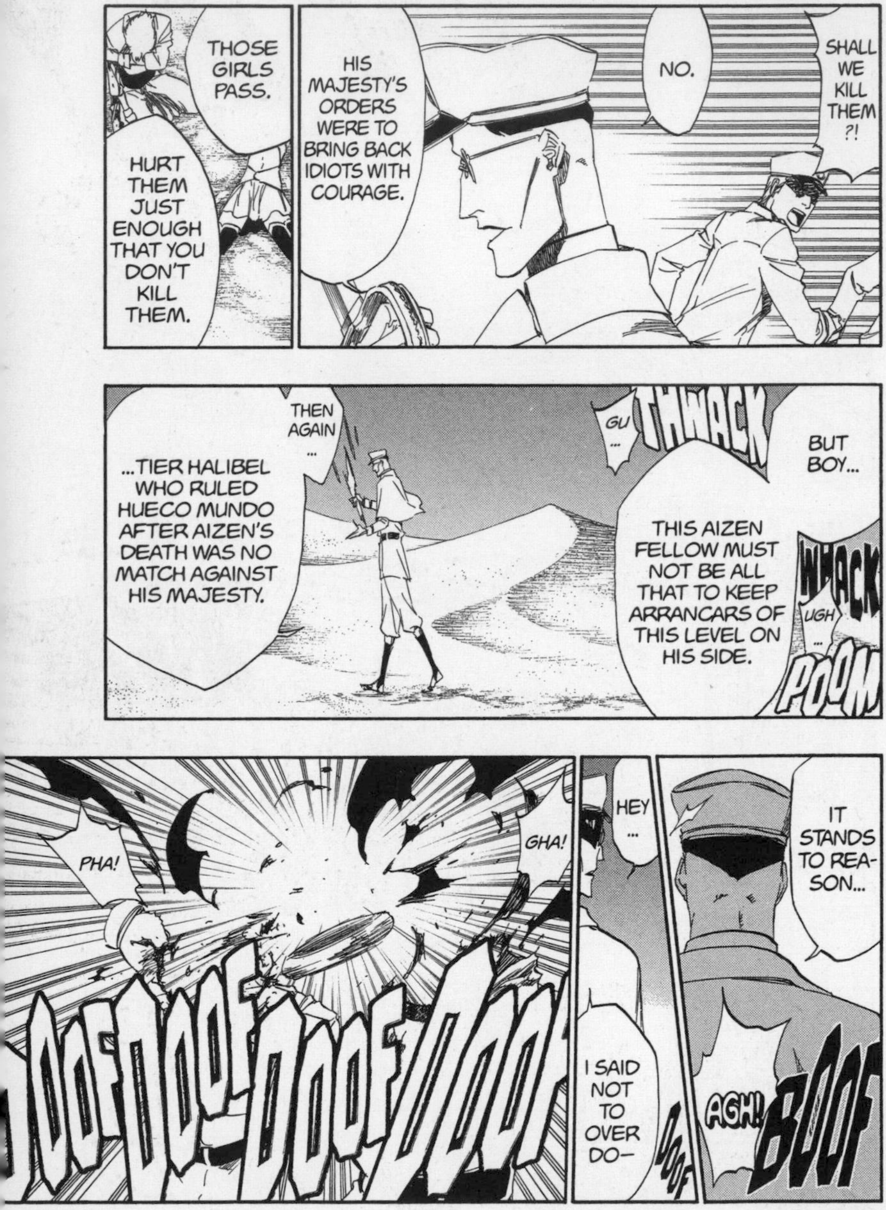
SHALL WE KILL THEM ?!
NO.
HIS MAJESTY'S ORDERS WERE TO BRING BACK IDIOTS WITH COURAGE.
THOSE GIRLS PASS.
HURT THEM JUST ENOUGH THAT YOU DON'T KILL THEM.
GU ...
THWACK
BUT BOY...
THIS AIZEN FELLOW MUST NOT BE ALL THAT TO KEEP ARRANCARS OF THIS LEVEL ON HIS SIDE.
WHACK
UGH ...
POOM
THEN AGAIN ...
...TIER HALIBEL WHO RULED HUECO MUNDO AFTER AIZEN'S DEATH WAS NO MATCH AGAINST HIS MAJESTY.
IT STANDS TO REA-SON...
AGH!
BOOF
HEY ...
I SAID NOT TO OVER DO–
DOOF
GHA!
PHA!
DOOF DOOF DOOF DOOF

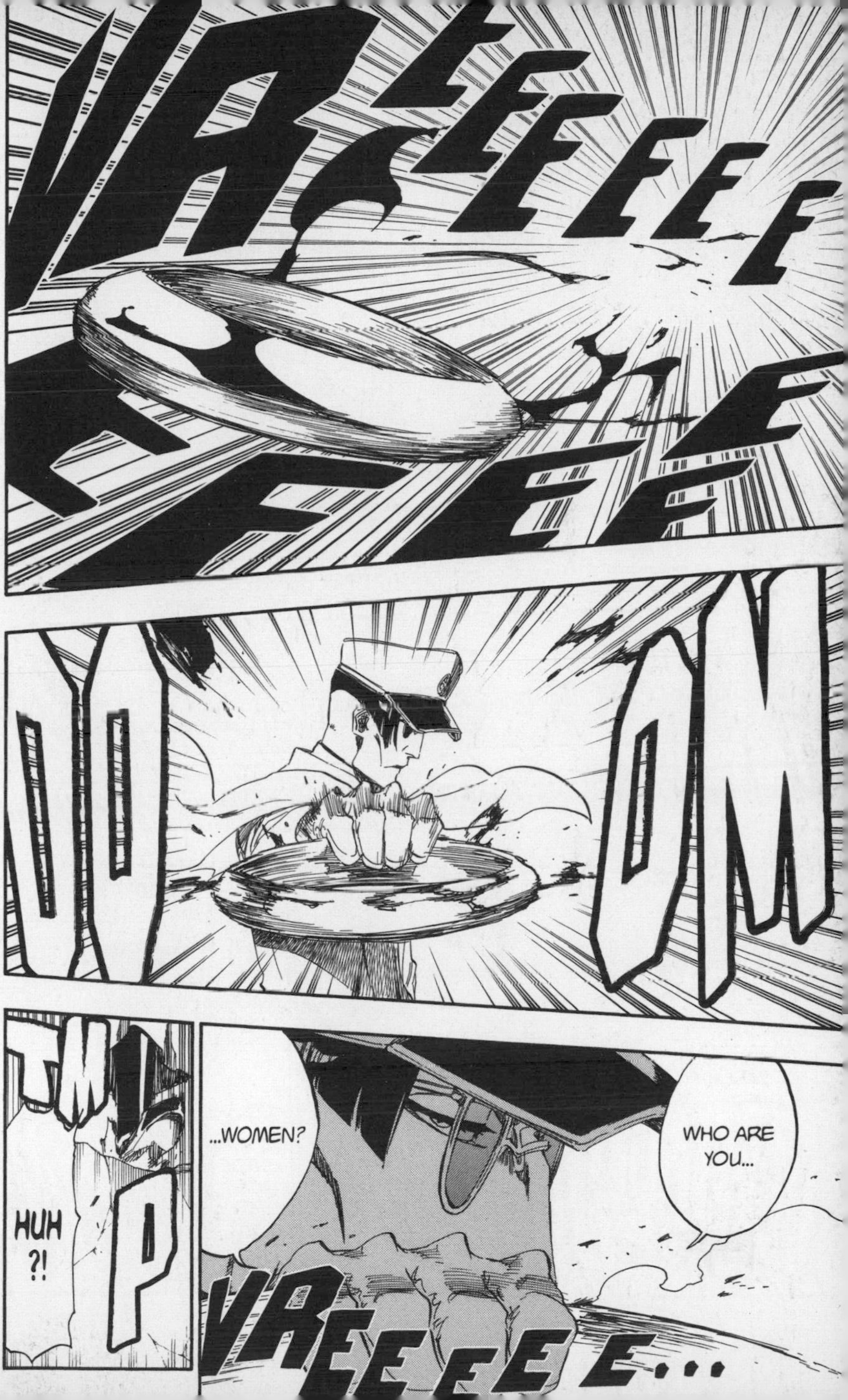
WHO ARE YOU...
...WOMEN?
VREEEEE...
HUH ?!

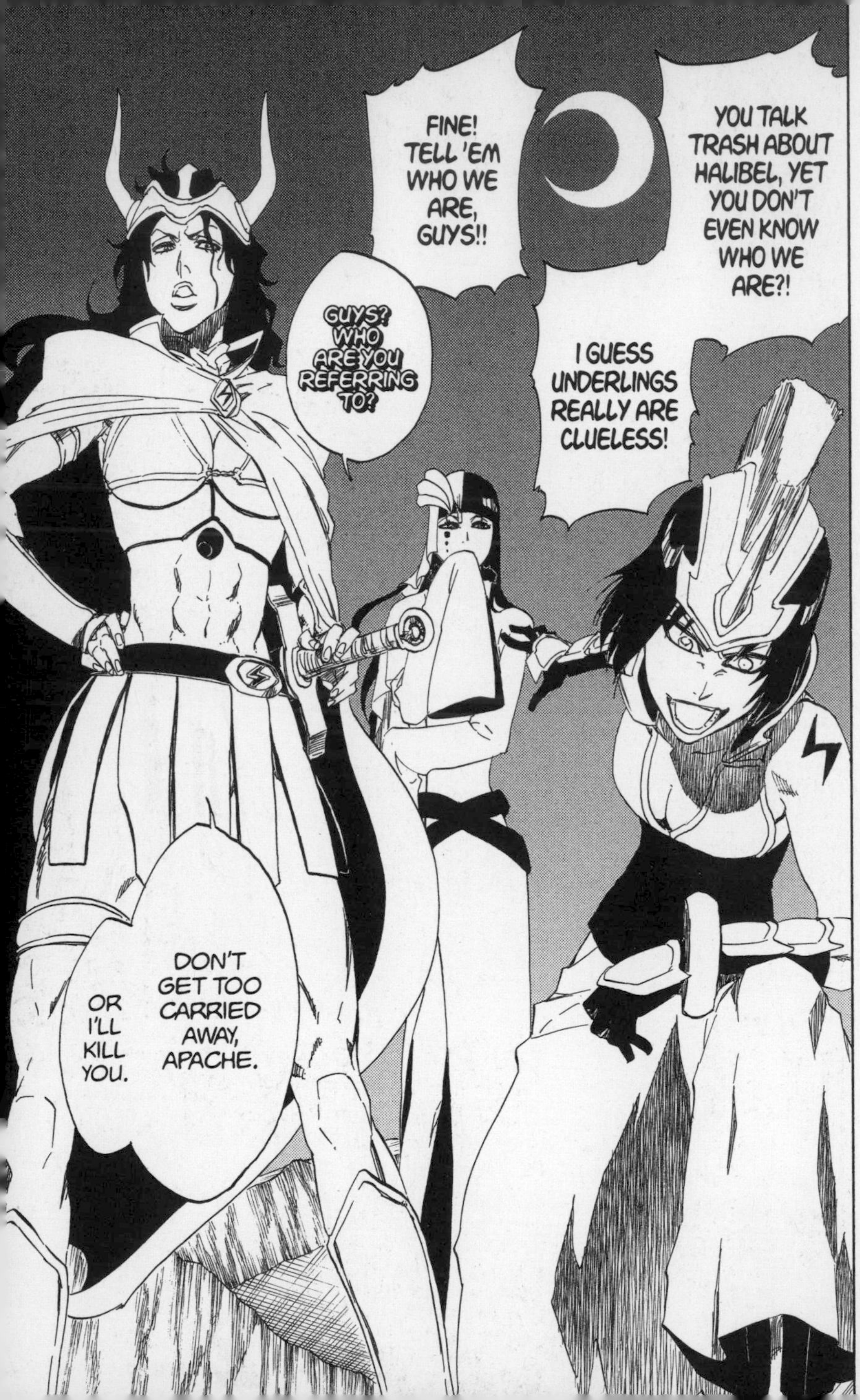
YOU TALK TRASH ABOUT HALIBEL, YET YOU DON'T EVEN KNOW WHO WE ARE?!
I GUESS UNDERLINGS REALLY ARE CLUELESS!
FINE! TELL 'EM WHO WE ARE, GUYS!!
GUYS? WHO ARE YOU REFERRING TO?
DON'T GET TOO CARRIED AWAY, APACHE.
OR I'LL KILL YOU.

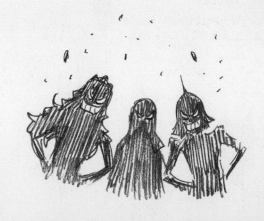

488. BOND BEHIND BLAST

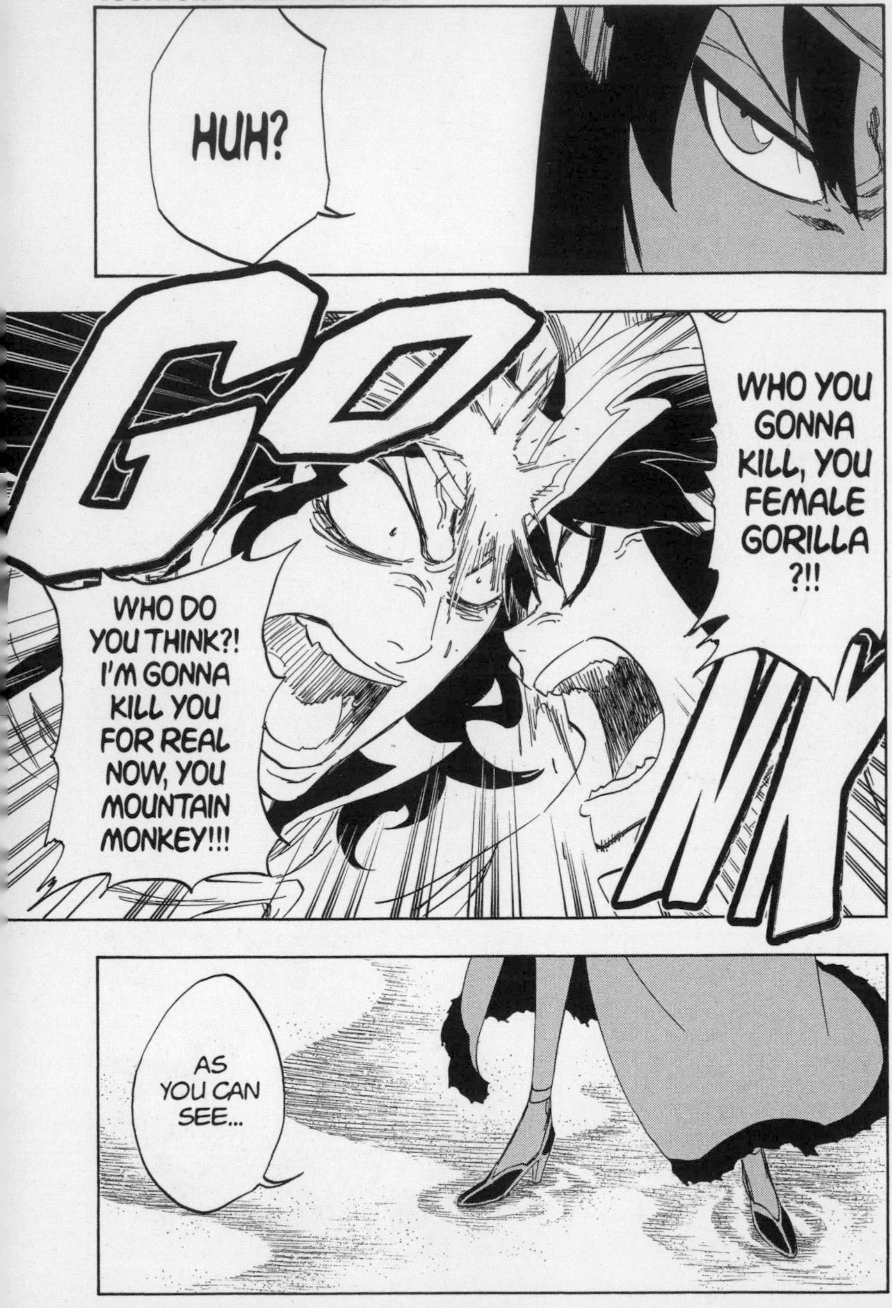
HUH?
WHO YOU GONNA KILL, YOU FEMALE GORILLA?!!
WHO DO YOU THINK?! I'M GONNA KILL YOU FOR REAL NOW, YOU MOUNTAIN MONKEY!!!
AS YOU CAN SEE...

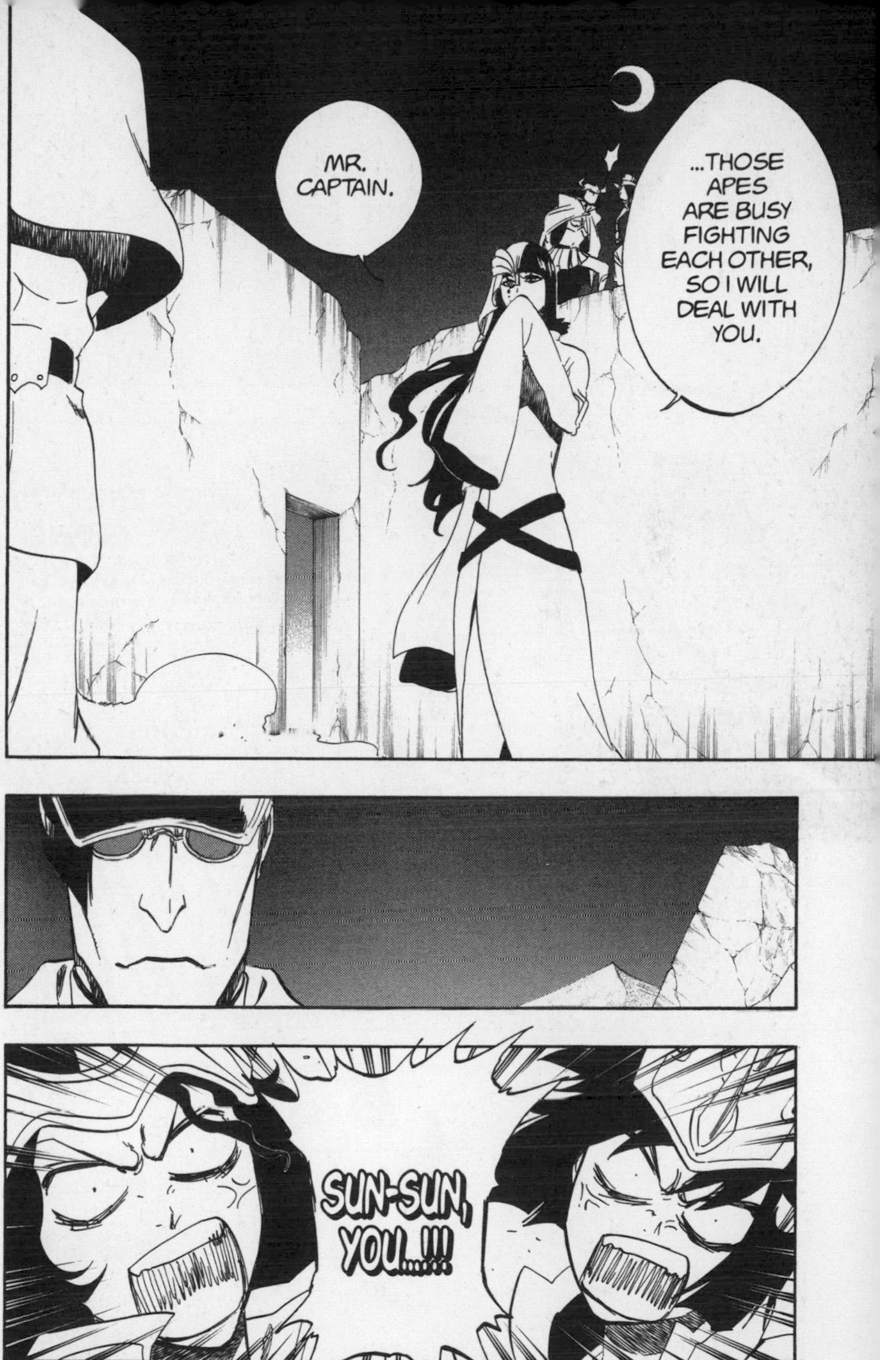
...THOSE APES ARE BUSY FIGHTING EACH OTHER, SO I WILL DEAL WITH YOU.
MR. CAPTAIN.
SUN-SUN, YOU...!!!

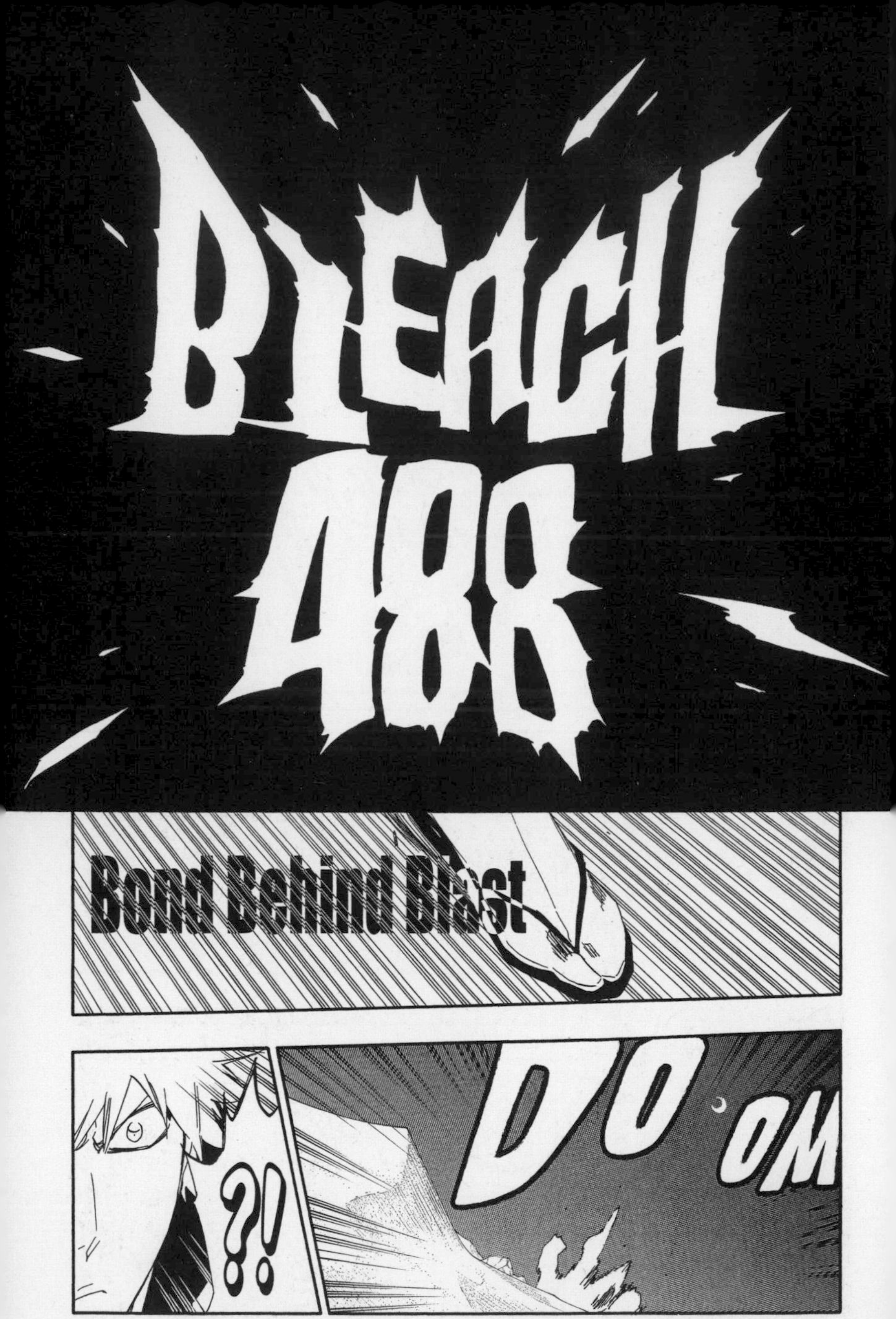
BLEACH 488
Bond Behind Blast
DOOM
?!

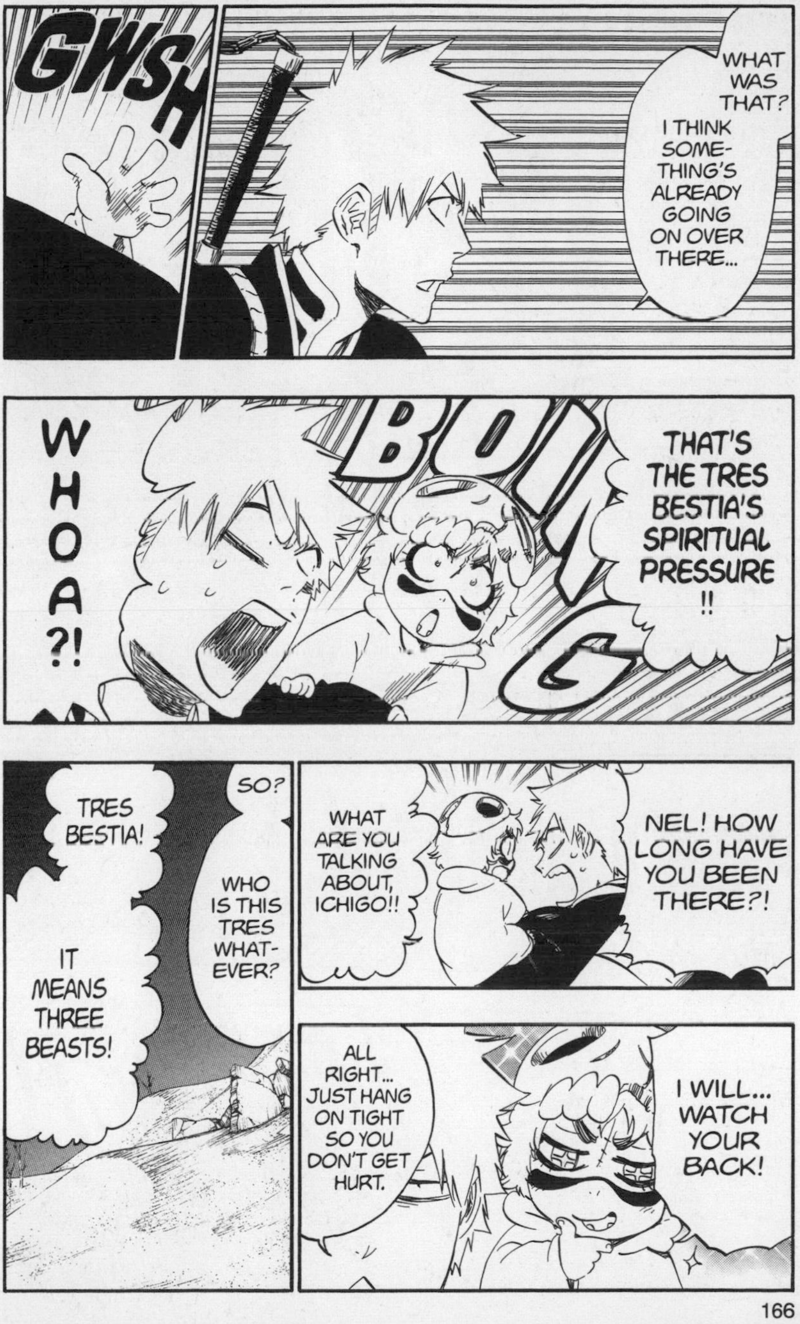
WHAT WAS THAT?
I THINK SOMETHING'S ALREADY GOING ON OVER THERE...
GWSH
THAT'S THE TRES BESTIA'S SPIRITUAL PRESSURE!!
BOING
WHOA?!
NEL! HOW LONG HAVE YOU BEEN THERE?!
WHAT ARE YOU TALKING ABOUT, ICHIGO!!
ALL RIGHT... JUST HANG ON TIGHT SO YOU DON'T GET HURT.
I WILL... WATCH YOUR BACK!
SO?
TRES BESTIA!
WHO IS THIS TRES WHATEVER?
IT MEANS THREE BEASTS!

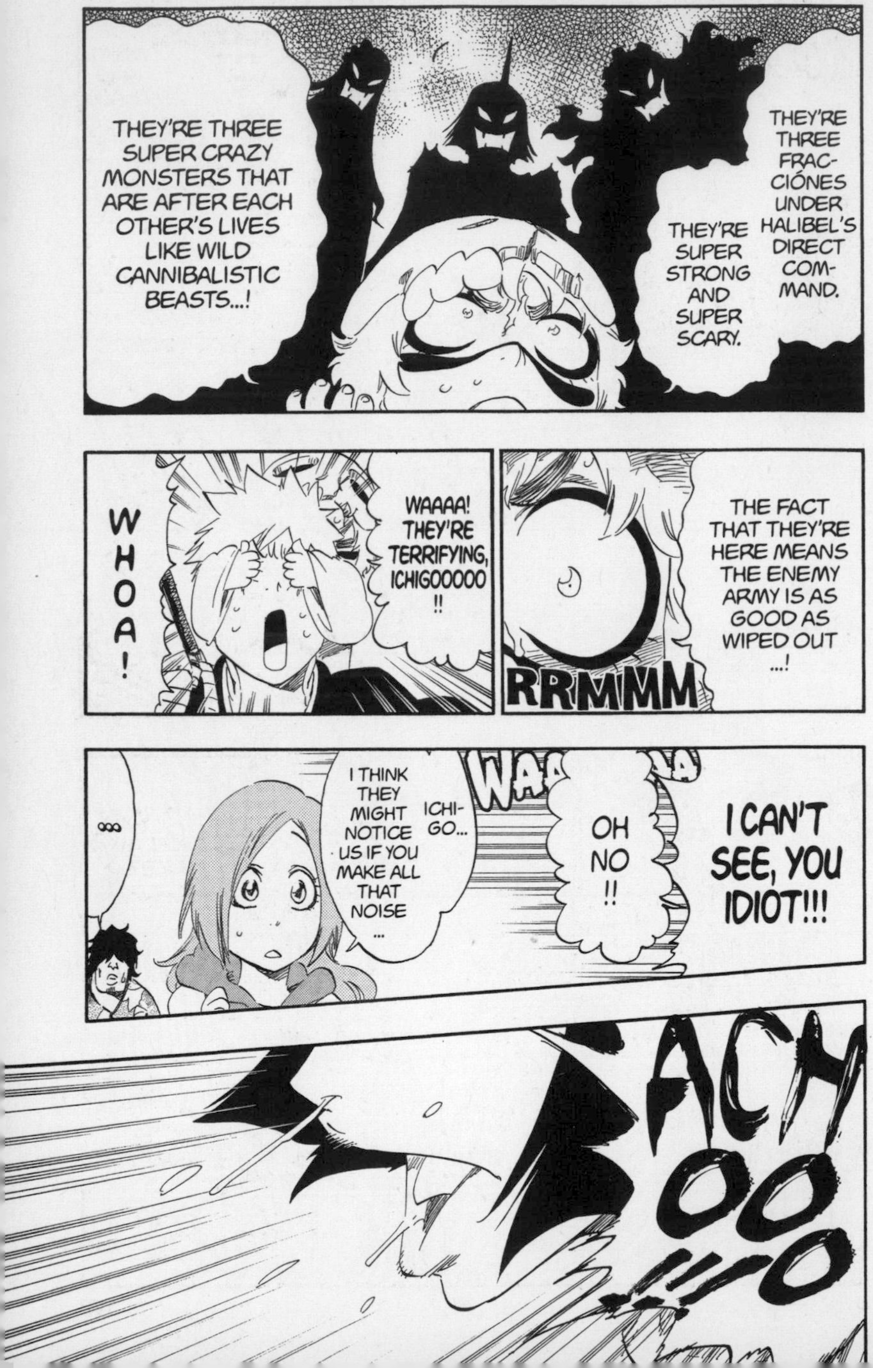
THEY'RE THREE FRACCIÓNES UNDER HALIBEL'S DIRECT COMMAND.
THEY'RE SUPER STRONG AND SUPER SCARY.
THEY'RE THREE SUPER CRAZY MONSTERS THAT ARE AFTER EACH OTHER'S LIVES LIKE WILD CANNIBALISTIC BEASTS...!
THE FACT THAT THEY'RE HERE MEANS THE ENEMY ARMY IS AS GOOD AS WIPED OUT ...!
RRMMMM
WAAAA! THEY'RE TERRIFYING, ICHIGOOOOO!!
WHOA!
I CAN'T SEE, YOU IDIOT!!!
OH NO!!
ICHIGO...
I THINK THEY MIGHT NOTICE US IF YOU MAKE ALL THAT NOISE...
...
ACHOO!!

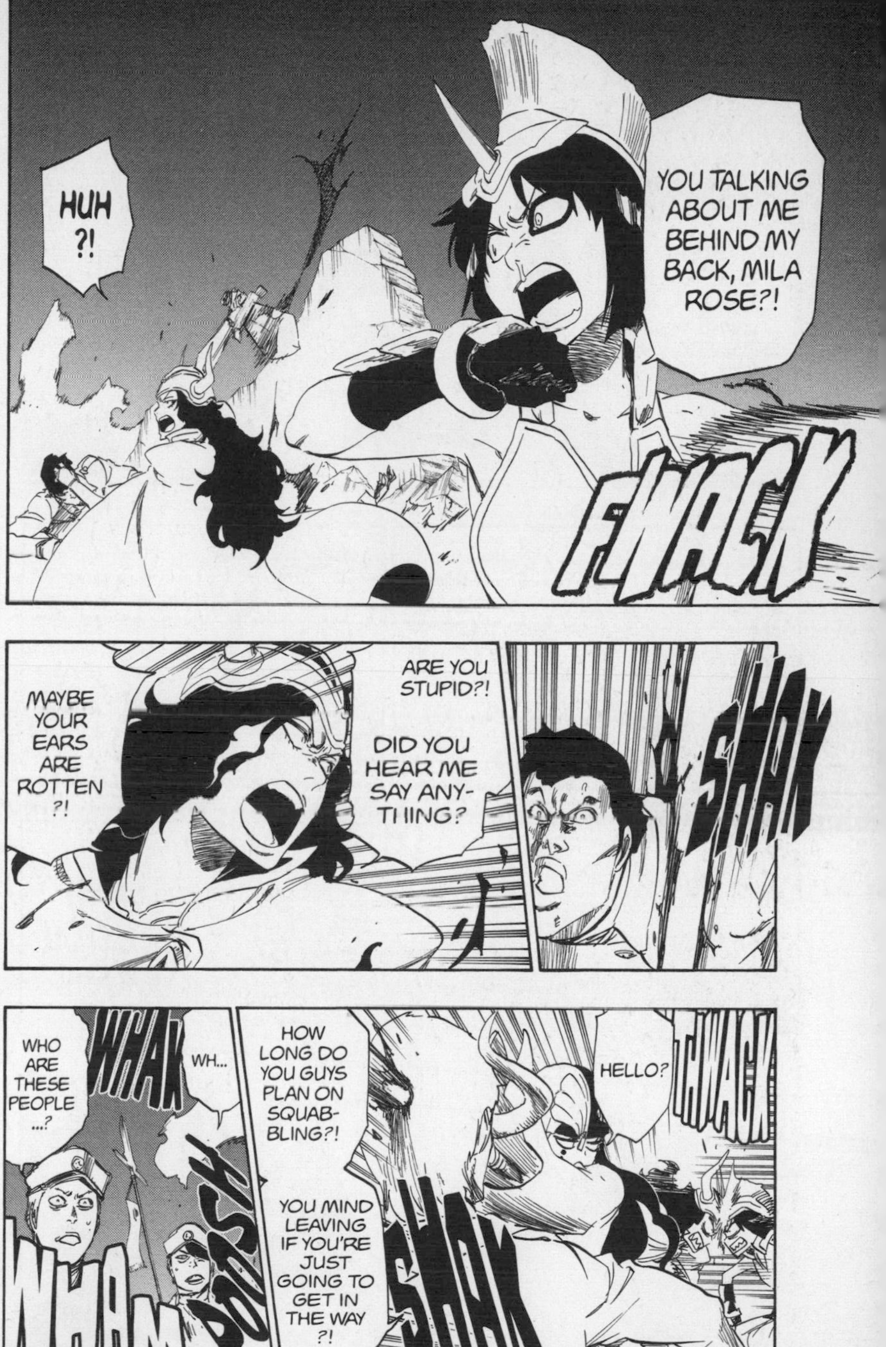
YOU TALKING ABOUT ME BEHIND MY BACK, MILA ROSE?!
FWACK
HUH ?!
SHAK
ARE YOU STUPID?!
DID YOU HEAR ME SAY ANY- THING?
MAYBE YOUR EARS ARE ROTTEN ?!
THWACK
HELLO?
HOW LONG DO YOU GUYS PLAN ON SQUAB- BLING?!
YOU MIND LEAVING IF YOU'RE JUST GOING TO GET IN THE WAY ?!
SHAK
WH...
WHAK
WHO ARE THESE PEOPLE ...?
DOOSH
WHAM

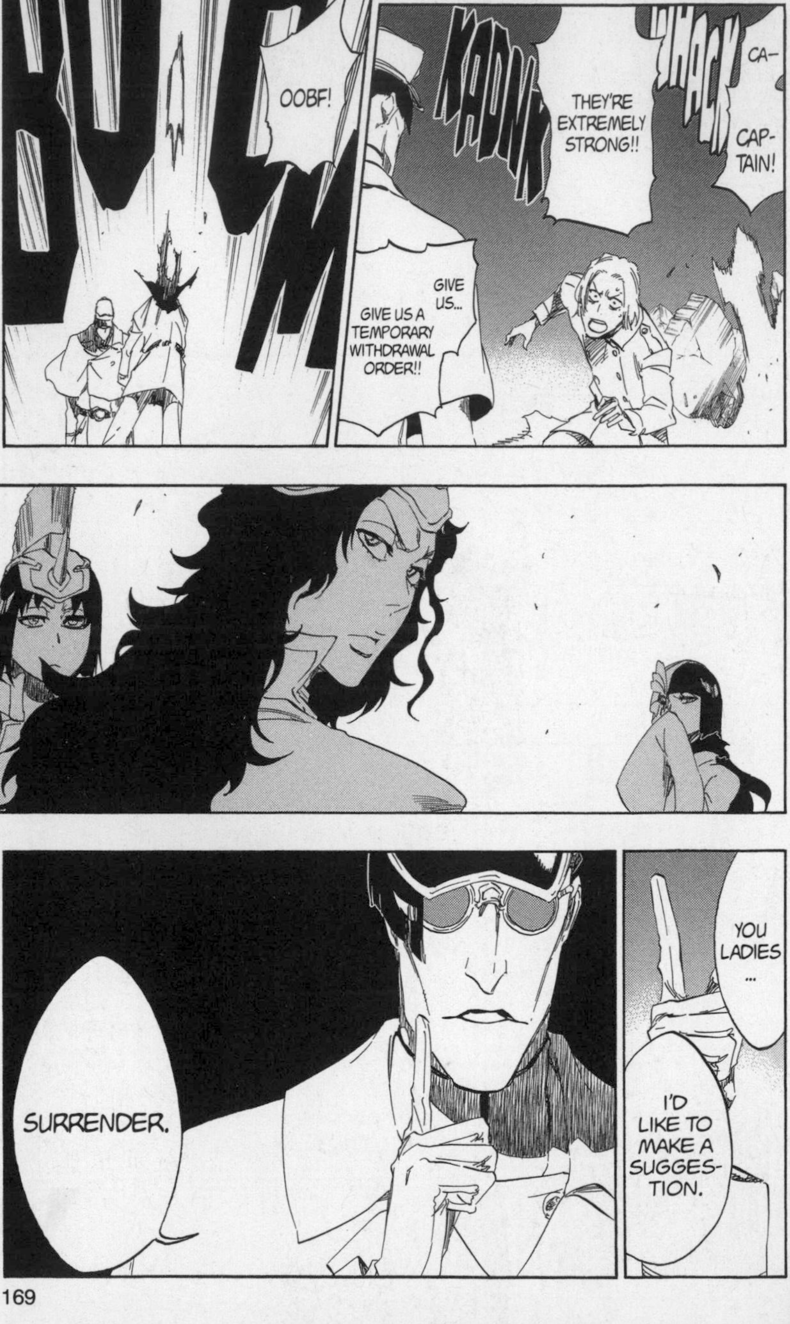
CA—
CAP-TAIN!
WHACK
THEY'RE EXTREMELY STRONG!!
KADUNK
GIVE US...
GIVE US A TEMPORARY WITHDRAWAL ORDER!!
OOBF!
BOOM
YOU LADIES ...
I'D LIKE TO MAKE A SUGGESTION.
SURRENDER.

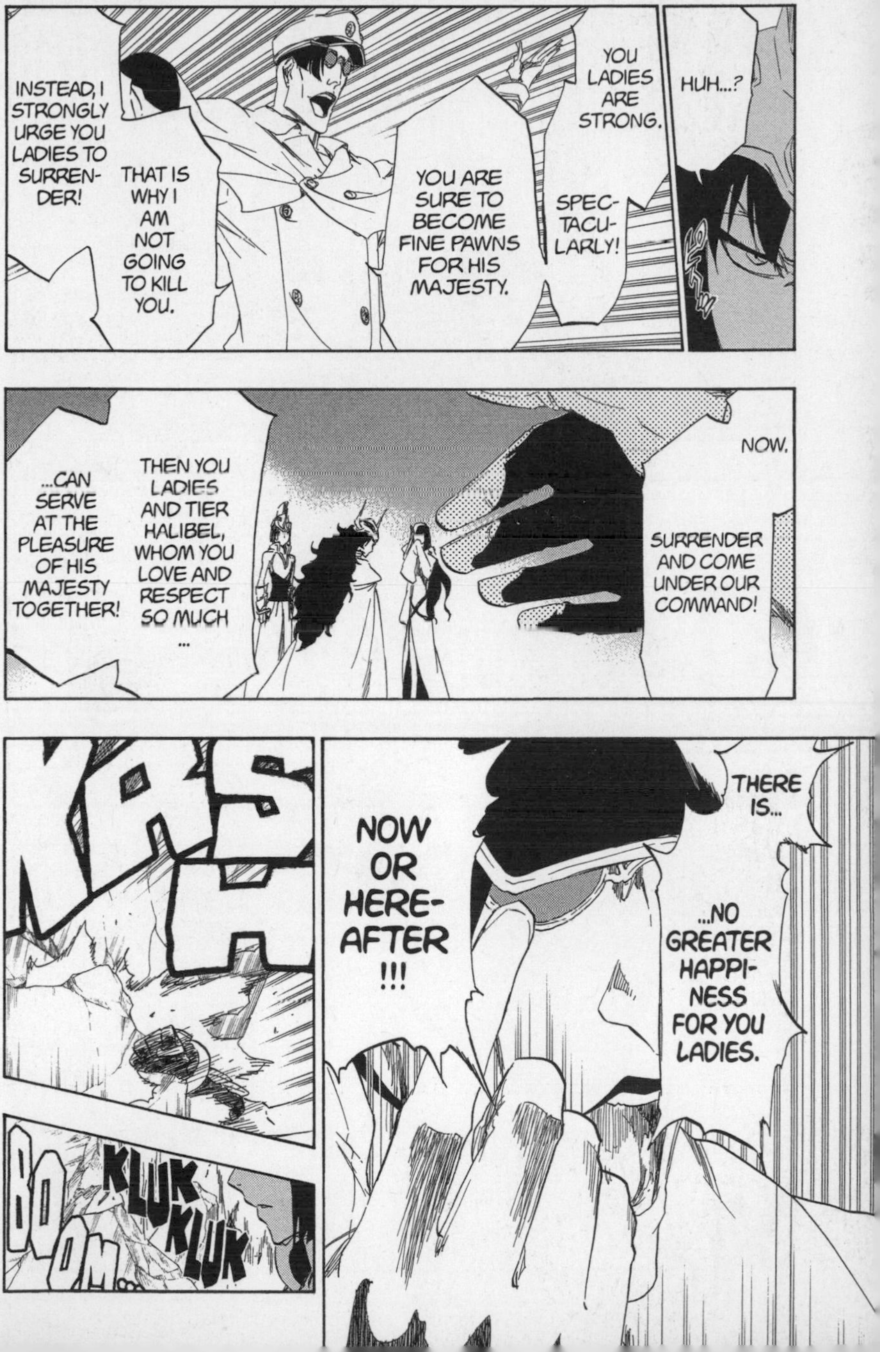
HUH...?
YOU LADIES ARE STRONG.
SPECTACULARLY!
YOU ARE SURE TO BECOME FINE PAWNS FOR HIS MAJESTY.
THAT IS WHY I AM NOT GOING TO KILL YOU.
INSTEAD, I STRONGLY URGE YOU LADIES TO SURRENDER!
NOW.
SURRENDER AND COME UNDER OUR COMMAND!
THEN YOU LADIES AND TIER HALIBEL, WHOM YOU LOVE AND RESPECT SO MUCH ...
...CAN SERVE AT THE PLEASURE OF HIS MAJESTY TOGETHER!
THERE IS...
...NO GREATER HAPPINESS FOR YOU LADIES.
NOW OR HEREAFTER!!!
KRASH
BOOM...
KLUK KLUK KLUK

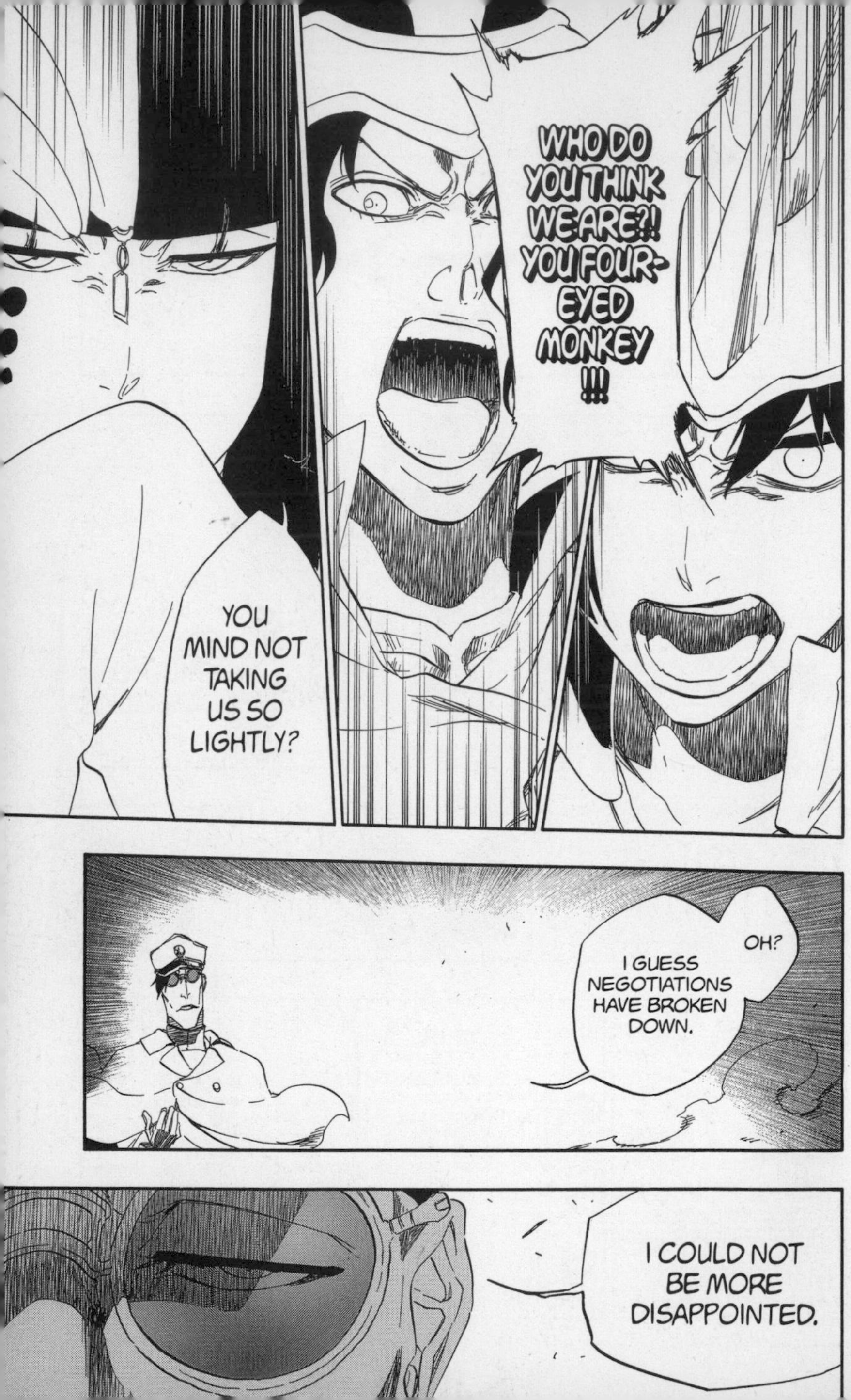
WHO DO YOU THINK WE ARE?! YOU FOUR-EYED MONKEY !!!
YOU MIND NOT TAKING US SO LIGHTLY?
OH?
I GUESS NEGOTIATIONS HAVE BROKEN DOWN.
I COULD NOT BE MORE DISAPPOINTED.

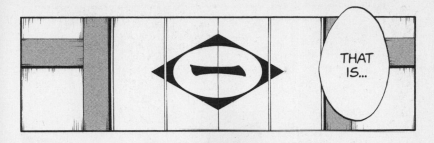

THAT IS...

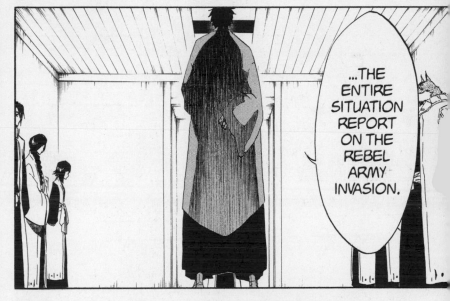

...THE ENTIRE SITUATION REPORT ON THE REBEL ARMY INVASION.

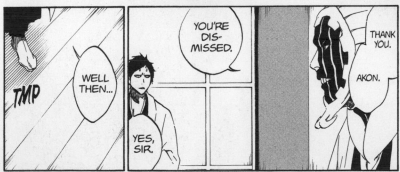

TMP

WELL THEN...

YOU'RE DISMISSED.

YES, SIR.

THANK YOU.

AKON.

READ THIS WAY

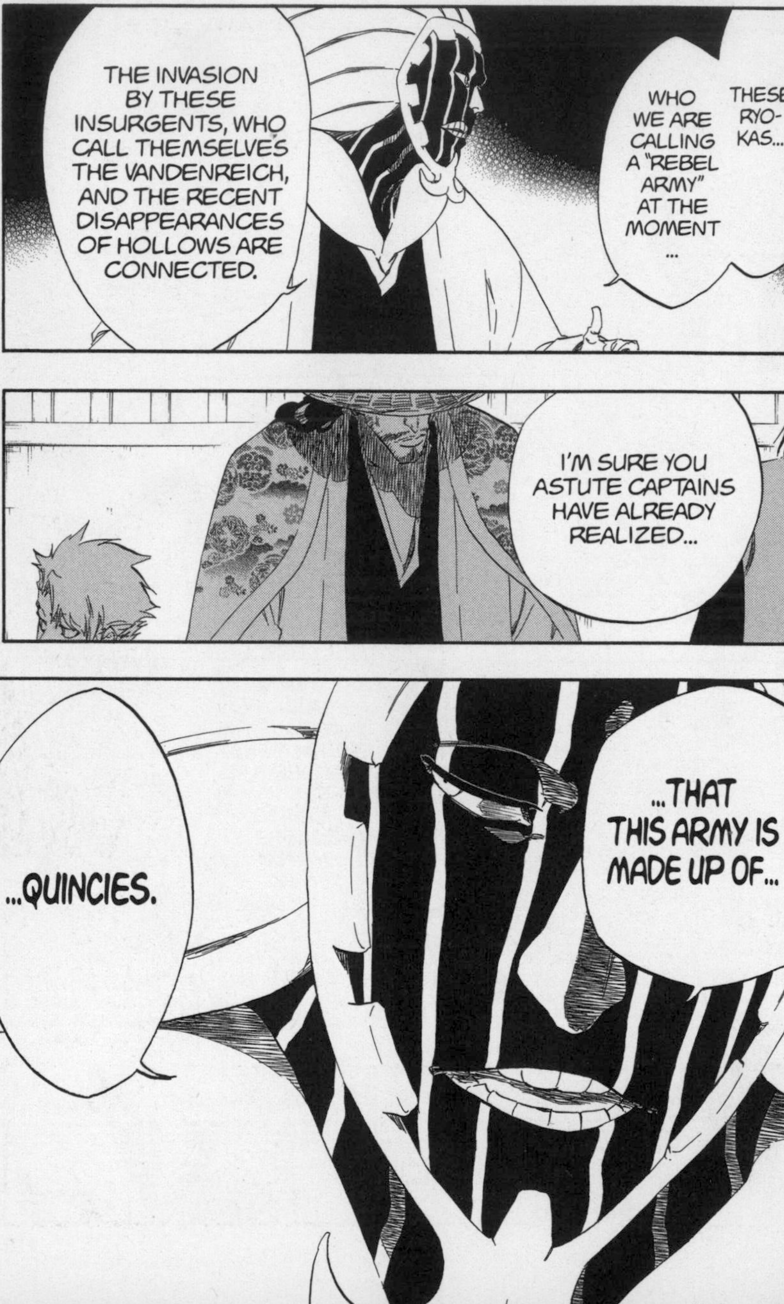
THESE RYO-KAS...
WHO WE ARE CALLING A "REBEL ARMY" AT THE MOMENT ...
THE INVASION BY THESE INSURGENTS, WHO CALL THEMSELVES THE VANDENREICH, AND THE RECENT DISAPPEARANCES OF HOLLOWS ARE CONNECTED.
I'M SURE YOU ASTUTE CAPTAINS HAVE ALREADY REALIZED...
...THAT THIS ARMY IS MADE UP OF...
...QUINCIES.

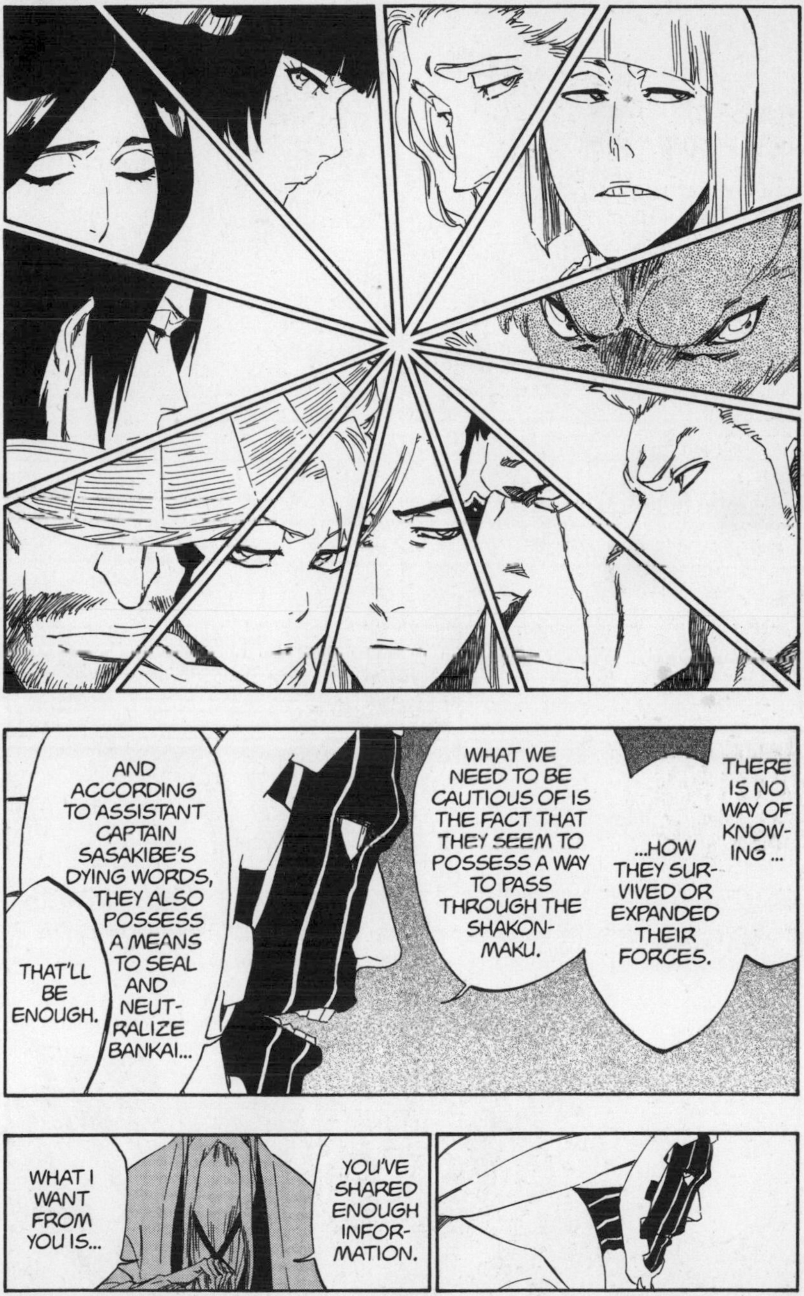
THERE IS NO WAY OF KNOW-ING ...
...HOW THEY SUR-VIVED OR EXPANDED THEIR FORCES.
WHAT WE NEED TO BE CAUTIOUS OF IS THE FACT THAT THEY SEEM TO POSSESS A WAY TO PASS THROUGH THE SHAKON-MAKU.
AND ACCORDING TO ASSISTANT CAPTAIN SASAKIBE'S DYING WORDS, THEY ALSO POSSESS A MEANS TO SEAL AND NEUT-RALIZE BANKAI...
THAT'LL BE ENOUGH.
YOU'VE SHARED ENOUGH INFOR-MATION.
WHAT I WANT FROM YOU IS...

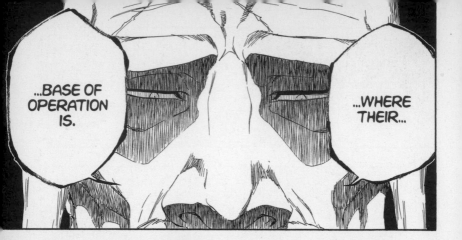

...WHERE THEIR...
...BASE OF OPERATION IS.
UNFOR-TUNATE-LY...
...WE HAVE NOT YET...
I SEE...
SO WE HAVE NO WAY OF ATTACKING THEM.
KLONK...
I'M ORDERING ALL CAP-TAINS...
...TO PREPARE FOR BATTLE.

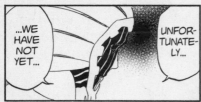

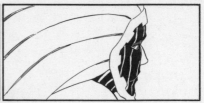

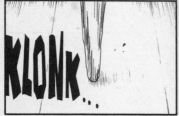

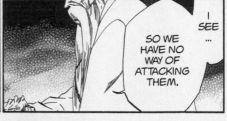

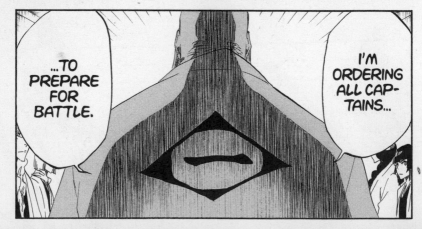

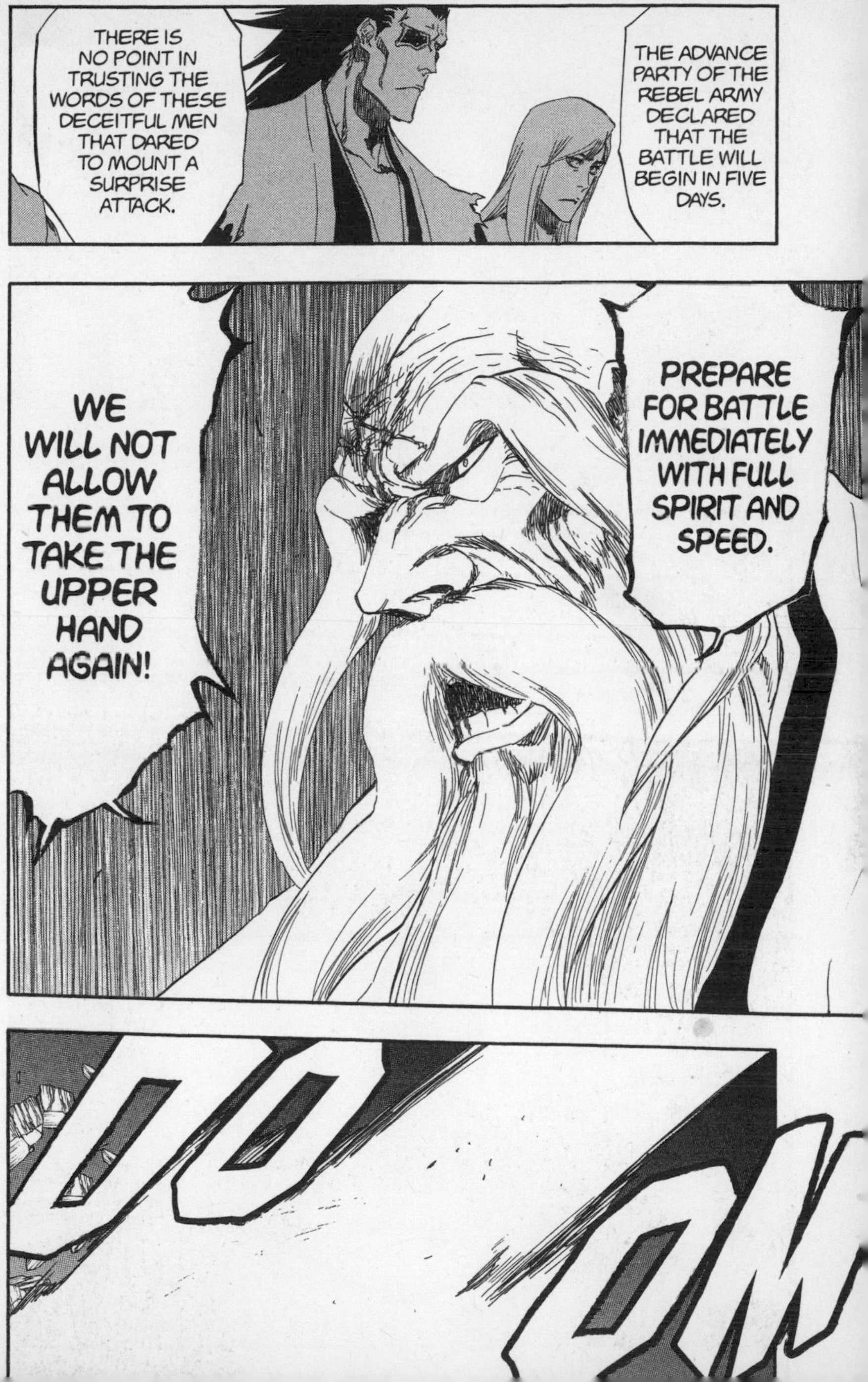
THE ADVANCE PARTY OF THE REBEL ARMY DECLARED THAT THE BATTLE WILL BEGIN IN FIVE DAYS.
THERE IS NO POINT IN TRUSTING THE WORDS OF THESE DECEITFUL MEN THAT DARED TO MOUNT A SURPRISE ATTACK.
PREPARE FOR BATTLE IMMEDIATELY WITH FULL SPIRIT AND SPEED.
WE WILL NOT ALLOW THEM TO TAKE THE UPPER HAND AGAIN!

READ THIS WAY

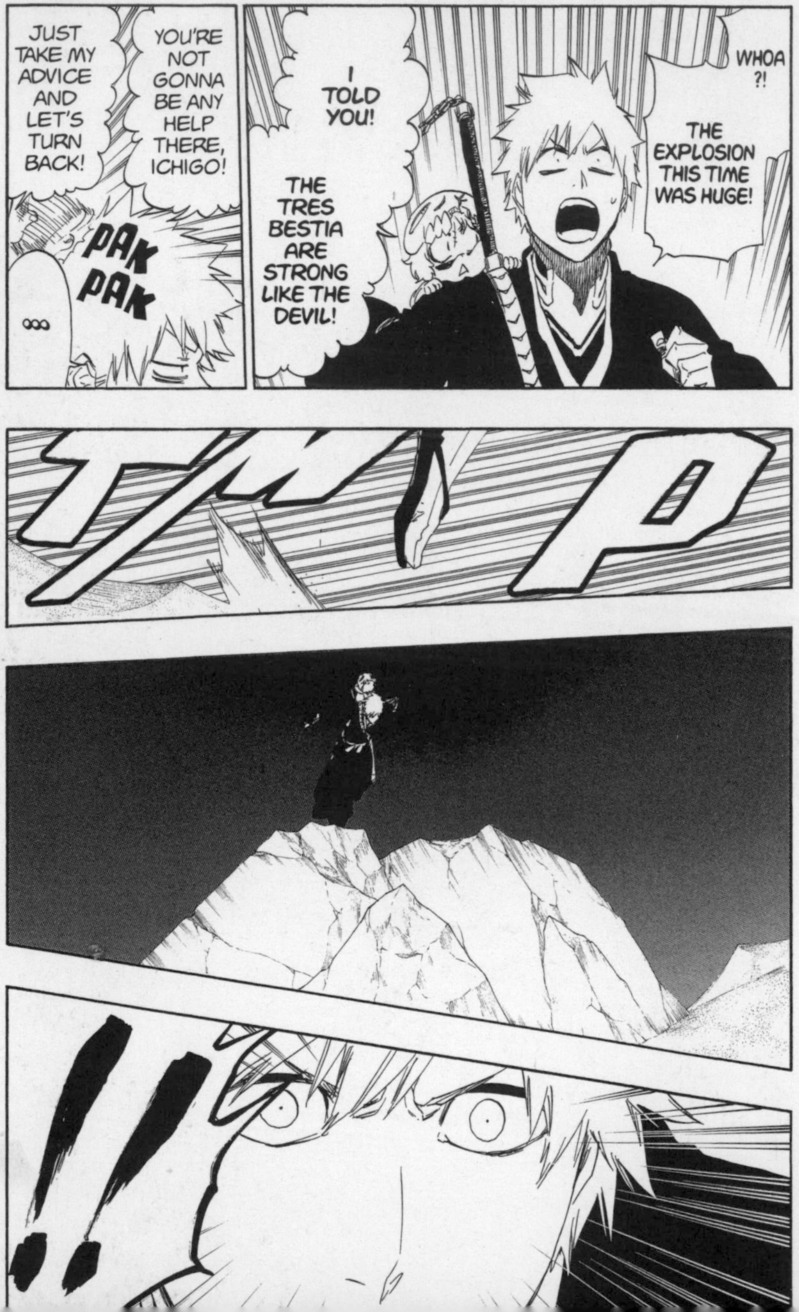
WHOA ?!
THE EXPLOSION THIS TIME WAS HUGE!
I TOLD YOU!
THE TRES BESTIA ARE STRONG LIKE THE DEVIL!
YOU'RE NOT GONNA BE ANY HELP THERE, ICHIGO!
JUST TAKE MY ADVICE AND LET'S TURN BACK!
PAK PAK
...
TMP
!!

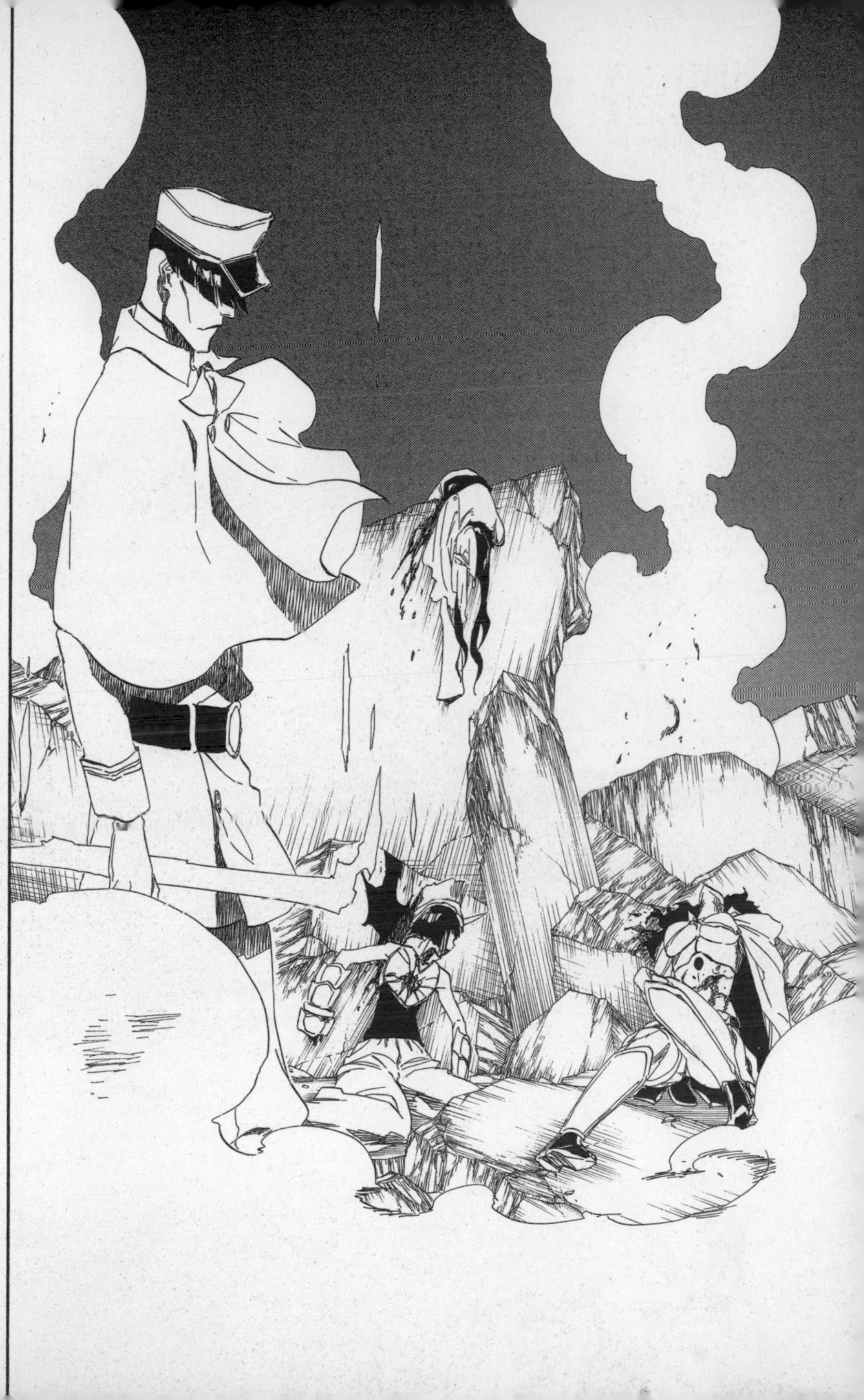

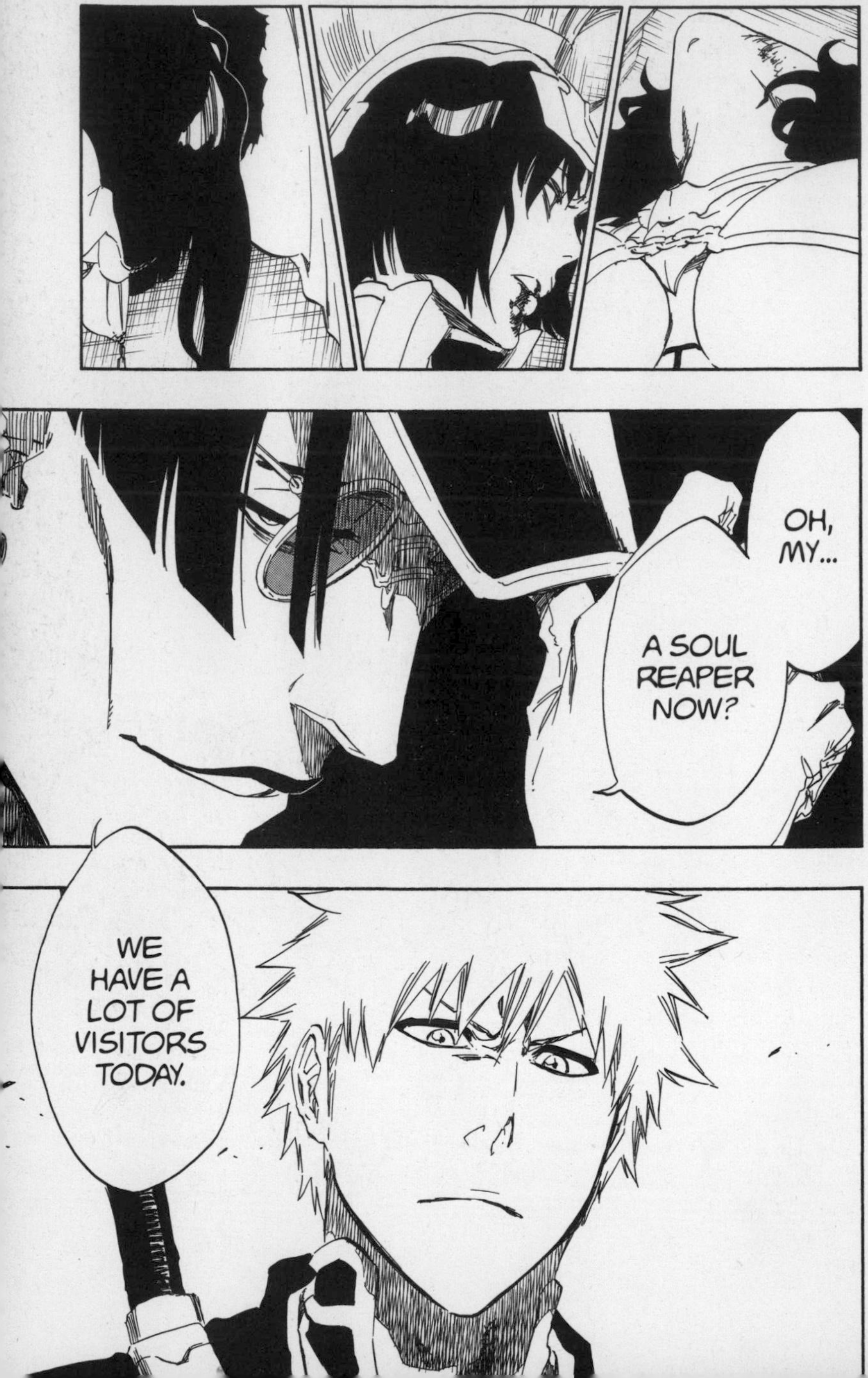
OH, MY...
A SOUL REAPER NOW?
WE HAVE A LOT OF VISITORS TODAY.

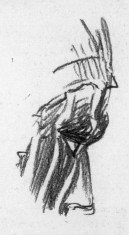

489. MARCH OF THE STARCROSS

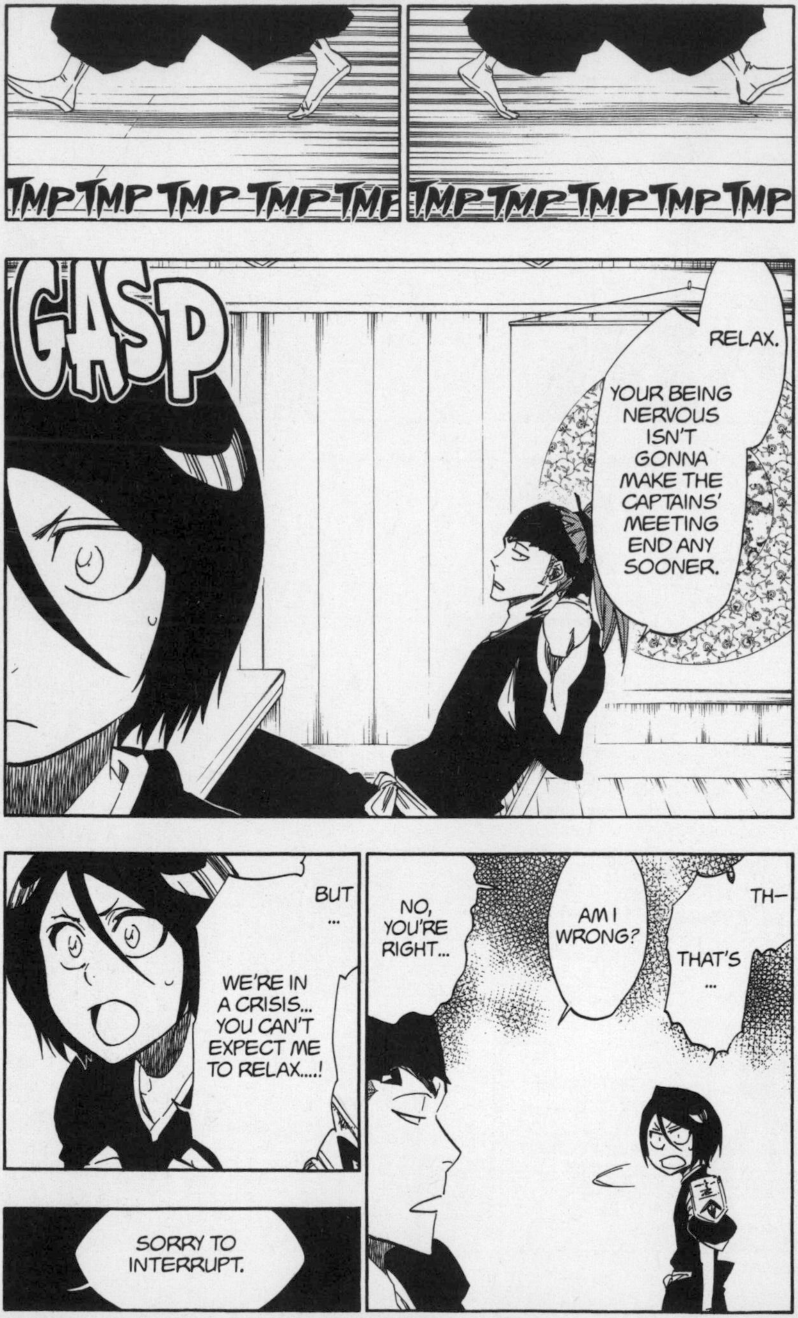
TMP TMP TMP TMP TMP
TMP TMP TMP TMP TMP
RELAX.
YOUR BEING NERVOUS ISN'T GONNA MAKE THE CAPTAINS' MEETING END ANY SOONER.
GASP
TH—
THAT'S ...
AM I WRONG?
NO, YOU'RE RIGHT...
BUT ...
WE'RE IN A CRISIS... YOU CAN'T EXPECT ME TO RELAX....!
SORRY TO INTERRUPT.

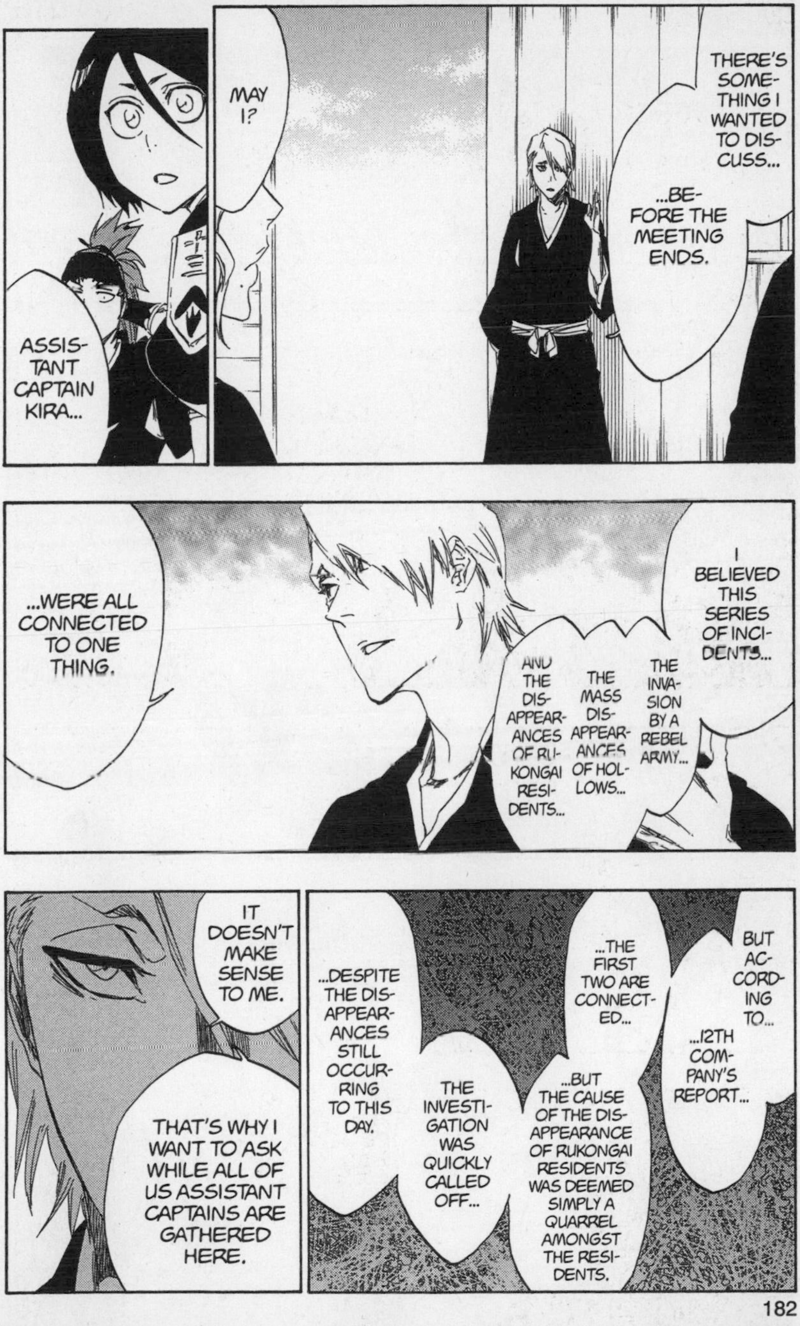
THERE'S SOMETHING I WANTED TO DISCUSS...
...BEFORE THE MEETING ENDS.
MAY I?
ASSISTANT CAPTAIN KIRA...
I BELIEVED THIS SERIES OF INCIDENTS...
THE INVASION BY A REBEL ARMY...
THE MASS DISAPPEARANCES OF HOLLOWS...
AND THE DISAPPEARANCES OF RUKONGAI RESIDENTS...
...WERE ALL CONNECTED TO ONE THING.
BUT ACCORDING TO...
...12TH COMPANY'S REPORT...
...THE FIRST TWO ARE CONNECTED...
...BUT THE CAUSE OF THE DISAPPEARANCE OF RUKONGAI RESIDENTS WAS DEEMED SIMPLY A QUARREL AMONGST THE RESIDENTS.
THE INVESTIGATION WAS QUICKLY CALLED OFF...
...DESPITE THE DISAPPEARANCES STILL OCCURRING TO THIS DAY.
IT DOESN'T MAKE SENSE TO ME.
THAT'S WHY I WANT TO ASK WHILE ALL OF US ASSISTANT CAPTAINS ARE GATHERED HERE.

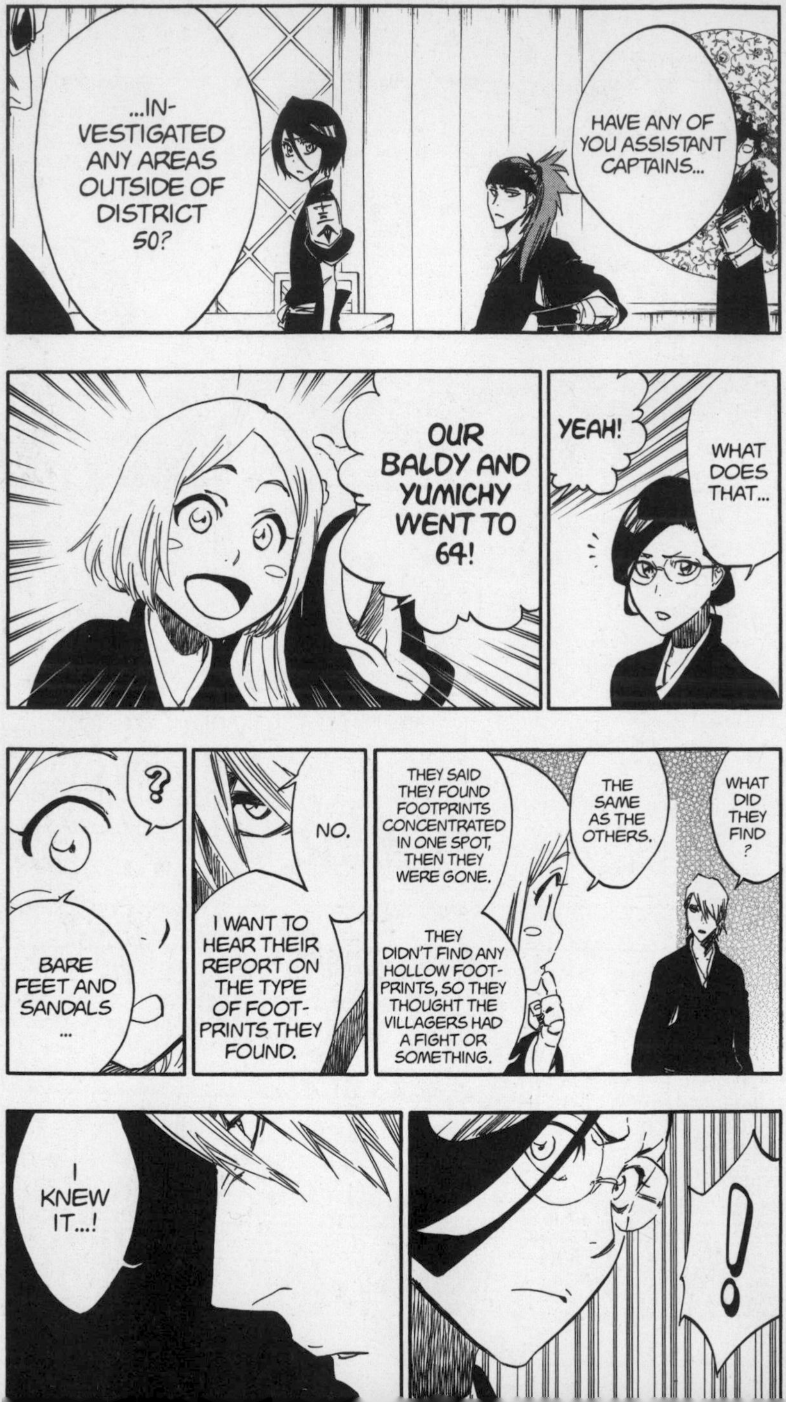
HAVE ANY OF YOU ASSISTANT CAPTAINS...
...IN-VESTIGATED ANY AREAS OUTSIDE OF DISTRICT 50?
WHAT DOES THAT...
YEAH!
OUR BALDY AND YUMICHY WENT TO 64!
WHAT DID THEY FIND?
THE SAME AS THE OTHERS.
THEY SAID THEY FOUND FOOTPRINTS CONCENTRATED IN ONE SPOT, THEN THEY WERE GONE.
THEY DIDN'T FIND ANY HOLLOW FOOT-PRINTS, SO THEY THOUGHT THE VILLAGERS HAD A FIGHT OR SOMETHING.
NO.
I WANT TO HEAR THEIR REPORT ON THE TYPE OF FOOT-PRINTS THEY FOUND.
?
BARE FEET AND SANDALS ...
!
I KNEW IT...!

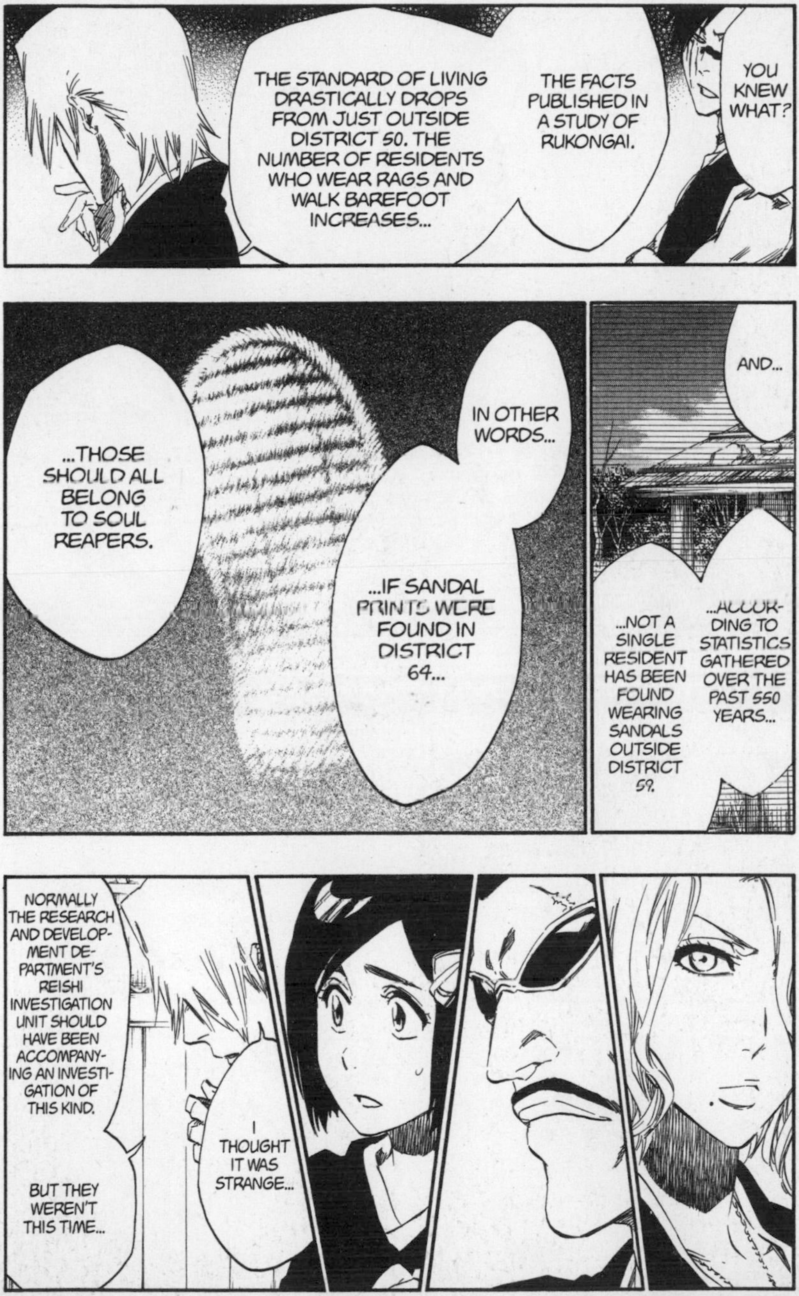
YOU KNEW WHAT?
THE FACTS PUBLISHED IN A STUDY OF RUKONGAI.
THE STANDARD OF LIVING DRASTICALLY DROPS FROM JUST OUTSIDE DISTRICT 50. THE NUMBER OF RESIDENTS WHO WEAR RAGS AND WALK BAREFOOT INCREASES...
AND...
...ACCORDING TO STATISTICS GATHERED OVER THE PAST 550 YEARS...
...NOT A SINGLE RESIDENT HAS BEEN FOUND WEARING SANDALS OUTSIDE DISTRICT 59.
IN OTHER WORDS...
...IF SANDAL PRINTS WERE FOUND IN DISTRICT 64...
...THOSE SHOULD ALL BELONG TO SOUL REAPERS.
NORMALLY THE RESEARCH AND DEVELOPMENT DEPARTMENT'S REISHI INVESTIGATION UNIT SHOULD HAVE BEEN ACCOMPANYING AN INVESTIGATION OF THIS KIND.
I THOUGHT IT WAS STRANGE...
BUT THEY WEREN'T THIS TIME...

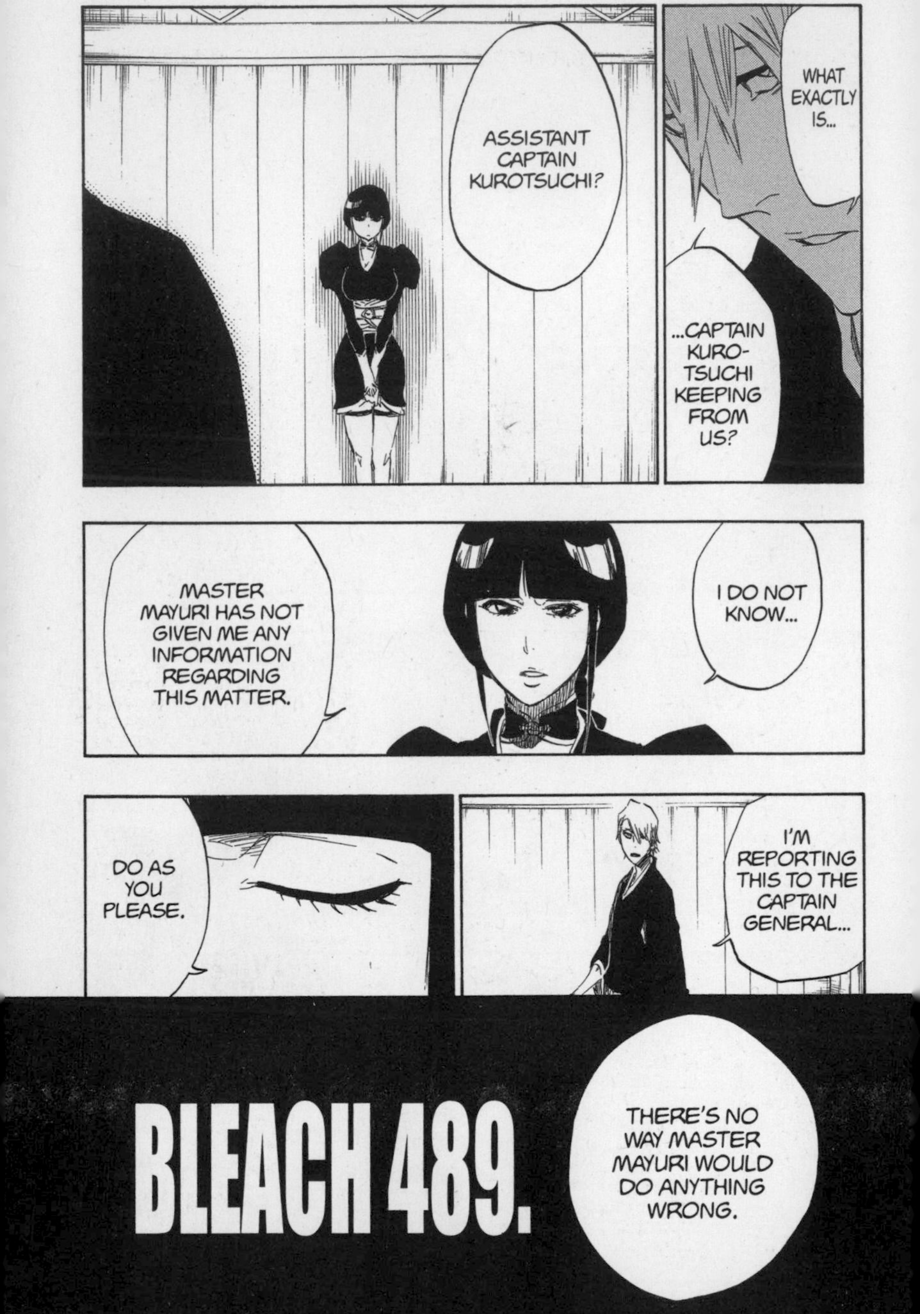
WHAT EXACTLY IS...
...CAPTAIN KURO-TSUCHI KEEPING FROM US?
ASSISTANT CAPTAIN KUROTSUCHI?
I DO NOT KNOW...
MASTER MAYURI HAS NOT GIVEN ME ANY INFORMATION REGARDING THIS MATTER.
I'M REPORTING THIS TO THE CAPTAIN GENERAL...
DO AS YOU PLEASE.
THERE'S NO WAY MASTER MAYURI WOULD DO ANYTHING WRONG.
BLEACH 489.

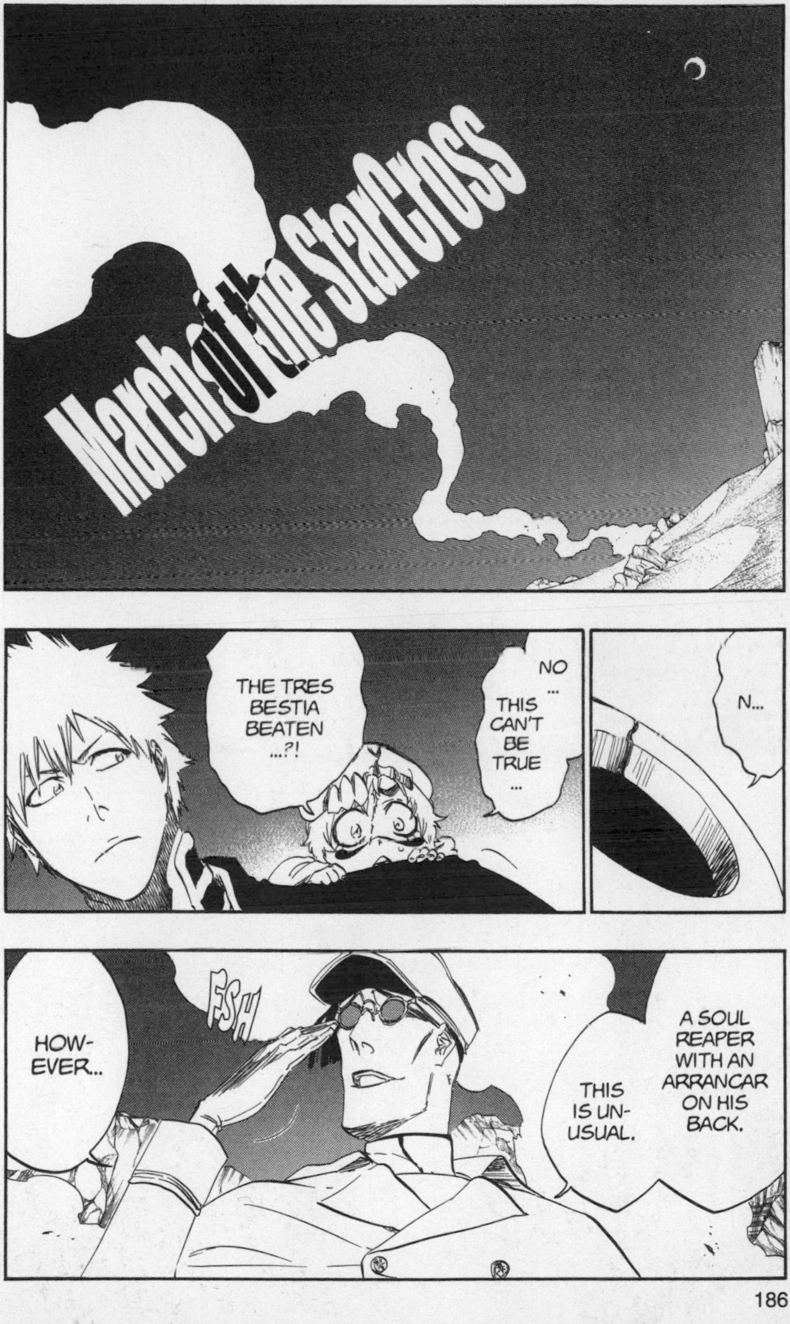
March of the StarCross
N...
NO ... THIS CAN'T BE TRUE ...
THE TRES BESTIA BEATEN ...?!
A SOUL REAPER WITH AN ARRANCAR ON HIS BACK.
THIS IS UN-USUAL.
FSH
HOW-EVER...

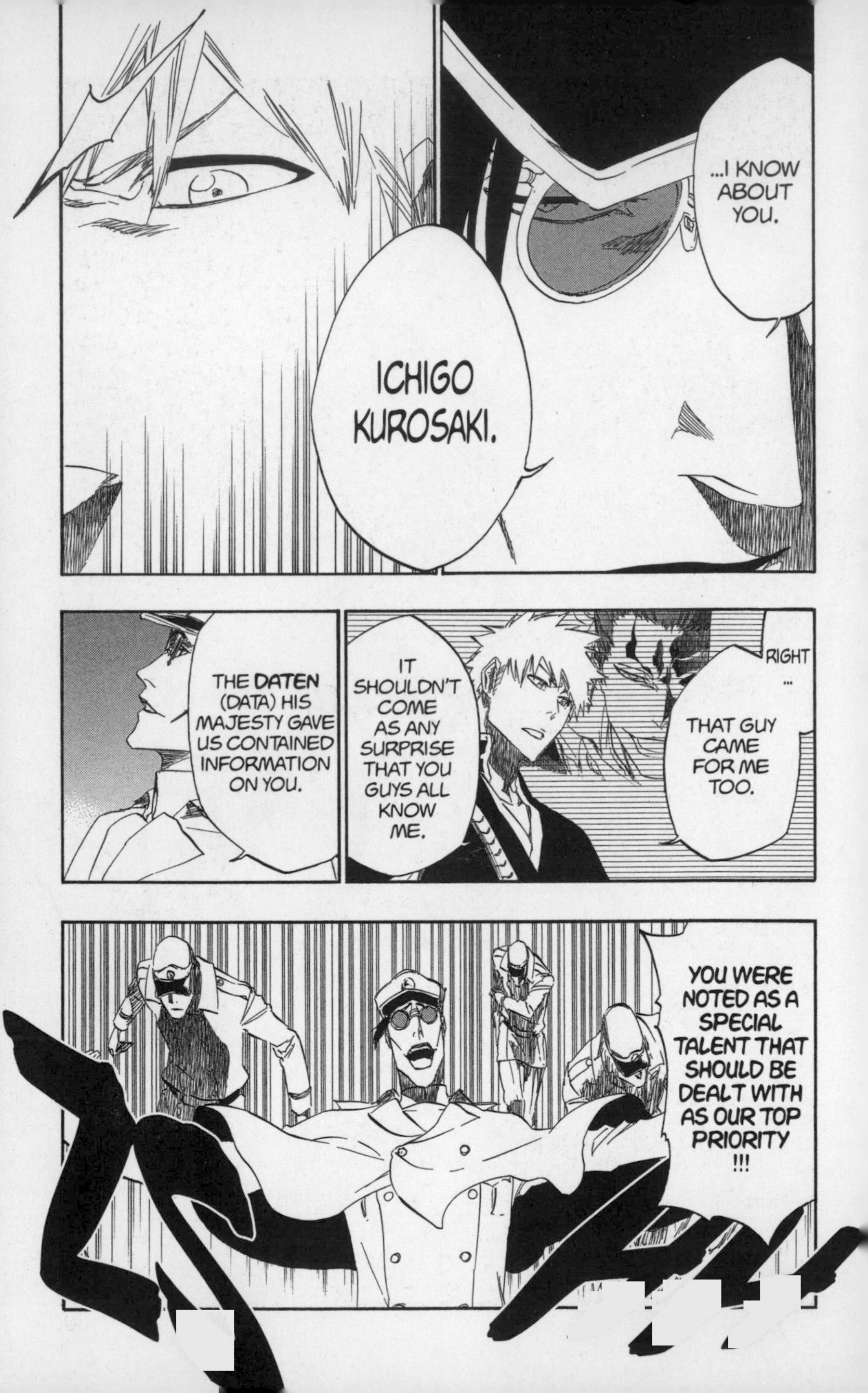
...I KNOW ABOUT YOU.
ICHIGO KUROSAKI.
RIGHT...
THAT GUY CAME FOR ME TOO.
IT SHOULDN'T COME AS ANY SURPRISE THAT YOU GUYS ALL KNOW ME.
THE DATEN (DATA) HIS MAJESTY GAVE US CONTAINED INFORMATION ON YOU.
YOU WERE NOTED AS A SPECIAL TALENT THAT SHOULD BE DEALT WITH AS OUR TOP PRIORITY!!!

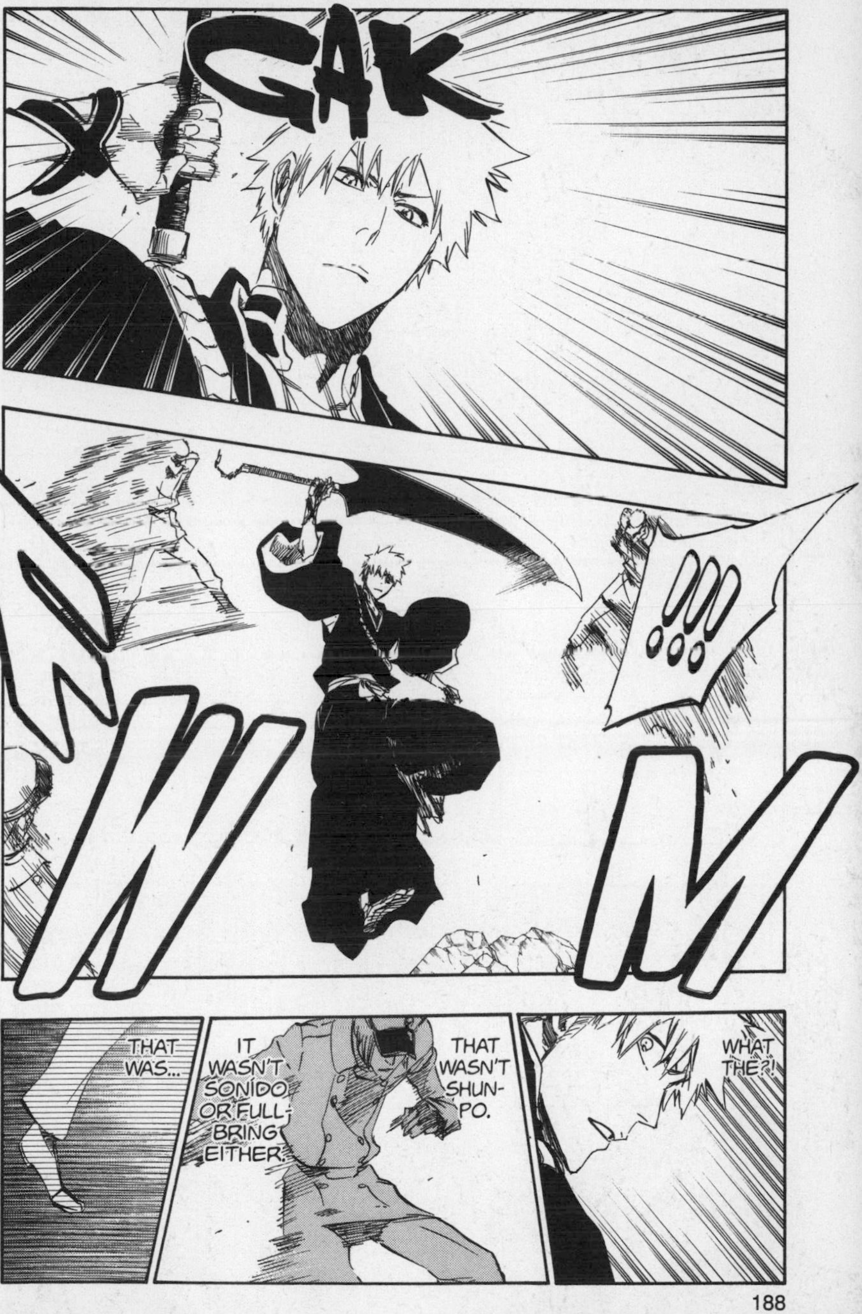
GAK
!!!
WHAT THE?!
THAT WASN'T SHUN-PO.
IT WASN'T SONIDO OR FULL-BRING EITHER.
THAT WAS...

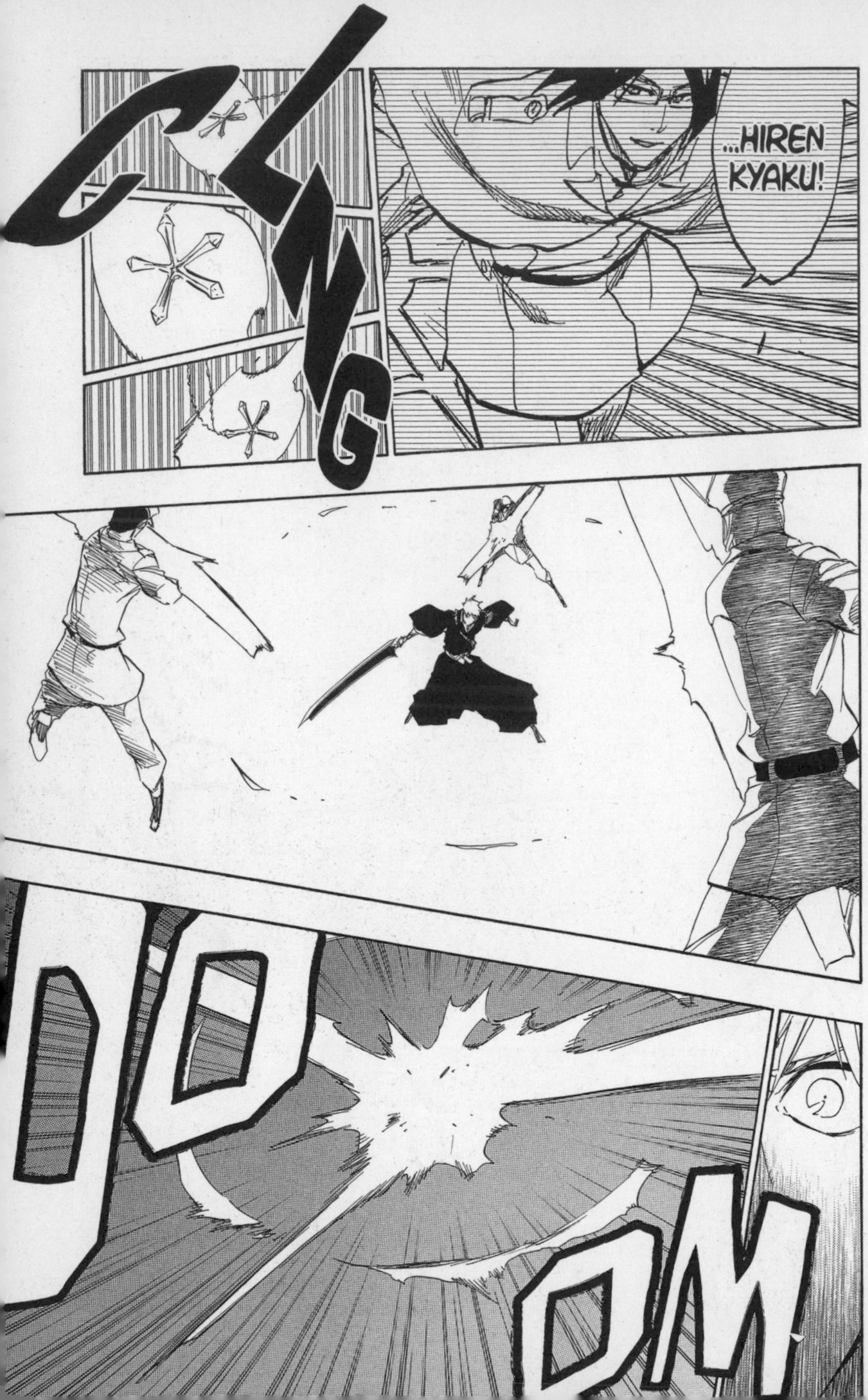
...HIREN KYAKU!
CLING
DOOM

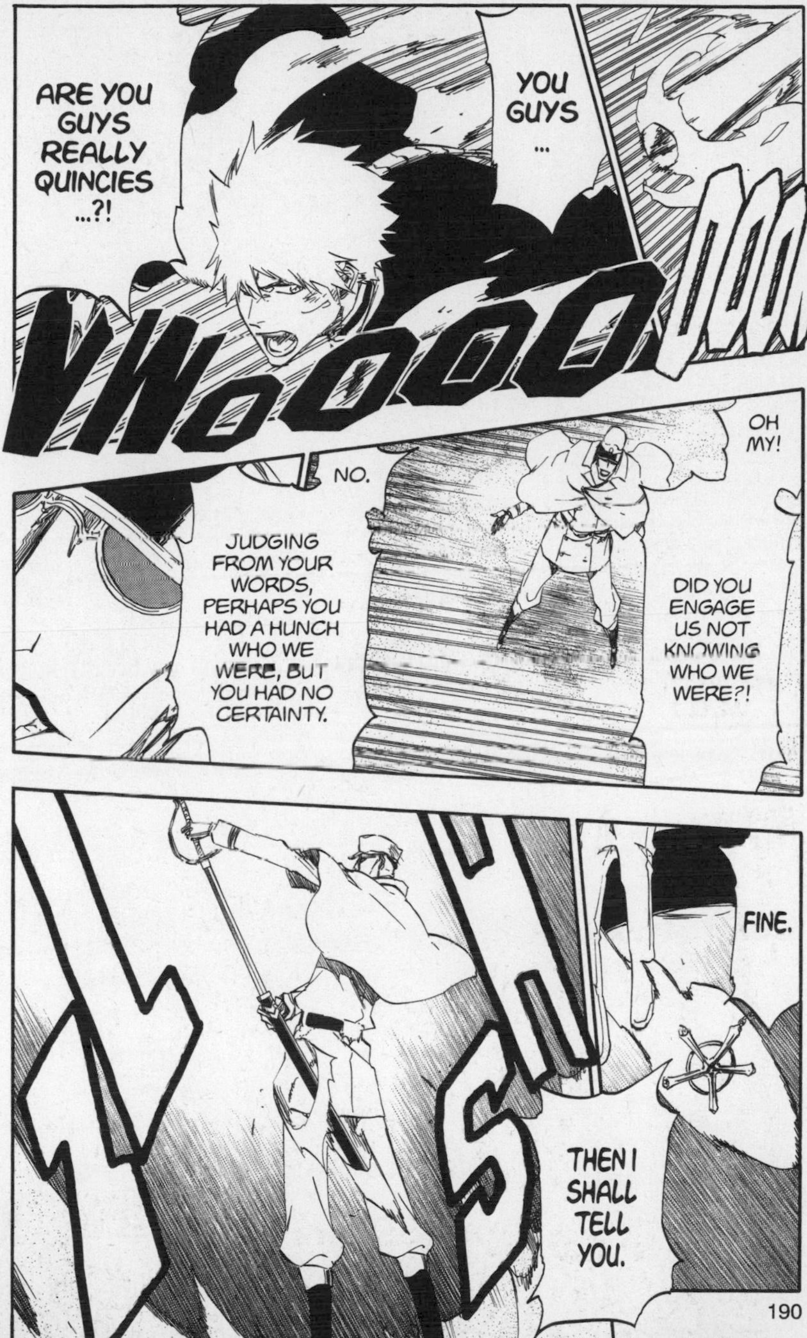
DOOOM
YOU GUYS ...
ARE YOU GUYS REALLY QUINCIES ...?!
WHOOOOO
OH MY!
DID YOU ENGAGE US NOT KNOWING WHO WE WERE?!
NO.
JUDGING FROM YOUR WORDS, PERHAPS YOU HAD A HUNCH WHO WE WERE, BUT YOU HAD NO CERTAINTY.
FINE.
THEN I SHALL TELL YOU.

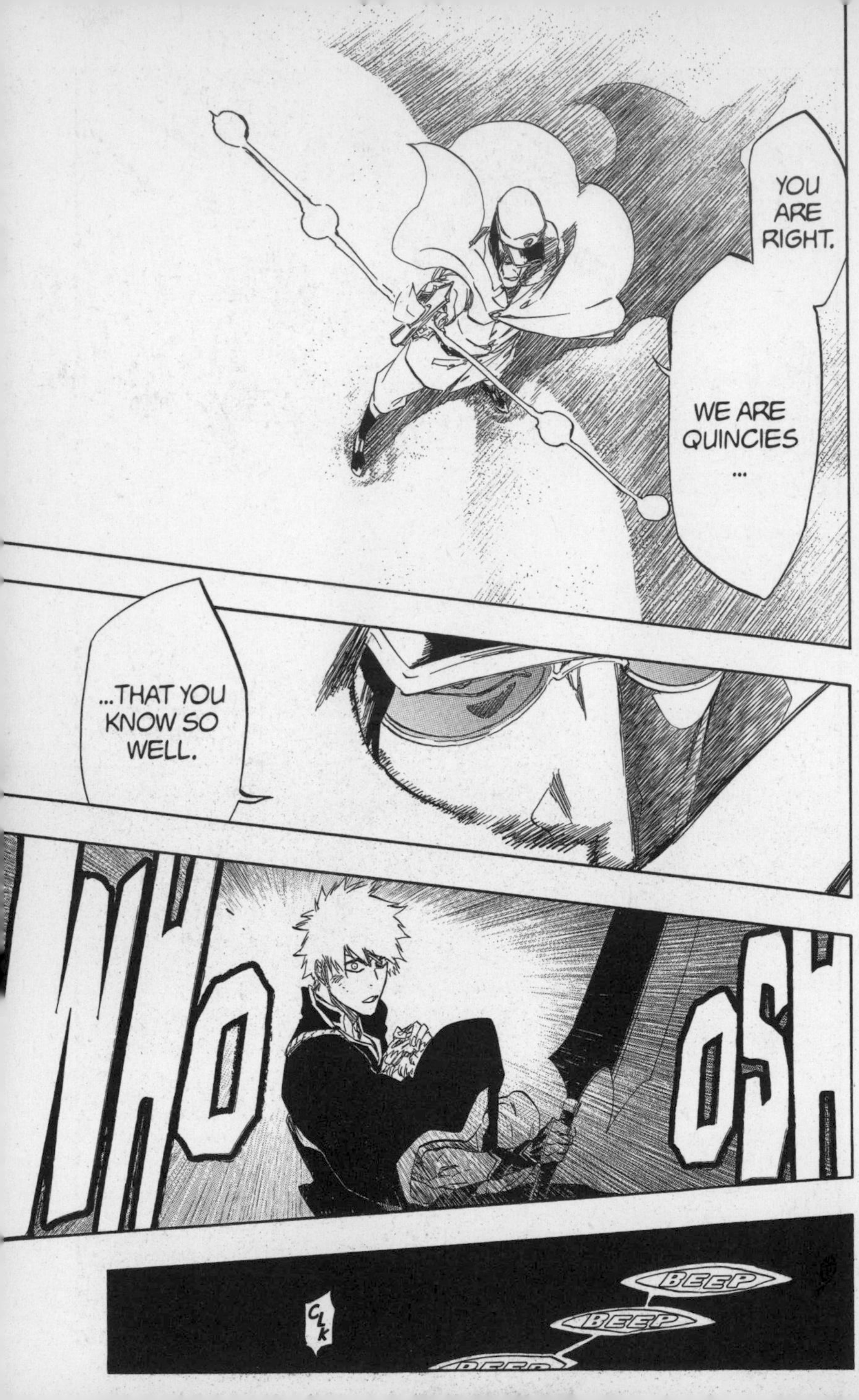
YOU ARE RIGHT.
WE ARE QUINCIES ...
...THAT YOU KNOW SO WELL.
WHOOSH
BEEP
BEEP
CLK

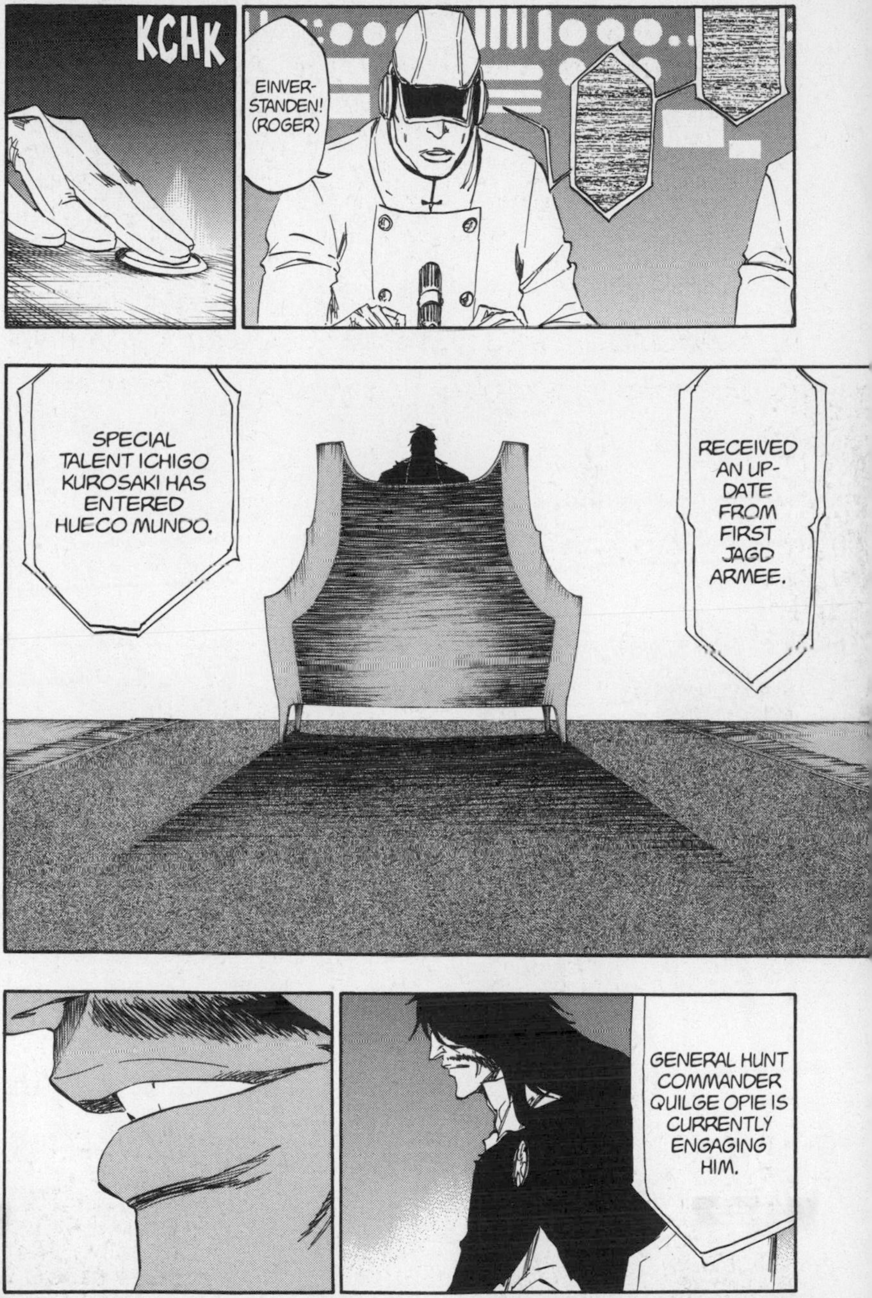
EINVER-
STANDEN!
(ROGER)
KCHK
RECEIVED AN UP-DATE FROM FIRST JAGD ARMEE.
SPECIAL TALENT ICHIGO KUROSAKI HAS ENTERED HUECO MUNDO.
GENERAL HUNT COMMANDER QUILGE OPIE IS CURRENTLY ENGAGING HIM.

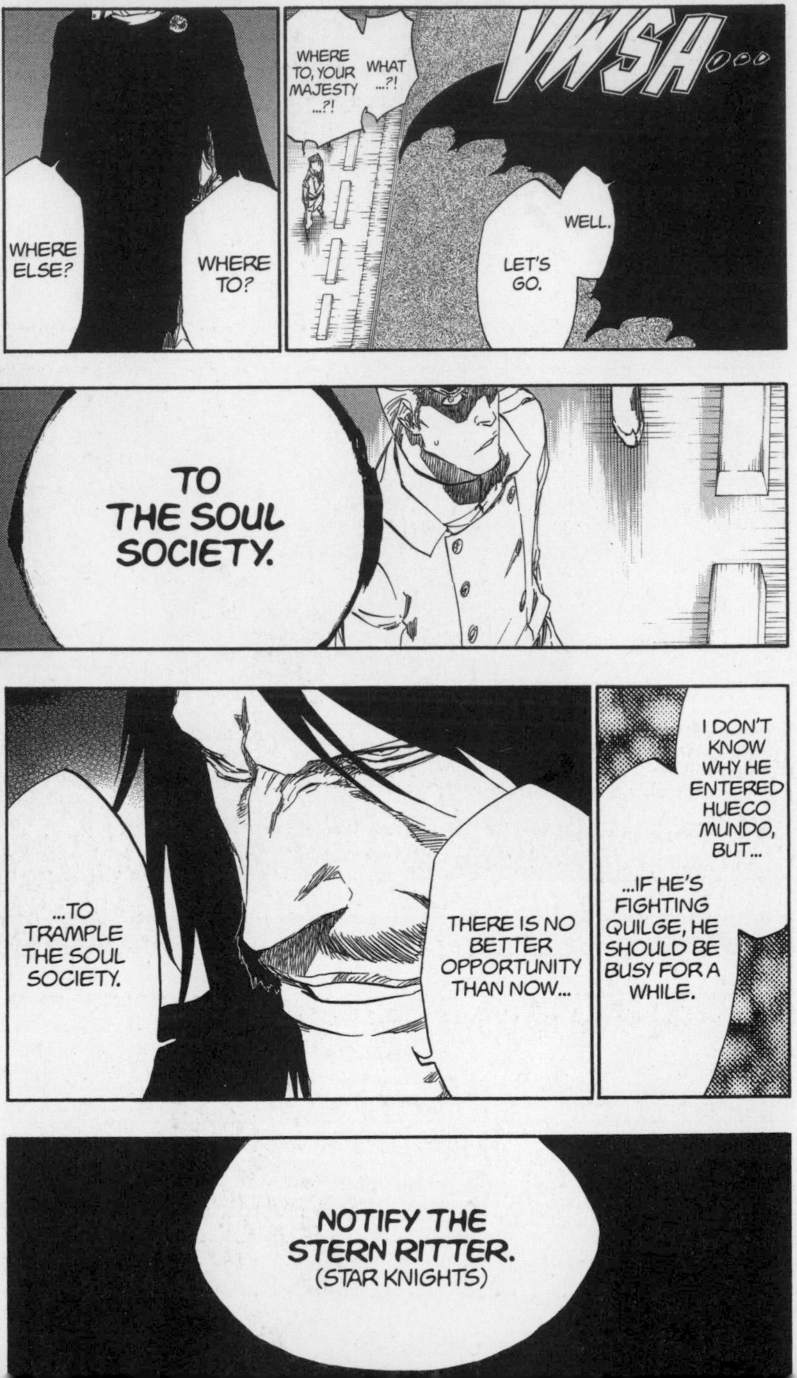
VWSH...
WELL.
LET'S GO.
WHAT ...?!
WHERE TO, YOUR MAJESTY ...?!
WHERE TO?
WHERE ELSE?
TO THE SOUL SOCIETY.
I DON'T KNOW WHY HE ENTERED HUECO MUNDO, BUT...
...IF HE'S FIGHTING QUILGE, HE SHOULD BE BUSY FOR A WHILE.
THERE IS NO BETTER OPPORTUNITY THAN NOW...
...TO TRAMPLE THE SOUL SOCIETY.
NOTIFY THE STERN RITTER.
(STAR KNIGHTS)

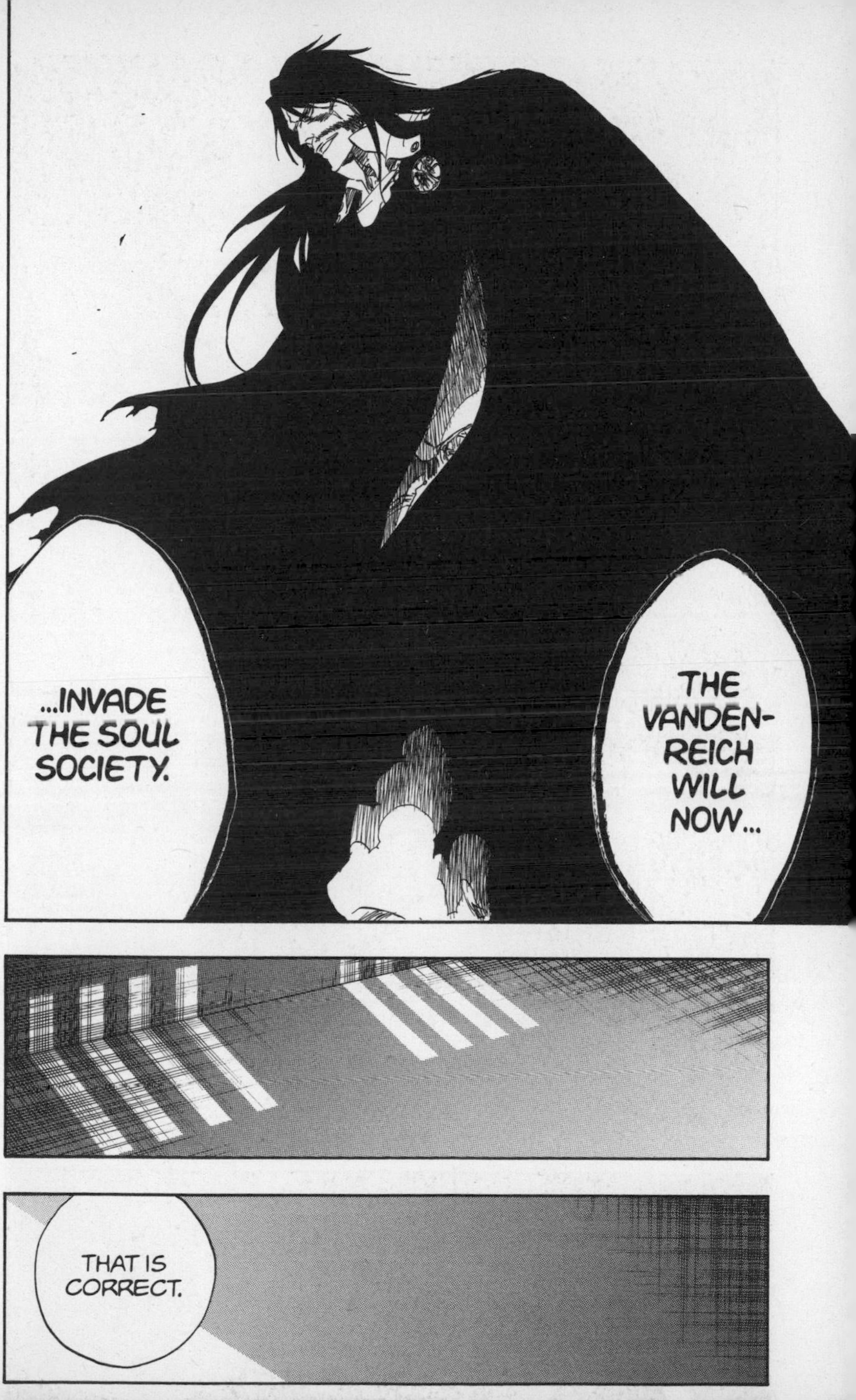
THE VANDEN-REICH WILL NOW...
...INVADE THE SOUL SOCIETY.
THAT IS CORRECT.

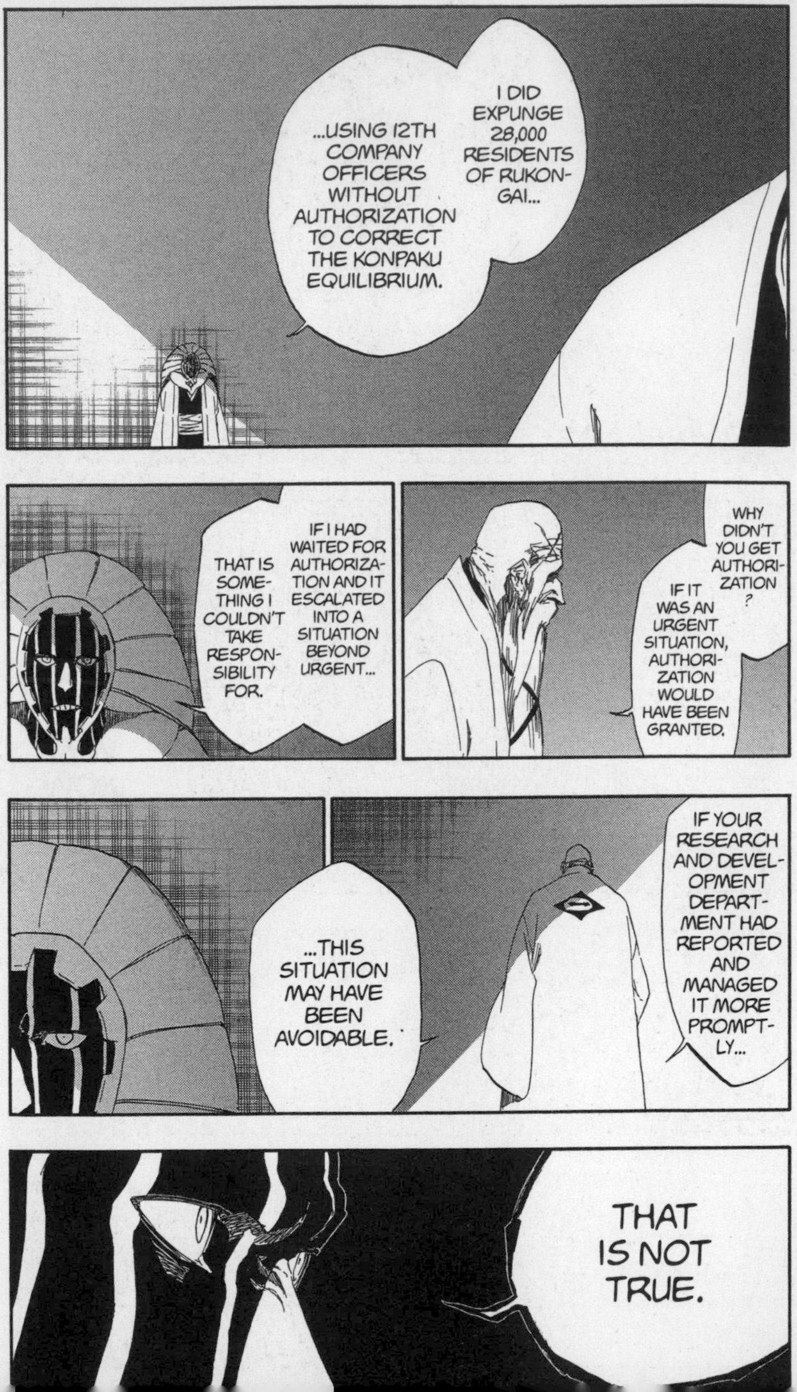
I DID EXPUNGE 28,000 RESIDENTS OF RUKON-GAI...
...USING 12TH COMPANY OFFICERS WITHOUT AUTHORIZATION TO CORRECT THE KONPAKU EQUILIBRIUM.
WHY DIDN'T YOU GET AUTHORIZATION?
IF IT WAS AN URGENT SITUATION, AUTHORIZATION WOULD HAVE BEEN GRANTED.
IF I HAD WAITED FOR AUTHORIZATION AND IT ESCALATED INTO A SITUATION BEYOND URGENT...
THAT IS SOMETHING I COULDN'T TAKE RESPONSIBILITY FOR.
IF YOUR RESEARCH AND DEVELOPMENT DEPARTMENT HAD REPORTED AND MANAGED IT MORE PROMPTLY...
...THIS SITUATION MAY HAVE BEEN AVOIDABLE.
THAT IS NOT TRUE.

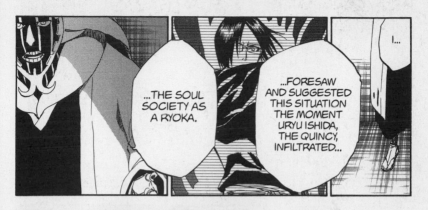

I...
...FORESAW AND SUGGESTED THIS SITUATION THE MOMENT URYU ISHIDA, THE QUINCY, INFILTRATED...
...THE SOUL SOCIETY AS A RYOKA.
IT WAS YOU WHO DIS-REGARDED THAT AS BEING ABSURD.
ISN'T THE PRINCIPLE CAUSE OF THIS SITU-ATION...
BECAUSE YOU...
...YOU, CAPTAIN GENERAL?

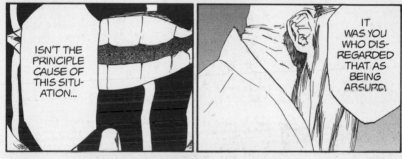

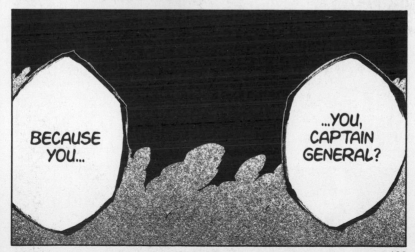

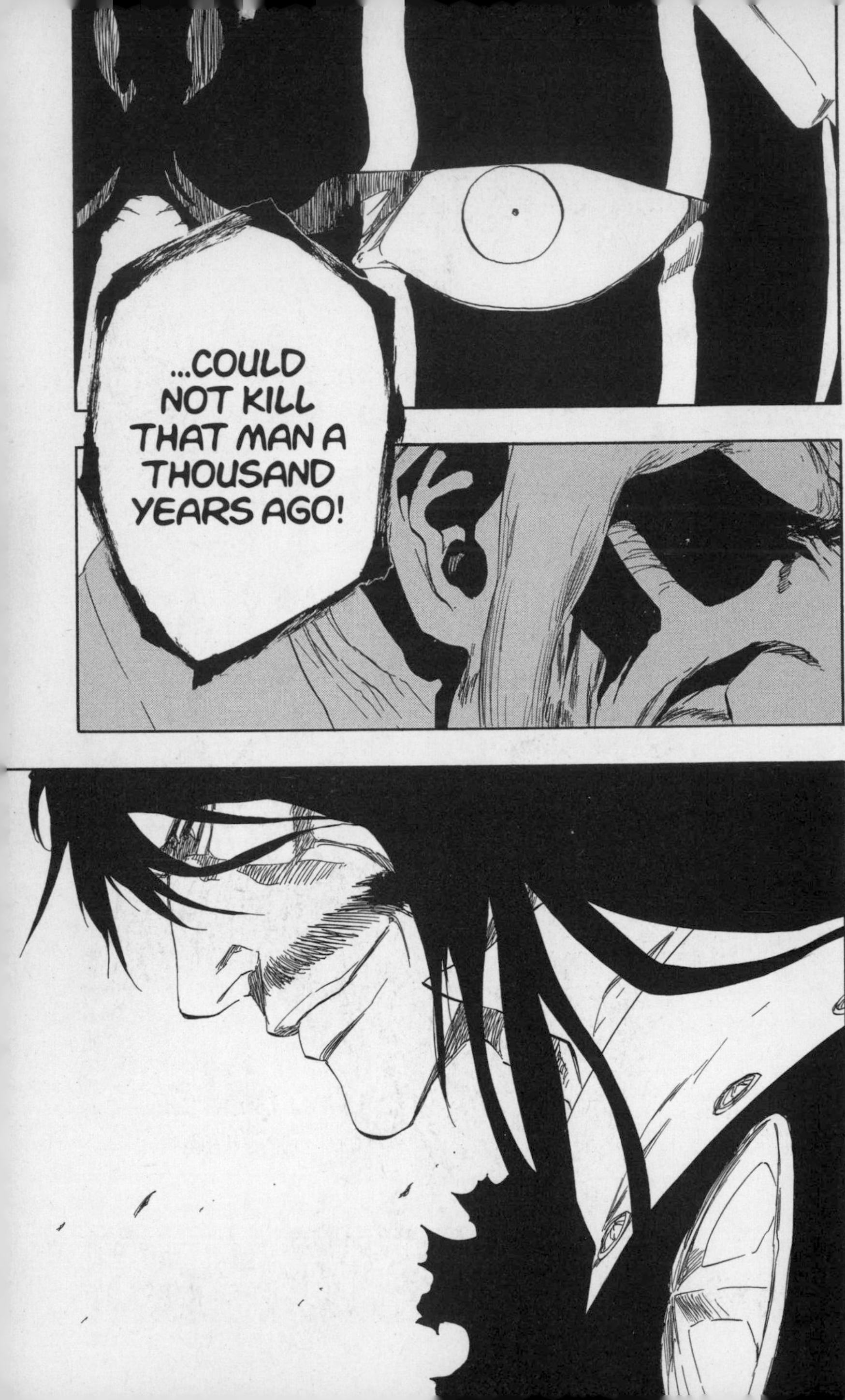
...COULD NOT KILL THAT MAN A THOUSAND YEARS AGO!

CONTINUED IN BLEACH 56

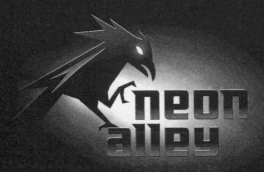
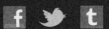

You're Reading in the Wrong Direction!!

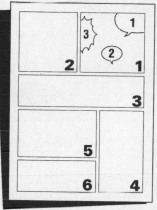

Whoops! Guess what? You're starting at the wrong end of the comic!

…It's true! In keeping with the original Japanese format, **Bleach** is meant to be read from right to left, starting in the upper-right corner.

Unlike English, which is read from left to right, Japanese is read from right to left, meaning that action, sound effects and word-balloon order are completely reversed… something which can make readers unfamiliar with Japanese feel pretty backwards themselves. For this reason, manga or Japanese comics published in the U.S. in English have sometimes been published "flopped"—that is, printed in exact reverse order, as though seen from the other side of a mirror.

By flopping pages, U.S. publishers can avoid confusing readers, but the compromise is not without its downside. For one thing, a character in a flopped manga series who once wore in the original Japanese version a T-shirt emblazoned with "M A Y" (as in "the merry month of") now wears one which reads "Y A M"! Additionally, many manga creators in Japan are themselves unhappy with the process, as some feel the mirror-imaging of their art skews their original intentions.

We are proud to bring you Tite Kubo's **Bleach** in the original unflopped format. For now, though, turn to the other side of the book and let the adventure begin…!

—Editor

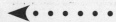

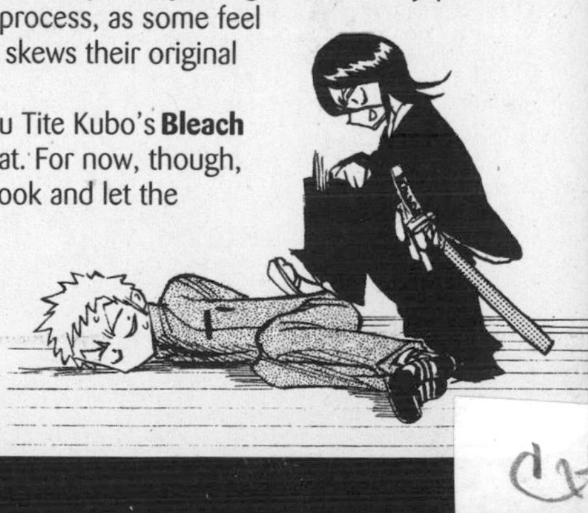